MACROECONOMICS 96/97

Eleventh Edition

Editor

Don Cole
Drew University

Don Cole, Professor of Economics at Drew University, received his Ph.D. from Ohio State University. He has served as consultant to a variety of public and private organizations, and is cofounder of the Drew University Semester on the European Union in Brussels, Belgium. An innovator in the use of computer-assisted instruction in economics, Dr. Cole is the author of articles on various subjects, including economic policy, monetary theory, and economic education. He is also the editor of other Dushkin Publishing Group/Brown & Benchmark Publishers publications, including *The Encyclopedic Dictionary of Economics* and two other anthologies in the *Annual Editions* series, *Economics* and *Microeconomics.*

A Library of Information from the Public Press

Cover illustration by Mike Eagle

**Dushkin Publishing Group/
Brown & Benchmark Publishers
Sluice Dock, Guilford, Connecticut 06437**

Distributed in the United States by Richard D. Irwin, Publishers

The Annual Editions Series

Annual Editions is a series of over 65 volumes designed to provide the reader with convenient, low-cost access to a wide range of current, carefully selected articles from some of the most important magazines, newspapers, and journals published today. Annual Editions are updated on an annual basis through a continuous monitoring of over 300 periodical sources. All Annual Editions have a number of features designed to make them particularly useful, including topic guides, annotated tables of contents, unit overviews, and indexes. For the teacher using Annual Editions in the classroom, an Instructor's Resource Guide with test questions is available for each volume.

VOLUMES AVAILABLE

Abnormal Psychology
Africa
Aging
American Foreign Policy
American Government
American History, Pre-Civil War
American History, Post-Civil War
American Public Policy
Anthropology
Archaeology
Biopsychology
Business Ethics
Child Growth and Development
China
Comparative Politics
Computers in Education
Computers in Society
Criminal Justice
Developing World
Deviant Behavior
Drugs, Society, and Behavior
Dying, Death, and Bereavement
Early Childhood Education
Economics
Educating Exceptional Children
Education
Educational Psychology
Environment
Geography
Global Issues
Health
Human Development
Human Resources
Human Sexuality

India and South Asia
International Business
Japan and the Pacific Rim
Latin America
Life Management
Macroeconomics
Management
Marketing
Marriage and Family
Mass Media
Microeconomics
Middle East and the Islamic World
Multicultural Education
Nutrition
Personal Growth and Behavior
Physical Anthropology
Psychology
Public Administration
Race and Ethnic Relations
Russia, the Eurasian Republics, and
   Central/Eastern Europe
Social Problems
Sociology
State and Local Government
Urban Society
Western Civilization,
   Pre-Reformation
Western Civilization,
   Post-Reformation
Western Europe
World History, Pre-Modern
World History, Modern
World Politics

Cataloging in Publication Data
Main entry under title: Annual editions: Macroeconomics. 1996/97.
     1. Macroeconomics—Periodicals. 2. Economics—Periodicals. 3. United States—Economic Conditions—Periodicals. I. Cole, Don, comp. II. Title: Macroeconomics.
ISBN 1-56134-431-1   339'73'05   75-20753

Eleventh Edition

Printed in the United States of America

Printed on Recycled Paper

Editors/ Advisory Board

EDITOR

Don Cole
Drew University

ADVISORY BOARD

Members of the Advisory Board are instrumental in the final selection of articles for each edition of Annual Editions. Their review of articles for content, level, currentness, and appropriateness provides critical direction to the editor and staff. We think you'll find their careful consideration well reflected in this volume.

Frank J. Bonello
University of Notre Dame

Sarah J. Bumgarner
University of North Carolina

Robert B. Catlett
Emporia State University

Lucinda Coulter-Burbach
Seminole Community College

Eleanor Craig
University of Delaware

Larry Frateschi
College of DuPage

Jo-Anne Gibson
Southeastern Louisiana University

Stephen K. Happel
Arizona State University

Matthew Marlin
Duquesne University

Joseph Meador
Northeastern University

Marshall D. Nickles
Pepperdine University

Kostis Papadantonakis
Essex Community College

Arthur J. Raymond
Muhlenberg College

Rolando Santos
Lakeland Community College

John M. Sapinsley
Brown University

Howard Stein
Roosevelt University

Evert Van Der Heide
Calvin College

Irvin Weintraub
Towson State University

Charles Zech
Villanova University

STAFF

Ian A. Nielsen, Publisher
Brenda S. Filley, Production Manager
Roberta Monaco, Editor
Addie Raucci, Administrative Editor
Cheryl Greenleaf, Permissions Editor
Deanna Herrschaft, Permissions Assistant
Diane Barker, Proofreader
Lisa Holmes-Doebrick, Administrative Coordinator
Charles Vitelli, Designer
Shawn Callahan, Graphics
Lara M. Johnson, Graphics
Laura Levine, Graphics
Libra A. Cusack, Typesetting Supervisor
Juliana Arbo, Typesetter
Jane Jaegersen, Typesetter

To the Reader

In publishing ANNUAL EDITIONS we recognize the enormous role played by the magazines, newspapers, and journals of the *public press* in providing current, first-rate educational information in a broad spectrum of interest areas. Within the articles, the best scientists, practitioners, researchers, and commentators draw issues into new perspective as accepted theories and viewpoints are called into account by new events, recent discoveries change old facts, and fresh debate breaks out over important controversies.

Many of the articles resulting from this enormous editorial effort are appropriate for students, researchers, and professionals seeking accurate, current material to help bridge the gap between principles and theories and the real world. These articles, however, become more useful for study when those of lasting value are carefully *collected, organized, indexed,* and *reproduced* in a *low-cost format,* which provides easy and permanent access when the material is needed. That is the role played by *Annual Editions.* Under the direction of each volume's *Editor,* who is an expert in the subject area, and with the guidance of an *Advisory Board,* we seek each year to provide in each *ANNUAL EDITION* a current, well-balanced, carefully selected collection of the best of the public press for your study and enjoyment. We think you'll find this volume useful, and we hope you'll take a moment to let us know what you think.

Annual Editions: Macroeconomics is an anthology that provides up-to-date readings on contemporary macroeconomic issues. In view of the recent explosion of interest in economics, it is essential that students are given opportunities to observe how economic science can help them to understand major economic events in the real world. *Annual Editions: Macroeconomics 1996/97* is designed to meet such a need.

This anthology is divided into six sections, which generally correspond to the typical sequence of topics in macroeconomic textbooks:

Introduction to Macroeconomics. The first section provides a general survey of macroeconomic policy making since the days of John Maynard Keynes. It also contains an assessment of the *Economic Report of the President (1995)* and a discussion of the theoretical basis for making judgments about appropriate policies.

Measuring Economic Performance. Economists use economic data for the purpose of judging an economy's general health and making informed choices among policy alternatives. This section examines various problems associated with the gathering and interpretation of such data.

Fiscal Policy and the Federal Budget. Articles in this section deal with ways in which the federal government might use its spending and tax programs to achieve various macroeconomic goals. Major emphasis is placed upon problems of controlling federal budget deficits.

Money, Banking, and Monetary Policy. Federal Reserve efforts at containing inflation have proved very successful in the past decade. Yet, in view of persistent deficits and a series of bank failures, some economists question the overall soundness of both Federal Reserve policy and the financial system. This section considers possible responses to such challenges.

Unemployment, Inflation, and the Business Cycle. A major goal in the implementation of macroeconomic policy is the simultaneous achievement of high employment, stable prices, and vigorous economic growth. Articles selected for this section discuss the theoretical and policy issues involved in improving the economy's performance in these areas.

International Economics. In recent years the global economy has experienced a series of dramatic events unforeseen even a decade ago: the end of the cold war; ambitious market reforms in what were formerly centrally planned economies; an acceleration of the process of economic integration in the Americas, Western Europe, and the Pacific Rim; and increased use of protectionist measures by most major traders. This section examines key aspects of these developments.

Whether you are someone who is currently pursuing studies in economics, or just a casual reader eager to learn more about some of the major economic issues of the day, you will find *Annual Editions: Macroeconomics 1996/97* to be one of the most useful and up-to-date anthologies available. Your comments can be very valuable in designing the next edition. Please complete and mail the postpaid rating form at the conclusion of this book and let us know your opinions.

Don Cole
Editor

Contents

Unit 1

Introduction to Macroeconomics

Four articles examine some of the controversies that lie at the heart of macroeconomics.

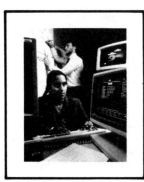

Unit 2

Measuring Economic Performance

Six articles consider the dynamics of the measurement and interpretation of economic indicators. Subjects examined include the validity of government statistics, productivity, and sustainable development.

The concepts in bold italics are developed in the article. For further expansion please refer to the Topic Guide, the Index, and the Glossary.

Unit 3

Fiscal Policy and the Federal Budget

Eight selections discuss the state of the federal budget. Topics include the current budget predicament, the dynamics of deficit, balancing the budget, and federal tax policy.

The concepts in bold italics are developed in the article. For further expansion please refer to the Topic Guide, the Index, and the Glossary.

Unit 4

Money, Banking, and Monetary Policy

Seven articles analyze the accountability of central
banking, how politicians influence federal policy, and
the money movement.

The concepts in bold italics are developed in the article. For further expansion please refer to the Topic Guide, the Index, and the Glossary.

Unit 5

Unemployment, Inflation, and the Business Cycle

Eight selections examine the interaction between
unemployment and inflation. Specific topics discussed
include employment rates, the effects of technology,
our standard of living, and inflation cycles.

The concepts in bold italics are developed in the article. For further expansion please refer to the Topic Guide, the Index, and the Glossary.

Unit 6

International Economics

Twelve articles consider how international trade, protectionism, trade deficits, foreign direct investment, the European Common Market, and the World Trade Organization affect the world economy.

The concepts in bold italics are developed in the article. For further expansion please refer to the Topic Guide, the Index, and the Glossary.

The concepts in bold italics are developed in the article. For further expansion please refer to the Topic Guide, the Index, and the Glossary.

Documents

The concepts in bold italics are developed in the article. For further expansion please refer to the Topic Guide, the Index, and the Glossary.

Topic Guide

This topic guide suggests how the selections in this book relate to topics of traditional concern to students and professionals involved with the study of macroeconomics. It is useful for locating articles that relate to each other for reading and research. The guide is arranged alphabetically according to topic. Articles may, of course, treat topics that do not appear in the topic guide. In turn, entries in the topic guide do not necessarily constitute a comprehensive listing of all the contents of each selection.

TOPIC AREA	TREATED IN:	TOPIC AREA	TREATED IN:
Balanced-Budget Amendment	2. Economic Report of the President 11. What's in Store? 12. Pitfalls of a Balanced Budget 14. Saving, Economic Growth, and the Arrow of Causality 15. Taxpayers Are Angry	Government Spending	9. Real Truth about the Economy 11. What's in Store? 13. Budget Blaster 14. Saving, Economic Growth, and the Arrow of Causality 16. True Tax Reform 17. Europeans Shrug as Taxes Go Up 32. Parties Skirmish over Budget
Banking Industry	22. Banking 23. Should the Feds Have Greater Control over State Banks? 24. Future of Money 25. Bank Failure	Inflation	2. Economic Report of the President 6. Taking the Measure of Economics 9. Real Truth about the Economy 20. The Fed: Wrong Turn in Risky Traffic 26. Our NAIRU Limit 31. Has Our Living Standard Stalled? 33. Long Wave in Inflation and Real Interest Rates 36. Global Growth Is on a Tear 37. From GATT to WTO
Business Cycles	1. Economics of My Times and Yours 8. Economy's Barometer 12. Pitfalls of a Balanced Budget 14. Saving, Economic Growth, and the Arrow of Causality 26. Our NAIRU Limit 30. Only a Paper Boon 33. Long Wave in Inflation		
		Interest Rates	14. Saving, Economic Growth, and the Arrow of Causality 16. True Tax Reform 20. The Fed: Wrong Turn in Risky Traffic 22. Banking 24. Future of Money 30. Only a Paper Boon 32. Parties Skirmish over Budget 33. Long Wave in Inflation and Real Interest Rates
Eastern Europe	34. Consolidating Capitalism 36. Global Growth Is on a Tear 37. From GATT to WTO		
Economic Indicators	5. Economy You Can't See 6. Taking the Measure of Economics 7. Services 8. Economy's Barometer 9. Real Truth about the Economy 10. Sustainable Development 29. Real Un(der)employment Rate	International Finance	20. The Fed: Wrong Turn in Risky Traffic 34. Consolidating Capitalism 37. From GATT to WTO 38. U.S. Trade Policy after the Cold War 40. U.S. Trade Deficits and International Competitiveness 41. Exporting the Truth on Trade
European Union	34. Consolidating Capitalism 36. Global Growth Is on a Tear 37. From GATT to WTO 38. U.S. Trade Policy after the Cold War 44. East Germany's Transitional Economy	International Trade	2. Economic Report of the President 10. Sustainable Development 18. Inequality Express 34. Consolidating Capitalism 35. Power and Policy 36. Global Growth Is on a Tear 37. From GATT to WTO 38. U.S. Trade Policy after the Cold War 39. Down in the Dumps 40. U.S. Trade Deficits and International Competition 41. Exporting the Truth on Trade 42. Cars and VCR's Aren't Necessarily the First Domino 45. Can a Socialist Republic Find Happiness?
Federal Deficit	2. Economic Report of the President 6. Taking the Measure of Economics 11. What's in Store? 12. Pitfalls of a Balanced Budget 13. Budget Blaster 14. Saving, Economic Growth, and the Arrow of Causality 16. True Tax Reform		
Federal Reserve System	2. Economic Report of the President 6. Taking the Measure of Economics 9. Real Truth about the Economy 19. Activist Monetary Policy for Good or Evil? 20. The Fed: Wrong Turn in Risky Traffic 21. It's Not Broke 24. Future of Money 32. Parties Skirmish over Budget		

TOPIC AREA	TREATED IN:	TOPIC AREA	TREATED IN:
Keynesian Economics	1. Economics of My Times and Yours 2. Economic Report of the President 4. Economic Possibilities for Our Grandchildren 12. Pitfalls of a Balanced Budget 19. Activist Monetary Policy for Good or Evil?	**Social Security**	11. What's in Store? 15. Taxpayers Are Angry 32. Parties Skirmish over Budget
		Supply-Side Economics	3. Revisionism in the History of Supply-Side Economics 15. Taxpayers Are Angry 26. Our NAIRU Limit
Long-Wave Theory	33. Long Wave in Inflation and Real Interest Rates	**Taxation**	3. Revisionism in the History of Supply-Side Economics 5. Economy You Can't See 11. What's in Store? 12. Pitfalls of a Balanced Budget 14. Saving, Economic Growth, and the Arrow of Causality 15. Taxpayers Are Angry 16. True Tax Reform 17. Europeans Shrug as Taxes Go Up
Monetarism	1. Economics of My Times and Yours 20. The Fed: Wrong Turn in Risky Traffic 21. It's Not Broke		
Monetary Policy	12. Pitfalls of a Balanced Budget 19. Activist Monetary Policy for Good or Evil? 20. The Fed: Wrong Turn in Risky Traffic 21. It's Not Broke 24. Future of Money 26. Our NAIRU Limit 32. Parties Skirmish over Budget	**Underground Economy**	5. Economy You Can't See
		Unemployment	9. Real Truth about the Economy 10. Sustainable Development 12. Pitfalls of a Balanced Budget 18. Inequality Express 26. Our NAIRU Limit 27. Technology and Unemployment 28. Flexibility Trap 29. Real Un(der)employment Rate 33. Long Wave in Inflation and Real Interest Rates
Newly Industrializing Countries (NICs)	10. Sustainable Development 34. Consolidating Capitalism 35. Power and Policy 36. Global Growth Is on a Tear 45. Can a Socialist Republic Find Happiness?		
North American Free Trade Agreement (NAFTA)	2. Economic Report of the President 38. U.S. Trade Policy after the Cold War 43. Changing Relationship between the State and the Economy in Mexico	**U.S. Income Distribution**	1. Economics of My Times and Yours 11. What's in Store? 13. Budget Blaster 15. Taxpayers Are Angry 18. Inequality Express 25. Bank Failure 28. Flexibility Trap 31. Has Our Living Standard Stalled?
Productivity	7. Services 9. Real Truth about the Economy 11. What's in Store? 27. Technology and Unemployment 28. Flexibility Trap 36. Global Growth Is on a Tear 40. U.S. Trade Deficits and International Competitiveness 42. Cars and VCR's Aren't Necessarily the First Domino		
		World Trade Organization	37. From GATT to WTO 45. Can a Socialist Republic Find Happiness?
Protectionism	35. Power and Policy 37. From GATT to WTO 38. U.S. Trade Policy after the Cold War 39. Down in the Dumps 40. U.S. Trade Deficits and International Competitiveness		
Regulation	18. Inequality Express 21. It's Not Broke 22. Banking 23. Should the Feds Have Greater Control over State Banks? 25. Bank Failure		

Introduction to Macroeconomics

Economics is a science of thinking in terms of models joined to the art of choosing models which are relevant to the contemporary world. (John Maynard Keynes)

This reader is about the ways in which economists think about economic problems and the advice they give to those who make economic policy. Its focus is on macroeconomics, the branch of economics that provides an overview of the ways in which an economy's major components—households, businesses, and governments—are related. Topics of investigation include such large, economy-wide variables as national output, the extent of unemployment, the general level of prices, and the rate of economic growth. Also considered are ways in which government policies might be used to promote various national goals, including high levels of employment, price stability, and an adequate expansion of output over time.

If you are a newcomer to the study of economics, you may be confused and dismayed by what you hear economists say about economic problems and policies. Someone once summed this up with the observation that "if all economists were laid end-to-end, they would never reach a conclusion." Outside observers want agreement on economic issues, and they are often discontent when they find that deep divisions exist within the economics profession. Why can't economists agree? they ask. The simplest answer is that economists, like other human beings, often have strongly held political and social beliefs. Professional quarrels are not primarily over scientific issues—in fact, most economists use the same scientific language in their debates. Rather, the disagreements among economists frequently reflect fundamental differences in value systems. This is particularly true where macroeconomics is concerned.

This is an exciting time to begin a study of economics. The last few decades have witnessed major changes in both the U.S. and the global economy. As they look back on this period of turbulence, today's economists—perhaps reflecting a more pragmatic, less ideological position—are asking: What have we learned from this experience that will guide us in understanding what needs to be done before the dawn of a new century? Like bruised combatants after a lengthy battle, they may be somewhat more tolerant of opposing views.

This unit begins with an article in which Herbert Stein, former chairman of the Council of Economic Advisors, surveys trends in macroeconomics over more than a half-century. For Stein this period is marked by fundamental changes in the sorts of problems with which economists must contend. The key issues of an earlier time (primarily macroeconomic stability and economic growth) have been displaced by new ones (including poverty and social pathology). The question for economists today is, what do they have to contribute for a solution of such problems?

Following that essay is an assessment by James Galbraith of the 1995 *Economic Report of the President*. This report (issued annually) conveys the core economic beliefs of the government's executive branch. Galbraith finds the 1995 edition flawed in both its overall analysis and handling of statistics.

In "Revisionism in the History of Supply-Side Economics," Robert Dunn Jr. and Joseph Cordes then trace the origins of "supply-side economics" (a topic in which there appears to be renewed interest today). They examine what the authors of this theory originally intended it to mean, and how its meaning has changed over time.

The unit concludes with "Economic Possibilities for Our Grandchildren," an essay written by John Maynard Keynes in 1930 offering a fascinating perspective on the future. Keynes's comment that "we are suffering now from a bad attack of economic pessimism" seems prophetic. The fact that he wrote this more than 60 years ago (prior to the Great Depression and all of the many economic difficulties since then) may trouble us. Yet, Keynes urges us to take a longer view, and he offers some much-needed hope. In 100 years he foresees the demise of the economic problem as we presently understand it. Instead, Keynes contends, filling leisure time in a meaningful way will prove to be our grandchildren's chief concern.

Looking Ahead: Challenge Questions

In his article, what does Herbert Stein say about the problems that concern economists? In what ways have these problems changed over the last half century?

What are the key points in James Galbraith's critique of the 1995 *Economic Report of the President*?

What is the original meaning of "supply-side economics"?

Do you agree with John Maynard Keynes's forecast of economic life in the year 2030? Why or why not?

Economics of My Times and Yours

Herbert Stein

Herbert Stein is a Senior Fellow at the American Enterprise Institute, Washington, DC, and a former Chairman of The Council of Economic Advisers. This paper was presented at the thirty-sixth Annual Meeting of NABE, Washington, DC, September 25-28, 1994 and was adapted from an article in *The American Enterprise*, September/October 1994.

Before about 1965, policy economics was concerned with flaws in the system due to inadequate and fluctuating demand, which could be addressed with fiscal and monetary tools. In the past twenty years, emphasis has shifted to issues of growth and the stagnation or decline in real income. Economists, working with other disciplines, will have to deal with a new problem — the capabilities, attitudes and behavior of the population.

I WOULD LIKE to give a thumbnail sketch of what has happened to policy economics during my lifetime as an economist and what I think is the present situation.

I entered economics near the beginning of what has been called "The Age of the Economist." It was a period of about thirty years of high and rising confidence in the ability of economists to solve the nation's problems.

In 1933, the year in which I decided to major in economics, the unemployment rate was 25 percent, the highest in history. We didn't know the number then, but we knew that is was very high. In 1935, the year I entered graduate school, Keynes' *The General Theory of Employment, Interest and Money* was published. These two events — high unemployment and Keynes' book — dominated economics for the next thirty years. That did not mean that we were all "Keynesians" in any narrow sense. But, as my contemporary at the University of Chicago, Al Hart, said, you could be pro-Keynesian or anti-Keynesian, but you could no longer be pre-Keynesian.

ECONOMIC PROBLEMS THEN

We had a certain view of our economic condition.

We had an efficient and potentially very rich economy. But there was some mechanical deficiency that kept us from realizing our potential. If that deficiency were corrected, people would pursue their own interests rationally and effectively and everything would be all right. Everyone would want to live by bourgeois values — studying and working hard, making provision for the future and taking responsibility for their families.

Also, we thought we knew what the flaw in the system was and how to correct it. The flaw was that aggregate demand was inadequate or fluctuated too much. We also thought that the correction could be found in some combination of fiscal and monetary measures — the fiscal measures associated with the name of Keynes and the monetary measures, which came into prominence later, associated with the name of Milton Friedman.

The distinction between fiscal and monetary policy is not important for my story, although it has absorbed much of the attention of economists. My point is that there was believed to be some macroeconomic button that could be pushed to make the machine run smoothly without fussing with its internal structure or operation.

This kind of thinking, both about what the problem was and about where the solution lay, was the basis for the Employment Act of 1946. That Act established the Council of Economic Advisers to the President and the Joint Economic Committee in the Congress and was a testament to public faith in economics.

Belief in this identification of the problem and confidence in that solution persisted for a long time, but both began to fade after 1965. Skepticism set in first with respect to fiscal policy, during the Vietnam War. Experience showed that economists did not forecast the economy and the effect of fiscal measures upon it well enough to keep demand very close to a predetermined path.

But there was a more fundamental difficulty, illustrated by President Johnson's reluctance to raise taxes to pay for the war. This revealed what should have been known all along. Taxes and expenditures are not value-free counters to be put on the scales of the economy, or taken off, by economists to achieve their notion of balance. They are policies in which taxpayers and recipients of benefits have strong interests that they are unwilling to subordinate to an economist's

mathematical model. And this unwillingness is correct, not ignorant.

Confidence in monetarism came along later and lasted longer. But anyone who reads the papers can see that there is no longer any faith in monetary economics. Instead faith has been displaced to the inscrutable oracle at the Federal Reserve. While this faith may be rewarded, it is not economics.

At the same time that we were losing faith in the ability of economics to solve it, the problem of inadequacy or instability of demand began to seem less overwhelming than we had thought since the Great Depression. Was this due to the success of economics? We really do not know, but there is now a body of research to suggest that the economy was just as stable before the Great Depression — say from 1869 to 1929 — as it has been since World War II. Only the Great Depression was unique. Otherwise, we have about the same degree of instability as we had before economists became so smart.

Also, we have become better adjusted to living with instability than we were. The problem in recessions, even in the great depression, was not that average incomes were absolutely low. The problem had two aspects. First, average incomes had fallen, so that, even though not low, they were lower than people were used to and expected. Second, the average was very unevenly distributed, so that the burdens were concentrated on the unemployed. But today people are better able to cope with a drop in their incomes because they have more assets, mainly in the form of owned homes and durable goods, so that they can get along better with some decline of income. Moreover, the burden of unemployment has been somewhat socialized. This is partly the result of unemployment compensation but even more the result of the prevalence of two-worker families.

In the past twenty years or so, the attention of economists and makers of economic policy has turned, or returned, to another problem. That is the problem of economic growth — of raising total output. This was the original Adam Smith problem, which he dealt with in *The Wealth of Nations*.

In 1928, Keynes, the great iconoclast, wrote an essay questioning the traditional value placed on growth. He calculated that in 100 years, at foreseeable rates of growth, per capita incomes in the developed countries would be from four to eight times as high as it then was. He thought that, when such a level of income was reached, further increase of income would not seem of much importance. We are now two-thirds of the way through Keynes' 100 years and three-fourths of the way to his forecast income level four times as high as in 1928. By his reasoning, we are close to the point at which more growth will be unimportant.

A Canadian economist, with the wonderful name of A.F.W. Plumptre, whom I knew during the war, disputed Keynes's conclusion. He said that wants are insatiable, so that, even if the forecast increase of income occurred, people would want more. That argument, however, leads to a paradox. Either we are going to become so rich that becoming richer will seem unimportant, or becoming richer brings us no closer to the satisfaction of our wants, which are infinite, so what is the point?

Moreover, at least two decades of worrying about economic growth have yielded very little knowledge about how to accelerate growth. Probably most economists in the past fifteen years have thought that reducing budget deficits would speed up growth, but estimates of the size of the effect vary widely, with the most plausible estimates being quite small.

So, at least in my opinion, the two problems, the instability problem and the growth problem, that have been the staples of economics as we know it, are not the critical problems, and we are not confident of our ability to contribute much to their solution.

ECONOMIC PROBLEMS NOW

Now we face the problems of an economy that is very rich and growing at a moderate pace. In my opinion these problems are summed up in the words poverty and social pathology. In spite of the increase in average per capita incomes in the past twenty years, the proportion of the population with incomes below an absolute measure of poverty has remained roughly stable — after fifty years in which it had declined substantially. The composition of the poverty population has changed, consisting increasingly of women with children and no husband present. Even among people with incomes that are low but not below the official poverty line, real incomes have stagnated or declined for twenty years. The share of total income received by the lowest fifth of the population has declined.

Many, but not all, of the poor people suffer from, or live in neighborhoods where a lot of other people suffer from, behaviors that are harmful to them and disdained by the mainstream population. Most significant is women bearing children at an early age and without the economic and emotional support of a man. Also there is neglect of educational opportunities, failure to seek employment vigorously, participation in crime, and drug and alcohol addiction. These economic, social and psychological problems are suffered disproportionately by Afro-American and Hispanic minorities, but not exclusively by them.

The question for economists today is what they have to contribute to the solution of those problems.

Three explanations are commonly offered for these conditions:

1. there has been a change in the demand for labor,

probably with a technological origin, that has reduced the demand for unskilled labor and consequently the earnings of the unskilled;

2. the various aspects of the welfare state have increased incentives to behave in unproductive ways, or at least weakened the disincentives against such behavior;

3. there has been a change in values that has weakened the internal and social forces making for stable families, hard work, provision for the future and responsibility for others.

All of these factors are probably at work. Moreover they reinforce each other. For example, if the welfare system reduces the cost of being an unmarried, teen-age mother, there will be more of them. But if there are more of them, and they become less exceptional, the stigma of being an unmarried mother fades away, and we have what looks like a change of values, and actually is.

Three kinds of remedies are proposed for the three causes of the problem. For the shift of demand away from unskilled labor, the proposed remedy is education and training. For the negative consequences of the welfare system, the remedy is welfare reform to reduce the reward for unconstructive behavior. For the values problem, the prescription is preaching.

There is probably merit in each of these remedial approaches. But some difficulties are also obvious. Some of the disadvantaged people are already so far behind in their education and so negative in their attitudes that only an extremely large investment in education and training would enable them to earn an income that the society will consider minimally adequate. It may be cheaper to support them than to educate and train them.

A similar difficulty afflicts welfare reform. This has already been encountered in the current proposals to require welfare recipients to go to work after two years on the rolls. It turns out that the costs of providing training, subsidized jobs and child care are very large, and the net results very uncertain. Similarly, it is proposed to try to change the payment system to discourage teen-age, out-of-wedlock childbirth. But there are already over 10 million children who are the product of such behavior, and even if the welfare reform should reduce the future number there will be some. The society will not put them out on the mountainside to die, and if they are supported, some incentive to produce more will remain.

As for the preaching, that may have some effect, but slowly. One problem is that the affected population does not listen much to Dan Quayle; very few of them are members of the Commonwealth Club of San Francisco, his favorite venue.

I do not mean to be negative about trying to deal with these problems. Indeed, I think we need to devote much more money and energy to them. But I want to suggest how different these problems are from those with which my generation of economists has been concerned.

Basically we looked at a world in which the population had the Puritan virtues. They took a long view, studied hard, worked, saved, and looked after their children. Productivity was distributed unequally, but given basic universal education the distribution would not be so unequal that many would be unable to earn an acceptable income. Moreover, the rising tide would lift all the boats. Economic policy had two main functions. It had to maintain macroeconomic conditions and open markets in which people could use their talents to the utmost. Beyond that it had to look after the widows and orphans — who would be the orphans of standard, two-parent families.

That is, the population was not the problem; the economic system was the problem. Today it is the population — its capabilities, attitudes and behavior — that is the problem. I want to avoid saying that in a judgmental way. If the market now rewards nimble fingers much more than a strong back, that does mean there is anything intrinsically inferior about a strong back. It is simply a fact about markets in the current stage of technological development. Even some of the attitudes that we typically regard as superior may have only local and temporary value. For example, Keynes regarded the anal propensity to save as a flaw both individually and socially.

Anyway, I think that we as economists are not now well prepared to deal with these problems. One possibility would be to leave them to sociologists, social workers, psychologists and preachers. That would be to rescue ourselves from the most important and interesting issues of our time. We would be, as Keynes said we might, like dentists, skilled at some essential but banal and repetitive tasks.

I do not, however, believe that this withdrawal by economists is necessary or desirable. Economists have techniques and a tradition of rigor, objectivity and far-sightedness that can be usefully applied to the new tasks, in conjunction with the work of other disciplines. But first economists will have to be seized with problems of their times, as we sixty years ago were seized with ours.

Economic Report of the President: A Review

James K. Galbraith

JAMES K. GALBRAITH teaches economics at the Lyndon B. Johnson School of Public Affairs, the University of Texas at Austin, and is co-author of *Macroeconomics,* a textbook from Houghton Mifflin.

This year's Economic Report of the President is a let-down. There appears to be a pervasive problem. Over the past two years, the spirit of Keynes has been driven altogether out of this administration and, as the Balanced Budget Amendment debate showed, out of the Democratic Party.

The defeat of the Balanced Budget Amendment in the U.S. Senate last month frames an interesting ethical question: When is a bad argument justified in a good cause? Plainly, the issue on which the final votes turned—that Social Security surpluses should be somehow walled off from the rest of the budget—was absurd. But on the other hand, the device worked. It gave Senators Kent Conrad and Byron Dorgan of North Dakota a hook.

I'm inclined to cheer Conrad and Dorgan on the ground that the Senate process is one to which stratagem and ploy are integral, and where substantive ends may well justify rhetorical means. The Balanced Budget Amendment was itself a poll-driven political text—a Republican wedge issue. In stopping it, Conrad and Dorgan acted as skilled politicians and developed a passable counterwedge. Surely, this is within the rules of engagement.

But the same rules cannot apply to official reports from expert agencies of the government—such as the Federal Reserve Board, the Congressional Budget Office, or (preeminently) the President's Council of Economic Advisers. Such documents are signed by figures of authority—not only in politics, but also in more general circumstances. They ought, therefore, to be held to the standards of argument that the signers would impose on themselves as independent professionals. They ought not be venues for apologia, rationalization, and hype.

How then to judge the following passages taken from the first two pages of the 1995 *Economic Report of the President?* "By most standard macroeconomic indicators, the performance of the U.S. economy in 1994 was, in a word, outstanding. . . . The economy's performance in 1994 is even more remarkable when viewed against the backdrop of the economic challenges confronting the nation around the time this administration took office. . . . This administration moved quickly and decisively to improve the economic situation, and the turnaround in macroeconomic performance has been dramatic. . . . At the same time, the administration

has acted to help reverse the long-term trends that continue to depress the incomes of many Americans . . . and has begun to move the nation in the direction necessary to again place the American dream within the grasp of all Americans."

When the 1994 *Economic Report of the President* appeared, I praised it in this magazine for its reasoned, nonpolemical tone. Indeed, that *Report* could have made a much sharper critique of preceding policies than it did. But it refrained from doing so—in part because, following the defeat of the early 1993 economic "stimulus" package, the Council did not expect the new President's policies to show much improvement. The 1994 growth forecast was for a bare 3 percent—no better than in 1993. And that was said to be contingent on a continuing reduction of long-term interest rates.

> How can we reconcile the administration's assurance that NAFTA will be good for everyone concerned—certainly Mexico—with its assertion that the collapse of the Mexican economy and peso was "brought on by Mexico's inability to finance its large current-account deficit?"

As it turned out, growth in 1994 was one percentage point better than expected. And this occurred despite the fact that the Federal Reserve broke faith with the administration's deficit-reduction program and spent the year raising interest rates. But why? The question remains unanswered. This year's Council grabs credit for a phenomenon it did not predict and does not explain.

In this case, the Federal Reserve Board's official account, transmitted to Congress on February 21, 1995, is more balanced and more honest: "The Federal Reserve continued to tighten policy over the course of the year and into 1995, as economic growth remained unexpectedly strong. . . . Developments in financial markets—for example, easier credit availability through banks and a decline in the foreign-exchange value of the dollar—may have muted the effects of the tightening of monetary policy." In other words, higher-than-expected growth arose under the circumstances for unexpected and at least partly unwelcome

reasons: (1) deeper indebtedness for firms and households; and (2) a falling dollar. This is not a course that the Federal Reserve itself intends to tolerate indefinitely. Nor will it "place the American dream within the grasp of all Americans" anytime soon.

ANALYSIS OR PROPAGANDA?

The distinction between analysis and propaganda comes to mind again and again as one peruses the new *Report*. For instance, we are told that: "One of the most fundamental lessons of economic history is that sustained economic expansion depends on sound fiscal foundations." The Council presents no evidence for this bit of wisdom. But that is not surprising, since American economic history from Roosevelt to Reagan contradicts it. Or again, on NAFTA: "Though the beneficial effects will take years to manifest themselves fully, the results, to date, confirm the view that NAFTA is good for the United States, Mexico, and Canada. So far, there is little evidence of the sucking sound that critics had alleged would accompany NAFTA. Indeed, the sounds most associated with NAFTA are those of trains, trucks and ships loading cargo, bound for destinations across the border."

How is this to be reconciled with the collapse of the Mexican economy and peso, which are described *on the same page* as "brought on by Mexico's inability to finance its large current-account deficit?" Two pages below, the *Report* answered: "It is also important to understand that NAFTA neither contributed to the peso devaluation nor in any way affected the U.S. government's response." In other words, NAFTA generated vast U.S. exports to Mexico—those trains, trucks, and ships (trains? . . . to Mexico?) —*without*, in any way, adding to the "large current-account deficit" of that country. As Robin McNeil might put it: "I see."

Sometimes the theology is laid on a bit thick, as in this passage at the end of a chapter that defends the existence of government: "Adam Smith published the Wealth of Nations in 1776; the same year, Thomas Jefferson wrote the Declaration of Independence. Since that time, the United States has become a vastly larger and more prosperous nation. One reason is that, throughout our history, government has worked in partnership with the private sector to promote competition, discourage externalities, and provide public goods."

Yes, quite.

THE CREDO

For all of its defects of form, the 1995 *Economic Report of the President* does convey, in structure and substance, the core economic beliefs of the present administration at midterm. And these provide insight into the state of thinking that passes for mainstream liberalism in the Clinton/Gingrich era.

Above all, the *Report* embraces a hydraulic model of capital accumulation, production, and productivity, based on a very strong form of Say's Law, in which saving is the social virtue above all else. Thus the emphasis on deficit reduction: "A primary economic reason for reducing the federal deficit is to increase national saving, in the expectation that increased saving will, in turn, increase national investment in physical capital. . . . The implication is that increased national saving should be associated with increased productivity." In contrast to last year's *Report,* the market mechanism that is usually supposed to link increased savings to investment—namely, a reduction in the long-term interest rate—is barely mentioned.

> For all of its defects of form, the 1995 *Economic Report of the President* does convey, in structure and substance, the core economic beliefs of the present administration at midterm. And these provide insight into the state of thinking that passes for mainstream liberalism in the Clinton/Gingrich era.

The *Report* is careful to state that deficit reduction is not an unlimited virtue. It insists that public investments are good and should not be cut, and that too much deficit reduction too soon is dangerous: ". . . because deficit reduction—whether accomplished through increases in revenue or decreases in spending—has a direct contractionary effect on aggregate spending. There are limits to the amount of deficit reduction the economy can be expected to withstand within a short period without endangering economic growth. Over the long run, deficit reduction makes room for additional private investment; but, in the short run, it depresses aggregate demand and as a result can actually depress private investment." In other words, we live in a world in which bad things

happening in a long sequence of short runs average out to be good things in the long run. The logic of this will be clear to professional economists, but to no one else. It is exactly the same as the logic that governs the businessman who loses a little on every sale, but makes up for it in volume.

PRICE MISMEASUREMENT

The remaining credo is laid out over Chapters Three through Six. It consists of four somewhat overlapping precepts: (1) increasing productivity; (2) more efficient markets and governments; (3) improving skills; and (4) free trade. The chapter entitled, "Increasing the Nation's Productive Capacity," begins by surveying the standard literature on growth accounting, with its famous findings that most productivity growth stems neither from labor nor capital but from the unknown "residual." It adds the collateral finding that virtually all of the measured productivity slowdown since 1972 also stems from the slowdown in the contribution of the residual. Declines in capital intensity had almost nothing to do with it, while the contribution to productivity from improved worker quality actually increased.

What then accounts for the declining residual? Failing infrastructure? Rising regulation? Oil prices? We do not know. And the *Report* admits that we do not know. Indeed, it goes a long way toward endorsing an argument that I and others have been making for nearly a decade—namely, that errors of price measurement may account for much of the alleged phenomenon of declining productivity growth: "Measurement of prices is *the* critical problem in the measurement of productivity. The output of the economy increasingly is shifting away from standardized commodities with easily definable characteristics that change little over time, toward goods and services for which issues of quality and even definition are of primary importance. And if the trend in prices is mismeasured, so will be the trend in output and hence productivity." But, if this is true to a substantial extent, then the "productivity slowdown" tends to disappear. The bits we can measure (mainly in computers) do suggest large effects overall.

Indeed, depending on just how much worse price mismeasurement became, it is not impossible that, in some real sense, productivity growth actually *accelerated* after 1972. It is also possible (even likely) that technological change became *capital-augmenting* over this time, as the real price of information tech-

nology plummeted and computer equipment virtually took over business capital investment.

But if the "productivity slowdown" disappears, so do all the reasons to be concerned with deficits, saving, investment, and supposed difficulties in the acquisition of skills. In that case, increased saving and investment, harder work, and abstinence are precisely the wrong prescriptions. What we need instead is an increase in leisure, a broader base of adequate mass consumption, and income security. Equally important would be direct attention to our deteriorating quality of life. These views are politically homeless nowadays, but they may well be right.

The Council marches on. Chapter Four contains an obligatory, mostly anecdotal section on the benefits of the National Performance Review. It also presents a review of progress toward deregulation in agriculture, farming, telecommunications, and transportation. There is no analysis of the administration's most far-reaching deregulatory proposal—the repeal of Glass-Steagall's wall between commercial and investment banking.

WAGES AND INCOME

Chapter Five returns to the human element in productivity improvement, under the guise of discussing the rapid rise in the inequality of wages and incomes. Its policy views are set from the beginning: "The large declines in the real wages of less-educated and lower-paid workers were associated with increased inequality in family incomes and with growing rates of poverty among working families." The pattern repeats itself here. The *Report* states facts but declines to draw conclusions. For example, the alleged effect of skill on earnings does not apply to black Americans: "In contrast to the decline of relative earnings and years of school completed, test scores among blacks have risen relative to whites. The difference in high school dropout rates between blacks and whites has narrowed sharply." As the Council states (though without documentation), it could be that a fall-off in antidiscrimination enforcement under Reagan did contribute to poor economic performance of African Americans. But isn't it possible as well that this glaring contradiction also shows the weakness of the skill-mismatch thesis and the associated sole reliance on education and training programs to fight inequality?

The skunk in the basement of the inequality issue is, of course, the influence of trade. The Council actu-

ally does admit that, "dramatic changes in technology and in global competition . . . have affected industrialized economies around the world, reducing the relative demand for workers with less education and training." But crucially, it overlooks the fact that the reverse is true of the *industrializing* regions, where the relative demand for workers with only a basic education has soared, indicating large-scale substitution of Southern for Northern labor. And it missed other facts laid out early last year in a landmark study by Adrian

> The fundamental reality is that it is trade, not technology or skills per se, that has driven the largest wedge between high and low pay in the United States since 1970.

Wood—*North-South Trade, Employment and Inequality*, Oxford University Press. (I vainly called the Council's attention to that study in my review of the 1994 *Report.*) With all this, the Council is able, once again, to deny the fundamental reality that it is trade, not technology or skills *per se*, that has driven the largest wedge between high and low pay in the United States since 1970.

The Council devotes this to the issue: "Intensifying global competition is also cited as a factor in putting downward pressure on wages of less-educated workers. However, a number of studies have found that the easily measured direct effects of trade on the wage distribution were small, implying that the vast majority of the demand shift originated domestically. . . . These effects of trade may be larger, if the internationalization of the U.S. economy also affects wages indirectly—for example, if the threat of increased import competition or of the relocation of a factory to another country undermines workers' bargaining power. It is not known how important such effects have been."

My translation follows:

• Some people disagree with us;

• when we restrict our focus to a few very easily measured effects (like the drunk under the streetlight), we can't find the influence of trade;

• these easily measured effects don't include the ones that actually count;

• we haven't read the studies that find much larger effects.

In truth, the Council just wants to go on believing (contrary to theory *and* evidence) that expanded trade can have virtually no bad consequences for anyone. The reason for this directed acquittal is clear from Chapter Six, "Liberalizing International Trade." It is a paean to GATT, the WTO, the NAFTA, the APEC, and every other reduction of trade barriers on the administration's agenda. With it, we get restatements of comparative advantage—assurances that free trade is, *ipso facto*, good for the environment. (To be sure, this is plausible in some cases.) It also offers reassurances that the disruptions of trade are always small, relative to the benefits. The *tour d'horizon* of these measures is useful; the analytical content is nil.

Interspersed through these pages are occasional boxes. They indicate that political reality hasn't entirely escaped notice. Among them are: "The Shortcomings of a Balanced Budget Amendment," "The Cost of Doing Nothing About Health Care," and "Scoring the Revenue Consequences of Tax and Expenditures Changes." These have the aspect of having been assembled in haste. No doubt, next year's *Report* could be devoted in its entirety to a serious discussion of similar issues.

THE DEEPER PROBLEM

Last year's *Economic Report of the President* was excellent. Why, then, is this one so bad? To be sure, the administration is in much worse trouble. Political demoralization may have left a mark—particularly on the rhetoric. One should not be too harsh. But it seems to me there is a deeper problem. Over the past two years, the spirit of Keynes has been driven altogether out of this administration and, as the Balanced Budget Amendment debate showed, out of the Democratic Party. It was driven out of fiscal policy, when the so-called "stimulus package" was allowed to die in early 1993. It was driven out of monetary policy in February 1994, when the Federal Reserve started raising rates and the President did not object. And (except to the meager extent of this year's bail-out loan to Mexico) it never got a start in international policy, where it is absolutely necessary as complement to a politics of free trade.

> *The administration abandoned the Keynesian spirit. It was driven out of fiscal policy, when the so-called "stimulus package" was allowed to die in early 1993. It was driven out of monetary policy in February 1994, when the Federal Reserve started raising rates and the President did not object.*

With no demand management to its policy, this administration has been forced into a pure form of supply-side economics, however liberal in tone. Deficit cuts are to boost the supply of savings and capital. Expenditure switching and incentives are to increase the supply of infrastructure and know-how. Education and training are to increase the supply of skills. And some lubricants are to make the markets—both domestic and foreign—work more efficiently.

That's it, folks. We've been handed a natural-law economics—the ideal and optimistic vision of Adam Smith. It is pre-Malthus, pre-Marx, and pre-Keynes. There are no false-color tax cuts here. This is the real thing—incentives and markets and nothing else. What we have here is the supply-side textbook, reduced to impotence by Democrats.

Somewhere out in California, I just know that Ronald Reagan and Art Laffer are laughing.

Revisionism in the History of Supply-Side Economics

Robert M. Dunn, Jr. and
Joseph J. Cordes

Professors of Economics, George Washington University

Although supply-side economics has largely faded from active discussion among economists, the recent increase in upper-bracket income tax rates and the approach of the 1996 presidential campaign may resurrect interest in its arguments.

In considering what supply-side economics may add to future debates over taxes, it would be useful to know what the original supply-siders actually said—a subject over which there has been some recent controversy.

Faulty memory

Many economists who are old enough to have followed policy debates in the 1978–81 period remember (or think that they remember) claims by proponents of supply-side economics that the incentive effects of a reduction in federal income tax rates would be so large that the Federal government would recapture all of the revenue losses, and that the reduction would result in no increase in the federal budget deficit. The U.S. tax system, it was argued, was beyond the peak of the Laffer curve, so that a tax cut would produce more (or at least no less) revenue.

The argument that high tax rates can depress economic activity, and perhaps government revenues, is not new. Arthur B. Laffer and Jan P. Seymour cited Ibn Khaldun, a 14th-century Arabic philosopher, as arguing that, because of disincentive effects, "At the end of the dynasty, taxation yields a small revenue from large assessments." They also noted that Henry George stressed the disincentive effects of high tax rates on production in 1879. They might have added Adam Smith, in *The Wealth of Nations*, to the list of early economists who argued that high tax rates provided a strong disincentive for productive activity.

Martin Anderson and Paul Craig Roberts, administration officials in the early Reagan years and defenders of Reaganomics, have recently argued that the view that a major tax cut would be fully self-financ-

From *Challenge*, July/August 1994, pp. 50-53. © 1994 by M. E. Sharpe, Inc., Armonk, NY 10504. Reprinted by permission.

ing is a gross misrepresentation of supply-side economics. A *Wall Street Journal* column by Martin Anderson (excerpted from his book *Revolution*), which presents this view, makes some rather serious charges of inaccuracy against a number of prominent economists who said that supply-siders had predicted that the Kemp-Roth tax cut would recapture all (rather than some) of its revenue losses through incentive effects.

These economists included Martin Feldstein, Walter Salant, Herbert Stein, Alan Blinder, William Branson, and Robert Solow. In corresponding with these economists (each of whom said that supply-siders had claimed that Kemp-Roth would recapture its revenue losses through incentive effects), Anderson describes himself as "feeling somewhat like Diogenes searching with a lantern in broad daylight for an honest man." The column concluded with the following:

"When eminent scholars from Harvard, Princeton, MIT, AEI, and Brookings make such consistently false charges openly to large audiences of their professional peers and not a peep is raised, there may be something more at work here than careless or shabby scholarship on the part of an individual professor or two. One has to seriously entertain the possibility that academic economists as a group have been driven to such an envious and resentful fury by Reaganomics, that they have, for a time, put aside their professional standards. Perhaps there is a nicer explanation for this intellectual malpractice; perhaps they meant well, but were just careless. Unfortunately, in the world of scholarship, the result of both carelessness and lying is the same." The

Roberts arguments were put less harshly, but they concluded, "Thus there is literally no basis for the caricature of supply-side economics as the belief that tax cuts pay for themselves."

Searching for the truth

Who is correct? Those of us who remember (or believe that we remember) the claim that the Kemp-Roth tax cut would produce no increase in the federal budget deficit? Or are the recent defenders of Reaganomics correct? They protest that no such claim was ever made and that, instead, all that was promised was that *some* of the revenue losses would be recaptured?

A trip to the library produces quite different answers to this question—depending on what one reads and on when it was written. Writings by supply-side economists and their congressional testimony in support of Kemp-Roth during the 1980–81 period are impressively restrained. There were no claims of full revenue-recapture in the testimony of Jack Kemp, Don Regan, and Arthur Laffer; and revenue forecasts were prepared in a surprisingly orthodox fashion.

When Arthur Laffer testified before the House of Representatives Committee on Ways and Means in support of the Kemp-Roth bill on March 4, 1981, the late Joseph Pechman, who was the next witness, congratulated him on his restraint by saying: "I was pleased to hear that Arthur Laffer did not exaggerate some of the things that have been attributed to supply-side economists. What he told us was that if you reduce taxes or increase the net return to saving and to labor, there will be an increase in in-

centives to work and to save. I think that every economist, regardless of his persuasion would agree with that."

If all that Laffer and the other supply-siders meant was that lower tax rates meant stronger incentives for productive activity that would provide partial revenue-recapture, how could so many economists have gotten the impression that they predicted full revenue-recapture because the U.S. tax system was in the prohibitive range of the Laffer curve?

The truth exposed

The answer can be found by going back to 1978, when supply-side economics and the Laffer curve first entered public discussion. The admirable restraint of the 1980–81 period was decidedly lacking in public presentations of supply-side economics and of the Laffer curve during 1978. The April 10, 1978 issue of *Fortune* ran a lengthy article on Jack Kemp's proposed tax cut which said, "Lowering tax rates from such counterproductive levels can increase government revenue by stimulating greater output. That is why Kemp has no fear that his tax proposals would result in a bigger federal deficit." The same *Fortune* article contained an inserted box entitled, "Professor Laffer's Famous Curve," which said, "When tax rates are in this counterproductive range—and Laffer thinks that is the case in the United States today—cuts in taxes should bring increased economic activity and higher, not lower, tax revenues." This article was reprinted in the Laffer and Seymour book, but with an interesting omission. The box within the article, which

cites Laffer as predicting full revenue-recapture, is missing in the reprint volume that was co-edited by Laffer a year later.

The introduction to that volume, however, concluded on page 2 by arguing that, "As often as not a cut in tax rates will lower deficits. With more goods and less deficit-financing, inflation will fall. For classical analysis, correctly constituted tax rate reductions do provide the proverbial 'free lunch.'"

In June of 1978, *Newsweek* ran a feature article on Arthur Laffer which said, "Laffer believes the United States is now operating in the 'prohibitive' range and that a tax cut would actually increase revenues by spurring the incentive to spend and invest." It included a drawing of the Laffer curve, with an arrow to a point in the prohibitive range which says, "where we are now," and included a list of those contributing to its preparation. One of those listed was described as "traveling with Laffer," suggesting that the contents of the article were based on conversations with Laffer rather than on secondary sources.

In December of 1978, the *Wall Street Journal* ran an article on Laffer by Alfred Malabre which said, "Mr. Laffer's theory holds in essence that a large tax cut, far beyond the recent federal legislation, would spur economic growth, increase tax revenues, and curb inflation—all without a painful cut in federal spending." Later in the article, Malabre said, "Mr. Laffer contends that taxation in America today has moved appreciably beyond the optimal point on his curve. Further increases in tax rates, he maintains, would only reduce tax revenues. Conversely, he argues that substantial tax cuts would increase incentive, and so production and revenues." The ar-

ticle noted that Laffer was pleased with the article in *Newsweek* and that "multiple copies are displayed in his office," which hardly suggests that *Newsweek* misrepresented his views. The Malabre article is datelined Los Angeles, and the reference to copies of *Newsweek* in Laffer's office indicated that it was based on a personal interview.

The 1978 views of Jack Kemp, the co-author of the supply-side tax cut that was passed in 1981, are expressed quite clearly in a *U.S. News and World Report* interview in July of that year, in which he responded to a question about his tax proposal by saying, "I think that it would generate enough growth to offset the revenue loss." Later in the same article, Kemp was quoted as saying, "When tax rates go beyond 25 percent—as they have in America and particularly in New York State—revenues are lost." A *Newsweek* article on Kemp earlier in 1978 said, "In Kemp's perfervid view, income taxes should be slashed about one-third lower than Carter's proposed rates—to perhaps 50 percent at the top and 8 percent at the bottom. This will generate so much additional capital, disposable income, and incentive, he argues, that the U.S. Treasury will net higher revenues—even at a lower rate—permitting the full range of government programs that the electorate has come to expect."

It is easy to see how economists of that era, including those whose accuracy is impugned in the Anderson column, got the impression that Laffer and Kemp, the leading supply-siders of the period, thought that large tax cuts would recapture all of their revenue losses through incentive effects. The idea became widespread, because Laffer and Kemp were quoted as

having said it—not once, but a number of times—in places such as the *Wall Street Journal, Fortune, U.S News and World Report,* and *Newsweek.* Unless all of these publications misquoted Laffer and Kemp (and there is no indication that claims of such misquotation were made in 1978), the conclusion is unavoidable that the early supply-siders argued that a large reduction in U.S. income tax rates would be self-financing.

Bait and switch?

How could supply-siders have been so careful and prudent in supporting the Kemp-Roth tax cut in 1980–81, after they had made such extravagant claims for the incentive effects of tax cuts in 1978? Perhaps it was the exuberance of youth. They had a new concept that had not been fully thought through, and it was tempting to exaggerate in order to attract an audience. When they thought more carefully about the realities of the U.S. economy, particularly when testifying before skeptical congressional committees, they became more prudent. A more cynical alternative is that they played a game of "bait and switch," using the "bait" of a self-financing tax cut to attract support for Kemp-Roth. As passage became more likely, they "switched" to predictions of lower revenues that would require expenditure cuts, if large budget deficits were to be avoided. Decades in Washington make it difficult to resist the attractions of a cynical explanation, but one cannot read minds—particularly those operating sixteen years in the past. To be gracious, perhaps we should retain our belief in the exuberance and innocence of youth.

Whatever the explanation of the contrast between the extravagant promises of 1978 and the prudence of 1980–81, the recent defenders of Reaganomics, who claim that supply-siders never said that the Kemp-Roth tax cut would be self-financing, are simply wrong. These predictions were made during 1978 in a number of widely read publications; and they were made by Laffer and Kemp, who were the dominant supply-siders of the period. Other supply-siders, who were more prudent, may protest that it was only Laffer and Kemp who made these claims; but

the curve is named after Laffer and the tax bill after Kemp, so what they said matters.

On August 1, 1978, Paul Craig Roberts proposed a somewhat different version of supply-side economics in a *Wall Street Journal* column—namely, that a tax cut would encourage economic growth, which would produce both *partial* revenue-recapture and increased savings. The combination of partial revenue-recapture and increased private savings would mean that a tax cut would produce no increase in interest rates, rather than no increase in the federal

deficit. He said that proponents of the Kemp-Roth bill held his view, despite clear statements by Laffer and Kemp earlier in 1978 that they meant considerably more—namely, full revenue-recapture rather than merely the lack of any increase in interest rates.

In conclusion, attacks by Reagan Administration officials on mainstream economists, who correctly described early supply-side economics as predicting a painless and self-financing tax cut, can be dismissed. Indeed, Anderson and Roberts owe an apology to the mainstreamers.

Economic Possibilities for Our Grandchildren

John Maynard Keynes

We are suffering just now from a bad attack of economic pessimism. It is common to hear people say that the epoch of enormous economic progress which characterised the nineteenth century is over; that the rapid improvement in the standard of life is now going to slow down—at any rate in Great Britain; that a decline in prosperity is more likely than an improvement in the decade which lies ahead of us. . . .

My purpose in this essay, however, is not to examine the present or the near future, but to disembarrass myself of short views and take wings into the future. What can we reasonably expect the level of our economic life to be a hundred years hence? What are the economic possibilities for our grandchildren?

From the earliest times of which we have record—back, say, to two thousand years before Christ—down to the beginning of the eighteenth century, there was no very great change in the standard of life of the average man living in the civilised centres of the earth. Ups and downs certainly. Visitations of plague, famine, and war. Golden intervals. But no progressive, violent change. Some periods perhaps 50 per cent better than others—at the utmost 100 per cent better—in the four thousand years which ended (say) in A.D. 1700.

This slow rate of progress, or lack of progress, was due to two reasons—to the remarkable absence of important technical improvements and to the failure of capital to accumulate. . . .

For the moment the very rapidity of these changes is hurting us and bringing difficult problems to solve. Those countries are suffering relatively which are not in the vanguard of progress. We are being afflicted with a new disease of which some readers may not yet have heard the name, but of which they will hear a great deal in the years to come—namely, *technological unemployment*. This means unemployment due to our discovery of means of economising the use of labour outrunning the pace at which we can find new uses for labour.

But this is only a temporary phase of maladjustment. All this means in the long run *that mankind is solving its economic problem*. I would predict that the standard of life in progressive countries one hundred years hence will be between four and eight times as high as it is to-day. There would be nothing surprising in this even in the light of our present knowledge. It would not be foolish to contemplate the possibility of a far greater progress still. . . .

Now it is true that the needs of human beings may seem to be insatiable. But they fall into two classes—those needs which are absolute in the sense that we feel them whatever the situation of our fellow human beings may be, and those which are relative in the sense that we feel them only if their satisfaction lifts us above, makes us feel superior to, our fellows. Needs of the second class, those which satisfy the desire for superiority, may indeed be insatiable; for the higher the general level, the higher still are they. But this is not so true of the absolute needs—a point may soon be reached, much sooner perhaps than we are all of us aware of, when these needs are satisfied in the sense that we prefer to devote our further energies to non-economic purposes.

Now for my conclusion, which you will find, I think, to become more and more startling to the imagination the longer you think about it.

I draw the conclusion that, assuming no important wars and no important increase in population, the *economic problem* may be solved, or be at least within sight of solution, within a hundred years. This means that the economic problem is not—if we look into the future—*the permanent problem of the human race.*

Why, you may ask, is this so startling? It is startling because—if, instead of looking into the future, we look into the past—we find that the economic problem, the struggle for subsistence, always has been hitherto the primary, most pressing problem of the human race—not only of the human race, but of the whole of the biological kingdom from the beginnings of life in its most primitive forms.

Thus we have been expressly evolved by nature—with all our impulses and deepest instincts—for the purpose of solving the economic problem. If the economic problem is solved, mankind will be deprived of its traditional purpose.

Will this be a benefit? If one believes at all in the real values of life, the prospect at least opens up the possibility of benefit. Yet I think with dread of the readjustment of the habits and instincts of the ordinary man, bred into him for countless generations, which he may be asked to discard within a few decades.

To use the language of to-day—must we not expect a general "nervous breakdown"? We already have a little experience of what I mean—a nervous breakdown of the sort which is already common enough in England and the United States amongst the wives of the well-to-do classes, unfortunate women, many of them, who have been deprived by their wealth of their traditional tasks and occupations—who cannot find it sufficiently amusing, when deprived of the spur of economic necessity, to cook and clean and

mend, yet are quite unable to find anything more amusing.

To those who sweat for their daily bread leisure is a longed-for sweet—until they get it.

There is the traditional epitaph written for herself by the old charwoman:—

Don't mourn for me, friends, don't weep for me never,
For I'm going to do nothing for ever and ever.

This was her heaven. Like others who look forward to leisure, she conceived how nice it would be to spend her time listening-in—for there was another couplet which occurred in her poem:—

With psalms and sweet music the heavens'll be ringing,
But I shall have nothing to do with the singing.

Yet it will only be for those who have to do with the singing that life will be tolerable—and how few of us can sing!

Thus for the first time since his creation man will be faced with his real, his permanent problem—how to use his freedom from pressing economic cares, how to occupy the leisure, which science and compound interest will have won for him, to live wisely and agreeably and well.

The strenuous purposeful money-makers may carry all of us along with them into the lap of economic abundance. But it will be those peoples, who can keep alive, and cultivate into a fuller perfection, the art of life itself and do not sell themselves for the means of life, who will be able to enjoy the abundance when it comes.

Yet there is no country and no people, I think, who can look forward to the age of leisure and of abundance without a dread. For we have been trained too long to strive and not to enjoy. It is a fearful problem for the ordinary person, with no special talents, to occupy himself, especially if he no longer has roots in the soil or in custom or in the beloved conventions of a traditional society. To judge from the behaviour and the achievements of the wealthy classes to-day in any quarter of the world, the outlook is very depressing! For these are, so to speak, our advance guard—those who are spying out the promised land for the rest of us and pitching their camp there. For they have most of them failed disastrously, so it seems to me—those who have an independent income but no associations or duties or ties—to solve the problem which has been set them.

I feel sure that with a little more experience we shall use the new-found bounty of nature quite differently from the way in which the rich use it to-day, and will map out for ourselves a plan of life quite otherwise than theirs.

For many ages to come the old Adam will be so strong in us that everybody will need to do some work if he is to be contented. We shall do more things for ourselves than is usual with the rich to-day, only too glad to have small duties and tasks and routines. But beyond this, we shall endeavour to spread the bread thin on the butter—to make what work there is still to be done to be as widely shared as possible. Three-hour shifts or a fifteen-hour week may put off the problem for a great while. For three hours a day is quite enough to satisfy the old Adam in most of us!

There are changes in other spheres too which we must expect to come. When the accumulation of wealth is no longer of high social importance, there will be great changes in the code of morals. We shall be able to rid ourselves of many of the pseudo-moral principles which have hagridden us for two hundred years, by which we have exalted some of the most distasteful of human qualities into the position of the highest virtues. We shall be able to afford to dare to assess the money-motive at its true value. The love of money as a possession—as distinguished from the love of money as a means to the enjoyments and realities of life—will be recognised for what it is, a somewhat disgusting morbidity, one of those semi-criminal, semi-pathological propensities which one hands over with a shudder to the specialists in mental disease. All kinds of social customs and economic practices, affecting the distribution of wealth and of economic rewards and penalties, which we now maintain at all costs, however distasteful and unjust they may be in themselves, because they are tremendously useful in promoting the accumulation of capital, we shall then be free, at last, to discard.

Of course there will still be many people with intense, unsatisfied purposiveness who will blindly pursue wealth—unless they can find some plausible substitute. But the rest of us will no longer be under any obligation to applaud and encourage them. For we shall inquire more curiously than is safe to-day into the true character of this "purposiveness" with which in varying degrees Nature has endowed almost all of us. For purposiveness means that we are more concerned with the remote future results of our actions than with their own quality or their immediate effects on our own environment. The "purposive" man is always trying to secure a spurious and delusive immortality for his acts by pushing his interest in them forward into time. He does not love his cat, but his cat's kittens; nor, in truth, the kittens, but only the kittens' kittens, and so on forward for ever to the end of cat-dom. For him jam is not jam unless it is a case of jam to-morrow and never jam to-day. Thus by pushing his jam always forward into the future, he strives to secure for his act of boiling it an immortality. . . .

I see us free, therefore, to return to some of the most sure and certain principles of religion and traditional virtue—that avarice is a vice, that the exaction of usury is a misdemeanour, and the love of money is detestable, that those walk most truly in the paths of virtue and sane wisdom who take least thought for the morrow. We shall once more value ends above means and prefer the good to the useful. We shall honour those who can teach us how to pluck the hour and the day virtuously and well, the delightful people who are capable of taking direct enjoyment in things, the lilies of the field who toil not, neither do they spin . . . .

Measuring Economic Performance

Economic decision making involves an assessment of the economy's general health and the informed selection of policies from among many alternatives. Economic analysts, in both the public and private sectors, regularly watch such measures as gross domestic product (GDP), unemployment, and inflation. You are probably familiar with these terms, since they are frequently mentioned in news broadcasts and daily newspapers. However, the popular understanding of economic data is sometimes flawed, partly because the formulation and use of economic statistics is a normative process influenced by value judgments. Arthur Ross summarizes this point quite well:

> Let us recognize candidly that statistical truths, like the other truths about man's social life, are created rather than discovered. It may well be different when it comes to measuring the amount of rainfall or the population of redwood trees. These are physical phenomena. It is man who invents and defines these categories. It is man who selects a few dimensions that are capable of measurement and uses them to characterize complex social conditions and relationships. It is man who decides how much effort should be expended in measuring these dimensions or others that might be selected. ("Living with Symbols," *American Statistician,* June 1966)

The articles in this section address a number of important issues involving the measurement and interpretation of macroeconomic data. Policymakers must be concerned with the relevance and reliability of the statistical truths upon which they base their decisions. This presupposes a knowledge not only of the way in which government statisticians structure their data, but also of the official meaning of these statistics. Beyond this, policymakers need to develop a sensitivity to at least three issues: that economic data are often subject to wide margins of error (which sometimes cast doubt upon the reliability of such data); that discrepancies between different sets of statistics are common (thereby requiring policymakers to make choices about the relative importance of one sort of data over another); and finally, that not all economic phenomena can be measured (particularly where such issues as the quality of economic life are concerned). In the end, good policy making mandates a careful consideration of these issues.

This section begins with a discussion by Paul Starobin on the underground economy, where goods and services—some legal, and some not—are produced but not reported, and therefore escape the attention of government statisticians altogether. Next, Robert Heilbroner probes the national income accounts in search of the meaning behind the statistics. He finds disparities between what official data may intend to convey and what they actually do convey. Then, Ronald Schmidt examines trends in U.S. labor productivity. Some people ask, if productivity is lower in service areas than in manufacturing—and services are growing more rapidly—won't America someday become "a nation of hamburger flippers"? Schmidt shows why there are reasons to believe otherwise.

In "The Economy's Barometer," Robert Charles discusses the Index of Leading Economic Indicators, and he shows how it is used to predict upturns and downturns in the business cycle. "The Real Truth about the Economy" cautions us to use economic data carefully, and it sorts out the myths from the realities of official statistics.

The unit concludes with an article in which David Korten focuses on a relatively new field known as "ecological economics." A variety of trends—including rising

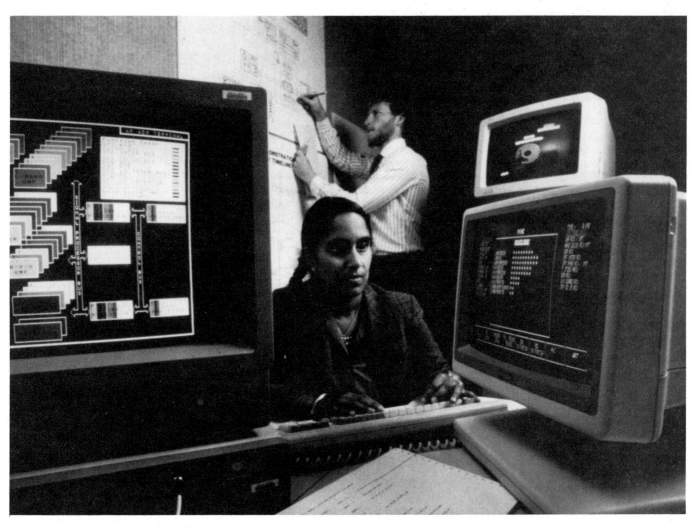

world poverty, global warming, ozone depletion, and loss of biodiversity—suggest that global production and consumption patterns are not sustainable. Korten offers an alternative vision for what he calls a sustainable society.

Looking Ahead: Challenge Questions

What is the underground economy, and why is it a troubling issue for policymakers?

Does the growth of the service sector imply a future of low U.S. productivity?

What is the Index of Leading Economic Indicators, and how is it used? Why are reliable statistics essential for good economic policy making?

What levels of consumption can Earth sustain, and when does having more cease to add to human satisfaction?

THE ECONOMY YOU CAN'T SEE

PAUL STAROBIN

Last year, the American economy produced $6.37798 trillion worth of goods and services, according to the Commerce Department's Bureau of Economic Analysis (BEA), the federal agency responsible for wrapping a tape measure around the economy.

Yeah, right. Don't be gulled: The precise-sounding number is as suspect as a Chesapeake Bay oyster left on the dock at midday. The truth is that nobody knows how big the economy is. Pressed by an interviewer, BEA director Carol S. Carson declined even to hazard a guess.

Nor does anyone know the level of family income in the United States, the extent of poverty or how many people lack jobs. And because nobody knows how much Americans earn and spend, nobody knows how much they save. Never mind that the government and others collect and publish statistics on every conceivable form of economic activity; that merely speaks to a modern society's wish for precision—or the illusion of precision. If you're looking for a reliable body of data, try baseball batting averages instead.

The main reason for the statistical squishiness is that murky mudpile known as the underground economy. BEA bean counters can count only the economic transactions that are reported to the government. That leaves out the zillions of transactions for which there isn't a paper (or electronic) trail. These include illegal activities, such as drug-peddling, as well as legal ones, such as babysitting, on which taxes or regulations are frequently evaded.

The underground sector wasn't born yesterday: Before America was even America, pirates were running West Indies rum past the colonial customs authorities. Tax evasion has been around as long as the tax man has—and prostitution and illicit gambling longer still. Nevertheless, there are many reasons to think

that over the past quarter-century, the underground economy has grown at a faster pace than the above-ground economy has, and there's almost no reason to think this trend will slacken over the next 25 years.

Seismic changes in the nation's economy and its culture—such as a shift from manufacturing to services and increased popular discontent with government—favor the continued growth of the underground sector. This may be an uncomfortable truth for an often-moralistic society, but an underground economy has become a permanent fixture of post-industrial American capitalism, as much a part of the economic infrastructure as Wall Street's gleaming skyscrapers. It's as if a seedling from Nairobi or some other Third World spot has taken root in the sidewalk cracks of the world's most sophisticated economy.

A SAFETY VALVE?

If the underground economy is viewed as some sort of out-of-control dandelion, then the solution might be to redouble enforcement efforts to eradicate tax dodging and the like. But aside from certain predatory activities, such as drug dealing, the shadow sector may not be all bad. Many analysts are coming to view it as a safety valve, a generator of jobs and business opportunities that holds frayed communities together.

In a public housing tenement on the South Side of Chicago, for example, welfare mothers get together on Sunday nights and bake breakfast rolls for sale to schoolchildren. They don't declare the income to Uncle Sam because if they did, they wouldn't get their welfare checks, according to John Kretzmann, a Northwestern University social policy analyst who has surveyed the housing project residents about their off-the-books-activities. "Almost everybody has some [underground] economic activity going on,"

Kretzmann said. "I think it's absolutely necessary for people's survival that they have these activities."

As usual, California seems to be leading the way. A recent study by economists at San Francisco-based Wells Fargo Bank concluded, "California's underground economy has taken its place with foreign trade, biotech, entertainment and health services as one of the few growth industries during the worst recession to hit the state since the 1930s."

New York, however, probably isn't far behind. Last year, a six-part series in *The New York Times* revealed a dizzying breadth of underground activities in New York City—such as illegal immigrants peddling T-shirts and mood rings on the sidewalks in front of the Immigration and Naturalization Service office in lower Manhattan.

The United States has plenty of company: Shadow economies are flourishing in Eastern Europe and in such supposedly law-abiding places as Canada, where a surge in tax cheating and cigarette smuggling has ignited a national soul search on the ethics of economic disobedience. Canada's finance minister, Paul Martin, recently declared: "The underground economy is not all smugglers. . . . It's hundreds of thousands of otherwise honest people who have withdrawn their consent to be governed, who have lost faith in government." Sound familar?

Common sense suggests that data on the reported economy not only understate the true scale of U.S. economic output, but also overstate the amount of unemployment. If nearly everyone on government relief earns off-the-books income, then alarmist reports on a widening income gap between rich and poor may need to be toned down—except, of course, if the wealthy are heavily misreporting income. No doubt there are plenty of fat cats who don't report capital-gains income on some spectacular investments. (Illegal misreporting

shouldn't be confused with legal tax avoidance, everyone's favorite sport in America.)

But don't put much stock in any of the estimates of the size of the underground economy. After all, secrecy and disguise are its defining characteristics.

The Wells Fargo analysis pegged California's underground sector at 18 per cent of the state's above-ground economy—but the author of the study, economist Gary Schlossberg, confessed in an interview that that number was no more than "a conjecture" based on a very crude analysis of the level of cash transactions in the economy. (Drug dealers, prostitutes and off-the-books carpenters usually don't take MasterCards.)

Using the same rubbery yardstick, Schlossberg estimated the national underground economy at about $1 trillion in 1993; that's nearly 17 per cent of the officially reported gross domestic product. Over the past two decades, other economists have produced guesstimates of the underground economy ranging from 1.4 per cent of the reported economy to 28 per cent. *(For a range of such estimates, see table.)*

The Internal Revenue Service (IRS) has thrown up its hands. Asked for an estimate of the underground economy, a spokeswoman said the IRS had long ago stopped trying to make any calculations. (Back in 1976, the IRS estimated the shadow sector at 8 per cent of reported economic output.) "It's too nebulous," the spokeswoman said. "You can't get a figure on it." One number that the IRS does spit out is the so-called tax gap—an estimate of the difference between what taxpayers should pay if they fully report all income from legitimate activities, and what they actually pay. For 1992 alone, the gap was pegged at $90 billion. (The BEA takes account of this estimate when it comes up with its economic-output calculation.)

THE PAPER MONEY TRAIL

With all the fuzziness, why do many analysts say the underground economy has grown rapidly over the past few decades? And why is it widely assumed that this trend will accelerate?

One clue is the curious staying power of paper money, just about the only acceptable means of payment, other than barter, in the underground economy. A little more than a decade ago, experts were hailing the arrival of the cashless society: "Paper currency will give way to electronic impulses," a soothsayer predicted. And in fact, the proliferation of plastic-money credit cards and bank debit cards now allows consumers to fill their carts at the grocery store and their

cars at the service station without ever removing a bill from their wallets. But cash hasn't disappeared: In fact, on a per person basis, paper-money holdings rose from $179 in 1950 to $1,142 in 1990, a 538 per cent increase that surpassed the 440 per cent increase in inflation over this period. The underground economy isn't the only reason for the persistence of cash—some people just can't leave their homes without that $10 bill in their side pocket—but it is certainly a very prominent one. The illegal drug economy alone probably accounts for a good deal of the continued popularity of $100 bills.

And how could the numbers racketeers ply their trade without cash? Despite the spectacular growth of legal gambling outlets all over the country, many people still prefer to take their winnings in nontaxable form. A few months ago, Manhattan prosecutors busted "Spanish Raymond" Marquez—a legendary numbers king with a fiefdom of 41 betting parlors that reportedly grossed $30 million annually.

Another spur to the underground economy is illegal immigration. Illegals are heavily employed in activities that can

easily be conducted off the books, such as peddling, taxi driving, day care and construction work. In New York City alone, unregulated garment sweatshops, drawing on a pool of cheap, often illegal immigrant labor, have multiplied from the hundreds to the thousands over the past 20-odd years, according to labor union estimates.

Then there are the changes that have rippled through the economy over the past quarter-century. The most important trend is a shift away from the production of tangible goods, such as automobiles and screwdrivers, toward the production of not-so-tangible services, such as business consulting and health care. It's usually easier for service providers than it is for manufacturers to conduct business without leaving a paper or electronic trail. (An important exception is financial services, which often do leave a trail.)

And with the decline of a manufacturing-based economy has come the decline of labor unions, which historically have offered protections against off-the-books business operators. What's more, jobs in the economy have been shifting away

THE SIZE OF THE UNDERGROUND ECONOMY

Estimates of how large the underground economy is vary widely, as shown by this comparison of studies over the past two decades by the Internal Revenue Service (IRS), academic economists Edgar L. Feige and Vito Tanzi, Federal Reserve Bank of Philadelphia economist Joel F. Houston, the Commerce Department's Bureau of Economic Analysis (BEA), U.S. Trust Co. economic consultant James J. O'Leary, author Harry I. Greenfield (from his book *Invisible, Outlawed and Untaxed*), the Labor Department and Wells Fargo Bank.

Study	Estimate (in billions)	Per cent of GNP*	Year of estimate
IRS	$145	8%	1976
Feige	600+	27	1979
Tanzi	118-159	4.5-6	1980
Houston	400	14.7	1980
BEA	184	5.4	1983
O'Leary	432	15.2	1985
Greenfield	350	6.7	1990
Labor	500	10	1992
Wells Fargo	1,000+	16.8	1993

*all estimates stated as a share of gross national product except Wells Fargo's, which is a share of gross domestic product

SOURCES: Federal Reserve Bank of Philadelphia (except for Wells Fargo data)

from large firms to small ones, including sole proprietorships, that can more easily disguise their books.

SORRY, BIG BROTHER

Also nurturing the underground economy is the growth of a postindustrial regulatory regime that has put all sorts of business activities under some form of government control. Keep in mind that some economic actors operate underground principally to escape burdensome requirements—restrictions against pollution, for example.

The tighter the clamps, the greater the incentive for underground activity. Many analysts predict that increased government controls on the health sector, now being considered by Congress, will spur the growth of off-the-books activities by doctors and others subject to new rules.

The White House has tried to deal with this possibility by calling for tough penalties—including prison terms—for doctors and patients who don't abide by new regulations. And yet, the Congressional Budget Office (CBO) didn't address the potential resort to underground activities as part of its economic and budgetary analysis of the Administration's health care bill. "I don't have any idea what the magnitude of this incentive might be," CBO director Robert D. Reischauer told a researcher

for the Federal Reserve Bank of Minneapolis who recently published a lengthy piece on the underground economy.

Likewise, efforts to set tighter controls on the gun market could drive a lot of the activity underground—and not necessarily prevent criminals from getting their hands on weapons.

For evidence of the power of economic incentives—the law be damned—consider the drug trade. The inner-city toughs who peddle crack cocaine are, in a sense, following a basic law of economics. "Returns in the regular [legal] sector can't match the returns in the illegal sector," observed economist Harry J. Holzer of Michigan State University, who has long studied the employment market for minority youths. "These people are making a fairly straightforward economic calculus." A rational actor, of course, might also weigh the short-term rewards against the long-term odds of survival. But the dealers behave according to a famous maxim of British economist John Maynard Keynes: In the long run, we're all dead.

Although the drug trade has thwarted every attempt to eradicate it, there's not much popular support for legalizing drug use. Nor does there appear to be much support for legalization of prostitution—a first step toward bringing it into the above-ground economy.

Many analysts and ordinary citizens say that the solution to evasion of taxes on legitimate activities is stepped-up enforcement by the authorities. And why not crack down on all those unlicensed peddlers in New York City?

But before the enforcement squad is doubled and given loads of fancy new equipment, the side effects should be contemplated. "A world of perfect enforcement could be an intolerable place," economist Frank A. Cowell warned in an essay published last year by the Washington-based Institute for International Economics. Think of the shadow sector, Cowell suggested, as "an economic ventilation shaft to enterprises in danger of suffocation. Plumbing, decorating and vehicle repair jobs may get done that would otherwise be unprofitable under an inappropriately austere tax regime."

On the principle that it is more difficult to disguise spending than to disguise income, Uncle Sam may want to consider a shift away from the income tax to a value-added consumption tax. Some economists already back this step as a way to encourage more saving. If the underground economy can't be legislated, moralized or otherwise Big Brothered into oblivion, maybe it's time to reconcile ourselves to its stubborn presence.

Taking the Measure of Economics

Economics needs to return to what it once was—the self-conscious means by which a capitalist social order explains itself to itself.

ROBERT HEILBRONER

Robert Heilbroner was the first person to be named as Scholar of the Year by the New York Council for the Humanities. This is a slightly amended version of his talk on that occasion.

Is economics a humanist discipline? The answer is *Yes*, but for reasons I think many economists would reject. The reasons are that economics, at its base, is inextricably connected with the exercise of social power, and that power in all its forms and uses is inextricably connected with social values and moral judgments. Are these not at the core of humanism? I do not see how a discipline that announces that its concern has always been the exploration of wealth can avoid the badge that other humanists wear with pride.

But I suspect that, if the question were put to the members of my profession, there would be an embarrassed clearing of throats. Of course, economics is devoted to the subject of wealth and would be, in fact, unimaginable without the concept of "income." That is a polite way of talking about wealth. But one of the hallmarks of economics lies in the fact that it does not pursue its subject from a "moralistic" point of view. Rather, it studies the problem of wealth objectively and dispassionately—the way a physical scientist studies the interaction of particles in a cloud of gas and determines whether the gas is expanding because the sun has come out or because it is part of a nuclear explosion. In the same way, economists study the processes by which wealth is generated and distributed, regardless of whether the end result is a poor society or a rich one, or whether it is a society with a lopsided distribution of income or an egalitarian one.

In other words, economists see themselves as observers of social processes, for whose moral workings they bear little or no responsibility. If the discipline of economics were itself involved in the design (as well as the outcome) of these processes, that argument might sound hollow. In the same manner, physicists would be hard pressed to deny any moral responsibility for the expansion processes they examined, if it were they who decided whether clouds would be made of water vapor or nuclear particles.

Are economists, in fact, nothing more than disinterested observers? I am afraid the answer is a discomfiting one. Economics—especially its modern-day variety —is directly responsible for important aspects of the phenomena it studies. The fact that this responsibility is largely unknowing makes all the more curious the uneasy reaction of economists to the charge that theirs is a humanist "science," whether they admit it or not.

Control of inflation

In an attempt to make this argument plausible, I offer the following examples. The first concerns the current discussion about the rationale for the Federal Reserve Board's policy of fighting inflation through raising interest rates. Every economist will tell you that the raising of rates is undertaken because it will discourage businesspersons and prospective homeowners from borrowing. In turn, economists will explain that this damper is needed to hold back the growth in spending. They also hold that it is the only way to forestall the dangerous process of inflation.

That certainly seems like a straightforward piece of economic analysis—one that is quite devoid of any question of moral responsibilities. Economists may disagree about how great an increase in interest rates is required to achieve the anti-inflationary goal; they may even argue about whether inflation is, at any moment in time, a real or imagined menace.

Nevertheless, if we accept that the Federal Reserve's estimates were made in good faith and with due care, where is the moral responsibility of the economics profession?

The answer involves an aspect of anti-inflation policy that we have not yet considered—that the Federal Reserve policy brings about the desired fall in spending because higher interest rates cause businesses to cut back expansion plans and families to forgo mortgages. Both of these result in fewer jobs (ordinarily a cause for dismay); but, in this case, they are accepted with a small sigh of regret as the price one must pay to hold inflation at bay. Meanwhile, our moral values are also being held at bay, because there is another, less unfair, means to control inflation. I am not referring to price controls—a clumsy and ineffective measure (save in emergencies). I mean using increases in federal taxes—both personal and corporate—to reduce the level of household and business spending to whatever degree is needed.

Why is there a moral issue at stake in choosing between interest rates and taxes to combat inflation? The answer is that a boost in interest rates reduces spending by drastically cutting the incomes of the unfortunates who are "let go," whereas a broad-based tax hike diminishes spending because most individuals will find their pay checks reduced. There will still be unemployment generated by an anti-inflation tax—the purpose of which is, like raising interest rates, to diminish spending. But, to some degree, all households will share in the cost. That is not the case when interest rates rise. By most people's moral standards, is that not the preferable course for a democracy to follow?

Then why is an anti-inflation tax not enthusiastically recommended by economists? Why does one, in fact, never hear of it as an alternative to Federal Reserve policy? The answer is that it would create too much political flack. That may not be a noble attitude, but it is an understandable one. Economists cannot expect that individuals or businesses will acquiesce meekly in higher taxes just because the profession explains that this is a fairer way of heading off inflation than interest rate hikes. But once more, a moral issue intrudes—namely, that economists can expect vehement protests against a tax policy with a high degree of certainty, *if they themselves have never offered any such explanation.* What I deplore is not that some economists hold values that are different from my own, but that they do not make these values explicit. Worse than that, I suspect that most

are not even aware that political issues, as well as technical ones, are involved in their policy positions.

The GNP

The second example which demonstrates that economics is a "humanist" discipline lies in the very definition of GNP. Economists do not need to be told that the term in their parlance that has most deeply permeated everyday talk is Gross National Product—Gross Domestic Product for the economically sophisticated. The profession rightfully takes pride in having popularized a framework of national accounting which clarifies the character, as well as the size (nearing $7 trillion a year), of the flow of goods and services that comprise our national wealth (sorry, income).

Alas, GNP also makes a profound negative contribution to the cause of national enlightenment by virtue of the manner in which its character is expounded to the general public by those in a position to do so—namely, economists. The negative contribution consists of serious misinformation about what the various components of GNP stand for and, therefore, what measures might best advance the public's welfare.

The least serious of these misleading treatments applies to the nearly $6 trillion component of GNP that is labeled "consumption." Over a hundred years ago, John Stuart Mill wrote in his *Principles of Political Economy* that consumption was, in fact, made up of two quite distinct kinds of expenditures. He called one "productive consumption" and the other "unproductive consumption." "Productive consumption" was comprised of those goods and services needed for the continuance of the national economy itself—adequate food and clothing and medical care, as obvious examples—whereas "unproductive consumption" was made up of goods and services which, however enjoyable to their users, brought no increase to national well-being. Indeed, it may have incurred some decrease. Mill would probably have placed alcoholic beverages in "unproductive consumption." Perhaps we can substitute cigarettes or handguns.

Breaking down the flow of "consumption" into "productive" and "unproductive" categories would undoubtedly pose a very difficult statistical (actually judgmental) task; but for all the unavoidable imprecision, would it not be of greater service than when we assume that all increases in "consumption," whether

for luxury restaurants or basic health care, yield equal additions to national well-being? And if it were too burdensome to make such a breakdown, would it not be useful to know whether the increase in spending was spread more or less evenly across the population? For instance, should we not announce that, during the 1980s, the real incomes (and presumably, the consumption) of more than two-thirds of all families fell, while that of the top one percent doubled? After all, these were real-time economic events of the times. Somehow, these aspects of GNP did not get much press, because economists did not make much of a fuss about them.

Investment

The next criticism is a good deal more important. It applies to the expenditures by which the private sector expands its operations. The overall flow of investment (running at just under $1 trillion a year) regularly receives the equivalent of apostolic blessings from economists who find here the source of the economy's growth. But this generally valid and useful clarification suffers from the same flaw as that which affects "consumption"—namely, the failure to apply a "productive/unproductive" distinction to the overall category. Thus, all construction, whether for a manufacturing facility, a luxury apartment house, or a gambling casino is counted as "investment," as candy and antibiotics are both in "consumption." As a result, when the nation applauds (no one louder than economists) because the total for "investment" is rising, I hear no economist's voice asking for more information about the makeup of the flow. Is that a technical oversight or a moral shortcoming?

But this is still of small account, compared with the case of the government component of GNP. Here, we find a wide assortment of goods and services that range from armaments through public education to the salaries of government officials—from the President to the cop on the beat. So large and varied an assortment might make more difficult any attempt to classify its elements as "productive" or "unproductive," but it breaks down easily enough into three major subgroups: (1) military expenditures of all kinds; (2) public investment from physical infrastructure to expenditures on research, health, and education; and (3) a general category of public consumption that ranges from air traffic control to the everyday running expenses of federal, state, and local government.

Such a tripartite division makes us recognize that all government spending cannot possibly be considered as exercising the same influence (good or bad) on the future flow of GNP. But, in general, that is not the way the economics profession handles the matter. In particular, little or no attention is paid to federal investment spending, including the federal financing of state and local investment. This crucial component of public spending is almost never stressed by economists. Instead, the profession usually treats all government expenditure as if it were only "consumption."

Hence, when economists discuss which flows in GNP ought to be discouraged in order to make way for growth, government spending is always the target. They forget that it includes dams as well as welfare. They forget that private investment includes factories that manufacture golf clubs, as well as computers. As a result, decisions concerning public policy are intrinsically biased by the presumption that government spending is less valuable than that of the private sector, always excepting the priority accorded to government spending during war.

It is, of course, by virtue of this implicit value-presumption that government spending is stymied by what is called the "deficit." I put quotations around the word because a deficit means one and only one thing—borrowing. Once that is said, it follows naturally that there is good and bad borrowing for public purposes, exactly as there is for private purposes. But the failure to recognize that government spending at all levels—state and local, as well as federal—normally contains an investment component blinds us to this fact. The deficit is, therefore, not viewed as borrowing to finance investment (to be examined for its usefulness or wastefulness), but as some kind of intrinsically wicked act. Unlike the private sector, where all borrowing that is undertaken for investment is presumed to be good, in the public sector (there being no recognition given to a category of "public investment"), all borrowing is presumed to be bad.

The problem, of course, is that the conventional treatment of government in GNP greatly increases the difficulty of making intelligent public decisions. The cry across the land is that the best deficit would be zero. That means that there should be no government borrowing and, thereby, implies that there is to be no government investment. Good-bye, Panama Canals of the future! So much for the "analytic" contribution of economics these days.

I may seem to have wandered far from the question of whether economics is a humanist discipline, but I presume that the reason is clear. Of course economics is humanist. The categories it establishes, and the policy positions it espouses, are unmistakably value-impregnated. The trouble, as I hope my examples have made clear, is that the values embodied in many of these mainstream economic policies are not in clear accord with those of a democratic society. Perhaps worse, I suspect most economists are not even aware of that fact.

Efficiency

Let me mention one last point. Economics proudly proclaims its dedication to the enhancement of efficiency. But how is efficiency measured? The answer is to compare the value of output against the value of input, the latter being mainly represented by labor. Yet, under a different set of values, labor itself would be counted, not as an input, but as an output. Here I can cite the views of an economist more revered than read—Adam Smith. In *The Wealth of Nations*, Smith wrote that exposure to the numbing routines of the division of labor makes laborers "as stupid and ignorant as it is possible for a human creature to become." From Smith's perspective, efficiency is not everything. One does not hear that so much these days.

Schism between values

It would not be difficult to add further examples. It is time to ask the question that must be in everyone's mind. How does economics find itself in such a situation of conflict between the values that most of its members would probably profess, and the values that these same members tacitly support in their professional pronouncements? One answer has to do with the evolution of the doctrine. The earlier economists—from Smith to Marx—were acutely aware of the social (that is, the value-laden) character of the field that was not yet described as "economics," but as political economy. Smith called the object of his investigations a *Society of Perfect Liberty*. These last words referred to the freedom of contract that separated such a social order from that of feudalism, with its rigidly construed lord-and-serf relationship. Marx subtitled *Capital* "A Critique of Political Economy," because he thought that its original expositors (including Smith) did not fully grasp the relations of sub- and superordination that remained in the post-feudal world. Indeed, Marx's signal contribution was to reveal that the forces of the market served to exercise power with the same effectiveness as the institution of serfdom, despite the freedom of social relations of which it so proudly boasted. The difference was that power was openly displayed in feudalism while, in capitalism, it is masked behind market "choice."

Mainstream contemporary economics has lost that penetrative and disturbing viewpoint. There are, of course, exceptions. One thinks not merely of Marxian writers, but of followers of that American iconoclast Thorstein Veblen, and of modern-day non-Marxian skeptics such as John Kenneth Galbraith. But the profession, as a whole, has lost its interest in economics as a veil. It sees it, rather, as a blueprint.

This brings us to a second reason for the moral myopia of my profession. It is the seductive appeal of analysis for its own sake. Unlike politics, sociology, or psychology, economics offers the prospect of giving us a "scientific" explication of social movement. That appeal cannot be overestimated. From the end of the 19th century, when Alfred Marshall introduced graphs and equations into his magisterial text (now called *Economics* without the "political" antecedent), the discipline has been increasingly viewed in terms of "models," the properties of which were most clearly revealed in geometrical and mathematical form. Marshall tactfully placed the first in footnotes and the second in appendices, but the expositional form was irresistible. Today, a neophyte might be forgiven if, picking up one of the leading economics journals for the first time, he or she construed it to be about physics. Not so incidentally, the term that one is least likely to encounter in skimming the contents of such economics journals is *capitalism*. The reason must be obvious. Economists feel more comfortable likening the object of their study to a "natural" system rather than a social system.

There is more here than mere political timidity. Capitalism is a distinct social order in history because it splits the formerly seamless web of political power into two: a public sphere of government in which the old considerations play their accustomed roles and to which moral judgments are therefore freely applied; and a private sphere, from which public authority is largely excluded, and which is, therefore, deemed to be immune from "political" scrutiny. Within the private sphere, power is expressed through competitive battle among institutions called firms and through antagonistic bargaining between employers and their employees. In this two-sided

contest, the explicit exercise of political power is largely excluded. An employer can fire a worker but he cannot jail him; an unsuccessful firm can seek to undersell its rivals, but he cannot destroy their property. The sphere of economic life is thus largely free of the uses of power that mark the political world, but this does not mean that power is, therefore, absent from a social realm in which some have the ability to offer income, and others have the necessity to obey the first in order to receive it.

It remains only to ask: Can economics again become an explicitly humanist discipline? Of course it can. Will it? That is less certain. There is a comfortable security in the cocoon of "pure" economics. Its highest ambition is the display of rigor. And as I never weary of saying, it also manifests, as a symptom of that rigor, signs of mortis.

Fortunately, there is increasing evidence of an uneasiness—even a bad conscience—with regard to the isolation of economics from sociological studies of institutions and psychological studies of behavior. What we have yet to see is that same unease with respect to the political aspects of economic society. But there are some signs of change there, too, under the leadership of a few brave souls and strong-minded editors. Thus I have hopes, although I would not say high expectations, that economics will again become what it once was—the self-conscious means by which a capitalist social order explains itself to itself.

Services: A Future of Low Productivity Growth?

The question is so common lately, it has become trite: "Is America turning into a nation of hamburger flippers?" The cause for concern is a potentially disturbing pair of trends. First, employment in the United States increasingly has shifted away from manufacturing toward services. In 1963 manufacturing accounted for 30 percent of all jobs, but in 1991 that share had fallen to less than 17 percent.

Second, "real" productivity increases (that is, adjusted for inflation) have been significantly lower in services than in manufacturing. Between 1963 and 1986, real output per worker in manufacturing rose at an annual rate of 2.6 percent, while real output per worker in the services sector rose by only 0.2 percent. Taken together, these trends suggest dire consequences: a sector with negligible productivity gains is rapidly becoming the most important source of new jobs, while the more productive manufacturing sector is losing employment. The inference many observers draw is that America faces stagnation, with most of its labor force engaged in employment that exhibits little productivity growth, and hence, provides little increase in its standard of living.

This *Letter* takes a closer look at the data. After combining the results of other researchers with evidence from data on compensation, it appears that the fundamental data on which these dire predictions are made may be misleading. While the evidence is not conclusive one way or the other, data on compensation at least raise the possibility that the opposite is true: that labor productivity is growing faster in services than it is in manufacturing.

The source of the "real" evidence
Concern about lack of productivity growth in the service sector emerges from the data released by the U.S. Department of Commerce's Bureau of Economic Analysis (BEA) on nominal output, real output (that is, adjusted for inflation), and employment for each industry. Using these data, it is possible to compute "real" output per employee.

The difficulty facing BEA in determining changes in real output per worker is daunting. In many cases, outputs are not directly priced, and often it is difficult or impossible to measure the quantity of the output. This is particularly true in the service sector. For example, bank customers receive services from tellers and loan officers, but they do not pay directly for those services; instead they pay indirectly with interest rate spreads and fixed service charges. Similarly, service industries producing information (such as research) generate a product that is consumed by the public, but the product is often not priced and there is no way to count how many people benefit from that information.

Adding to the complexity is the problem of quality changes. With the exception of a few agricultural products, nearly all products change over time, with most embedding improved features. For example, a 1992 car cannot be compared directly with a 1972 car. We can count the number of cars sold and observe the prices charged, but counting the change in output—the stream of benefits derived from the car—will not be correct unless it is possible to standardize the car with earlier models, to distinguish and count improvements in dimensions of quality, safety, and emissions as well as the number of units produced.

BEA's methodology
Because of limitations on data collection, BEA must extrapolate from available information on prices and production to calculate price or quantity indexes for each industry. In the case of most manufacturing industries, BEA has information available about input costs, prices of some final products, and output indexes. Although the problem of quality remains, and not all final product prices are recorded, most manufacturing industries produce a physical output that is countable, which makes the process less abstract.

BEA faces the same conceptual problems in services that it does in manufacturing, but fewer data typically are available for services. Quantity

indexes usually are not available—in fact, there often is no physical ''good'' to count—and prices also are not observed directly. To derive ''real output,'' therefore, BEA must extrapolate using indirect measures of input costs as proxies for price changes. In other industries, such as banking and recreation, measures of inputs are used—often the number of employees—to proxy for changes in the level of production.

While this approach is perhaps the only available strategy in some industries, the effects on productivity measurements are predictably biased. When real output is calculated for industries using labor quantities as an important measure of output, then *by definition* the industry will show no productivity growth. Moreover, price indexes based on input costs ignore potential quality improvements—such as higher skilled labor and better capital—and hence, may attribute quality improvements inaccurately to price increases rather than output increases.

Evidence from compensation data

Several researchers have looked at the validity of BEA's inter-industry productivity comparisons. Denison (1989) argues that BEA's approach could not accurately distribute output gains to industries when intermediate products (that is, products developed by one manufacturer and used by another for producing final consumer products) are involved. Moreover, Baily and Gordon (1988) used a case study analysis and questioned BEA's measurement of output gains attributed to each industry, suggesting a bias toward manufacturing. This bias also was noted by Smith (1972), who found that the data consistently pushed measured productivity gains toward the manufacturing sector and away from the service sector.

Unfortunately, these criticisms typically are qualitative rather than quantitative, making it difficult to reject BEA's conclusions. It is possible, however, to provide a quantitative check of the BEA data by using data on compensation growth by industry.

One of the central conclusions of economic theory is that wages are determined by the marginal value of labor's contribution to that output. Thus, changes in compensation should be related to changes in labor's marginal productivity. Research on inter-industry wage differentials offers some support to this proposition. Empirical research has found that a large portion of these wage differentials is related to observable labor quality factors—experience and education, for example—and other differentials are attributed to unobservable quality differences.

Compensation growth per worker in an industry, therefore, should be related to the growth in the

productivity of its labor force. If workers are paid the value of their marginal product, the growth in compensation per worker in an industry reflects the growth in the average marginal product of that industry's labor force.

The accompanying chart compares real compensation growth per worker (the BEA's compensation series deflated by the consumer price index) to BEA's real output measure for manufacturing and several service-producing industries. In many cases, there are wide disparities in the relative growth rates for compensation and output.

Real Compensation and Output per Worker, Selected Industries
(Average Annual Percent Growth: 1963-86)

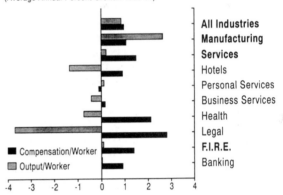

Consider the comparison between services and manufacturing. In contrast to the BEA real output data, compensation data indicate higher gains in services than in manufacturing. Service industry compensation per worker rose at a 1.5 percent annual rate, compared to 1.1 percent for manufacturing. In fact, manufacturing reported compensation gains just slightly above the average for all industries.

Other important differences are worth noting. Banking is found in the output data to have virtually no productivity growth, yet compensation growth matches the average for all industries. Moreover, output growth per worker in the health care and legal industries is reported to have been negative according to the real output series while recording higher increases in compensation growth than are found in any other industries.

Which measure is right?

Compensation is not a direct measure of productivity either, however. Economic theory shows that changes in compensation over time can be split roughly into two parts: changes in the relative output price of the final good and changes in the marginal productivity of the labor used to make the good.

If output prices rise for a particular product, that may feed into compensation to workers in the form of raises and bonuses. Over time, though,

the ability of labor to capture increases in output prices is determined by labor's ability to restrict the entry of new laborers. If higher wages are not the result of higher marginal productivity by the firm's labor force, those higher wages will attract new workers and bid down those wages unless the existing labor force can effectively restrict entry through unions or licensing restrictions.

The second source of compensation increases, linked to productivity gains, would appear where the firm has raised the quality of its labor force over time. Hiring larger proportions of skilled labor would raise the relative compensation growth of that industry.

Determining whether compensation increases are due to productivity gains or to output price gains, therefore, can be problematic. Nevertheless, one factor seems to be useful in distinguishing between the two effects: labor mobility. In some of the more heavily unionized and licensed industries (manufacturing, transportation, legal, and health care), compensation increases may be less useful as a measure of productivity gains. In other industries, however, where employment growth has been rapid, it is likely that compensation gains do reflect the market's evaluation of the relative productivity of those workers.

Moreover, in industries where capital/labor ratios have changed dramatically, compensation may provide a superior measurement of changes in labor productivity. BEA's simple measure of labor productivity growth—output per worker—is not adjusted for total productivity gains that are the result of increased productivity of non-labor inputs. Thus, in industries that have become more capital intensive, gains in average output per worker may reflect increasing productivity of other factors, not just labor. Compensation, which is a payment to labor for its contribution to total productivity gains, provides the market's assessment of the value produced by those workers.

For many industries, therefore, differences between the compensation growth rates and measured real productivity gains may signal measurement errors. Particularly in the case of service industries, where output and prices are nearly impossible to observe directly, compensa-

tion may offer an alternative measure of productivity gains. While it is clear that compensation growth is not a perfect measure of productivity growth, trends in compensation raise an important question: If productivity growth is so low in some sectors, why are employers willing to pay the workers so much? If market participants are relatively rational, the payment workers receive may be a better indicator of the market's evaluation of their productivity than is the traditional BEA measure.

Conclusions

Concern about the observed shift of employment toward service industries often is based on the assumption that services have lower productivity growth than manufacturing. The BEA real output data are used to support this proposition. As shown in this *Letter*, however, data on real compensation per worker provide conflicting evidence, at least suggesting the possibility that services have had faster productivity increases than manufacturing.

The compensation data are not a perfect measure of productivity growth either, but the fact that the data differ so dramatically from the output data is disturbing. At a minimum, the compensation data, along with results from other researchers looking at particular industries, suggest that the inter-industry productivity comparisons made with the "real" output data are biased and potentially misleading.

Ronald H. Schmidt
Senior Economist

References

Baily, Martin N., and Robert J. Gordon. 1988. "The Productivity Slowdown, Measurement Issues, and the Explosion of Computer Power." *Brookings Papers on Economic Activity*, vol. 2, pp. 347-420.

Denison, Edward F. 1989. *Estimates of Productivity Change by Industry: An Evaluation and an Alternative*. Washington, DC: The Brookings Institute.

Smith, A.D. 1972. *The Measurement and Interpretation of Service Output Changes*. Washington, DC: National Economic Development Office.

The Economy's Barometer

The Index of Leading Economic Indicators has 11 components that together predict upturns and downturns in the business cycle.

Robert B. Charles

Robert B. Charles is a lawyer at the Washington, D.C., law firm Weil, Gotshal & Manges.

You have heard it mentioned at White House press briefings, in front-page stories, and by Peter Jennings. You have seen economists speak reverently of it, stockbrokers bandy it about like sailors eyeing the night sky, and politicians refer to it authoritatively, as if everyone knew just what it is, how it works, and where it comes from.

But what is the Index of Leading Economic Indicators? What does this much-loved term mean and measure? How is it assembled, and by whom? What are the components that the assemblers think central, and why? Most important, what authority does this Leading Index (as it is often called) merit? Does it really predict the future, or is it, like so many econometric models and other presumed gauges of the economy, just another oversold bellwether?

Those are questions usually not answered (or asked) by anchormen, securities brokers, and podium-pounding politicians. Still, they are key questions for anyone who wants to make use of the Leading Index in day-to-day life.

Does the latest report mean my variable mortgage interest rate is headed up again? Maybe. Does it mean prices are likely to rise? Could be. Does it tell me what other consumers are thinking? Yes. So, how does it work?

Unlike most individual signs of economic performance (such as the monthly unemployment rate, personal savings rate, federal government purchases, consumer prices, or current interest rates), "composite indexes," or multiple-factor indexes, provide a sort of over-the-horizon view of where the economy is headed. The Leading Index is the most famous of these composite indexes.

While there are three main composite indexes (the other two being the Lagging and Coincident indexes), the Leading Index is generally seen as the one with the greatest predictive value over the coming six to nine months and thus a good guide for decisions to be made in that period.

What the indexes measure

All three composites are compiled and released monthly by the Bureau of Economic Analysis (BEA) of the U.S. Department of Commerce. The Leading Index is aptly considered the economy's "barometer"—not rain gauge or decennial almanac, since it offers not immediate or far-distant insights but a midterm view.

But a word on composite indexes, generally. First, the way they work is that each measures, in the BEA's words, average behavior for a different group of "economic time series"; that is, each measures a "series" of values over time for differing economic activities or components. So, the Lagging Index measures such things as the "ratio of manufacturing and trade inventories to sales," "commercial and industrial loans outstanding," and changes in "labor cost per output," focusing on the longer term.

The Coincident Index measures components like "personal income less transfer payments" and "employees on nonagricul-

tural payrolls," excluding other predictors.

Each index measures activities that tend to "show similar timing at business cycle turns," or components that bundle well together. Last, components are "weighted" to "neutralize the tendency of more volatile time series to dominate the average" and to smooth out erratic factors. Each of the composite "time series" is then used to chart trends and business cycles.

To understand how the Leading Index works, one needs first to look closely at what goes into it, then at what people think they see coming out of it.

Like a good beef stew, there is more in the Leading Index than meets the eye. This index is composed of 11 "leading indicator components," each describing a significant, but individually inconclusive, aspect of U.S. economic performance.

The 11 components are measurable over the short run, that is, by the week or month. They offer historically accurate bases from which to extrapolate, or in the BEA's words, "predict peaks and troughs in the business cycle" (and thus things like whether there will be inflationary pressure on wages and prices or interest rate hikes to counter anticipated inflation).

The 11 components? Here they are: (1) average weekly hours of manufacturing production (work week), (2) average weekly initial claims for unemployment insurance, (3) manufacturers' new orders for consumer goods and materials, (4) vendor performance, as measured by speed of deliveries, (5) contracts and orders for new capital-enhancing equipment, (6) new private housing units authorized by local building permits, (7) the change in manufacturers' unfilled orders (month to month), (8) the change in sensitive (raw) material prices, (9)

■ *Economic metaphor:* **Just as well-proportioned ingredients produce a savory beef stew, the 11 weighted components of the Index of Leading Economic Indicators maximize the measure's predictive power.**

stock prices (for 500 common stocks), (10) money supply, and (11) consumer confidence (based on University of Michigan continuing research).

These components were last set in 1989 but were revised in December 1993 to introduce new data and methodology (including a change in "weights" accorded various components). Without assessing every component, you can see that each is a likely predictor of future economic performance, even if variables such as stock prices and consumer confidence are highly subjective.

Consider some examples. If first-time unemployment claims are up over time, that means several things. First, labor in certain industries is falling, and the price of labor likely with it. That means job insecurity and possibly less purchasing and lower consumer confidence (note: these variables are not independent). It also means that the government will be spending more in unemployment benefits.

But what if local building permits are up? That means that, very shortly, first-time home sales may be on the march,

and construction jobs and purchases with it. It also means people are not afraid to borrow at current or anticipated interest rates, and that could mean that either the economy will keep growing apace or that the Federal Reserve will have to step in, boost rates, and slow the growth to stem inflation. That is the stew, if you will.

But what do people expect from the Leading Index, once these components have been recorded, charted, weighted, and extrapolated in the aggregate? In short, economists, businessmen, governments, and consumers want greater certainty. Is it better to borrow at today's rates or wait? Better to save at low long-term rates or wait for higher ones? Will my employer be part of the up-drift, or are we all headed south? Of course, none of these microeconomic questions gets a full answer from the Leading Index, or takes account of election-year politics, for that matter (often the enemy of predictable economics).

A sterling record

But there is good news: The

Leading Index has a steady record and is worth watching for. Here is a piece of the record. By December 1990, the Leading Index had fallen for five consecutive months, and with it orders by manufacturers for equipment and factory orders for durable goods—10 percent in November alone. At the same time, first-time unemployment claims were continuing to rise. A prediction in the aggregate? Deepening recession. And that is what we got.

However, by April 1992 the Leading Index was recording an uptick of 0.3 percent. By May 1992, the uptick was 0.6 percent. Moreover, 5 of the 11 component indicators were up, each indicating rising demand and an end to the recession. Climbing components included the price of raw materials, a longer work week, slower delivery times from increased orders, rising stock prices, and improved consumer confidence.

The reasonable conclusion? Something was going right, and somewhere between November 1992 and February 1993 stronger economic growth could be expected. Nevertheless, much of the media stressed that the Leading Index was sluggish and presaged only a slow recovery.

Did the Leading Index predict accurately? Announcements in December 1992 showed October construction spending up a full percentage point, reaching its highest level in two years. Residential spending was up 2.3 percent in October 1992, and retrospectively up 5.7 percent over the first 10 months of 1992.

In addition, December 1992 numbers showed a rise of between 5 and 8 percent in retail spending, causing the *Financial Post*, for example, to say that the news "suggests the U.S. economy is returning to solid growth." All of this was, of course, too late to be factored

Economic Crystal Ball

The Index of Leading Economic Indicators:

➡ Is compiled by the Commerce Department's Bureau of Economic Analysis.
➡ Is released monthly.
➡ Is a powerful predictor of economic trends over the next six to nine months.
➡ Can suggest whether citizens will have to pay more on variable-rate mortgages.
➡ Can augur whether consumer prices will be going up or down.
➡ Gives insight into what other consumers are thinking.
➡ Can suggest answers to a whole host of other questions of a down-to-earth, practical nature.

■ *Not enough:* **Many months of sunny Leading Index forecasts failed to ameliorate the November election debacle experienced by President Clinton's Democratic Party.**

Since July 1993, the Leading Index has climbed 10 times and remained unchanged 3. This means the economy is on a solid growth track.

Recipe for an Index

The 11 components of the Leading Index are:

1. Average work week in the manufacturing production field.
2. Average weekly initial claims for unemployment insurance.
3. New orders to manufacturers for consumer goods and materials.
4. Vendor performance, as measured by speed of deliveries.
5. Contracts and orders for new capital-enhancing equipment.
6. New private housing units authorized by local building permits.
7. The month-to-month change in manufacturers' unfilled orders.
8. The change in sensitive raw-material prices.
9. Stock prices for 500 common stocks.
10. Money supply.
11. Consumer confidence (based on University of Michigan continuing research).

into the 1992 election cycle but certainly bears out the predictive value of the Leading Index.

Where has the Leading Index taken us to date? Well, announcements in October 1994 showed that the Leading Index rose 0.6 percent in August 1994, suggesting a strong spring 1995 but more. That increase represented the 13th straight month without a decline. Since July 1993, the Leading Index has climbed 10 times and remained unchanged 3. What does this mean? For one thing, the economy was and is on a solid growth track. By November 1994, despite 5 consecutive increases in short-term interest rates by the Federal Reserve, the national press was able to report that "the economy grew at a healthy 3.4 percent rate" in the last quarter; that sales, orders, and consumer confidence were up; that first-time unemployment claims were not up; and that stocks finished October with a 55-point one-day gain.

The final question: What does such news mean? Well, for one thing, as a student of the Leading Index you can now watch the next White House press briefing, read the next front-page article, or enjoy the next Peter Jennings report and know which direction the Leading Index is probably headed. And looking over its 11 components, you will also know why.

THE REAL TRUTH ABOUT THE ECONOMY

Are government statistics so much pulp fiction? Take a look

Wondering about yesterday's weather in Tallahassee? No problem, ask the Weather Bureau. Interested in who won last night's ball game? Just check the newspaper. Want to know how the economy did last month? Uh-oh.

The economic statistics that the government issues every week should come with a warning sticker: User beware. In the midst of the greatest information explosion in history, the government is pumping out a stream of statistics that are nothing but myths and misinformation. Most of the surging information economy—including software, telecommunications, and entertainment—is poorly covered by the data. While figures such as a 5.9% unemployment rate or a 3% inflation rate seem to have a reassuring solidity, in fact the connection between the government's statistics and the reality is getting more tenuous every year. Such official measures as gross domestic product (GDP), producer price index (PPI), or capacity utilization say far more about what's happening in old-line manufacturing industries than they do about such leading-edge companies as Microsoft, Disney, MCI, Fidelity, and Intel.

Based on BUSINESS WEEK analysis and recent economic research, it becomes clear that the real economy is vastly different from the one painted by the government's numbers. The true rate of inflation is at least a percentage point lower than the official consumer price index, which misses changes in consumer buying habits and gains from product improvements. Business investment in equipment, after adjusting for depreciation, is a full 30% bigger than the government statistics say, as the data only captures a fraction of the money companies spend on software and telecommunications equipment. And productivity growth is also twice the official rate, which omits rising productivity in most of the service sector. Taken together, this means that GDP growth is stronger than the numbers show, the nation's productive capacity is a lot higher, and the dangers of inflation are far lower.

NOT WORKING. A true picture of the economy would also show that Americans are right to be worried about jobs these days, despite the low official unemployment rate. Increasingly, the labor market is filled with surplus workers who are not being counted as unemployed. The rate of labor force participation—those working or looking for work—has dropped sharply for men since 1989. Estimated conservatively, some 1.1 million more prime-age male workers are out of the labor force compared with five years ago. Adding those workers back in would push the real unemployment rate to 6.8%, from its

reported 5.9%. And there are at least 500,000 more workers with some college who have jobs but are underemployed compared to 5 years ago. That's an enormous pool of surplus labor available to fuel the economy's growth.

The bum numbers are costing the country a bundle. Wall Street, corporate executives, and Washington policymakers continue to make bad decisions based on the official—but incorrect—statistics. And the potential for harm is increasing as the statistics become ever less accurate.

The biggest danger right now is that the government's numbers are scaring the Federal Reserve and bond market vigilantes into raising interest rates. If overstated inflation numbers and misleading investment numbers induce the Fed to unnecessarily slow growth by 1%, that alone would take almost $70 billion off GDP.

OFF BY BILLIONS. Bad data hit the economy hard in other ways. Inaccurate readings of the economy's health may lead companies to unnecessarily cut back on production or to produce far more than is needed, at an average annual cost of some $5 billion. Because entitlements and income tax brackets are indexed to inflation, a 1% overstatement of the CPI raises the federal budget deficit by an estimated $5 billion each year. And an overstated CPI will lead workers and businesses to demand bigger wage and price increases, which will impose an additional $5 billion drag on the economy. This brings the toll from bad statistics to an average of some $15 billion a year in incorrect business and consumer decisions, according to BUSINESS WEEK estimates.

The shortcomings of the economic statistics also leave economists fumbling with major policy questions. Is real pay falling or rising? Is productivity improving or stagnating? Health care, trade, welfare reform, income inequality: All suffer from the

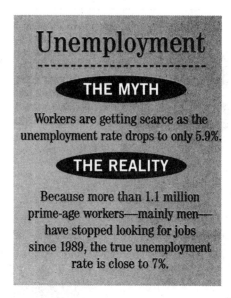

Unemployment

THE MYTH

Workers are getting scarce as the unemployment rate drops to only 5.9%.

THE REALITY

Because more than 1.1 million prime-age workers—mainly men—have stopped looking for jobs since 1989, the true unemployment rate is close to 7%.

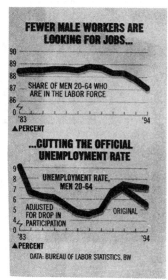

FEWER MALE WORKERS ARE LOOKING FOR JOBS...

SHARE OF MEN 20-64 WHO ARE IN THE LABOR FORCE

'83   '94
▲PERCENT

...CUTTING THE OFFICIAL UNEMPLOYMENT RATE

UNEMPLOYMENT RATE, MEN 20-64

ADJUSTED FOR DROP IN PARTICIPATION   ORIGINAL

'83   '94
▲PERCENT

DATA: BUREAU OF LABOR STATISTICS, BW

same lack of accurate information. "You need the data to do real research on what interventions help and which ones don't," says Zvi Griliches, an economist at Harvard University. "The biggest problem is the system itself is not measuring the concepts people care about," adds Michael J. Boskin of Stanford University, head of the Council of Economic Advisers under George Bush. "And that divergence is growing over time."

Paradoxically, aggregate economic statistics are becoming more and more important even as they become less reliable. It used to be that a business could focus on a narrow set of markets. But as the economy gets more complex and interconnected, having good information about other markets and other parts of the country is essential. Businesses base their hiring and investment decisions, in part, on expectations of future sales and costs. Chrysler Corp, for example, tracks the different components of the producer price index to estimate what will happen to its cost of materials.

Consumers, too, worry about future income when deciding how much to buy or save. "People's expectations don't come out of thin air," says Thomas Juster, an economist at the Institute for Social Research at the University of Michigan at Ann Arbor. "Information that relates to job security and inflation-rate prospects has a significant cumulative impact on people's decisions."

Take inflation, for example. The CPI is used to set cost-of-living increases for union contracts and Social Security payments, while the producer price index is often used to index commercial contracts. Moreover, corporations and workers often use the published inflation rate as a benchmark for determining what constitutes a fair pay increase, even in the absence of an explicit contract. Some 76% of corporations use the CPI to help determine how much to increase their salary budget, according to a recent survey by Hewitt Associates. "The CPI helps determine people's ideas of what kind of raises that they ought to get," says Larry Ball, an inflation expert at Johns Hopkins University.

As a result, if the official CPI is stuck around 3%, that level of inflation can actually become a self-fulfilling prophecy, since

workers want to keep up with inflation. But if the official number reflected the reality of a 2% inflation rate, that might encourage companies and workers to hold down wage and price increases, thus lowering the true rate of inflation. "If there is upward bias in the CPI and you get rid of it," says Ball, "people might be happier with smaller wage increases."

An inaccurate CPI number does other damage, too. Federal Reserve Board Chairman Alan Greenspan has argued that higher inflation slows productivity growth by making it more difficult for businesses to plan ahead. An overstated CPI, by raising the actual inflation rate, could cut one- or two-tenths of a percentage point off of productivity growth. That might not seem like much, but it is worth $5 billion to $10 billion of GDP.

As much as 10% of the ups and downs of industrial production is a reaction to economic statistics that are later revised, according to a recent study by Michael Waldman of Cornell University and Seonghwan Oh of Seoul National University. For example, says Waldman, a series of pessimistic economic data in the first half of 1989 helped persuade businesses and consumers to cut back on spending. The statistics were later revised up—but by then, the damage had been done, costing the economy at least $10 billion in lost production.

"PREHISTORIC." Companies are also concerned with the accuracy of the more detailed statistics that the government publishes about individual industries. Texas Instruments Inc., for example, uses industrial production numbers issued by the Federal Reserve to help project revenues for its various businesses. But Vladi Catto, chief economist for TI, has reservations about these numbers, which are calculated in part by measuring electricity consumption. "That's prehistoric," says Catto.

Catto also worries about the trade statistics, especially since the government no longer classifies exports and imports by whether they are for final sale or just for assembly purposes. So now it's not clear whether chips shipped to Korea will just be plugged into a VCR for sale in Topeka, Kan., or in Seoul. "It's much more difficult to trace exports and imports," says Catto.

The stream of economic statistics, whether accurate or not, helps shape the political climate in which policy is made. Take the debate over the 1988 trade law, which provided U.S.

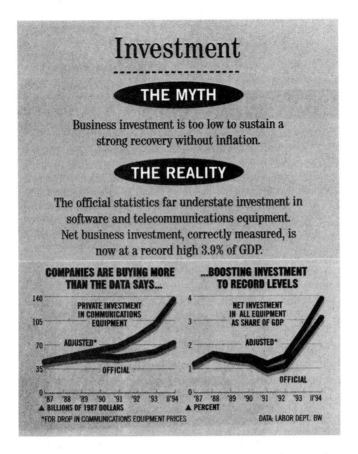

Investment

THE MYTH

Business investment is too low to sustain a strong recovery without inflation.

THE REALITY

The official statistics far understate investment in software and telecommunications equipment. Net business investment, correctly measured, is now at a record high 3.9% of GDP.

COMPANIES ARE BUYING MORE THAN THE DATA SAYS...

PRIVATE INVESTMENT IN COMMUNICATIONS EQUIPMENT

ADJUSTED*

OFFICIAL

▲ BILLIONS OF 1987 DOLLARS

*FOR DROP IN COMMUNICATIONS EQUIPMENT PRICES

...BOOSTING INVESTMENT TO RECORD LEVELS

NET INVESTMENT IN ALL EQUIPMENT AS SHARE OF GDP

ADJUSTED*

OFFICIAL

▲ PERCENT

DATA: LABOR DEPT., BW

Where the Statistics Dollar Goes

FISCAL YEAR 1994*
MILLIONS OF DOLLARS

AGRICULTURE DEPT.	$294
BUREAU OF LABOR STATISTICS	280
CENSUS BUREAU	276
NATIONAL CENTER FOR EDUCATION STATISTICS	135
ENVIRONMENTAL POLICY ADMINISTRATION	107
ENERGY INFORMATION ADMINISTRATION	89
NATIONAL CENTER FOR HEALTH STATISTICS	88
BUREAU OF ECONOMIC ANALYSIS	44
FUNDING FOR OTHER FEDERAL STATISTICS	1,346
TOTAL FEDERAL FUNDING FOR STATISTICS	2,659
PERCENT OF FEDERAL BUDGET	0.2%

*Estimate   DATA: OFFICE OF MANAGEMENT & BUDGET

industries with new weapons to protect themselves against foreign competition. At the time, the merchandise trade deficit for 1987 was reported as $171 billion. Since then, revisions and the inclusion of services in the trade numbers have pushed the trade gap for 1987 down to $151 billion. "The debates over the trade bill would have been less vitriolic if people had had the real data," says Boskin.

Certainly, the problems in the numbers are affecting Fed policy. Not because Greenspan is ignorant of the potential biases: Indeed, he is the ultimate sophisticated consumer of economic statistics. As he recently testified before Congress: "The list of shortcomings in U.S. economic data is depressingly long." Publicly, Greenspan has often said the CPI probably overstates inflation, while in private he has been very critical of GDP figures, especially the quarterly figures. Instead, the Fed, when setting monetary policy, now relies heavily on anecdotal evidence of inflation, hiring, and other economic trends collected from the 12 regional Fed banks, and on reports from industrial, service, and financial companies.

But this dependence on anecdotes rather than statistics raises two problems. First, policy necessarily gets less precise when less information is available. Second, as psychologists and lawyers well know, anecdotes can be biased and colored by the viewpoint of the questioner. If the Fed is looking for examples of inflation and labor shortages, it will certainly be able to find them.

But no matter how many anecdotes the Fed says point to shortages, the evidence is overwhelming that the U.S. is not suffering from tight labor markets and other bottlenecks. True, the unemployment rate has now fallen to 1988 levels. But the

index of help-wanted ads is down 25% compared with then, and jobs seem much scarcer. Just ask new college graduates. "Students are working a lot harder at the job search," says Laurie Paul, director of career services at Drew University in Madison, N.J. "They'll take a little bit less job and hope they can move up. These students are a lot more realistic now."

Indeed, a look behind the numbers explains the change in attitude. After a decade of stability, the labor force participation

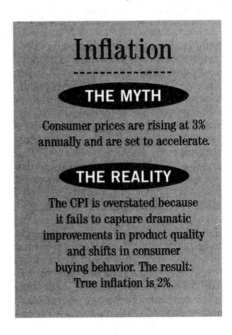

Inflation

THE MYTH

Consumer prices are rising at 3% annually and are set to accelerate.

THE REALITY

The CPI is overstated because it fails to capture dramatic improvements in product quality and shifts in consumer buying behavior. The result: True inflation is 2%.

of men has fallen off sharply, and the erosion is continuing this year, despite the apparent surge in new jobs. At the same time, underemployment is on the rise for workers with some college or more. In 1988, 46.2% of these educated workers held executive or professional jobs. By 1993, the percentage holding good jobs had dropped to 43.5%, with the decline much larger for men than for women. Adds Wayne Wallace, director of the career resource center at the University of Florida: "Getting a job is not the issue. The real issue: Is it an appropriate job?"

And even the payroll employment numbers, which have been growing at a rate of about 300,000 a month, are suspect. Out of that growth, about 50% is coming from what BLS calls the "bias adjustment," which is simply a fixed number added to the published number each month to take account of the fact that the payroll number historically gets revised upward each year. So even if job creation were to slow sharply, it would not show up in the bias adjustment for months. "That's a little unsettling," admits Katharine Abraham, BLS commissioner.

RELIABILITY FACTOR. The situation with the CPI is, if anything, even worse. By now, almost everyone from Greenspan to the Congressional Budget Office to the BLS agrees that CPI growth is too high. "I think the inflation rate is overstated by 1%," says Boskin. The reasons for upward bias in the CPI include technical problems with the calculation of the index and sluggishness in picking up changes in consumer shopping behavior. But the biggest problem with the CPI is that it doesn't reflect the improved quality of many products. New automobiles, for example, are far more reliable than they were a few years ago, yet this increase in quality—which pays off in fewer visits to the repair shop—is not accounted for in the CPI.

The producer price index suffers from the same problem. The BLS reports that the price of such telecommunications equipment as fax machines, video-conferencing gear, and modems has gone up in recent years. But that's not the experience of anyone who has gone shopping for these products. Adjusting for the tremendous gain in power and speed, true prices have actually dropped substantially for most types of communications equipment. In the case of pharmaceuticals, the inability of the BLS to properly account for generics and new drugs means the PPI for prescription drugs is overstated by some 50%. And there is no price index for software at a time when software is the single largest nonlabor expense for some companies.

Similarly, high-tech investments such as telecommunications equipment and software are either undercounted or not counted at all in the official investment figures. To put it another way, the 10 largest software companies have a total market capitalization of $80 billion—yet, according to the government, none of them produces any investment goods.

If the government is undercounting investment, it's not surprising that the capacity-utilization numbers are skewed as well. In the past, companies added to capacity by building new plants, which the government could easily track. But now Corporate America is trying to boost capacity by reorganizing production, something that the official statistics have no way of measuring. By reducing cycle time and improving manufacturing yields, "in just the first half of this year we 'created' an 'invisible factory' the size of one of our $400 million fabs—

Capacity Utilization

THE MYTH

U.S. factories are working at some 84% of capacity, close to the point where shortages start to develop and prices start to rise.

THE REALITY

The numbers are overstated because increased productivity allows manufacturers to get more output without adding new factories. Moreover, the capacity-utilization numbers are based only on domestic production, which makes little sense in an increasingly global world.

without any new brick and mortar," says Texas Instruments Chief Financial Officer William A. Aylesworth. "That kind of thing is probably happening throughout the chip industry, and throughout Corporate America." TI's goal is to free up another factory's worth of capacity in the next year.

The globalization of many industries is also distorting the capacity-utilization figures, since the Federal Reserve's figures include only domestic factories. But increasingly, corporations move production back and forth across national boundaries. Consider GE's Electrical Distribution & Control business in Plainville, Conn., which makes circuit breakers, panel boxes, and other industrial gear. According to President and CEO Lloyd Trotter, back in 1989 his foreign customers were mainly supplied from U.S. factories. But now the percentage has reversed. Exports account for only 20% of overseas sales, while the rest come from foreign factories in places such as Singapore—which are not counted in U.S. capacity.

And what about the country's productivity statistics, which purport to measure how fast output per worker is growing? They are "a horror show," says Juster of the University of Michigan. "They're widely regarded as the worst kind of numbers that have ever existed." The government has no good way of measuring output in a whole range of industries, including banking, software, legal services, wholesale trade, and communications—all of which have invested heavily in information technology. And without a good number for output, the official productivity numbers for these industries are sus-

Productivity

THE MYTH

Long-term productivity growth is only a meager 0.8% annually.

THE REALITY

The published number undercounts productivity gains in more than two-thirds of the economy, including financial services, communications, and health care. The actual productivity growth in the economy is twice that number.

STATISTICS CAN'T BE DAMN LIES ANY LONGER

Data! Data! Data! I can't make bricks without clay.
—Sherlock Holmes, *The Adventure of the Copper Beeches*

In the poorer countries of the world, investment and commerce are blossoming. From emerging capitalist nations of the former Soviet empire to the developing countries of Latin America and Asia, new opportunities are tantalizing and economies booming.

But by how much? Officially, China's economy has been expanding at an average 12% rate over the past several years. Yet a recent Chinese government investigation uncovered more than 60,000 cases of falsified and mistaken figures. Gross statistical errors were found in a slew of major economic sectors: industrial output, grain yield, farmers' per capita income, capital construction investment, inflation, and birth rates. These mistakes call into question whether Beijing has an accurate picture of just how fast its economy is surging ahead.

MASSAGING DATA. China isn't alone. The official numbers for the Czech Republic's gross domestic product and industrial production portray a weak economy, but strong growth in the country's entrepreneurship belies that picture. Some developing nations have suspiciously permanent 2% unemployment rates, and figures on education and labor skills are frequently unreliable. From Moscow to Caracas, local officials and corporate executives alike twist data to meet bureaucratic objectives or to avoid paying hefty taxes.

Still, statistical shenanigans are becoming much less pervasive than before. In much of the world, there are genuinely impressive efforts under way to improve the quality of economic statistics, often with the advice of outside consultants and international agencies. And for good reason. It takes accurate numbers to institute free-market reforms. When rigid command economies crumble and highly decentralized markets take over, governments suddenly need sound data to run their fiscal and monetary policies, says Jan Svejnar, economist at the University of Pittsburgh and economic adviser to Czech President Vaclav Havel.

And as foreign investors and multinational corporations expand their presence in developing countries, they require better guideposts on wages, prices, and other critical variables before committing millions in equity investments or in new factories. "Countries which develop a reputation for not having reliable statistics may pay a price in the international capital markets," says William Sterling, international economist at Merrill Lynch & Co. Adds Carlos Jarque, president of Mexico's National Institute of Statistics, Geography & Informatics (INEGI): In today's world, "we think a country without statistics can't develop."

Indeed, when free-market technocrats gain power in an emerging capitalist country, one of the first things they do is overhaul data collection. Mexico's President Carlos Salinas de Gortari, for example, made modernizing INEGI a priority when he came to power in late 1988. The institute has gone from 30 personal computers to 4,000, revised much of its methodology, and is busy compiling numbers on previously neglected parts of the economy. A top priority for the Chinese government is improving its data on everything from population to industry. Russia and the East European nations are working on better capturing emerging private-sector activities. Says Rudi Dornbusch, economist at Massachusetts Institute of Technology and BUSINESS WEEK columnist: "In the 19th century, the great effort was to draw up a map of a country. The 20th century equivalent is to get a good set of economic statistics."

Clearly, the stakes are high. Economic statistics are not only a barometer of current conditions. They can play a vital role in increasing the future wealth of nations.
By Christopher Farrell in New York, with Joyce Barnathan in Hong Kong and Elisabeth Malkin in Mexico City

---

pect. Most economists now believe that productivity growth in these industries is substantially understated by the government figures. As a result, overall productivity growth for the economy is understated by "something around the order of one-half to one percentage point a year," says W. Erwin Diewert, an economist at the University of British Columbia.

And the list of problem statistics goes on and on. The Fed no longer relies on M2 as a good indicator of where the economy is going. Nobody knows how much currency is held abroad. Even the savings rate is "terribly unreliable," says David Bradford, an economist at Princeton University. What the U.S. should be interested in, he says, is not savings but the creation of wealth—which the government statistics system is simply not designed to measure.

STOPGAP SOLUTION. To be sure, the primary agencies that generate national statistics have seen a moderate budget in-

crease in recent years. That meant, for example, that the Bureau of Labor Statistics was able to update the monthly survey that generates the unemployment numbers. The BLS also has started collecting its monthly payroll employment figures from companies by letting them punch in the data by phone, which has drastically decreased the number of large revisions. The Census Bureau and Bureau of Economic Analysis were able to add service exports and imports to the trade numbers. And on Oct. 21, the BLS announced that it would revise the CPI starting in January, 1995.

But these initiatives, however necessary, address only a fraction of the problems with the statistics. The agencies do not have the funds needed to deal with an information-based economy. Indeed, they never caught up with the rapid growth of the service sector in the 1970s and 1980s. Even the upcoming CPI revision is only a stopgap solution—it will better track food

THE SPAWNING OF A THIRD SECTOR: INFORMATION

From employment to trade, almost all of the government's economic data is based on dividing the economy into two sectors: businesses that produce goods and businesses that provide services. But with the dawn of the Information Economy, this traditional split no longer makes sense. The service sector has become a confusing mishmash of everything from software giants such as Microsoft Corp. to the neighborhood day-care center.

It makes a lot more sense to create a new statistical system designed for the Information Age. It would consist of three economic sectors: goods-producing, services, and information. Services would include only businesses where personal contact with the ultimate consumer is essential—the day-care center is in the service sector, while Microsoft is not. Instead, the software giant would go in the information sector, along with other businesses that provide, move, or manipulate information—including most financial services, communications, and publishing companies such as McGraw-Hill, publisher of this magazine, which are currently counted as manufacturers.

The new classification shows that the big job creators in the economy are in the service industries, not the information sector (table). Yet strong productivity gains are largely in the information sector, not in services. After all, it's hard to imagine huge productivity gains in a barber shop.

Measuring the Information Economy won't be easy. But it would be worthwhile considering the growing role information plays in the U.S. economy.

A New Way To Split The Economy

	SHARE OF EMPLOYMENT, 1993	GROWTH IN EMPLOYMENT, 1989-93
GOODS	14.7%	−6.5%
Includes mining, utilities, and most manufacturing		
SERVICES	70.0%	5.2%
Includes people-oriented services such as auto repair, banking, and hotels; most health care; state and local government; elementary and secondary education		
INFORMATION	15.3%	3.2%
Includes information-oriented services such as advertising and entertainment; communications; publishing; software; computers; higher education; medical diagnosis; securities industry		

DATA: BUSINESS WEEK

prices but won't come close to capturing the gains from rapid technological progress. And it's coming far too late. "The CPI should have been redesigned years ago," says Janet Norwood, long-time commissioner of the BLS and now a fellow at the Urban Institute. "The American people don't want to spend money on statistics."

Still, there's a lot that could be done to make the official statistics more accurate. One easy change would be to reallocate statistics money from the Agriculture Dept., which gets far more than its share. Then the BLS, for example, could update the PPI more quickly. "We don't have a pot of new money for developing new indices in the service sector," says the bureau's Abraham. "If we had a few extra millions we could use it fruitfully."

But ultimately it will take hundreds of millions of dollars to get an accurate picture of today's economy. "It's one thing to collect data from huge factories," says Norwood. "It's another thing to go to a bunch of service establishments, which tend to be much smaller." And the problem is compounded in the information economy, where it's hard to even figure out how to value the product.

But it's well worth doing. American companies and workers are going through wrenching readjustments as they gear up to compete in the new world economy. Without good statistics, we don't know whether what we're doing is working. Better economic data will mean better economic policymaking by government, better decisions by investors and corporations and, ultimately, a higher standard of living for everybody—and we'll even be able to measure it.

By Michael J. Mandel in New York, with bureau reports

Sustainable Development
Conventional versus Emergent Alternative Wisdom

David C. Korten

David C. Korten is the founder and president of The People-Centered Development Forum 14 E. 17th St., Suite 5, New York, NY 10003, U.S.A., Fax (1-212) 242-1901.

An important starting point in any discussion of sustainable development is to clarify the basic assumptions we each bring to the table. While the views on sustainable development cover a broad spectrum, the following contrast of the conventional wisdom and the emergent alternative wisdom on this subject helps to define the range. Most of the economists, governments and official agencies (including the World Bank, IMF, and the GATT) that define national and global policies profess the conventional wisdom. A growing number of alternative economists, independent thinkers, and citizen organizations concerned with economic justice and environmental issues are engaged in articulating and elaborating the alternative wisdom as the foundation for policies they hope will prove to be more people and environment friendly. Which best captures your view of sustainable development?

Sustainable Development

Conventional: Sustainable development is about achieving the sustained economic growth needed to meet human needs, improve living standards, and provide the financial resources that make environmental protection possible.

Alternative: Little of the growth of the past twenty years has improved the quality of human life. Most of the benefit has gone to the very wealthy and the remainder has been offset by the costs of resource depletion, social stress, and environmental health and other problems caused by growth. Sustainable development is about creating: 1) sustainable economies that equitably meet human needs without extracting resource inputs or expelling wastes in excess of the environment's regenerative capacity; and 2) sustainable human institutions that assure both security and opportunity for social, intellectual, and spiritual growth.

Sustainable Lifestyles

Conventional: Adopting less resource intensive lifestyles means going backwards, accepting a lowered standard of living. Given the current trend toward declining rates of population growth, any apparent limits to growth will be eliminated by continuing technological advance and the operation of market mechanisms. Responding to ill advised calls to end growth is not necessary and would be a tragic error condemning billions of people to perpetual poverty.

Alternative: Consumption of environmental resources already exceeds sustainable limits. The central task of development must be to reallocate the use of sustainable resource flows. This will require that current high consumers significantly reduce their per capita resource consumption. This may reduce their standard of living as defined by physical consumption, but it also offers opportunities for an improved quality of personal, family, and community life. Necessary reductions can be accomplished in part by reforming production systems to maximize recycling and minimize dependence on inputs from and water disposal to the environment. Some nonessential forms of consumption may need to be eliminated.

Helping Poor Countries Become Sustainable

Conventional: Once poor countries are on the path to sustainable growth an expanding economic pie will allow them to address a wide range of needs, including environmental protection and the elimination of poverty. Achieving sustainable growth in the South depends on accelerating economic growth in the North to spur demand for Southern exports and thus stimulate Southern economies. Of course, if it is to fully benefit the South, accelerated growth in the North must be combined with the removal of trade barriers and increases in foreign investment and foreign aid — including environmental lending.

From *Human Economy,* Summer 1994, pp. 1, 8, 14. © 1994 by Human Economy, a quarterly newsletter of new economics. Reprinted by permission.

Alternative: Environmental problems are in large part a consequence of Northern countries exporting their ecological deficits to the South through trade and investment. The appropriation of environmental resources and sinks to service Northern overconsumption limits the per capita shares of these resources available in Southern countries to meet domestic needs and pushes the economically weak to marginal ecological areas. Much of existing foreign aid, loans and investment, create Southern economies that are deeply in debt to the North and dependent on the continuing import of Northern technology and products. This creates demands for ever greater foreign exchange earnings for imports, debt service and repatriation of profits by foreign investors that can be obtained only through further depletion and export of environmental resources. Sustainable development in poor countries depends on: 1) increasing the availability, accessibility, and quality of sustainable natural resource flows to meet the basic needs of their own people: and 2) the political, institutional, and technical capacity to use their resources efficiently and sustainedly and to distribute the benefits equitably among all members of current and future generations. Northern countries best contribute to achieving this outcome in Southern countries by: 1) limiting their own consumption to reduce Northern dependence on environmental subsidies extracted from the South and release resources for use by the poor to meet their basic needs; and 2) facilitating unrestricted Southern access to socially and environmentally beneficial technologies.

Responsibility for Environmental Problems

Conventional: Poverty is the primary cause of environmental problems. Because of lack of education and economic opportunities the poor have too many children and lack the sensitivity and resources to provide the care for their environment that wealthier people and countries do. Environmental quality is a low priority among people whose survival is in question. They will become concerned about and invest in environmental conservation only once a certain level of income is attained. Stimulating economic growth

to increase employment opportunities and incomes must be the foundation of environmental protection.

[There is not a clear alternative consensus. Alternative I is the more prevalent among alternative thinkers, particularly in the South.]

Alternative 1: The overconsumption of Northern countries is the problem. Therefore Northern population growth is an issue because of the substantial consumption each additional Northerner adds. The poor consume very little so their numbers are not environmentally important and Southern population growth is not a consequential issue.

Alternative 2: Inequality is the fundamental cause of environmental problems. Because of their much greater relative power in a market economy, the wealthy are able to pass on the social and ecological costs of their overconsumption to the poor. Since the poor are the first to suffer from environmental degradation, they are in many localities becoming the leading advocates of more environmentally responsible resource management practices. Where poverty appears to be the cause of environmental destruction it is usually because the poor have been deprived of other means of livelihood and thus have been pushed in desperation to over exploit environmentally fragile lands. Often their lack of any other source of security creates an incentive to have many children. Eliminating inequality by distributing resource control more equitably is a fundamental condition for sustainability.

Population

Conventional: Population will stabilize naturally at somewhere between 12 and 15 billion people. While this will create some strains, with adequate economic growth it should not be a consequential problem.

Alternative: In the absence of radical economic reforms intended to rapidly accelerate reductions in fertility by increasing equity, social security, and investment in female education, female livelihood opportunities, health, and family planning services, the global population will be naturally stabilized well below 12 billion by catastrophic events as social and ecologi-

cal stress result in mass starvation and violence. Given current dependence on the depletion of nonrenewable ecological reserves, it is doubtful that even the world's current population is truly sustainable if minimum acceptable levels of consumption are to be maintained.

Economic Management Goals

Conventional: The primary goal of economic policy is the efficient allocation of resources. The internalization of production costs is a precondition to efficient allocation by markets and therefore must also be a goal of policy. Equity is a secondary by-product of economically efficient markets.

Alternative: There are three basic goals that economic policy must seek to optimize. In order of relative importance these are: a scale of resource use consistent with ecological regenerative capacities, a fair distribution of resources, and the economically efficient allocation of resources. Efficient market allocation requires the internationalization of all costs of production, including the social and environmental costs.

Jobs

Conventional: Jobs are created through economic growth.

Alternative: We have entered an era of jobless growth in which technology and reorganizations are eliminating good jobs faster than growth is creating them. The new jobs being created are often low paying, temporary, and without benefits — creating an under-

....

"As a society we hold on to the idea of economic growth with the kind of unreflective tenacity that marks the presence of a deeply neurotic structure. Very few people — including very few economists — understand what growth means, and what its long-term implications are, let alone whether it is a wise concept to hold as a central social dogma."

— James Thornton
....

lying sense of insecurity throughout society that deeply stresses the social fabric. Furthermore, many of the jobs

provided by the conventional economy are based on unsustainable rates of resource extraction and are therefore temporary in nature. We must begin to thin in terms of providing people with sustainable livelihoods based on sustainable production for sustainable markets to support sustainable lifestyles. There is a great deal of useful, environmentally friendly work that needs to be done that could readily eliminate involuntary unemployment if we chose to do so. Furthermore, in most instances sustainable production methods and technologies provide more livelihood opportunities than do their alternatives.

Trade and the Environment

Conventional: Free (unregulated) trade increases economic efficiency through comparative advantage. Economic efficiency means better use of resources, which is environmentally advantageous. Increased trade also increases overall economic growth, thereby producing the resources needed for environmental protection. The greater the volume of trade the greater the benefit to the environment.

Alternative: Trade is useful where gains from comparative advantage are real. More than half of all international trade involves exchanges of the same goods, which suggests there is little or no comparative advantage involved. To be fair and economically efficient, trade must be carried out within a clear framework of rules that: 1) internalize total costs (production, social and environmental costs, including the full costs of transport); and 2) maintain balanced trade relations. Free (unregulated) trade leads to competition between localities in need of jobs to reduce costs of local production by suppressing wages and allow-

ing maximum externalization of environmental, social, and even production costs — which is both inefficient and highly damaging to the environment and to social standards.

Markets and Governments

Conventional: Markets allocate resources most efficiently when there is the least government interference. Consumers express their preferences through their purchasing decisions, with the consequence that in the aggregate the market reflects the value preferences of the society as to how scarce resources are best allocated. When governments intervene they distort the price signals and allocative efficiency is reduced. In performing most any given function markets tend to be more efficient than governments. Therefore it is desirable to privatize functions wherever possible, while providing incentives to private investors to create jobs and increase foreign exchange earnings.

Alternative: The market is an essential institution in any workable economic allocation system. However, by its nature, the market reflects only the preferences for private goods of those who have money. Without the intervention of government and a vigilant civil society, a free (unregulated) market takes no account of optimal scale or the needs of those without money, neglects essential needs of public goods, externalizes a significant portion of real production costs, and tends toward monopoly control of allocation decisions by the market's winners. When conventional wisdom calls for incentives for private investors, it is in fact calling for subsidies that commonly take the form of agreeing to let firms increase their private gain by transferring a larger portion of their

production costs to the public. To achieve social justice and environmental sustainability, government must intervene to set a framework that assures full costs are internalized, competition is maintained, benefits are justly distributed, and necessary public goods are provided. A vigilant and vigorous civil society is required to assure the accountability of both government and market to the public interest and to provide leadership in advancing social innovation processes.

Scientific Foundations

Conventional: The conventional wisdom is grounded in accepted theory that has stood the test of time and been validated by extensive historical observation and measurement.

Alternative: The conventional wisdom represents an ideology, not a science, and largely contradicts both the theoretical foundations of market econom-

....

The answers to human problems of ecology are to be found in the economy. And the answers to the problems of the economy are to be found in human culture and character.
— Wendell Berry

....

ics and empirical experience — which contrary to the claims of the conventional wisdom strongly favor the alternative wisdom. Indeed, the conventional wisdom may itself be the single greatest barrier we face to progress toward sustainability.

Originally prepared for the Office of Technology Assessment, United States Congress. Revised May 10, 1994

Fiscal Policy and the Federal Budget

Discussion of federal budget policy in the United States has fallen to an abysmally low level. It consists wholly of bumper-sticker slogans, sound bites, lip reading. It finds public expression in shibboleths like no new taxes, balance the budget, don't raid Social Security. Prescriptions for dealing with the budget evade the central problem, which is making choices. (Herbert Stein, "Governing the $5 Trillion Economy," *The Brookings Review*)

Prior to the 1930s, fiscal policy—changes in taxes and government spending for the purpose of smoothing out the business cycle—was not used explicitly by policy makers in their pursuit of macroeconomic goals. In fact, the conventional wisdom of the day held that the best fiscal policy was a balanced budget. Most economists (known as "Classicists") maintained that a market economy had enough built-in mechanisms so that any downturns in economic activity would be quickly reversed; according to this line of reasoning, recessions were temporary departures from an economy's normal state of affairs, which was noninflationary full employment. In the Classical view, since the economy would perform better if the government did not intervene, annually balanced budgets—which served to constrain government—were a good idea.

Classical reasoning was shattered by the events of the Great Depression, a period of prolonged and widespread joblessness, falling incomes, bankruptcies, and political turmoil. In 1936 the British economist John Maynard Keynes attacked the Classical view in his *General Theory of Employment, Interest, and Money*. Keynes demonstrated how market economies could normally produce less than acceptable levels of employment and output. In Keynes's view, a healthy economy (operating at full employment and full production) could only come about if fiscal policymakers were permitted to administer the right medicine (in the form of carefully unbalanced budgets). As Keynes's ideas gained general acceptance over the next few decades, a national consensus emerged on the need for the federal government to intervene actively in the pursuit of macroeconomic goals. This view was officially sanctioned in the Employment Act of 1946 (which established a federal commitment to policies aimed at achieving "maximum production, employment, and purchasing power").

Although the goals mandated by the 1946 act are relatively clear-cut, actual policy-making experience since World War II demonstrates the difficulties the United States faces in implementing them. It also reflects the limitations of both economic ideology and the political system. Curiously, the mid-1990s echo with the same question originally raised by Keynes and the Classicists more than a half century ago—are balanced federal budgets a good idea? The challenge to fiscal policy is that this question is being asked at a time when the national debt (the product of accumulated federal deficits) has reached unprecedented heights.

This unit begins with a discussion of the Republican "Contract with America," which calls for tax cuts, deep spending cuts (except for Social Security and defense), and a balanced budget by 2002. Daniel Sichel asserts that promising a budget balance without pain merely postpones the process of finding answers to the nation's long-term economic problems. Then, Louis Uchitelle, in "The Pitfalls of a Balanced Budget," discusses potential risks associated with implementing proposals that mandate an annually balanced budget. In the opinion of many economists, the primary danger is that the government would become a destabilizer of the economy rather than a stabilizer. As a result, national rates of saving, investment, and growth may actually be reduced, as Robert Eisner demonstrates in "Saving, Economic Growth, and the Arrow of Causality."

In the essay "Budget Blaster," the reader has an opportunity to try to cut the federal budget. Using data from the nonpartisan Congressional Budget office, and assuming that existing laws will remain in effect, the goal is to balance the budget by 2002. The widespread appeal of balanced budgets may reflect the popular belief that government wastes vast amounts of tax revenues on pork barrel projects and handouts to an ungrateful underclass. However, in "Taxpayers Are Angry. They're Expensive, Too," Michael Wines points out that the largest beneficiaries of government largesse are ordinary, middle-class citizens. Wines surveys evidence on federal spending for entitlements and tax expenditures.

Few would doubt that the federal tax system has many problems, particularly to the extent that they discourage saving and investment. In the next article, Murray Weiden-

baum argues for a complete overhaul of the federal tax system in "True Tax Reform: Encouraging Saving and Investment." Nathaniel Nash provides additional insights into this complex issue by contrasting American and European attitudes toward taxes. The European willingness to pay high taxes may reflect the wider range of services their governments provide, including free medical care, nearly free university education, and generous pension and unemployment safety nets.

The unit concludes with a survey of trends in U.S. income distribution by Barry Bluestone. In recent years, the gap in earnings between those who are well educated and those not-so-well educated has increased steadily, while the real standard of living for a large portion of the workforce has sharply declined. Bluestone discusses the major explanations that economists offer for the rise in U.S. income inequality.

Looking Ahead: Challenge Questions

What are the major economic aspects of the "Contract with America?" How does the federal budget affect the economy?

Is the rapid growth of the national debt since 1980 a legitimate cause for concern? What should be done about it?

Are U.S. taxes too high? Too low? How can one explain the differing attitudes toward taxes in the United States and in Europe?

Describe and explain recent trends in U.S. income distribution.

What's in Store?

The GOP Contract for Tax Cuts and a Balanced Budget

DANIEL E. SICHEL

Daniel E. Sichel is a research associate in the Brookings Economic Studies program. He is completing a book on the effect of computers on U.S. business productivity.

On November 8, for the first time in more than 40 years, American voters handed Republicans the keys to the Capitol. Although the causes of this dramatic shift will long be debated, frustration over long-standing economic problems was surely a key element. In the minds of many, fiscal disarray in Washington was a powerful symbol of the government's inability to solve these problems.

As their solution, Republicans offered voters a 10-point "Contract with America." And since the election they have quickly gone to work on the contract, important parts of which focus on how the government conducts its business: how it taxes, how it spends, and how it operates. In particular, the contract calls for tax cuts, deep spending cuts except for defense and Social Security, and a balanced budget by 2002.

Although the balanced budget amendment in the contract floundered and was defeated in the Senate over the issue of how to treat Social Security, the fiscal promises in the contract are likely to set the political agenda for some time to come. Senate Majority Leader Robert Dole has vowed to bring the balanced budget amendment up again later this year, and pressure to reduce the deficit is unlikely to diminish. Moreover, the balanced budget amendment was just a promise to balance the budget. Congress can still pursue a fiscal path leading to budget balance by 2002, even without a constitutional amendment in force.

Thus, the fiscal promises in the contract are still front and center. And the key question remains: what must happen between now and 2002 to balance the budget and fulfill the other fiscal promises in the contract? But before looking ahead, it is helpful to look back a bit.

How Did We Get into the Deficit Mess?

Large budget deficits in peacetime are a relatively new feature on the U.S. economic landscape. By and large, deficits were small before the 1980s, except during wars and recessions. But in the early 1980s, the nation spun the fiscal roulette wheel: taxes were cut and defense spending raised without substantial spending cuts in other areas. At the time, the hope was that these changes would not boost the deficit because tax cuts would actually boost revenues. But the nation lost that fiscal gamble, and the government's budget deficit soared. As each year's hefty deficit was added on to those of past years, the total debt of the federal government surged upward as well.

Figure 1 shows the ratio of total federal debt to gross domestic product (GDP) since the end of World War II. Following heavy wartime deficit spending, the ratio fell rapidly through the early 1970s and was roughly stable over the next decade. If the diagram ended in 1980, one would not conclude that the federal household was mismanaged. On the contrary, the record until then showed that small deficits and robust economic growth had combined to cause the debt to shrink as a share of GDP. This point bears emphasis. The deficit problem is not age-old. It was created by the policy mistakes of the early 1980s. At that time, large budget deficits pushed the total stock of debt up much faster than the economy, and the ratio turned back up, reaching 70 percent by 1995.

Recent years have seen some progress on reducing the deficit and therefore slowing the rate at which total debt is growing. The deficit reduction agreements of 1990 and 1993 helped bring a 1992 deficit of $290 billion down to an estimated $176 billion by 1995. But

From *The Brookings Review*, Spring 1995, pp. 20-25. © 1995 by the Brookings Institution. Reprinted by permission.

the Congressional Budget Office (CBO) now projects that the deficit will rise to $320 billion by 2002, the year the contract promises a balanced budget.

Large deficits do not cause immediate harm to the economy. Rather, they eat away at its foundations. Saving and investment are key to future economic growth. Given the already low private saving rate in the United States, large deficits—or dissaving by the government—leave even less saving for other productive investments. Over extended periods, reduced investment implies less capital per worker and the gradual buildup of losses in labor productivity and wages. Of course, investments in the United States can be financed by borrowing overseas, but if foreigners help foot the bill—as they did during the 1980s—then they receive many of the benefits. Most economists agree that getting the deficit down would significantly improve the nation's long-run economic health.

How Does the Contract with America Address These Problems?

Let us assume that the fiscal promises contained in the Republican "Contract with America" are put into action. The budget is set on a path to balance by 2002, which of course can be done even without a balanced budget amendment. Taxes are cut. As pledged, Social Security is not touched. Given the overwhelming anti-tax sentiment expressed in the last election, Republicans in Congress seem committed to eliminating the budget deficit through spending cuts. Now we look ahead to 2002 to see how these pieces fit together.

As indicated earlier, the Congressional Budget Office projects a deficit of $320 billion in 2002 under current law. The pledge to balance the budget would bring that figure down to zero, implying a spending cut of $320 billion. But the actual task is much tougher because the contract also promises a tax cut.

In particular, the contract promises a lower capital gains tax, a $500 per child tax credit, more generous depreciation rules for businesses, and a cut in taxes paid by Social Security recipients. For this budget exercise, we will assume that all those tax provisions are enacted. Last December, the U.S. Treasury estimated that the cost of those tax cuts would average $40 billion a year over the first five years, surging to more than $100 billion a year for the next five. In 2002, the estimated revenue loss equals $100 billion. The tax cuts make balancing the budget in 2002 even harder, because $100 billion of spending must be cut just to stay even.

Thus, balancing the budget while paying for very expensive tax cuts means that $420 billion must be cut from projected spending in 2002. If the budget cutters set to work at once, rather than waiting until 2002, the debt on which interest must be paid would be lower over the next seven years and interest rates might be lower too, possibly saving as much as $100 billion in interest payments by 2002. Thus, the Republicans must find roughly $320 billion in annual programmatic cuts in 2002. (In subsequent years, the challenge is even more difficult for two reasons. First, CBO projects that under current law the deficit will rise even further by 2005, pushed up by rising health care costs. Second, the revenue loss from the tax cuts in the contract explodes in later years.)

Such a cut would be difficult enough if it came out of all programs. However, the contract shields Social Security and defense from the budget knife. Figure 2 highlights the significance of this exclusion, showing CBO's projected spending shares for 2002 under current law. Social Security, defense, and interest payments on the debt account for more than half of all federal outlays, a crucial but often overlooked point. Because

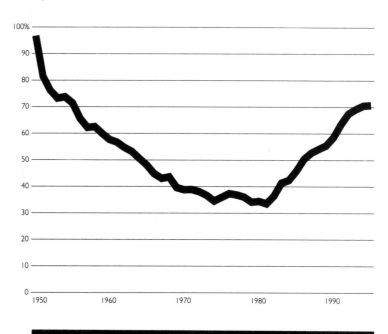

Figure 1. Federal Debt As a Share of GDP

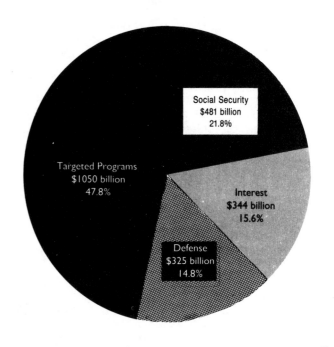

Figure 2. Projected Spending Shares, 2002

Social Security
$481 billion
21.8%

Targeted Programs
$1050 billion
47.8%

Interest
$344 billion
15.6%

Defense
$325 billion
14.8%

the contract promises to exclude these programs, the entire $320 billion cut in programs must come from the much diminished "targeted spending" category, implying a reduction of more than 30 percent.

Table 1 emphasizes the ramifications of placing a big chunk of spending off limits for cuts. The top line shows projected spending in 2002 for all programs except interest and shows the spending cut of $320 billion required to balance the budget under the promises of the contract. As the table shows, the excluded programs—Social Security and defense—are not to be touched, and therefore the targeted programs must be cut by almost one-third.

Within the targeted programs, the ultimate distribution of hits remains to be determined. Nevertheless, an examination of the components of the targeted spending category reveals who stands to lose under the contract, and who, therefore, might be expected to oppose the budget cuts. As the table shows, grants to cities and states account for about a quarter of the targeted spending category. These grants cover highway construction, support for education, health programs including Medicaid, disaster relief, and a host of other activities.

According to a recent Treasury Department study, some large states could be big losers if Social Security and defense are exempt from cuts and all programs in "targeted spending" are cut by nearly a third. For example, California—whose Republican governor Pete Wilson has been mentioned as a presidential hopeful—stands to lose as much as $10.5 billion by 2002. New York, whose newly elected Republican governor George Pataki has promised a large tax cut, would lose a similar amount; making up this lost revenue would require a state tax hike of more than 20 percent or substantial cuts in services. Governors and mayors may not go to the chopping block quietly.

Retirees also receive a big chunk of targeted spending, with Medicare and pensions (civilian and military) accounting for about 40 percent of the targeted category. Because retirees are a powerful political constituency, their programs may be spared the full force of the budget ax, but then, of course, the cuts in other programs would have to be that much greater.

Everything else in targeted spending is projected to cost $350 billion under current law. If painful choices elsewhere make this category the chief target of the budget cutters, spending would be virtually eliminated for such programs as federal prisons, the federal court system, the National Weather Service, NASA, cancer research, the National Parks, and most other federal government activities.

Figure 3 provides another perspective on the challenge facing budget cutters, highlighting the source of pressure on federal spending. This figure charts shares of federal spending back to 1965, broken down a little differently than in the pie charts. Social Security, defense, and interest payments have accounted for more than half of federal outlays for many years. The share of spending for Medicare and Medicaid has risen rapidly since 1970, pushed up, in large part, by the steep ascent in health care costs, which has also affected the private sector. Unless a way is found to limit price increases for health care, either recipients of government health care must pay more, access to government-financed care must be limited, or health care costs will continue to put pressure on the budget. The category of spending labeled "other"—outlays less Social Security, defense, interest, Medicare, and Medicaid—has actually been on a downtrend as a share of output since around 1980, a fact that may come as a surprise to those subjected to the drumbeat of rhetoric about government programs eating up more and more of the economy's resources.

Other Roads to a Balanced Budget

According to this budget arithmetic, it will be next to impossible to balance the budget if Social Security and defense are exempt from cuts and future tax hikes are ruled out. Some contend, however, that traditional budget arithmetic is the wrong way to frame the issue. Either they argue that the use of baseline spending assumptions makes budget balance look harder to achieve than it really is. Or they contend that this budget arithmetic implicitly—and wrongly—assumes a continuation of the current structure of federal spending. Does either critique offer an alternative road to budget balance?

Holding the Line on Current Spending

In the budget analysis summarized in the pie and bar charts, necessary spending cuts are calculated relative to a baseline budget, which itself is growing over time to take account of increases in population and inflation. Critics argue that if spending could just be frozen at current levels, then the budget would be in balance by the end of the century. This line of reasoning is correct in principle, but difficult in practice because most of the projected increases in spending are for interest payments on the debt and entitlements that will be politically painful to cut.

For example, spending for Social Security is projected to rise about 5 percent a year in nominal terms because the number of retirees increases and because benefits are indexed to inflation. If spending on Social Security were frozen at 1995 levels, benefits in 2002 would be more than 30 percent lower than they would be if every recipient received the benefit promised under current law. Even if Social Security were allowed to increase at 3 percent a year to cover inflation, benefits in 2002 would still be 14 percent below what current law promises.

Similarly, outlays for Medicare are expected to increase more than 10 percent a year. Just as for Social Security, the number of retirees on Medicare is expanding. And rapid increases in the price of medical care, accompanied by ever wider use of new technologies, push up anticipated spending quite rapidly. Even if increases in Medicare outlays were held to only 3 percent, benefits in 2002 would have to be cut by more than a third relative to what recipients would receive under current law. Medical services received by retirees would necessarily be cut back.

Simple formulas for achieving budget balance—such as holding current spending constant—entail extremely hard political choices.

Taking a Chain Saw to Federal Spending

The other frequent criticism of conventional budget analysis is that trimming around the edges of the current structure of federal spending will never work; solving the deficit problem requires taking a chain saw to entire programs. Consider estimated savings from the following list of programs sometimes mentioned as candidates for cuts.

Completely eliminating federal payments for Aid to Families with Dependent Children—the government's main welfare program providing cash benefits for the poor—would save an estimated $16.4 billion a year by the end of the decade. Zeroing out farm subsidy programs would save $10.8 billion a year. Stopping subsidies for urban mass transit would hold down yearly spending by $4.8 billion. Defunding the space station would save another $2.4 billion. Shutting down the Small Business Administration would save $550 million (yes, less than $1 billion). Eliminating federal support of Amtrak would save another $800 million or so. Switching off the subsidies received by the Rural Electrification Administration would keep spending down by another $90 million. At this point, a lot of political blood would have been spilled and the deficit would be down by only $36 billion, a long way from the hundreds of billions in spending cuts needed to balance the budget.

Should spending be carefully examined to eliminate fat? Yes. Will that balance the budget? No. The lesson of budget arithmetic is simple. Although spending can be cut and efficiency improved in many areas, balancing the budget will be virtually impossible without touching the big programs like Social Security, Medicare, and defense. Back in the 1930s Willie Sutton explained that he robbed banks because that's where the money is. If Willie were a member of the House or Senate Budget Committee today, he would be looking up addresses for these large programs.

What Happens Once the Budget Is Balanced?

The difficulty of balancing the budget, of course, is what led many in Congress to support a constitutional amendment to force the tough choices. But while getting the deficit down would be a definite plus for the economy's long-term health, doing so by amending the Constitution has some disadvantages. The likelihood that the issue will arise again despite its recent defeat in the Senate makes it important to keep four, in particular, in mind.

First, a balanced budget amendment could turn a mild economic slowdown into a major recession, because fiscal policy will lose its ability to stabilize the economy automatically. As jobs are lost and incomes fall during a slowdown, tax revenues will decline. As more jobless workers apply for unemployment insurance and other benefits, spending will rise. Falling revenues and higher spending could generate a very large temporary deficit. Under the old rules, such

Figure 3. Federal Spending as a Share of GDP

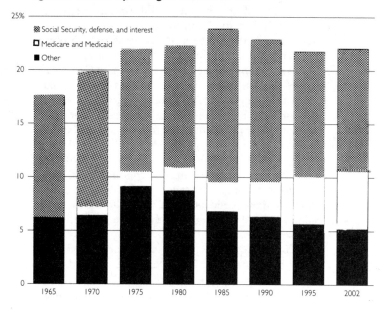

Table 1. Required Spending Cuts in 2002 under the Contract

(billions of dollars, except where noted)

	CBO PROJECTIONS UNDER CURRENT LAW	CUT REQUIRED UNDER CONTRACT	PERCENT CUT REQUIRED UNDER CONTRACT
Spending for programs (excluding interest)	$1856	$320	–
Excluded programs	806	0	0%
Social Security	481	0	0%
Defense	325	0	0%
Targeted programs	1050	320	30%
Cities and states*	265	?	?
Retirees†	435	?	?
Everything else	350	?	?

Source: CBO, Treasury, and author's calculations.

* Medicaid and other grants.

† Medicare, civilian, and military pensions.

deficit spending would automatically boost the weakened economy. But under the new rules, the budget must be balanced. Congress would have to slash spending or raise taxes, either of which would push the economy deeper into recession. And the negative effects of a downturn can linger for a long time, as they did after the most recent recession, which officially ended in the spring of 1991.

But in the amendment just considered by Congress, a three-fifths majority of the House and Senate could waive the budget balance requirements. And often they surely would. But given the uncertainties of economic forecasting, would Congress always act before serious economic damage was done? Would a determined minority in either house ever block a move to waive the budget rules in time of economic crisis, perhaps to delay recovery and weaken the election prospects of the president? Such damage to the nation's economy could all be done in the name of defending the Constitution.

Second, requiring year-to-year budget balance would hold Washington to an extreme standard. Although it is often said that the federal government should balance its budget just as families do, most households do not. Few families pay cash to buy homes, cars, and college educations; they borrow. Businesses borrow to finance inventories or invest in plant and equipment. States issue bonds (borrow) to finance capital expenditures like highways. Year-to-year budget balance would require that the federal government's purchases of long-term capital (buildings, highways, defense equipment) be paid for in full in the year of purchase, a very peculiar accounting standard.

Third, a balanced budget amendment could lead to increasingly outlandish budget shenanigans. Many tools are available to Congress besides direct spending. Congress could declare certain government expenses to be off-budget. It could impose requirements on state

The fundamental economic challenges facing the nation, including sluggish growth in real wages and productivity for today's workers, diminished economic prospects for our children and grandchildren, and a further falling behind of those at the bottom of the income distribution, go well beyond the budget deficit.

and local governments or on the private sector, perhaps with off-budget loan guarantees to sweeten the pot. Such maneuvers would further undermine the budget process, dragging the debate even deeper into procedural muck and creating even more voter cynicism.

Fourth, a balanced budget amendment raises difficult enforcement questions. Suppose spending exceeds revenue in 2004? Would the federal courts enforce the balanced budget amendment? Would they raise income taxes? cut Social Security benefits? Would they, as Bill Frenzel, a former Republican Congressman now at Brookings, puts it, "send the U.S. marshals in to arrest the check writers?" Whatever the case, Congress and the president would have ceded much of their authority to unelected judges. Suppose instead that the amendment is simply ignored or sidestepped with creative accounting, something like Prohibition earlier this century. Although such a move might ease a temporary budget crisis, it would damage respect for the rule of law and voters' confidence in their government.

A Challenge Unmet

The fundamental economic challenges facing the nation, including sluggish growth in real wages and productivity for today's workers, diminished economic prospects for our children and grandchildren, and a further falling behind of those at the bottom of the income distribution, go well beyond the budget deficit. Any solution to these problems will require greater investments in our future, and deficit reduction—which frees up the nation's savings for productive investment—is surely a step in the right direction.

But the "Contract with America" may not move us in that direction. It does not specify how the budget would be balanced, and once Social Security and defense are taken off the cutting table and future tax hikes are ruled out, budget balance will be extremely difficult to achieve. And tax cuts today—unless paid for by spending cuts or tax hikes elsewhere—only make it harder to balance the budget.

Nevertheless, most Americans support the concept of a balanced budget amendment. A January 12 *Wall Street Journal* opinion poll showed approval at almost 70 percent. Americans do not, however, support the painful deficit reduction that the analysis here shows will be necessary to actually balance the budget. The same opinion poll finds that 60 percent of Americans oppose the amendment if it entails substantial cuts in entitlement programs such as Medicare, Medicaid, and veterans' benefits.

The contract perfectly mirrors this inconsistency in public opinion, promising budget balance without pain. Its failure to come to grips with budget arithmetic perpetuates the myth that the nation's fiscal problems can be solved without sacrifice by most Americans. The contract's supporters, Republicans and Democrats alike, are merely deferring the political debate we must one day have over how to get the deficit down and how to improve the nation's long-run economic prospects.

The Pitfalls of a Balanced Budget

Dismantling a Decades-Old System for Softening Recessions

Louis Uchitelle

The unemployment rate, which peaked at 7.7 percent after the last recession, could have reached 9 percent if a balanced budget had been required, Government and private economists estimate. And a laid-off worker who collected $12,000 in unemployment pay might have received only $7,000 or so.

Such estimates of the potential economic impact are not emphasized very much, however, in the debate over the balanced budget amendment. So far, the battle has focused on its value as a tool to shrink government or to discipline spending. But if the amendment is enacted, the side effect would be huge: a system that has softened recessions since the 1930's would be dismantled.

"There are risks associated with a balanced budget, and I don't think anyone should deny them," said William Hoagland, the Republican staff director for the Senate Budget Committee. "Nevertheless, the debate on the floor has been dominated by what we must do to get the budget in balance, not what the risks of a balanced budget amendment might be."

Mr. Hoagland expressed surprise that the biggest risk—deeper, more painful recessions—had not figured significantly in the debate, although Senator Daniel P. Moynihan, Democrat of New York, and Senator Paul

S. Sarbanes, Democrat of Maryland, had called attention to the risk in several floor speeches. "The reason must be that the advocates of a balanced budget see the benefits to the economy as far outweighing the negatives associated with cyclical downturns," Mr. Hoagland said. "That must be what is going on."

No benefit seems to hold more sway than the view that the amendment would shrink the Federal Government by restricting its power to tax and to spend. A dollar not collected and spent by the Government is a dollar left in the hands of the private sector. And the private sector invariably invests money more efficiently than the Government, this view holds.

"The people have spoken clearly that government is too big and we need to do something about it," said Robert Hall, a Stanford University economist who favors smaller government. "The problem is that the balanced budget amendment is a heavy-handed solution and risky."

Is monetary policy enough to bolster the U.S. economy in tough times?

The biggest risk is to the nation's "automatic stabilizers," which have made recessions less severe than

they were in the century before World War II. The stabilizers, an outgrowth of Keynesian economics, work this way: When the economy weakens, outlays automatically rise for unemployment pay, food stamps, welfare and Medicaid. Simultaneously, as incomes fall, so do corporate and individual income tax payments. Both elements make more money available for spending, thus helping to pull the economy out of its slump.

The problem, of course, is that the stabilizers make the deficit shoot up—by roughly $65 billion as a result of the 1990–1991 recession, according to the Treasury Department. Under the balanced budget amendment, Congress and the Administration would be required to get the budget quickly back into balance, through spending cuts, higher tax rates, or a combination of the two—perhaps even in the midst of a recession.

"The Government would become, almost inevitably, a destabilizer of the economy rather than a stabilizer," said Joseph Stiglitz, a member of the President's Council of Economic Advisers. Many economists share that view.

Absent the stabilizers, every 73-cent drop in national income in the last recession would have become a $1 drop, said Bradford DeLong, deputy assistant Secretary of the Treasury, who as a Harvard economist studied this dynamic and recently updated his research. Of the 27 cents

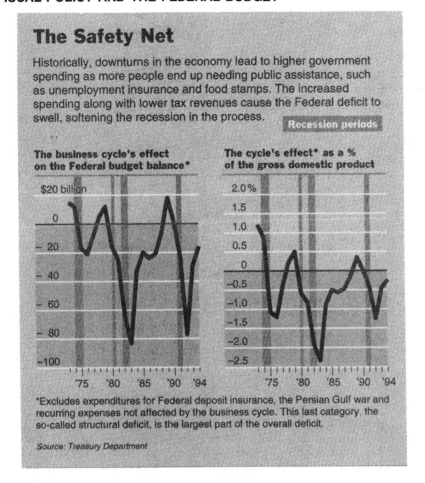

The Safety Net

Historically, downturns in the economy lead to higher government spending as more people end up needing public assistance, such as unemployment insurance and food stamps. The increased spending along with lower tax revenues cause the Federal deficit to swell, softening the recession in the process.

Recession periods

The business cycle's effect on the Federal budget balance*

The cycle's effect* as a % of the gross domestic product

*Excludes expenditures for Federal deposit insurance, the Persian Gulf war and recurring expenses not affected by the business cycle. This last category, the so-called structural deficit, is the largest part of the overall deficit.

Source: Treasury Department

A move seen by some as a heavy-handed solution to big Government.

in cushioning, 20 cents came from falling tax revenue and 7 cents from the higher spending.

Economists outside the Government offer similar estimates. Ray Fair of Yale University, for example, said for every $10 billion decline in national income during a recession, the deficit rises by $2 billion, as the stabilizers kick in with their higher spending and lower tax revenue.

"We ought not to give up the stabilizers," Professor Fair said. "That would be very Draconian."

Nearly every economist agrees that the American economy requires, if not stabilizers, some substitute method for offsetting recessions in an era of balanced budgets. And those who favor the amendment are no exception.

"It would be a disaster to lose the stabilizers," said C. Fred Bergsten, director of the Institute for International Economics, who endorses the amendment as a necessary step if the nation is to afford the high cost

of Social Security and Medicare for the baby boom generation, which reaches retirement age early in the next century.

Mr. Bergsten notes that the amendment, as now worded, would permit Congress to bring back the stabilizers by a three-fifths vote in both houses. The vote would permit the necessary deficit spending to finance the stabilizers.

While a three-fifths vote is a big hurdle, Mr. Bergsten and others argue that Congress would get used to authorizing the necessary deficits during recessions. Nevertheless, he would prefer a different solution. Once through a painful process of balancing the budget by 2002, as required by the amendment, then the Government should run budget surpluses in years of strong economic growth and full employment, Mr. Bergsten said.

The surpluses would cover the rising costs of the stabilizers during recessions. "You could go down to a

balanced budget in the hard years, and still give the economy a little stimulus," he said.

The Congressional Budget Office has estimated that the surplus needed to pay for the stabilizers during a recession as severe as that of 1981–1982, the worst since World War II, would be 1 percent of the national income during robust periods of full employment, and perhaps as much as 1.5 percent.

That would mean an annual surplus in today's dollars of $70 billion to $100 billion, rather than the nearly $200 billion of so in annual deficits expected under current policy. Most of the $200 billion is to help pay for programs like highway construction and new weaponry that have fixed costs and do not fluctuate with the ups and downs of the economy, as unemployment pay, food stamps, tax revenues and the other stabilizers do.

Some economists—including Milton Friedman, a Nobel laureate in economics who is with the Hoover Institute—hold that the stabilizers, despite the ballyhoo, are no longer so important. The Federal Reserve, through monetary policy, can more than offset their disappearance by lowering interest rates an extra notch or two to give the economy an additional stimulus in hard times.

"I have looked at many episodes in the world in which monetary policy went one way and fiscal policy the other, and I have never found a case in which monetary policy did not dominate," Mr. Friedman said. He favors a balanced budget amendment that would shrink the Federal Government by putting a ceiling on

the tax increases that could be enacted to balance the budget.

But the Clinton Administration and even Federal Reserve officials question whether monetary policy could alone handle the task of reviving an economy in recession. The stabilizers, they note, kick in automatically—before the Federal Reserve and most economists often realize that the economy is falling toward recession.

A recession might be well along and getting deeper before the Fed recognized the problem and began to drop rates. The lower rates, in turn, would not be felt in the economy for a year to 18 months, the traditional lag. And even if the Fed acted quickly enough, the economy would behave in new and different ways without the stabilizers.

"My guess is that we would get it wrong the first time we went into recession, making that recession much deeper than it should be," said a Federal Reserve official, who spoke on condition that he not be identified. "But we would learn from that experience and do a better job thereafter."

BUDGET BLASTER

Welcome to Budget Blaster, the game that lets you cut the deficit. Reducing this shortfall is crucial and requires hard work. But the labor is worth it because of the resulting growth. When you play Budget Blaster, you'll use data from the nonpartisan Congressional Budget Office. The CBO's forecast lifts spending caps after 1998 and assumes that existing laws remain in effect. These numbers don't include GOP proposals and differ from the president's new budget. Good luck!

Unless you succeed in cutting the deficit, you won't be able to increase net national savings, lower interest rates and spur economic growth.

▼

In order to bring the deficit under control, you will have two major tools at your disposal: cutting spending and/or increasing taxes.

▼

Future spending will be driven by federal outlays for mandatory programs such as Social Security, Medicare, Medicaid and welfare payments.

▼

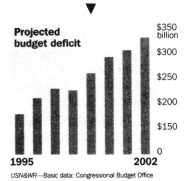

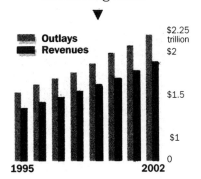

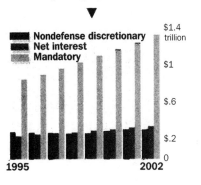

USN&WR—Basic data: Congressional Budget Office

MEET THE FISCAL FAMILY

To help you understand how a balanced budget would affect your family, community and country, we'd like you to meet the Fiscal family, which lives in Deficitville.

FRED AND FRANCES FISCAL

This married couple has a combined family income of about $40,000. Fred has been running his own small business in Deficitville for years. Frances, a part-time nurse, works closely with a doctor who serves the community's large elderly population.

FRED'S PARENTS

The couple, both retired, live across town in Deficitville and depend on Social Security benefits as a major source of income.

FRED'S BROTHER

A Vietnam veteran, he spent 20 years in the military and now works at an aerospace plant.

DEFICITVILLE

Deficitville is a small city that has relied on federal grants to improve its water system. It has also received education grants from Washington for its schools. Rising interest rates have dramatically increased the community's municipal-debt costs.

FRANCES'S PARENTS

This hard-working couple still labors on a big farm outside the city of Deficitville. The harvest includes wheat and corn.

FRED'S SISTER

She was abandoned by her husband and is now unemployed. Her child needs frequent medical care because of a severe disability.

FRED'S UNCLE

This very wealthy businessman has been pulling down a healthy six-figure income for many years.

The object of the game is to balance the budget by 2002, as many in Congress now propose to do. According to the CBO, this will require about $1.2 trillion in deficit reduction. The CBO has set deficit targets for each of the next seven years. If you hit the annual targets, you balance the budget and win the Fiscal Patriot Award.

HOW TO PLAY BUDGET BLASTER

■ Scan the spreadsheets, which detail federal spending programs and tax provisions. The pages list the CBO's projected budget numbers for discretionary and mandatory outlays as well as key revenue sources.
■ You may cut or increase spending and taxes as much as you like, but you may adjust the "Other" category by only 15 percent a year so that your budget decisions are not arbitrary.
■ Cutting the deficit yields interest savings on the national debt. But calculating the savings for different deficit reduction levels is very complex. In lieu of a sophisticated computer model, we provide annual interest-savings figures on your work sheets that assume you have hit the previous year's deficit target. This means you can't change net interest numbers.
■ After you make your fiscal decisions for each year, total the numbers from the spreadsheets and enter

them on the work sheets. You must hit annual deficit targets to keep playing. A Budget Blaster bonus will be awarded for surpassing a deficit target. You will receive a $1 billion credit for each $1 billion in excess deficit cuts. These points carry over to the next year. The bonus reflects the benefits that accrue from slashing programs early in this deficit reduction cycle.

A NOTE ON SOCIAL SECURITY

■ By law, Social Security's two trust funds are officially "off budget" for the purpose of making all budget calculations. Still, so-called consolidated budget estimates include the annual surpluses in Social Security—estimated at $69 billion in 1995—in order to reflect the true net borrowing needs of the government. Without today's Social Security surplus, the total federal budget deficit would be much higher than it is. But the surplus will dwindle into deficit by 2013—causing an explosion in federal borrowing—unless benefits are reduced, cost-of-living adjustments are trimmed or payroll taxes are increased. Many politicians have vowed not to touch Social Security, and some senators want to modify the proposed balanced-budget amendment by prohibiting cuts in the program. But Congress can still change Social Security, and our rules also allow you to adjust this program.

BUDGET BLASTER SPREADSHEETS

This menu lays out spending and revenues through 2002. To balance the budget, you can change outlays and/or taxes. Tally your numbers here and transfer the totals to the work sheets that follow.

OUTLAYS

DISCRETIONARY

Housing assistance	*Gives rental aid to people in 79,000 low-income-housing units and funds other housing activities.*
Federal aid to highways	*Funds the construction, revitalization and maintenance of the nation's highway system.*
Elementary, secondary schools	*Distributes grants for disadvantaged, delinquent and migrant students, among others.*
Space flight and research	*Major U.S. program for operating the space shuttle and developing the orbiting research lab.*
Health research and training	*Supports the National Institutes of Health, which deals with diseases ranging from AIDS to cancer.*
Air transportation	*Helps provide funding for 570 civilian airports around the country.*
International development	*These aid programs aim to promote growth in developing nations such as the former Soviet Union.*
Federal law enforcement	*Funds operations at the FBI, Immigration and Naturalization Service, Customs and other agencies.*
Student financial assistance	*The key program for aiding about 7 million students a year through grants and loans.*
Pollution control and abatement	*Helps communities construct waste-water-treatment facilities.*
International security assistance	*Aids countries, such as Israel and Egypt, seeking to acquire U.S. military equipment and services.*
Federal judicial activities	*Funds operations for several federal courts, including the U.S. courts of appeals.*
Conservation and land	*Supports 156 national forests and 20 national grasslands while protecting endangered species.*
Training and employment services	*Provides funding for the economically and educationally disadvantaged.*
Water resources	*Assists the U.S. Army Corps of Engineers in operating and maintaining flood-control procedures.*
Conduct of foreign affairs	*Facilitates the diplomatic and consular programs run by the Department of State.*
Community development grants	*Provides grants to state and local governments aimed at revitalizing urban cities and counties.*
General science, research	*Enables researchers to study a variety of subjects, including genetic engineering and polar ice-caps.*
Federal correctional activities	*Allows for the maintenance and operation of 94 federal prisons across the United States.*
Area and regional development	*Finances water disposal, telecommunications services and computer networks in rural areas.*

DEFENSE

Operations and maintenance	*Supplies funds for operation and maintenance of the U.S. armed forces.*
Military personnel	*Pays the salaries and expenses of active-duty forces and reserves.*
Procurement	*Finances acquisition of weapons, supplies and munitions by the Defense Department.*
Research and development	*Supports military modernization through R&D activities.*
Atomic energy defense activities	*Funds maintenance and improvement of the nation's nuclear arsenal.*
Military construction	*Aims to improve or replace obsolete facilities and provide installations for new weapons systems.*

1995	1996	1997	1998	1999	2000	2001	2002

ALL FIGURES ARE IN BILLIONS

1995	1996	1997	1998	1999	2000	2001	2002
$27	$29	$31	$33	$35	$37	$38	$39
19	19	20	20	21	21	22	23
15	16	16	17	17	18	18	19
13	13	14	14	14	15	15	16
11	12	12	12	13	13	14	14
10	10	10	11	11	11	12	12
8	9	9	9	9	10	10	10
8	8	8	9	9	9	10	10
7	7	8	8	8	9	9	9
6	7	7	8	9	9	9	9
6	6	6	6	6	7	7	7
5	5	6	6	6	6	7	7
5	5	5	5	5	6	6	6
5	5	6	6	6	6	6	7
5	5	5	5	5	5	5	5
4	4	4	5	5	5	5	5
4	4	5	5	5	5	5	5
4	4	4	5	5	5	5	5
3	3	3	3	3	3	3	3
2	3	3	3	3	3	3	3
$88	$94	$97	$101	$105	$109	$113	$117
71	70	75	76	79	82	85	87
55	50	47	47	48	49	50	52
35	36	37	38	39	41	42	44
10	11	11	11	12	12	12	13
6	6	6	6	6	6	6	6

The budget deficit is expected to rise from $207 billion to $322 billion between 1996 and 2002.

OUTLAYS (CONTINUED)

MANDATORY

Medicare	*This health program provides insurance to an estimated 37 million elderly recipients.*
Medicaid	*Funded jointly by Washington and the states, this health program offers insurance to the poor.*
Civil-service retirement	*Provides pensions to nearly 2.5 million retired and disabled federal employees and their survivors.*
Veterans' benefits	*Former military personnel are eligible for a number of programs including disability and hospitalization*
Military retirement	*More than 1.5 million military retirees collected federally funded pensions in 1994.*
Supplemental Security Income	*Aids elderly, blind or disabled low-income citizens.*
Food stamps	*Provides low-income households with coupons for the purchase of groceries.*
Unemployment compensation	*Funded by Washington and the states, this program provides temporary compensation to the unemployed*
Earned-income tax credit	*Offers monetary assistance through tax credits to low-income working families with children.*
Family support payments	*Known as AFDC, the government's welfare program offers benefits to about 14 million people a month*
Farm income stabilization	*This program compensates farmers for commodity-price drops, helping to support over 700,000 farms*
SOCIAL SECURITY	*This broad-based entitlement program delivers benefits to 94 percent of all elderly families.*
OTHER	*Incorporates all other federal spending programs. You may adjust this category by only 15 percent a year.*
NET INTEREST	*Includes federal interest payments to the public and, as an offset, government interest income on loans*

TOTAL OUTLAYS

REVENUES

INDIVIDUAL INCOME TAX

Earning less than $25,000	*This group accounted for some 8.1 percent of total income tax in 1993.*
Earning $25,000-$49,999	*This segment generated about 22.7 percent of total income tax in 1993.*
Earning $50,000-$99,999	*This slice of taxpayers provided some 30.9 percent of total income tax in 1993.*
Earning $100,000-$199,999	*This upper-income group accounted for about 15.4 percent of total income tax in 1993.*
Earning more than $200,000	*These wealthy taxpayers generated about 22.8 percent of total income tax in 1993.*
CORPORATE TAX	*Corporate taxes as a share of GDP shrank from 4.3 percent in 1960 to 2.1 percent in 1994.*
PAYROLL TAX	*These taxes are withheld from wages and go to programs such as Social Security and Medicare.*
OTHER	*Incorporates all other taxes. You may adjust this category by only 15 percent a year.*

TOTAL REVENUES

DEFICIT

DEFICIT

Note: Some spending numbers for 2001 and 2002 are *U.S. News* estimates adjusted for inflation; income tax segments are estimates based on 1993 IRS data and adjusted gross income; deficit may not exactly equal outlays minus revenues because of rounding; tax distributions may not add to 100 percent because of rounding; trust fund surpluses are part of total federal budget.

1995	1996	1997	1998	1999	2000	2001	2002

ALL FIGURES ARE IN BILLIONS

1995	1996	1997	1998	1999	2000	2001	2002
$ 176	$ 196	$ 217	$ 238	$ 262	$ 286	$ 314	$ 344
90	100	111	123	136	149	164	179
38	39	41	43	45	47	48	50
35	34	37	38	39	43	44	46
28	29	31	32	35	37	38	39
27	27	32	35	38	43	44	46
25	26	27	29	30	31	32	33
24	25	27	28	30	31	32	33
17	20	23	24	25	26	27	28
17	18	18	18	19	19	20	21
10	10	9	8	9	9	9	9
334	352	371	390	411	433	456	481
43	48	30	15	15	15	14	16
235	260	270	279	294	310	325	344
$1531	**$1625**	**$1699**	**$1769**	**$1872**	**$1981**	**$2084**	**$2202**

1995	1996	1997	1998	1999	2000	2001	2002
48	51	53	56	59	63	66	70
135	143	149	157	166	175	185	196
184	194	203	214	226	239	252	266
92	97	101	107	113	119	126	133
136	143	150	158	167	176	186	196
149	151	155	161	167	173	182	192
494	517	539	565	590	618	650	682
117	122	125	128	130	134	140	145
$1355	**$1418**	**$1475**	**$1546**	**$1618**	**$1697**	**$1787**	**$1880**

1995	1996	1997	1998	1999	2000	2001	2002
$ 176	$ 207	$ 224	$ 222	$ 253	$ 284	$ 297	$ 322

Note: Spending caps are eliminated after 1998; discretionary programs may have elements of mandatory spending and vice versa; mandatory spending is controlled by permanent laws and is constrained by "pay as you go" rules; discretionary spending is controlled through annual appropriations.

BUDGET BLASTER WORK SHEETS

Enter your total annual outlays and revenues below. Compute your deficit; compare it with the deficit target. If your deficit is lower than the target, put the difference on the bonus line and carry it forward.

1996

NET INTEREST	$ 260	YOUR OUTLAYS	▶ $	
TOTAL OUTLAYS	1625	INTEREST SAVINGS	▶ —	1
TOTAL REVENUES	1418	YOUR REVENUES	▶ —	
PROJECTED DEFICIT	207	YOUR DEFICIT	▶	
DEFICIT TARGET	174	BLASTER BONUS 1996	▶	

1997

NET INTEREST	$ 270	YOUR OUTLAYS	▶ $	
TOTAL OUTLAYS	1699	INTEREST SAVINGS	▶ —	4
TOTAL REVENUES	1475	YOUR REVENUES	▶ —	
PROJECTED DEFICIT	224	BLASTER BONUS 1996	▶ —	
DEFICIT TARGET	155	YOUR DEFICIT	▶	
		BLASTER BONUS 1997	▶	

1998

NET INTEREST	$ 279	YOUR OUTLAYS	▶ $	
TOTAL OUTLAYS	1769	INTEREST SAVINGS	▶ —	10
TOTAL REVENUES	1546	YOUR REVENUES	▶ —	
PROJECTED DEFICIT	222	BLASTER BONUS 1997	▶ —	
DEFICIT TARGET	116	YOUR DEFICIT	▶	
		BLASTER BONUS 1998	▶	

Note: All figures are in billions of dollars; years refer to fiscal years; totals may not add because of rounding; revenue data do not assume dynamic scoring; numbers do not assume changes in economic activity from CBO base-line forecast.

FAMILY FORTUNES

Your budget choices will affect the Fiscal family's future.

FOOD STAMPS
Until Fred's sister finds a job, she will rely on food stamps to feed herself and her son.

MEDICARE
Fred's mother was alarmed when she heard that Medicare premiums might increase.

TAXING THE RICH
Taxes for Fred's uncle went up in 1993; he's afraid that the affluent will get hit again.

VETERANS' HEALTH
Fred's brother received free surgery on his lower back at a local veterans' hospital last year.

Keep attacking the deficit! You are halfway to your goal of balancing the budget. Remember: The Blaster bonus will help you win the game.

1999

NET INTEREST	$ 294	YOUR OUTLAYS	▸ $	
TOTAL OUTLAYS	1872	INTEREST SAVINGS	▸ −	19
TOTAL REVENUES	1618	YOUR REVENUES	▸ −	
PROJECTED DEFICIT	253	BLASTER BONUS 1998	▸ −	
DEFICIT TARGET	71	YOUR DEFICIT	▸	
		BLASTER BONUS 1999	▸	

2000

NET INTEREST	$ 310	YOUR OUTLAYS	▸ $	
TOTAL OUTLAYS	1981	INTEREST SAVINGS	▸ −	31
TOTAL REVENUES	1697	YOUR REVENUES	▸ −	
PROJECTED DEFICIT	284	BLASTER BONUS 1999	▸ −	
DEFICIT TARGET	59	YOUR DEFICIT	▸	
		BLASTER BONUS 2000	▸	

2001

NET INTEREST	$ 325	YOUR OUTLAYS	▸ $	
TOTAL OUTLAYS	2084	INTEREST SAVINGS	▸ −	46
TOTAL REVENUES	1787	YOUR REVENUES	▸ −	
PROJECTED DEFICIT	297	BLASTER BONUS 2000	▸ −	
DEFICIT TARGET	26	YOUR DEFICIT	▸	
		BLASTER BONUS 2001	▸	

All figures are in billions of dollars; totals may not add because of rounding; AFDC stands for Aid to Families with Dependent Children.

FAMILY FORTUNES

Washington touches many aspects of the Fiscal family's life.

AFDC
Fred's sister lost her job and is now receiving a monthly AFDC check until she can find work.

SOCIAL SECURITY
Fred's parents fear that their annual Social Security cost-of-living increase might be trimmed.

TAX CUTS
Tax cuts will add to the deficit, and they might not put much money in Fred and Frances's pocket.

DEFENSE SPENDING
Defense cutbacks have led to layoffs at the aerospace plant where Fred's brother works.

One more year to go! The projected deficit keeps rising because of the dramatic increase in mandatory federal spending. To balance the budget, you'll have to make some very difficult choices.

2002

NET INTEREST	$ 344	YOUR OUTLAYS	▶	$
TOTAL OUTLAYS	2202	INTEREST SAVINGS	▶ –	64
TOTAL REVENUES	1880	YOUR REVENUES	▶ –	
PROJECTED DEFICIT	322	BLASTER BONUS 2001	▶	
DEFICIT TARGET	0	YOUR DEFICIT	▶	

FAMILY FORTUNES

Deficit reduction is hard but beneficial.

FARM SUPPORTS
Frances's parents worry that a cut in crop subsidies would reduce their farm income.

GAME OVER!

Congratulations! If you penciled in a zero on the deficit line for 2002, you have successfully balanced the budget in seven years and earned U.S. News's Fiscal Patriot Award. Your patience and persistence have spurred growth in Deficitville. Although Washington no longer subsidizes many of the city's projects, the dramatic drop in interest rates has enabled the community to finance many of its own civic improvements. For their part, members of the Fiscal family have had to make sacrifices to help achieve this budgetary health. Fred's sister has seen her AFDC benefits cut; Medicare premiums for Fred's parents have shot up dramati-

cally, and Fred's wealthy uncle is now paying higher taxes.

ECONOMIC BOOST. Your deficit reduction efforts have also boosted the national economy. By cutting federal debt levels, the country saves billions of dollars in interest costs. In addition, a tighter fiscal policy should enable the Federal Reserve to cut short-term interest rates, and the financial markets should slice long-term rates. This combination should eventually increase investment, boost productivity and raise living standards.

TALK TO US. After finishing Budget Blaster, clip your work sheets

and the coupon below. Send this to us, and we'll deliver it to your congressional representative. The full text and graphics from this article are available in U.S. News Online on CompuServe. And for those who are interested, look for "Uncle Sam's Budget Balancer," along with the full text of the president's 1996 budget, in the resources library of the U.S. News Forum on CompuServe.

NAME

ADDRESS

CITY   STATE   ZIP

CONGRESSIONAL REPRESENTATIVE

Budget Blaster was developed by William Meyers, Robert F. Black, David Fischer and Timothy M. Ito

Saving, Economic Growth, and the Arrow of Causality

Robert Eisner

ROBERT EISNER is the William R. Kenan Professor Emeritus at Northwestern University and a past President of the American Economic Association. This article was adapted from a statement that he presented to the Senate Finance Committee on January 31, 1995.

The vast public investment, and particularly investment in intangible capital, will prove to be our engine of growth. It will pull private tangible investment along with it. A well-qualified labor force will offer the best incentive to business to invest in the capital that makes full use of its talents.

Saving and growth are inextricably intertwined. You can't have one without the other. But which is cause and which is effect? Does saving generate growth or does growth generate saving? And, to the extent that saving does contribute to growth, what should and can be done to have more saving and more growth? Which measures would work? Which measures would have little or no effect? And which measures are likely to be counterproductive?

THE ARGUMENTS

In the economy as a whole, saving is the accumulation of assets—or investment. Indeed, saving and investment are identical. If investment adds to our productivity or productive capacity, *and if that capacity is utilized*, it adds to growth. That tells us that saving which corresponds to unproductive investment does nothing for growth. It also tells us that an economy that does not provide enough purchasing power to buy the products of new investment robs that investment of its potential contribution to growth.

Indeed, it probably causes it to decline in the future. Business will not continue to invest, if it can't sell its products.

If we understood this, our view of the futility of many measures to "promote saving" would become clear. Individuals may be persuaded to save more by some "tax incentive." But that might be more difficult to accomplish than some think. This means that individuals would be persuaded to consume (spend) less of their income. But unless this reduction of their consumption led business to decide to invest more (that is, to buy more new machines or construct additional plant or accumulate additional inventories), there would be no new investment. Thus, there can be no additional saving in the economy as a whole. Individual thriftiness, whether motivated by self or government, might not add up to national saving.

What happens is that one individual's decision to consume less merely results in another individual earning less income. For example, say the individual decides to forgo a haircut. As a consequence, a second individual—in this case, the

barber—saves less, since his saving equals his income minus his consumption. If the barber chooses to cut his consumption in order to maintain his saving, the chain (referred to in textbooks as a "multiplier chain") merely goes on undisturbed. If somehow, investment increases, income will be maintained. Someone else earns more, produces new machinery, and compensates for the barber's loss of income. Or there may even be an increase of income from which will emanate the increased saving. But you can't get more saving without more investment.

DON'T WORRY

The old classical argument (resurrected in some quarters today) was: "Don't worry." If one individual decides to save more, he offers to lend his free money—directly or through a bank. This lowers interest rates and hence brings about the increase in investment that corresponds to the increased saving. But if the effects of interest rates on most investment are modest, and if lower consumption has a more chilling effect on business and its investment than lower interest rates can offset, the classical argument surely fails. And if we want lower interest rates to stimulate investment, that can best be achieved by the Federal Reserve relaxing its constraints.

In addition, the traditional measures (the intention of which was to encourage more individual saving) are of doubtful efficacy. People save to provide for expected future needs—such as to send a child to college and, most important, to provide the resources required to maintain their consumption during their retirement years. Considerable saving is also undertaken (intentionally or unintentionally) to provide for one's heirs or (at least among the wealthy) to give away their wealth to charity at death. None of these components of saving appears to be much affected by the returns to be expected. These returns might be influenced by changes in interest rates or in tax provisions which would alter any remaining differences between the after-tax and before-tax return on savings. There is even some suggestion that increasing the return might lower the individual propensity to save. Those saving for retirement, for example, might find that, because of the increased return on their accumulated savings over the years, they need to set aside less each year (to save less), in order to have enough to provide the standard of living to which they would aspire in their later years.

This indicates that the way to get more private saving may well be to approach it from the other side of the saving-investment identity—to raise investment. As I have indicated, that might be done by lowering real interest rates. Real interest rates are, of course, the real borrowing cost to business and the real returns to lenders. They are the nominal interest rates minus the expected rate of inflation. We can lower real interest rates by increasing the rate of expected inflation with nominal interest rates rising less, or by lowering the nominal rate with expected inflation falling less, remaining the same, or even rising. The second alternative—with less inflation—seems preferable. But it should be noted that past periods of high inflation have generally been periods of very low, or even negative, real interest rates and of relatively high investment. Whatever other complaints we might voice about inflation, it has tended to be good for investment, and therefore good for saving. *That* said, however, the direct impact of interest rates on investment

> *The way to get more private saving may well be to approach it from the other side of the saving-investment identity—to raise investment. That might be done by lowering real interest rates.*

(except, probably, investment in housing) has not been that great. And *that* said, low real interest rates are likely to have a further desirable effect on investment by contributing to more spending of all kinds, thereby providing general prosperity and a sufficiency of purchasing power.

FISCAL STIMULATION

Given the limited direct impact on investment of interest rates and monetary policy in general, there have been periodic efforts to stimulate investment with fiscal measures—that is, with tax "incentives." These have included, in particular, accelerated depreciation for tax purposes (and currently, again, "neutral recovery systems," which may not prove so neutral) and investment tax credits. In studies over many years, these incentives have proven to have very limited effect. When Robert Chirinko and I reexamined the major econometric models for the Treasury a decade ago, we reported that each dollar of lost Treasury revenue tended to result in perhaps 40 cents more of investment. There would have been more bang for the buck, if the Treasury had merely paid the entire bill

for new investment and given the machines and plants to business free of charge.

There is a further question to be raised about so-called "incentives" for investment. As stated above, investment contributes to growth, if it is productive—that is, if it adds to productivity or *utilized* productive capacity. But if opportunities for such productive investment exist, we should expect profit-seeking firms in a market economy to undertake it without special tax favors. If they do not, we must presume that the investment we would promote is not really expected to be sufficiently productive on its own. I am fond of pointing out the folly of an investment tax credit of $10 million that induces a firm to acquire new machinery that costs $100 million, with an expected pay-off of $95 million without the tax credit. Fostering such investment will lead us, not to growth, but to national decline.

INADEQUATE RATES OF SAVING

It has been argued frequently that the United States suffers from inadequate rates of saving and investment. This purported inadequacy is said to be related, in considerable part, to our federal budget deficits. While gross saving is identically equal to gross investment, much of private saving goes to finance public dis-saving—that is, to buy the Treasury bills, bonds, and notes that are sold to finance the deficit. If, for example, last year's deficit of about $200 billion had been eliminated, gross private investment would have equaled approximately $1,000 billion of private saving, rather than the actual approximately $800 billion—$200 billion less.

This argument is repeated widely. But it is essentially without merit. Of course, if private saving remained the same while the deficit were eliminated, gross private investment would have been increased by the amount of the deficit. But that is what exactly frames the question. Would, or could, private saving remain the same, if the deficit were eliminated? Suppose we could eliminate it by raising taxes. Would this not lower private saving, as taxpayers would have to pay Uncle Sam a portion of what they would have saved? And as they cut their spending to pay these increased taxes, would that not slow the economy and discourage investment, thereby *lowering* saving? If taxpayers decided not to buy new cars (as a result of increased taxes and reduced after-tax income), would that cause GM, Ford, and Chrysler to invest more, or less?

I have done extensive work relating the underlying, real structural deficit to saving and investment (see "National Saving and Budget Deficits" in For Further Reading). I have found, on the basis of data stretching over a 35-year period, that real deficits have actually contributed to gross private domestic investment and to national

> *Much of private saving goes to finance pubic dis-saving—that is, to buy the Treasury bills, bonds and notes that are sold to finance the deficit.*

saving. The reason is clear. During most of this period, the economy had slack resources. The real deficits tended to stimulate the economy by offering more purchasing power to use idle capacity. That promoted both economic growth and investment. And as long as there is idle capacity (as there is now), it is possible to have more consumption *and* more investment.

Perhaps it is confusing that larger deficits have generally been associated with recessions and therefore with lower growth and less investment. But that again is a confusion relating to cause and effect. The underlying, real structural deficit affects the economy. But the economy also affects the deficit. When the economy slumps, the deficit soars (as it did in 1982–83 and 1991–92). Tax receipts, based largely on individual and corporate income, decline. Outlays—such as unemployment insurance payments—rise.

This, by the way, underlines one of the follies of the so-called "Balanced Budget Amendment" that, happily, was blocked (if only all too narrowly) in the Senate on March 2nd. If unemployment were to rise by two percentage points (it has fallen 2.2 percentage points since June 1992), it would raise the deficit by at least $110 billion. Suppose the amendment were in effect, and by some miracle (or sleight of hand), we were to begin the year with the plan for a balanced budget. Suppose, then, that unemployment rose. In violation of the constitution, outlays would immediately begin to exceed the declining receipts. Again in violation of the constitution, the Treasury would have to borrow to finance government operations. What would we do?

Stop paying unemployment benefits? Delay social security checks? Send our armed forces home or lay off the border patrol? Default on interest payments on the existing debt? Or raise taxes? All of these measures are clearly outlandish if not disastrous, even including the last one—raising taxes. All would bring

on new misery in one direction or another and would hurt the economy. They might indeed plunge the economy so much deeper into recession that the deficit would not be eliminated but would actually increase. Herbert Hoover discovered this, when he tried to balance the budget in the 1930s. And all of these measures, we can be sure, would prove to be a new disaster for saving and investment.

The lament that national saving is too small is generally misdirected. For one thing, there are significant measuring problems. In fact, gross private domestic investment represents a high proportion of gross domestic product. It is running currently at about 15.5 percent in current dollars and 18 percent in constant dollars. The latter figure takes into account the major technological advance in capital equipment—particularly computers. In 1990, the current dollar ratio was 14.6 percent and the constant dollar figure was only 15.2 percent. If we exclude highly variable and frequently involuntary inventory investment, we find that constant dollar fixed investment is currently running at just about 17 percent of GDP—17.23 percent in 1994-IV—as against 15.1 percent in 1990. Of course, much of the growth over the past four years relates to the recent recovery of the economy. But that is, indeed, always the major factor that determines investment.

But the argument that national saving is too low usually turns on measures of net investment. There are two problems here. First, the difference between gross and net is our estimate of "capital consumption"—or depreciation. But this is notoriously difficult to come by. It essentially relates to accounting conventions and practices. My own inference is that accounting allowances for depreciation have grown more than is warranted by real depreciation. The only nonarbitrary measure we have is for gross investment. Even here, when we look for constant dollar measures, we run into uncertainty.

GROWTH GENERATES SAVING

More fundamentally, what can we really expect for net saving or net investment? The incentives for both are closely related to economic growth. As Franco Modigliani reminded us in his Nobel lecture, distilling the results of years of development of the life-cycle theory of consumption, growth in income will generate a major portion of national saving, even if each individual (or household) has no net saving over his (its) lifetime. The national saving results from the fact that, with growing incomes, the younger cohorts will save more for their retirement out of their higher

incomes than the older cohorts, who are retired, will dis-save out of the wealth they have accumulated from their lower incomes. If incomes were not growing—either from increase in population or increase in income per capita—unless each generation bequeathed more than it had received, there would be no net national saving.

But can we have any net investment without growth? After all, net investment is the increase in our capital stock. In a free economy, business acquires additional capital stock essentially in order to produce more. If there is no growth, there is no increase in production. Therefore, there is no need for more capital, and hence no net investment. It is conceivable that, for a while, we can switch to a more capital-intensive economy (presumably by moving to more long-lived, more expensive capital) without a concomitant increase in current production. But we can hardly expect that to continue indefinitely. If we are to

> *Growth in income will generate a major portion of national saving, even if each individual (or household) has no net saving over his lifetime.*

believe the depreciation figures, we have probably been moving the other way in recent years—to shorter-lived capital with faster obsolescence. That would mean more gross investment but less net investment.

But more investment demands higher growth. It is frequently pointed out that Japan and other countries have higher net saving ratios than do we. But this undoubtedly reflects the fact that they have been growing more rapidly—in considerable part, going through a period of catch-up to the greatest economic power in the world. As they complete their catch-up and their rates of growth slow, their net saving and investment rates will also fall.

For the United States to have markedly higher saving and investment rates will require that the U.S. economy grow more rapidly. The way to achieve that more rapid growth is not by futile and wasteful tax incentives for saving. Nor is it by weak and dubious incentives for business investment. Both individual saving decisions and business investment decisions would be better left to free choice. That choice, however, must not be restricted by artificially high interest rates which have been engineered in an effort to fight an invisible inflation, or by a lack of purchasing

power sufficient to the output of our existing resources of labor and capital.

IGNORED INVESTMENT

The propelling force to growth is largely to be found in the major (indeed, dominant) components of investment. They are all too often ignored in discussions such as these. Even I have not mentioned them thus far. What I have in mind are the vast amounts of investment other than in business tangible investment or gross private domestic investment. These include non-profit investment and investment in owner-occupied housing. These also include all of public investment in infrastructure of roads, bridges, harbors, airports, our land, water, and air, and the domestic security that makes all other investment possible. And they include business and nonprofit and public investment in the research that underlies new technology and economic progress. Most important of all, I have in mind the investment in our human capital—the education of our young and the training of a work force essential to production in a modern, technologically advanced society. I have estimated that all of this investment (outside of the conventional measures) comes to some 75 percent of total investment (see *The Misunderstood Economy: What Counts and How to Count It* in For Further Reading).

I have argued that private saving and private business investment in tangible capital should be left to the free choice of those involved—with a minimum of government intervention. But all of this vast public investment, and particularly investment in intangible capital, is very much a matter of public policy choice. This investment will prove to be our engine of growth. It will pull private tangible investment along with it. A well-qualified labor force will offer the best incentive to business to invest in the capital that makes full use of its talents.

We shall not be able to compete favorably in the world, or have much growth or investment, if we continue to have perhaps one-fifth of a generation growing up functionally illiterate. Right now, we are coping (or failing to cope) with schools and neighborhoods where our youngsters are challenged to survive—let alone learn. Nor shall we have much growth or investment, if we continue to have the 13-year-olds who populate our good suburban neighborhoods score last in tests in

math and science, when compared with children in other parts of the world—Asia, Europe, and Canada.

It is to this vast area of investment in human capital (much of it publicly supported) that we must look for renewed sources of that growth which will come with greater public and private investment. When we recognize this, and when we recognize that so much of it depends on government support, we will also recognize the folly of current obsessions with reducing the role and functions of government—with little care about what is reduced. And when we see that this investment—whether public or private—will have its

> *We will recognize the folly of current obsessions with reducing the role and functions of government— with little care about what is reduced.*

payoff in the future, we may understand that it is folly to try to prevent government borrowing to finance investment in that future. We would not dream of telling business that it cannot borrow to finance its investment. And we would not dream of telling individuals that they cannot borrow to invest in new houses or in their children's education.

Relating all this to the current topic of political discourse, it is the utmost folly to amend the supreme law of the land to restrict the powers of the federal government to borrow without discriminating at least (as state and local governments do) between borrowing for current operations and borrowing for capital investment.

For Further Reading

The following books and articles may be of interest to readers who would like to explore the topics in this article more fully.

ROBERT S. CHIRINKO and ROBERT EISNER, "The Effects of Tax Parameters in the Investment Equations in Macroeconomic Econometric Models," in MARSHALL BLUME, JEAN CROCKETT, and PAUL TAUBMAN, eds., *Economic Activity and Finance,* Ballinger, 1982.

ROBERT EISNER, "National Saving and Budget Deficits," *The Review of Economics and Statistics,* February 1994.

_____, *The Misunderstood Economy: What Counts and How to Count It,* Harvard Business School Press, 1994.

_____, *The Total Income System of Accounts,* University of Chicago Press, 1989.

Taxpayers Are Angry.
They're Expensive, Too.

Michael Wines

WASHINGTON

Americans believe that their Government wastes vast wads of cash on pork-barrel highways, naval bases in the landlocked home states of important Senators and handouts to an ungrateful underclass—and that wiping out all this would balance the budget.

After the election of 1994, few Republicans or even Democrats deny that the voters have a point.

But like most truths, this one is not absolute. Sure, Congress is a certain soft touch. But the biggest beneficiaries of the benefits mandated by law are not grifters or crack addicts or well-connected defense contractors: they are mostly average folk, like you. Or me.

Direct aid to the Government-certified poor—food stamps, Medicaid, Supplemental Security Income, Aid to Families with Dependent Children—totals about $140 billion a year. That is

roughly what the Government spends on Medicare, providing services to the elderly at roughly one quarter of their actual cost.

And payments to the poor add up to less than the three largest tax breaks that benefit the middle class and wealthy: deductions for retirement plans, the deduction for home mortgage interest and the exemption of health-insurance premiums that companies pay for their employees.

DON'T TOUCH

Perhaps more important, most tax breaks and payments to the well-situated are practically exempt from the debate over controlling expenditures.

There are some arguments in favor of this. Cutting Social Security and tax-deferred retirement plans could push some of

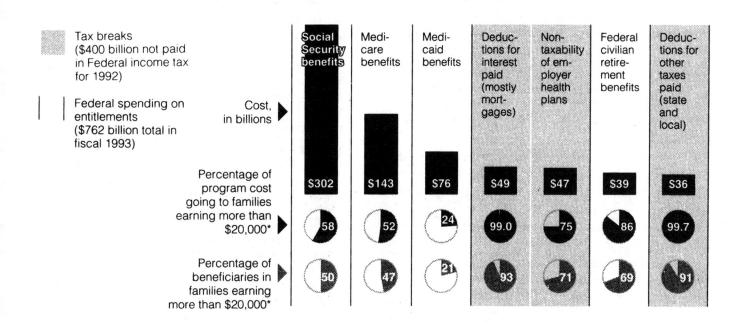

The pie charts show benefits going to middle- and upper-class families. The $20,000 threshold is one and a half times the poverty level ($13,359 for a family of four in 1990), so it includes the working poor.

the elderly below the poverty level. Curbing the mortgage interest break would devalue homes and crimp sales.

And politically, the principle known in budgetese as "means-testing" seems a dead letter. Republicans and Democrats alike say they won't seek limits in the largest entitlement, Social Security, although a large share goes to people who live in relative comfort. When Mr. Clinton's budget director, Alice Rivlin, floated the idea of limiting some popular middle- and upper-class tax breaks, like the mortgage deduction, Republicans pounced on the Democratic "tax-and-spend" philosophy, and the White House disavowed her.

Some experts say that ignores the Willie Sutton law of accounting: to balance the budget, you go where the money is, and the money these days is put mostly in the hands of people who are not poor. "My view of life is, you rule out taxes and Social Security and most Medicare, and you're not serious" about balancing the budget, said Charles Schultze of the Brookings Institution, who was chairman of the Council of Economic Advisers under President Carter. "I don't care what you say. You're not really playing the game."

Entitlements vs. Tax Breaks

Percentage of households that received Federal entitlement benefits in 1990.	Percentage of tax filers that received a tax break for 1992 (Everyone gets at least one deduction.)
49%	100%
Average benefits per recipient family: **$10,320**	Average tax break per filer: **About $5,000**

Sources: Congressional Budget Office; Internal Revenue Service; Office of Management and Budget

The New York Times

Now that Republicans control Congress, there will be some pressure to fulfill one of the promises of the "Contract With America"—a balanced budget. Back in the early Reagan years, balanced budget promises were accompanied by stories of welfare mothers buying vodka with food stamps. Now the watchword is welfare reform. Either way, the implication is that cracking down on the poor will bring about big savings.

But once budget committees start looking at Federal costs, both in direct payments and in money the Government doesn't take in through tax breaks, they'll find that there are precious few poor people's programs to cut. The bulk of the money goes to the politically potent middle class.

Below are figures for some Federal spending programs in fiscal 1993 and tax breaks given for individuals in 1992 and filed in 1993, based on early review of the returns.

Unemployment benefits	Military retirement benefits	Food stamps	Tax exemption of Social Security benefits	Supplemental security income (poor elderly and disabled)	Deductions for contributions to charity	Veterans benefits	Welfare and family support	Farm price supports	Deductions for extreme medical costs	Earned income tax credit
$35	$26	$25	$24	$21	$17	$17	$16	$16	$3	$1
75	99.5	14	70	18	99.7	70	25	74	95	15
69	99.0	14	n.a.	14	92	60	23	n.a.	69	31

*Tax break figures are for 1992; entitlement figures are for 1990. The figure for farm support payments is the percentage of farm families making $25,000 from all sources of income in 1990.

Sources: Congressional Budget Office; Internal Revenue Service; Congressional Research Service; Office of Management and Budget; Employee Benefit Research Institute; Department of Agriculture; Census Bureau.

True Tax Reform: Encouraging Saving and Investment

Murray Weidenbaum

Murray Weidenbaum is Mallinckrodt Distinguished University Professor and Director of the Center for the Study of American Business at Washington University in St. Louis, Missouri. He is indebted to Samuel Hughes, the Frederick Deming Fellow at the Center, for extremely helpful research assistance.

The federal government needs to change the tax code by overhauling the entire income tax system, not by adopting other forms of taxation.

The United States would benefit greatly by reforming the national system of taxation to encourage more saving and investment. Such a transformation would help achieve faster economic growth, higher levels of employment, improved standards of living, and smaller budget deficits. Specifically, a savings-exempt income tax on individuals and families and a companion cash-flow tax on business should replace the existing federal income taxes.

The idea proposed here deals with the missing link in the budget debate. Until now, most proposals to reduce the deficit have focused either on cutting spending or raising taxes. But there is a third alternative: improving the way the tax system functions. The twin proposals made here—the savings-exempt income tax and the business cash-flow tax—would initially raise the same amount of revenue as the existing tax system with far less damage to the economy. This means that over the years the nation would achieve a faster-growing economy. The direct benefits would be threefold: (1) more people at work, (2) lower federal outlays for unemployment payments and so on, and (3) more income to the Treasury from a growing tax base with no future change in tax rates.

All this cannot be attained by tinkering with the details of the Internal Revenue Code. Instead, the present federal income tax system must be overhauled so it exempts saving and investment, which constitute the seedcorn for economic expansion. This is not an argument for a new tax, such as a value-added tax (VAT), but a sea change in the existing income tax structure.

Going beyond the present array of detailed proposals that would modify the income tax in a piecemeal fashion, let us consider instead making a fundamental transformation in the federal revenue system: Abandon the whole idea of taxing income and shift to a consumption-based tax as the primary federal revenue source. This notion indeed was a key recommendation of the recent report of the Commission for Strengthening America, co-chaired by Senators Sam Nunn and Pete Domenici.

Economists have offered several basic arguments over the years for shifting the primary base of taxation from income to consumption in an effort to achieve greater equity as well as economic efficiency. Consumption-based taxes put the fiscal burden on what people *take* from society—the goods and services they consume— rather than on what they *contribute* by working and saving, as income taxes do. Thus, under a consumption-based tax system, saving—and long-term investment—is encouraged at the expense of current consumption. Of course, over a period of time, the society is likely to achieve higher levels of saving *and* consumption. This is because the added investment, by generating a faster-growing economy, will lead to a bigger income "pie" to be divided among the various participants in economic activity.

A constant theme voiced by tax reformers is the need for increased incentives for saving, capital formation, and economic growth. It is common knowledge that the United States saves and invests far less than other industrialized countries. In 1990, the U.S. net savings rate as a percentage of GDP was only 2.2 percent, the lowest of any member country of the Organization for Economic Cooperation and Development (OECD). In contrast, the OECD average net savings rate was 8.3 percent. Standing alone, this fact might not

From *Business Horizons*, May/June 1995, pp. 4-10. © 1995 by the Foundation for the School of Business at Indiana University. Reprinted by permission.

appear terribly harmful. However, among the major industrialized nations, there is a clear and positive correlation between the share of GDP going to investment and the pace of economic growth. This is not a transitory or fleeting relationship. The close fit between investment and growth shows up in the data for the past three decades.

In that light, let us examine the ramifications of consumption-based taxation and the major alternative approaches to structuring a new consumption-based tax.

PROMOTING INVESTMENT AND ECONOMIC GROWTH

Under a consumption-based tax, the basic way to cut taxes—legally—is for individuals and families to save more and for companies to invest more. To minimize tax liability under the existing tax structure, taxpayers have to earn less. This fundamental fact reduces the incentives for taxpayers to work, save, and invest. By increasing the amount we save and invest, the proposed tax system would augment the forces that create the formation of capital.

To many citizens, any discussion of capital formation immediately brings to mind visions of greedy bankers, wealthy coupon clippers, and—to use what is to many a pejorative word—capitalists. Nevertheless, capital plays a pivotal role in providing the basis for the future standard of living of any society. Capital is essential for increasing productivity and thus providing the basis for rising real incomes. Increased capital formation also enhances our competitiveness in an increasingly global marketplace.

A rising stock of capital is necessary for a growing society. It is really a basic matter of how much we want to eat, drink, and be merry today, and how much we want to set aside for tomorrow. Boiled down to its fundamentals, assuring an adequate flow of saving and investment is little more than demonstrating a proper concern for the future.

A slow pace of capital formation in the United States is especially troublesome at a time of heightened global competition, when modern, state-of-the-art machinery and equipment are necessary to match foreign firms with low-wage structures. The increasingly international nature of business competition requires updating the American tax system to face up to these global realities. Unfortunately, the United States has much lower rates of saving and business investment than do our economic competitors.

The reason for this shortcoming is clear: The current U.S. tax code is biased in favor of current consumption and against saving. For the average citizen, the existing personal income tax structure favors consumption over saving. In effect, the

current system taxes saving twice, once when the income is earned and second when the saving generates interest, dividends, and so forth.

CHANGING THE TAX STRUCTURE

The United States uses consumption taxes to a far lesser degree than most other developed Western nations. In 1991, the 24 OECD members obtained an average 30 percent of their revenue from taxes on consumption. For the United States, the ratio was 17 percent.

The U.S. Treasury proposed a "spending tax" in 1942 as a temporary wartime measure to curb inflation. The proposal was rejected by Congress on the grounds that the exemption of saving would favor the rich, since they are better able to save large portions of their incomes. Some believe that this would lead to greater concentrations of wealth in the hands of a few. As we will see, proponents of a consumption tax respond that some versions can be made as progressive as desired.

Another objection to consumption-based taxation is that such a system would favor the miser over the spendthrift, even when both have similar spending power or ability to pay. The response offered to this argument is that consumption uses up the resources available to the nation, while saving adds to these resources. Thus, people should be taxed on what they take out of society's pool of resources, not on what they put into it.

Tax experts have devised, and criticized, a variety of specific consumption-based taxes. No consensus has yet been reached on the details. It is likely that three interrelated clusters of issues will receive increased public attention in the 1990s:

1. the general desirability of a tax on consumption;

2. the specific form it should take ("top-down" or "bottom-up"); and

3. whether it should replace or augment an existing tax.

There are two major types of consumption-based taxes. One is a "bottom-up" tax on individual purchases of goods and services. The United States provides many examples in the form of general sales taxes. In Western Europe and other industrialized areas, a variation known as a value-added tax (VAT) is customary. Like general sales taxes, a VAT is comprehensive. Essentially, value-added is the difference between a business's sales and its purchases from other companies. The VAT is paid by each enterprise in the chain of production—manufacturer, wholesaler, and retailer. Duplication is avoided by taxing only the added value that the firm contributes to the goods or services it produces.

The second approach to consumption taxation is a "top-down" variation. Over the years,

this proposal has been called an expenditure tax and a consumed-income tax; the current nomenclature is a "savings-exempt income tax." Based on the current income tax, it exempts all savings, in effect changing the income tax into a consumption-based tax. As will be shown, this form of taxation avoids many of the negatives associated with the VAT while capturing most of the benefits. Conceptually, the base of the two types of consumption-based taxes is the same (the value of goods and services purchased) and the yields from these taxes could be very similar.

THE VALUE-ADDED TAX

A value-added tax represents a very different way of collecting a general tax than most Americans are familiar with, focusing on the sales of goods and services to consumers by individual companies. It is, in effect, a sophisticated and comprehensive sales tax that avoids the double counting otherwise inevitable when the same item moves from manufacturer to wholesaler to retailer. In total, a VAT should be equivalent in yield to a single-stage sales tax levied at the retail level.

Essentially, a firm's "value-added" is the difference between its sales and its purchases from other firms. Value-added can also be estimated by adding labor and capital inputs supplied by the firm itself—represented by wages and salaries, rent and interest payments, and profit.

Reasons for Favoring a VAT

Proponents of the VAT maintain it is economically neutral, because ideally it would be levied at a uniform rate on all items of consumption. It would not distort choices among products or methods of production. In that regard, the VAT is indeed superior to the existing array of selective excise taxes.

Advocates of the value-added tax also point out that, in contrast to an income tax, there is no penalty for efficiency—profits are taxed equally as wages—and no subsidy for waste (a dollar of expense saved becomes a dollar of profits and, again, is taxed equally). Moreover, the VAT is neutral between incorporated and unincorporated businesses and, theoretically, between public and private enterprises. By focusing on consumption, it avoids a double tax burden on the returns from capital.

This kind of tax starts off with no exclusions or exemptions and thus, at least initially, provides a broader and fairer tax base, one that the underground economy will have more difficulty evading. Consumption taxes such as the VAT are levied on the returns to labor (wages and salaries) equally with the returns on capital (rent, interest, and profits). Thus, shifting to a more capital-intensive and perhaps more profitable method of

production would not influence a firm's tax burden.

Another argument in favor of a value-added tax is that many other nations have adopted this form of taxation. It therefore fits in better than conventional taxes with the growing international character of production. Almost every industrialized economy in Europe imposes the VAT, and it has spread throughout the Third World as well. The members of the European Union have used VAT taxation since the late 1960s or early 1970s. In 1989, Japan imposed a broad-based 3 percent sales tax.

However, unlike recent attempts to overhaul the U.S. tax code, the adoption of a tax on value-added was true reform in Western Europe. The VAT typically replaced an extremely inefficient form of consumption tax that was already in place: a cascading sales or turnover revenue system. Those latter taxes apply to the total amount of a firm's sales rather than only to its value-added. Sales taxes, therefore, would be paid over and over again on the same items as they moved from firm to firm in the various stages of the production and distribution process. Such cascade-type taxes favored integrated firms (that could legally avoid one or more stages of the tax), but they severely discriminated against independent companies that operate at only one phase of the production process.

An additional and much-cited reason for adopting a VAT is the anticipated foreign trade benefits. Unlike an income tax, a sales-based tax can be imposed on goods entering the country and rebated on items leaving, thereby supposedly encouraging exports and discouraging imports. Thus, at first blush, a VAT would seem to help reduce this nation's presently large deficit. However, most economists believe that fluctuations in exchange rates would largely offset these initial effects and result in little change in the balance of trade.

Reasons for Opposing a VAT

Opponents of a value-added tax offer an extensive list of shortcomings. They contend that a VAT is inherently regressive—those least able to pay face the highest rates because, on average, the higher your income the smaller proportion you spend on current consumption. Such regressivity can be softened by exempting food and medicine or by offering refunds to low-income taxpayers, but such variations make the collection of the tax much more complicated. They also provide an opportunity for people in the underground economy to avoid paying taxes.

Because the VAT is included in the price of purchases, it registers in the various price indices and, hence, exerts an inflationary force on the economy. The counterargument to this charge is that any price increases would be only a one-

time effect, occurring when the tax is enacted or increased. However, there would be secondary inflation effects resulting from the operation of automatic escalators in wage and price agreements. That inflationary impact could in turn be offset by appropriate changes in monetary policy, albeit at times with an adverse effect on the levels of production and employment.

Opponents also charge that a VAT would invade the area of sales taxation, traditionally reserved for state and local governments. However, most states and some localities have come to rely on income taxes despite heavy use of the same tax base by the federal government.

Turning to the administrative aspects, imposition of a VAT in the United States would require establishing a new tax-collection system by the federal government and additional recordkeeping on the part of business taxpayers. This would be a vast and expensive undertaking. The Treasury Department, based on European experience, believes it would need 18 months after enactment to begin administering a VAT.

Several different approaches have been suggested for collecting a new VAT, the simplest of which is the credit method. Using this approach, the tax is computed initially on a company's total sales and the firm is given credit for the VAT paid by its suppliers. To a substantial degree, such a VAT would be self-enforced. Each company would have a powerful incentive to ensure that its suppliers paid their full share of the tax, because any underpayment would have to be made up by the next firm in the chain of production and distribution.

THE UNLIMITED SAVINGS ACCOUNT

A new approach to a consumption-based tax has been proposed by Senators Pete Domenici (R-New Mexico) and Sam Nunn (D-Georgia) in the form of a savings-exempt income tax. This is popularly referred to as the Unlimited Savings Account.

Taxes on Individuals and Families

As we have seen, the VAT suffers from a number of possible complications, such as inflation, regressivity, and administrative burden. In contrast, a savings-exempt income tax would be collected much as income taxes currently are. It would be levied directly on the taxpayer. The annual taxpayer return would continue to comprise the heart of the collection system, containing exemptions and deductions, as it does now. However, one fundamental change would be instituted: The portion of income that is saved would be exempt from taxation.

This type of tax has been known by a variety of names, a fact that can unnecessarily complicate policy debates. Many prefer to call it a con-

sumption tax, for the intent is to tax what people spend, not what they save. Another frequent name is expenditure tax. The most recent congressional labels attached to this proposal are the unlimited savings allowance or the savings-exempt income tax.

Figure 1 provides a hypothetical example of a "short form" version of a reformed income tax return showing how the difficult bookkeeping requirement to tally all consumption outlays could be structured. Because of the notion that income equals consumption plus saving, consumption can thus be readily estimated, indirectly but accurately, merely by deducting saving from income. And taxpayers are used to developing estimates of their incomes. The new schedule of saving during the year would include changes in bank balances and in holdings of bonds, stocks, and similar investment assets.

To a typical taxpayer, a savings-exempt income tax is essentially the equivalent of a universal but simplified Individual Retirement Account (IRA), using an amended rate table. Each taxpayer would decide how much to save and in what form. Many benefits would result. Consider the current tax treatment of housing. A bigger

---

Figure 1
Savings-Exempt Income Tax: Illustrative Tax Return

Income and Other Receipts — *Amounts*
1. Wages, salaries, tips, etc. _____
2. Dividends _____
3. Interest _____
4. Rents and royalties _____
5. Pensions and annuities _____
6. Net receipts of sole proprietorships _____
7. Withdrawals from partnerships _____
8. Receipts from:
   a. sales of financial assets _____
   b. gifts and bequests _____
   c. insurance _____
9. Net decrease (if any) in bank accounts _____
10. Total (add lines 1 through 9) _____

Unlimited Savings Allowance
11. Purchases of financial assets _____
12. Capital contributed to partnerships _____
13. Net increase (if any) in bank accounts _____
14. Other investments (equity in a home) _____
15. Total (add lines 11 through 14) _____
16. Net Income (subtract line 15 from line 10) _____

Deductions
17. A. Itemized deductions
    or
    B. Standard deduction _____
18. Exemptions _____
19. Total deductions (add lines 17 and 18) _____

Tax Base
20. Taxable Income (subtract line 19 from line 16) _____
21. Tax from rate table _____

down payment, and thus lower interest payments, gives a home buyer a smaller tax break. But why should tax policy discourage investing in a home? Under a savings-exempt income tax, down payments and payments of principal would be fully deductible (as would a limited amount of interest on the mortgage). After all, building equity in a home or business is a form of saving and investment. Home equity loans that tap into this investment would not be rewarded with tax deductions, as they are under current tax law.

The first reaction by many people to exempting all savings from the income tax is that it is unfair because it must be regressive. If this were the case, poorer people would end up paying a larger share of their income in taxes than would wealthier Americans. However, the savings-exempt income tax need not be regressive at all. As with the existing income tax, each taxpayer would face a rate table that could be made as progressive as desired. Under the revenue-neutral shift from the traditional income tax contemplated here, the average taxpayer would experience no change in tax burden. However, at each income level, above-average savers would pay less than they do now and below-average savers would pay more.

To deal with the concern over regressivity, lower-income families (those with combined earnings of less than $25,000) would also receive a tax credit for some portion of their contributed payroll taxes. This credit would be phased out for mid-income families (earnings of $25,001-$50,000), while high-income families (those earning more than $50,000) would receive no payroll tax credit.

The Nunn-Domenici plan also expands the earned income tax credit by about 30 percent and exempts households with low incomes from the savings-exempt income tax altogether. For example, a family of four might not pay any federal taxes on their first $25,000 of consumption. A graduated rate schedule provides further assurance that the savings-exempt income tax is a progressive tax.

The basic idea is that the new tax structure would raise as much federal revenue as the existing system (this is known as being "revenue neutral"). In the longer run, the reformed income tax could generate more revenue—or permit rate reductions—to the extent that the added savings stimulate economic growth, which in turn increases the tax base while reducing the demand for unemployment benefits and other government spending.

Most important, the reformed income tax is not a new or an added tax; it is a simple change in the existing IRS tax collection system. Current restrictions on IRAs and other specialized forms of investment would be eliminated. *All* savings would be exempt from taxes. Thus, the savings-exempt income tax does not suffer from the ad-

ministrative burden associated with a VAT, which would require setting up a new tax-collection system and new recordkeeping, causing overhead costs to rise in both the public and private sectors. From the viewpoint of the taxpayer, the current bookkeeping and administrative requirements would actually be reduced under a savings-exempt income tax system.

For example, the Nunn-Domenici version of fundamental tax reform does not differentiate among different income sources; wages, salaries, interest income, capital gains, and dividends are all treated equally. We may never again achieve the level of simplicity offered by the original 1913 income tax. Its 1040 form was three pages long, accompanied by one page of instructions, and filed by only one percent of the population. However, the Nunn-Domenici proposal would eliminate about three-fourths of the current individual tax code that is estimated to cost taxpayers $50 billion in compliance costs annually.

Because the savings-exempt income tax is not a new tax, it will not generate an added source of income for the U.S. Treasury. Thus, its enactment would not encourage the further expansion of the public sector. A VAT, by contrast, is a new tax that would be an addition to the current array of taxes levied by the federal government.

For a while, the United States was moving toward a form of exempting savings from federal taxation, albeit indirectly and in modest steps. The establishment of IRAs enabled many federal taxpayers to defer paying taxes on amounts saved and invested in the accounts (up to $2,000 a year). Also, the first $100 of dividends per taxpayer was exempt from income taxation. The 1986 tax law, however, sharply cut back on IRAs and eliminated the dividend credit.

TAXES ON BUSINESS

Tax incentives to promote saving do not suffice in responding to the desire for more rapid economic growth. A larger amount of new investment is also necessary. To accomplish this, a business counterpart to the savings-exempt income tax should replace the current corporate income tax and provide greater stimulus to investment.

The Business Tax proposed by Senators Nunn and Domenici would levy a flat 10 percent tax on the cash flow (total sales minus purchases) of most businesses. Very small businesses—a group that files the majority of business tax returns but pays only a small fraction of the total tax collected—would probably be exempted from the cash-flow tax altogether, as would most nonprofit organizations. The earnings of unincorporated businesses would not be taxed until the money was withdrawn for personal use. Export sales would be excluded from the tax base and a tax

equal to the Business Tax rate would be levied on imports entering the country. Such a tax treatment is designed to provide a "level playing field" for products sold within the United States.

One important feature of the Nunn-Domenici proposal is its treatment of the current employer payroll tax. All firms are required to pay a 10 percent tax on their cash flow, including the amounts paid to employees as salaries and wages. However, firms are given a full credit for their payment of the 7.65 percent employer payroll tax for social security. This reduction of their payroll tax liability is designed to help offset the new tax on labor costs and other cash flow.

In computing the cash-flow tax, each firm would add up all its sales during the year, then deduct the cost of any purchases it made from other businesses during the year (plant and equipment, outside services, parts). The remaining cash flow would be the tax base, which would then be taxed at the designated rate (see **Figure 2** for a hypothetical computation of the Nunn-Domenici cash-flow tax). Remaining after-tax cash would be available to pay wages, salaries, dividends, and interest, or otherwise to be reinvested in the business.

The key characteristics of the Nunn-Domenici cash-flow tax are:

1. It would apply to all businesses, regardless of their legal form: corporation, partnership, individual proprietorship, and so on. Unincorporated firms currently taxed under the individual collection system would instead pay the business cash-flow tax. This would eliminate the incentives for companies to structure themselves in ways that are less productive just to take advantage of tax differentials.

2. Because it is a tax on cash flow, capital purchases would be treated the same as other expenditures: deducted in full at the time of purchase (that is, "expensed"). Because of this, firms would have strong incentives to invest in productivity-enhancing capital equipment. Furthermore, there would be no onerous accounting requirements for depreciation, estimates of an asset's useful life, or any of the other arcane complications required by the current tax system.

3. The current tax advantage afforded to borrowed capital compared to equity—because interest payments are now tax deductible but dividend payments are not—would be eliminated.

This type of cash-flow tax is superficially similar to a VAT in that both taxes use the same tax base of sales minus purchases. However, the cash-flow tax differs from the VAT in several important respects. First, the cash-flow tax is intended as a replacement for the corporate income tax, not as an additional sales tax. Second, the cash-flow tax lacks the administrative complexities of a VAT, which requires firms to track on an invoice-to-invoice basis the amount of tax attributable to each transaction.

Figure 2
Hypothetical Computation of Cash-Flow Tax

Total Sales ___

Deduct: Exports ___
Equals: Domestic Sales ___

Deduct:
  Purchases from other firms ___
  Capital outlays ___
Equals: Cash flow ___

Calculation of cash-flow tax:
  Cash flow times the tax rate ___
Equals: Gross tax ___

Deduct: Employer-paid social security tax ___
Equals: Cash-flow tax liability ___

Note: Cash flow covers employee compensation, dividend and interest payments, and retained funds.

Indeed, a cash-flow tax would drastically simplify the current business tax structure, allowing firms to devote fewer resources to complying with tax regulations (and devising creative methods to minimize their tax burden), and more resources to productivity-increasing investment. For example, the cash-flow tax would eliminate bizarre, complicated tax provisions such as the "amortization of intangible expenditures," a procedure that depreciates purchases of patents, licenses, and other intangibles. Such complicated law contributes to the high costs of tax compliance. The Tax Foundation estimated that business tax compliance costs in 1990 totaled $112 billion, a sum nearly equal to 75 percent of federal corporate income tax collections. The simplifications offered by a cash-flow tax would particularly aid small business.

The Nunn-Domenici proposal is designed to be revenue neutral. It does not initially provide the federal government with additional funds. Thus, there are no new taxes, but instead more efficient replacements for the current corporate tax. As with any major change in the tax system, in the period of transition from the old to the new, a variety of short-term adjustments would be necessary. But the short-run complications are likely to be far more than offset by the long-run advantages.

An Unlimited Savings Account, or savings-exempt income tax, would achieve many of the same budgetary and economic benefits associated with a VAT while avoiding its many shortcomings. Reforming the current income tax to exempt all savings—unlike adopting a new tax on value-added—does not require setting up an additional collection system.

Nor is it regressive or inflationary. In contrast, a value-added tax becomes extremely complicated if an effort is made to soften its inherent regressivity by exempting certain categories of expenditures, such as food and medicine, or taxing them at lower rates. Unlike a VAT, adopting an Unlimited Savings Account does not provide the federal government with a new revenue source. Therefore, the public sector has no special temptation to grow more rapidly.

It is not surprising that politicians in many countries favor sales-type taxation on the assumption that, politically, the best tax is a hidden tax. "Bottom-up" sales taxes such as a VAT are rarely identified separately, because the purchaser merely pays a combined product-plus-tax price. So that type of tax forces a business firm to act as the "middleman" between government and the consumer. Many companies marketing consumer products fear that the higher prices resulting from the imposition of a VAT would reduce their sales and earnings. Conversely, companies selling capital equipment and business services tend to take a more sympathetic attitude toward this form of government revenue, which would lighten the tax burden on their customers and, hence, tend to expand their markets.

The impact of the comprehensive savings-exempt income tax, in contrast, would not be shielded from the knowledge of the taxpayer and would not be apt to generate the differential reactions that flow from the VAT. In any event, a shift in emphasis in U.S. taxation from income-based to consumption-based should, on balance, generate positive results, especially in helping to move the economy to a more rapid expansion path. Thus it would enable the American people to enjoy a higher living standard while reducing the federal budget deficit.

The combination of a truly reformed personal income tax with an unlimited savings account and a companion business cash-flow tax would initially be revenue neutral, compared to the income tax system it displaces. However, over the years, it would generate more revenue for the U.S. Treasury. This is likely because such a tax system encourages more saving to finance additional investments in a growing economy. The tax reform proposed here is one of the few pain-free ways of reducing the federal budget deficit.

Europeans Shrug as Taxes Go Up

Nathaniel C. Nash

Special to The New York Times

DÜSSELDORF, Germany—Johann Scholtz sits in his white smock, hunched over his workbench 10 hours a day, stringing viola bows, repairing the necks of cellos and, when he has time, carving the maple back and front panels of his handmade violins. He says that often during his quiet labor, he remembers that more than 30 minutes of every hour go toward paying his taxes.

"I have no idea how much I pay," the 55-year-old master violin maker said. "It's so much. Only my tax accountant really knows. And the depressing thing is, my taxes are going up again this year."

Mr. Scholtz, who works in this German city known for its affluence and attention to style, has plenty of company. As Americans look to the new Republican-controlled Congress to cut taxes this year, taxes are going up across most of Europe.

Although European economies are expanding at a slower pace, European countries are shying away from cutting expenses because of the political dangers of threatening the quality of life. This has left little recourse but to raise taxes, despite the damping effect on economic growth.

In Spain the value-added tax, a kind of broad-based sales tax, rose one percentage point on Jan. 1, to 16 percent. Levies on electricity, gas-oline, tobacco, alcohol and stamps are also rising.

Switzerland introduced a 6.5 percent value-added tax to replace a 6.3 percent sales tax on a much smaller basket of goods. The change will cost the public $1.2 billion this year.

In Sweden, the highest income-tax bracket jumps to 56 percent, from 51 percent, affecting anyone earning more than $30,000 a year. And in Britain, excise taxes on wine and spirits, gasoline and diesel fuel are rising.

In Italy, economists predict that a ballooning budget deficit is almost certain to force higher taxes.

Even in France, where a presidential election this year has discouraged politicians from increasing taxes, critics say the country's deficit is growing so rapidly that an increase after elections is inevitable.

It is not that Europeans are happy about it. Recent studies of German taxpayer sentiment found that a growing number of Germans—known in Europe for their honesty about tax compliance—say they are willing to cheat because they feel they are getting less for their tax dollar.

But few are willing to stage a tax revolt that might risk big changes in their system of free medical and nursing home care, nearly free college educations and generous pension and unemployment safety nets.

"As long as you have a job and pay your taxes, you are protected and don't have to worry about your fu-ture," said Paul Breuer, a former manager of Merrill Lynch's Hamburg office, who left a year ago to open Bender Antiquariat, a rare book and manuscript dealer.

Most taxpayers in Europe feel they are getting their money's worth.

"The European knows that if he gets sick he can go to a good hospital and it won't bankrupt him," said Mr. Breuer, who added that his tax rate was approaching 60 percent. "He knows his child will get a good education. He knows if his old parent gets sick or they need someone to give them a bath or take them out for a walk, they're protected.

"To Americans, these can be financially disastrous. But we don't fear them. That is why we keep paying. That is why we say, we don't like it but the taxes are necessary."

Europeans also frequently refer to lower crime rates, cleaner streets, state-of-the-art mass transportation and less social instability in general, all of which they see as products of their willingness to pay higher taxes.

While tax revenues in the United States amount to 31.6 percent of the overall economy, the proportion paid by European taxpayers is more than 45 percent.

"There is a sort of an understanding that varies from country to country," said Richard Reid, chief economist for the Frankfurt office of the Union Bank of Switzerland.

"If your system works correctly, there is a willingness to pay taxes as long as you see what you are getting for it. In the United States, they don't have this strong association that you get tangible benefits from the taxes you pay."

If there is a country that typifies the acceptance of higher taxes, it is Germany, where the tax burden is rising almost 10 percent this year, by far the largest increase in Western Europe.

Germany's private wealth taxes are doubling, insurance taxes are rising 25 percent and a special 1 percent income tax to pay for old-age nursing care began on Jan. 1. Perhaps most controversial, a 7.5 percent tax increase, called the solidarity surcharge, will be extracted to pay for the rebuilding of the former East Germany.

And despite the new taxes already imposed this year, the Government of Chancellor Helmut Kohl is debating another $6.6 billion in energy taxes next year to subsidize coal mining.

In all, analysts say the tax bill for Germans will rise by $25 billion this year, when they are just recovering from the setbacks of the worst recession in Europe since World War II.

Yet many are philosophical about such taxes, particularly the solidarity surcharge.

"These are our brothers in the east and they need our help," Mr. Scholtz said. "We have to pay to let all of Germany prosper, and you can't risk the social problems of not caring for the eastern states. We can live with it."

But despite these high rates, taxes are not about to go down. The reason is that European governments are saddled with huge budget deficits coming out of the recent recession.

"There will be hardly any tax cuts in Europe through the end of the century," said Alfred Boss, economist with the Kiel Institute, an economic research group.

The European willingness to pay high taxes, compared with the frequent tax revolts that sweep the United States, also reflects a difference in the level of risks that Europeans seem to be able to stand, versus their American counterparts—attitudes that are seen clearly in their saving and investment behavior.

For example, while Americans readily live beyond their means, taking out large home mortgages, building up credit card debt and flocking to equities that carry a relatively high risk level, Europeans are quite different.

In general, they buy homes outright with no mortgage loans. They carry very little consumer debt and only reluctantly buy stocks, prefer-

---

COMPARE AND CONTRAST

Western Europe's Tax Burden

Taxes in Western Europe Are High . . .

Government tax revenues as a percent of gross domestic product in 1994.

Denmark	58.6%
Sweden	56.2
Norway	55.2
Finland	54.0
Netherlands	51.2
Belgium	50.0
France	49.6
Austria	48.0
Italy	46.3
Germany	46.1
Spain	39.5
Britain	36.4
United States	31.6
Western Europe	45.5

Source: Organization for Economic Cooperation and Development

. . . And Many Countries Plan New Taxes in 1995

BRITAIN

4 percent rise in excise tax on alcohol. Small rise in gasoline and diesel taxes.

GERMANY

7.5 percent income tax surcharge for rebuilding of East Germany. Doubling of wealth tax to 1 percent. 25 percent jump in tax on insurance policies. 1 percent income tax to pay for elderly care.

FRANCE

Increase on gasoline taxes push prices up 5 percent. New taxes expected later in the year to combat big budget deficit.

ITALY

Large tax increase expected later in year to reduce growing budget deficit.

SPAIN
Value added tax jumps to 16 percent, from 15 percent. 2.5 percent rise in transporation taxes. 3.5 percent increase in alcohol taxes. Gasoline, electricity, tobacco and mail taxes all increase.

SWEDEN

Top tax bracket rises to 56 percent, from 51 percent. 2 percent payroll tax to pay for pension and health insurance. V.A.T. increases for postage and restaurants.

SWITZERLAND
6.5 percent V.A.T. on wide range of goods introduced, replacing narrower 6.3 percent sales tax.

ring the assured (though lower) rates of return offered by fixed-income securities.

The explanation is simple: most of today's American taxpayers did not witness the stock market crash of 1929 or the Depression years and have not known widespread financial calamity, whereas twice this century Europeans have seen their continent destroyed by war and felt its economic reverberations for years afterward.

"There is a perception in Europe that if you live beyond your means, that is bad," Mr. Reid said. "In the United States it is more growth mentality. Here it is control of inflation and preventing big deficits."

But such reliance on Government for cradle-to-grave care has its weaknesses, economists add. Europeans are producing fewer patents and fewer entrepreneurs than the United States.

And the "good life" in Europe may in the long run be threatened by such high taxes and such generous social benefits, economists say. For example, economists say high taxes are stifling consumer spending, leaving Europe possibly vulnerable to recession again.

The Government of Sweden, long known as the most generous social welfare state, had to calm financial markets by announcing plans to slash social spending, sending a sober warning that there are limits to the European welfare state.

"I think we are now at the threshold of pain," said Matina Miksits, a salesclerk at a book store here. "Any higher and you have to ask yourself, 'Why work?' "

Indeed, there is a rising tide of resistance to higher taxes, seen in more tax evasion. Evasion is rampant and growing in most Mediterranean countries, like Italy, Greece and Spain, economists say.

Even in Germany, public sentiment is turning toward ways to avoid taxes. The German Association of Taxpayers found in a recent survey that the attitude toward tax evasion was significantly less critical than in similar surveys in 1977 and 1984.

"Germans are well on the way to losing their reputation as the most honest taxpayers in the world," said Karl Heinz Däke, the association's president. "Two-thirds of the population sees tax evasion not as criminal behavior, but merely as clever."

But no fundamental changes are seen in the near future. Despite more audible grousing, Europeans are far from revolt.

"Look at the German railroads and you can see what our tax dollar does," Mr. Scholtz said. "Look at my career. I have no fear that I will go bankrupt. I pay my taxes and know that if I have problems, the state will help."

The Inequality Express

Barry Bluestone

Barry Bluestone is Frank L. Boyden Professor of Political Economy at the University of Massachusetts, Boston, and senior fellow at the John W. McCormack Institute of Public Affairs. His latest book is Negotiating the Future: A Labor Perspective on American Business.

In his 1958 book, *The Rise of the Meritocracy, 1870–2033*, British sociologist Michael Young predicted that growing inequality in Britain's income distribution would spark a great populist rebellion in the year 2034. As British society moved closer to realizing the ideal of equal opportunity, Young wrote, it would also abandon any pretense of equal outcome: Each individual's socioeconomic status would depend less on lineage, family connections, and political influence, and more on intelligence, education, experience, and effort. Outright racial and gender discrimination and iniquitous privilege would be gone; inequality based on merit would take their place. The victims of this new inequality—those who were once protected by good union wages, civil service status, or seniority—would then take to the barricades.

We haven't seen any such revolution yet, but the rest of Young's prophecy today seems uncomfortably prescient. Virtually every number cruncher who has perused contemporary income data from the United States and the United Kingdom reports three clearly defined trends, each consistent with Young's forecast. First, the distribution of earnings in both countries increasingly reflects the distribution of formal education in the workforce. Second, the gap in earnings between the well educated and the not-so-well educated is steadily increasing. And finally, the real standard of living of a large proportion of the workforce—particularly those with less than a college degree—has steadily and sharply declined.

Universal acceptance of these trends has not, however, led to any agreement about their source. Some scholars emphasize increasing demand for skills in a high-technology economy. Others claim globalization of the economy has thrown workers in high-wage countries into competition with workers in low-wage ones.

Still others indict deindustrialization, the decline of unions, rising immigration, and the proliferation of winner-take-all labor markets. This lack of consensus about causes has produced a lack of consensus about remedies.

Here we will attempt to solve the mystery of rising wage inequality, and in so doing consider what might be done to stymie it. The best primer for this exercise is Agatha Christie's *Murder on the Orient Express*.

MERIT OR MARKET?

When Young penned his satire, there appeared little reason to heed his warning. In the immediate postwar period, while Europe and the United States were enjoying the heady days of rapid growth, economic expansion almost always spawned greater equality. Class warfare was giving way to an implicit and generally peaceful social contract. The big trade-off between equality and growth so elegantly detailed by the American economist Arthur Okun seemed to hold more true in theory than in practice. In the U.S., real average weekly earnings would grow by 60 percent between 1947 and 1973. Median family income literally doubled. And over the same period, personal wages and family incomes became tangibly more equal, not less. Along with growth and greater equality, poverty declined across the nation. Those at the bottom of the distribution gained more—on a percentage basis—than those at the top. The higher wages of unionized workers did not come at the expense of other workers' living standards. If anything, the rising wages of higher-paid labor were extracted from the profits that traditionally went to the wealthy.

There is little dispute that by 1973 this trend had come to an end. Inequality actually rose, especially during the 1980s. Many initially blamed a slowdown in overall economic growth. But the expansion of the economy after the 1980–82 recession suggested a new dynamic at work: Faster growth no longer reduced inequality or did much to increase the earnings of those at the bottom of the skill ladder. Wage dispersion returned to levels not seen since before the 1960s. By

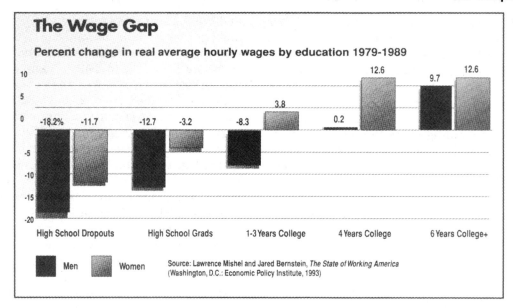

The Wage Gap

Percent change in real average hourly wages by education 1979-1989

High School Dropouts: -18.2% (Men), -11.7 (Women)
High School Grads: -12.7 (Men), -3.2 (Women)
1-3 Years College: -8.3 (Men), 3.8 (Women)
4 Years College: 0.2 (Men), 12.6 (Women)
6 Years College+: 9.7 (Men), 12.6 (Women)

■ Men ▦ Women

Source: Lawrence Mishel and Jared Bernstein, *The State of Working America* (Washington, D.C.: Economic Policy Institute, 1993)

the late 1980s, family income inequality was higher than at the end of World War II.

Wage dispersion, of course, is not the only source of economic inequality. Another source is demographic trends, such as the simultaneous rise in the number of dual income couples and single-parent families. The tremendous increase during the 1980s in nonwage sources of income for the well-to-do—interest, dividends, rent, and capital gains—plays an important role as well. But whatever role these other causes may play, changes in the distribution of wages and salaries are clearly a primary factor in rising inequality.

Racial and gender discrimination continue to be the basis of large earnings differences. However, as the influence of more virulent prejudices has declined in the labor market, differences in education and skill have had a greater impact on wages. One manifestation of this trend is the increasing wage ratio of college-educated workers to high school dropouts. In 1963, the mean annual earnings of those with four years of college or more stood at just over twice (2.11 times) the mean annual earnings of those who had not completed high school. By 1979, this ratio had increased to 2.39. This was but a harbinger of things to come. By 1987, the education-to-earnings ratio had skyrocketed to nearly three to one (2.91). The trend continues today.

In fact, the entire pattern of wage growth during the 1980s reflects a remarkable labor market "twist" tied to schooling. (See "The Wage Gap."). During this decade, the average real wage of male high school dropouts *fell* by over 18 percent, while male high school graduates suffered nearly a 13 percent real earnings loss. At the other end of the distribution, men who completed at least a master's degree emerged as the

only real winners. Their earnings rose by more than 9 percent. Note that even men who had attended college without graduating saw a serious erosion in their earning power. And men who completed college discovered that their undergraduate degrees merely served to prevent a decline in inflation-adjusted wages. Women fared better than men in terms of overall wage growth, but the imprint of a labor market twist is clearly discernible here as well.

That three out of four U.S. workers have not completed college provides some indication of how large a proportion of the entire labor force has been adversely affected by the new meritocratic distribution. If we take some liberty with Robert Reich's definition of symbolic analysts—people such as research scientists, design engineers, and public relations executives whose work focuses on problem-solving, problem-identifying, and strategic brokering activities—and limit the use of this term to those with two or more years of schooling beyond the bachelor's degree, the successes in the new economy account for just 7 percent of the U.S. labor force. If we include men with the equivalent of at least a master's degree plus women with at least a bachelor's, we could say the proportion of real earnings winners includes about 15 percent of the workforce. The extreme losers in this new meritocratic society— those with no more than a high school diploma—still comprise more than half of all U.S. workers.

In economic terms, the "return" of education, or how much one earns with a given level of education, has diverged sharply from its "rate of return," or how much an additional year of education is worth. What we have seen is a reduction in the return of education—a decline in earnings for high school graduates, for example—while the increment in earnings due to a little more schooling pays off a whole lot, most notably at the

high end. This is why the college degree for men has become a defensive good. It provided almost no wage growth during the entire decade of the 1980s, but at least it kept college graduates from suffering the nearly 13 percent loss sustained by those with only a high school diploma. For men, completing college during the 1980s became the equivalent of donning a brand new pair of running shoes to go bear hunting with a companion. If the bear ends up attacking you, you cannot outrun it. But in order to survive you need to outrun your friend. Anyone who has visited a vocational guidance counselor lately will recognize this as the principal underlying message. The college degree still outfits women with the equivalent of a new pair of Reeboks, but any less schooling leaves women trying to run in quicksand.

THE ECONOMISTS' LINEUP

To explain this crisis, economists have offered up ten suspects:

Suspect One: Technology. Robert Lawrence of Harvard's John F. Kennedy School of Government and Paul Krugman, now at Stanford University, are the leading advocates of this position. They believe that the new information technologies skew the earnings distribution by placing an extraordinary premium on skilled labor while reducing the demand, and hence the wage, for those of lesser skill. This, they contend, is about all you need to explain current earnings trends.

The problem is that no one has any direct measure of the skill content of technology. Proving this hypothesis would require proving not just skill-biased technological change but also a tremendous acceleration in new technology during the 1980s. After all, at least some level of technological change occurred in earlier decades without such an adverse impact on earnings equality. What's so different about technology in the 1980s and 1990s? According to David Howell ("The Skills Myth," *TAP*, Summer 1994, No. 18), and Lawrence Mishel and Jared Bernstein in an Economic Policy Institute working paper, there is little evidence that the pace of innovation—the speed at which new machines are brought to factories and new products are developed—was any faster than during the 1960s or 1970s. Most businesses are not introducing technology that requires vastly improved skill. Many are simply paying less for the same skills they have been using all along while others are hiring better educated workers at lower wage rates to do the work previously relegated to lesser-educated employees.

Suspect Two: The service-based economy. Other researchers, including George Borjas of the University of California at San Diego, have argued that a primary suspect is deindustrialization—the shift of jobs from goods-producing sectors to the service sector. In previous writings, I have estimated that between 1963 and 1987 the earnings ratio between college graduates and high school dropouts working in the goods-producing sector (mining, construction, and manufacturing) increased from 2.11 to 2.42—a jump of 15 percent. In the service sector, however, the education-to-earnings ratio mushroomed from 2.20 to 3.52—a 60 percent increase. All of the employment growth in the economy during the 1980s came in the services sector, where wages were polarizing between high school dropouts and college graduates four times faster than the goods-producing industries. Hence, this could explain at least part of the dramatic increase in earnings inequality.

Suspect Three: Deregulation. Government deregulation of the airlines, trucking, and telecommunications industries very likely has produced the same effect. In each of these industries, intense competition from new non-union, low-wage entrants, such as the short-lived People Express in the airline industry, forced existing firms to extract large wage concessions from their employees to keep from going bankrupt. How much this has contributed to overall earnings inequality remains an open question.

Suspect Four: Declining unionization. Unions have historically negotiated wage packages that narrow earnings differentials. They have tended to improve wages the most for workers with modest educations. As Richard Freeman of Harvard and a number of other economists have noted, the higher rate of union membership is one of the reasons for the smaller dispersion of wages found in manufacturing. That unions have made only modest inroads into the service economy may explain in part why earnings inequality in this sector outstrips inequality in the goods-producing sector.

Suspect Five: Downsizing. The restructuring of corporate enterprise toward lean production and the destruction of internal job ladders as firms rely more heavily on part-time, temporary, and leased employees is still another suspect in this mystery, according to Bennett Harrison of Carnegie Mellon. The new enterprise regime creates what labor economists call a "segmented" labor force of insiders and outsiders whose job security and earnings potential can differ markedly.

Suspect Six: Winner-take-all labor markets. The heightened competitive market, which forces firms toward lean production, may also, according to Robert Frank and Philip Cook, be creating a whole new structure of free-agency, "winner-take-all labor markets. As Frank has explained ("Talent and the Winner-Take-All Society," *TAP*, Spring 1994, No. 17), in winner-take-all markets "a handful of top performers walk away with the lion's share of total rewards." The difference between commercial success and failure in such markets may depend on just a few "star" performers—in movies the director and leading actor or actress; in the O. J. Simpson trial the conduct of just one or two trial attorneys. Given the high stakes involved in a multi-

million dollar movie project or a murder trial involving a well-to-do client, investors are willing to pay a bundle to make sure they employ the "best in the business."

Today, the fields of law, journalism, consulting, investment banking, corporate management, design, fashion, and even academia are generating payoff structures that once were common only in the entertainment and professional sports industries. Just a handful of Alan Dershowitzes, Michael Milkens, and Michael Eisners can have a sizeable impact on the dispersion of wages in each of their occupations. There is considerable evidence that inequality is not only rising across education groups but within them, very likely reflecting such winner-take-all dynamics.

Suspect Seven: Trade. Even more fundamental to the recent restructuring of the labor market—and a likely proximate cause of deindustrialization, deunionization, lean production, and perhaps even the free-agency syndrome—is the expansion of unfettered global trade. According to trade theory, increased trade alone is sufficient—*without* any accompanying multinational capital investment or low-wage worker immigration—to induce the wages of similarly skilled workers to equalize across trading countries. Economists call this dynamic "factor price equalization." As the global economy moves toward free trade, lower transportation costs, better communications, and the same "best practice" production techniques available to all countries, factor price equalization is likely to occur.

Unfortunately, in a world like ours where there is a plentiful supply of unskilled labor juxtaposed to a continued relative scarcity of well-educated workers, this "price equalization" *within* skill categories leads to a "wage polarization" *between* skill categories. The gap between the compensation of low-skilled workers and high-skilled workers everywhere will tend to grow. According to the well-respected trade theorist Edward Leamer of the University of California at Los Angeles, freer trade will ultimately reduce the wages of less-skilled U.S. workers by about a thousand dollars a year, partly as a result of NAFTA. If factor price equalization is a chief source of wage dispersion today, just consider the implications when China and India with their immense unskilled workforces enter fully into global markets.

Suspect Eight: Capital mobility. Freer trade generally provides for the unrestricted movement of investment capital across borders. This inevitably accelerates the process of growing wage inequality. Modern transportation and communications technologies, combined with fewer government restrictions on foreign capital investment, have led to increased multinational capital flows between countries. To the extent that companies move to take advantage of cheaper unskilled labor, transnational investment adds to the effective supply of low-skilled workers available to American firms, thus reinforcing factor price equalization.

Suspect Nine: Immigration. Increased immigration potentially has the same effect, if a disproportionate share of new immigrants enters with limited skills and schooling. This is true at least for legal immigrants. The typical legal immigrant in the U.S. today has nearly a year less schooling than native citizens. Undocumented immigrants surely have even less. As such, while many immigrants to the U.S. come here with excellent education and skills, there is little doubt that the large number of Central American, Caribbean, and Southeast Asians seeking refuge in this country has had the unfortunate side effect of at least temporarily boosting the supply of low-skill workers seeking jobs.

Suspect Ten: Trade deficits. The trade gap has contributed to the decline in those sectors of the economy that have in the past helped to restrain earnings inequality. Moreover, trade data indicate that the import surplus itself is disproportionately composed of products made by low-skilled and modestly skilled labor. This boosts the effective supply of workers at the bottom of the education-to-earnings distribution and thus depresses their relative wages.

WHODUNNIT?

Thus, in our rogue's gallery we have ten suspects: skill-biased technological change, deindustrialization, industry deregulation, the decline of unions, lean production, winner-take-all labor markets, free trade, transnational capital mobility, immigration, and a persistent trade deficit. Quantitatively parsing out the relative impact of all of these forces on wage distribution is fraught with enormous difficulty. Still, Richard Freeman and Lawrence Katz have attempted to do something like this, at least for the wage gap between men with a college degree and those with a high school diploma. The results of their research—and that of some other economists—are summarized in the chart, "Sources of Inequality."

What do these results suggest? If the Freeman and Katz estimates are in the right ballpark, the answer to our mystery is the same denouement as Agatha Christie's in *Murder on the Orient Express*. They all did it. Every major economic trend in the U.S. contributes to growing inequality largely linked to merit. None of these trends shows the least sign of weakening.

Each trend reflects the growth of market forces and the decline of institutional constraints on competition. This was Young's essential message more than 30 years ago. Increased reliance on domestic market dynamics as the sole determinant of earnings produces inequality. Heightened competition within these markets, as a consequence of fuller integration into the global economy, exacerbates this wage dispersion. While it may be sinister, there is nothing conspiratorial about this phenomenon. It is embedded in the very nature of laissez-faire market dynamics. For this

reason, meritocratic inequality is much harder to remedy than overt forms of discrimination based on race and sex.

Sources of Inequality

Factors responsible for the increase in the male college/high school wage differential during the 1980s

Technological Change	7% - 25%
Deindustrialization	25% - 33%
Deunionization	20%
Trade and Immigration	15% - 25%
Trade Deficit	15%

Source: Richard B. Freeman and Lawrence F. Katz, "Rising Wage Inequality: The United States vs. Other Advanced Countries," in Richard Freeman, ed., *Working Under Different Rules*. Russell Sage, 1994.

POLICY ENDGAMES

Even economists who tout the merits of the market have come to recognize the need to soften the potentially devastating social impact of current income trends. Yet given the long-standing resistance to most forms of public intervention in the marketplace, the search for solutions has been restricted to just three types of countermeasures: education and training, immigration reform, and direct tax-and-transfer policy.

In theory, education can offset the effect of skill-biased technological change and factor price equalization. If somehow we could produce a true glut of symbolic analysts in place of high school dropouts, meritocratic inequality would begin to resolve itself. Education reduces the surplus of low-skilled workers and relieves the shortage of skilled workers. If this strategy also happens to increase the overall level of education, it has the added advantage of improving overall labor productivity and ultimately real wages.

A number of education and training programs have widespread appeal. These include expanding the Head Start program for disadvantaged preschool children, levying a corporate tax to finance on-the-job training, instituting a national apprenticeship program, and converting current grant and loan programs into income-contingent loans for college and university students. Other possibilities under consideration for education reform include setting national standards for school performance, introducing merit systems to reward successful teaching, instituting voucher systems, and increasing teacher and parent control over schools.

Legal restriction of immigration is a second possible means of reducing wage inequality. Canada has a higher rate of immigration than the United States. But immigration laws in the two countries have produced very different effects on their respective labor markets. Since the 1960s, U.S. policy has stressed family reunification. Canada, in contrast, employs a point system designed to produce a more skilled immigrant labor pool. This approach has produced legal immigrants in Canada who average 1.3 more years of education than native Canadians. If we ignore the thorny ethical issues surrounding the rights of political refugees and judgments about the worthiness of individuals seeking to immigrate—a whole other debate—one could imagine tilting immigration policy toward greater use of skill-based criteria.

Finally, if immigration control and education cannot do the job, there is the old standby of progressive tax-and-transfer policy to effect greater equality after wages are paid. Traditionally, most contemporary liberal economists have favored this method, for it entails the least interference with market forces.

On the surface, this complement of liberal policies seems germane for coping with meritocratic inequality. Not surprisingly, all three policies are at the top of the domestic agenda of the Democratic Party. Yet, given the powerful set of national and global forces at work in the economy, these policies may not be enough.

A case in point is education and training. Greater equality in schooling does not by itself produce more equal earnings. The distribution of education has become significantly more even over the past three decades. Among year-round, full-time workers, the overall variation in completed years of schooling has declined by more than 25 percent since 1963. The performance of black students and other minorities on the Scholastic Aptitude Test (SAT) is further evidence of this convergence. In 1976, the average verbal SAT score for blacks stood at the 74th percentile of whites; by 1990 the average score was up to the 80th percentile. Math SAT scores for black students improved by the same amount.

But even as education backgrounds have converged, the importance of small differences in education has increased—enough so to offset any equalizing effect education would otherwise have. Recall the distinction between the return and the rate of return of schooling. As such, no matter what other benefits might flow from increased schooling, expanded education is not, by itself, a certain cure for inequality.

Job training programs have made even less headway. While the federal government has experimented with a bevy of programs from the original Manpower Development and Training Act (MDTA) of the Great Society to the Job Training and Partnership Act (JTPA)

of the 1980s, repeated evaluations suggest mixed results at best. Some programs like the Job Corps, which provide long-term training opportunities to disadvantaged youth, have been cost effective. The vast majority, however, have provided dubious returns. And even when these programs are deemed successful, the earnings advantage they give participants produces only the slightest deviation in the trend toward income inequality.

James Heckman of the University of Chicago has estimated just how small this deviation really is. Assuming a generous 10 percent rate of return on investment, he calculates that the government would need to spend a staggering $284 billion on the U.S. workforce to restore male high school dropouts to their 1979 real incomes. To restore education-based wage differentials to 1979 levels without reducing the real incomes of existing college-educated workers would take more than $2 trillion.

Future investments in human capital programs may have a somewhat better track record than past attempts, particularly if they are well targeted. But one cannot ignore the enormous increases in inequality that have already taken place. And to keep inequality from growing even more quickly, government would have to expand these programs at a frenetic pace. This is not to say that there is no role for training in solving America's labor market problems. While more training may not significantly reduce inequality, it is nevertheless useful for raising overall productivity, providing individual workers with a defense against further wage decline, and for rectifying specific skill shortages which could otherwise lead to wage-led inflation.

Immigration reform may also have a marginal impact on the earnings distribution, but any improvement will be largely limited to regions of the country where immigration flows have been disproportionately large—California, Texas, Florida, and perhaps a few states in the Northeast.

That leaves tax-and-transfer programs as the centerpiece for adjusting distributional outcomes. On paper, a suitably progressive set of tax rates combined with sufficiently generous transfer assistance could radically redistribute income after it is earned in the market. But in practice even such hard-to-win liberal measures as President Clinton's 1993 tax initiative produce relatively little redistribution. In 1977, when the federal tax system was significantly more progressive than today, the richest fifth of American families had 9.5 times the pretax total income of the poorest fifth. Federal taxes reduced the overall gap in relative shares by less than 20 percent; regressive state and local taxes wiped out this improvement. Given increased reliance on regressive payroll taxes and an aversion to any further increase in progressive income taxation, the tax system is unlikely to do much more.

The same is true of public transfer programs. Over the past 20 years, the New Deal safety net of unemployment insurance and welfare assistance has come under attack. Unemployment insurance covered more than 60 percent of the jobless during the 1961 and 1975 recessions. Despite the greater severity of the 1982 recession, only 43 percent of jobless Americans collected unemployment benefits. During the 1991 recession, coverage was down to 40 percent. While the Clinton administration implemented important reforms of the federal unemployment insurance system, the states and the federal government are unlikely to greatly expand coverage of the unemployed. As for the traditional welfare system, including Aid to Families with Dependent Children (AFDC), real benefit levels have been cut in many states and the government has imposed greater eligibility restrictions. Most of the proposed reforms of the AFDC program would change the dynamics of dependency, but do nothing to change the final distribution of income—and they could, by forcing welfare recipients off the roles after two years, make matters worse.

Education and immigration reform, as well as redistributive tax-and-transfer policy, could contribute to reducing inequality, but they are by themselves—even under the best of political scenarios—no match for the concerted forces now driving the labor market. Indeed, relying exclusively on redistributive tax-and-transfer schemes to redress the growing inequality problem would likely require tax rates and transfer sums so large that there would be not only massive political resistance but real economic costs in terms of disincentives to investment and growth.

THE END OF INEQUALITY?

There is, however, an additional policy agenda which a progressive government could embrace. This agenda would focus attention on the market forces that generate greater inequality. First, there is direct regulation of the labor market. As the empirical evidence demonstrates, the growth in earnings inequality has materialized in part because of a serious erosion in wages at the bottom of the skill distribution and a sharp decline in unionization. Higher minimum wage standards are one way government can affect the distribution of employee compensation. While raising the mandatory wage minimum theoretically entails some trade-off in the form of job loss, some recent studies prove the positive earnings impact of modest increases in the statutory minimum far outweigh any unemployment effect. Thus, the aggregate wage bill paid to less-skilled workers increases, improving the living standards of those on the bottom rungs of the earnings ladder.

Labor law reform makes it easier for unions to organize workers and provides an indirect method of accomplishing the same objective. While there are many reasons why union membership is dwindling, the recent *Fact Finding Report* of the U.S. Commission on the Future of Worker-Management Relations found undeniable evidence that the playing field is tilted heavily toward employers. Employers can permanently replace striking employees, which reduces the ability of unions to organize and to freely negotiate collective bargaining agreements. Unions do not have free access to employees during membership drives, and the penalties for employer unfair labor practices are trivial. To remedy this, government could ban permanent striker replacements, permit union organizers access to in-plant bulletin boards and public forums, impose more costly penalties on employers who violate the rights of union organizers, expedite legal remedies, and authorize binding arbitration for first contracts.

There are also industrial and trade policies to consider. Advocates of industrial policy can cite the success of the U.S. aircraft and agriculture industries, in which government purchases and research-and-development subsidies helped to create and maintain industries that now dominate world markets. The Carter administration's Chrysler loan guarantee, which provided an eleventh-hour reprieve from certain bankruptcy for the then-hapless automaker, turned around an old smokestack company and saved tens of thousands of well-paying jobs—not only at Chrysler but at hundreds of its suppliers. With a new lease on life, Chrysler has surged back as a world leader in automotive technology. There are, of course, many instances of failed industrial policy—the government's ill-fated Synfuels Corporation, for example—but there are an ample number of cases on the other side of the ledger. Maintaining the nation's manufacturing base would have a salutary effect on incomes.

The other policy that can bolster the goods-producing sector is implementation of fair-trade language in trade agreements. One way of doing this is to use tariffs and trade barriers designed to give *temporary* protection to key industries, promoting industrial revitalization and economic transition. Another form of managed trade would tie the offer of reduced protection to a trading partner's compliance with certain environmental and labor standards. Critics of NAFTA argued for side agreements that would have linked the pace of tariff reduction to the rate at which Mexican wages caught up with Mexico's rapidly rising productivity. To be sure, government-imposed limits on trade can have detrimental effects on prices and therefore reduce average real incomes from what they might be under a free trade regime. Nevertheless, a carefully crafted set of trade policies that condones temporary protection of selected domestic markets and sets minimum labor and environmental standards can soften the distributional impact of factor price equalization. The trick is to keep such protection from becoming permanent or prompting a trade war.

One last point: What about the use of macroeconomic stimulus to counteract inequality? As noted above, growth per se is no longer an antidote to increased wage dispersion. But it is important to realize that it is the sine qua non for providing the tax revenue and the political will to address inequality through government action. Hence, overzealous attacks on government deficits that reduce aggregate demand and overly restrictive monetary policies that unnecessarily boost interest rates can poison the environment for possible egalitarian reforms.

Is there any evidence that more aggressive structural policies can help? Critics like Mickey Kaus, the *New Republic* columnist and author of *The End of Equality,* think not. In declaring that "the venerable liberal crusade for income equality is doomed," Kaus argues that

> you cannot decide to keep all the nice parts of capitalism and get rid of all the nasty ones. You cannot have capitalism without 'selfishness,' or even 'greed,' because they are what make the system work. You can't have capitalism and material equality, because capitalism is constantly generating extremes of inequality as some individuals strike it rich . . . while others fail and fall on hard times.

This may sound sensible, but it will come as remarkable news to a large number of our foreign capitalist competitors. A comparison of earnings trends across countries suggests that different institutional frameworks, all operating within a capitalist framework, produce substantially different distributional outcomes.

Kaus confuses capitalism with laissez-faire economics. All nations now face nearly identical pressures from technological change and global competition. Yet not all are experiencing the same degree of growing income inequality. Those countries with stronger unions, national wage solidarity agreements, generous social welfare programs, and more vigorously pursued industrial and trade policies have greater wage equality than countries pursuing pure free-market strategies. Relying on an extensive review of comparative statistics, Richard Freeman and Lawrence Katz conclude that while educational and occupational skill-wage differentials were growing rapidly in the United States and the United Kingdom during the 1980s, the experience elsewhere was quite different. Wage equality increased in the Netherlands; wage differentials did not change noticeably in France, Germany, and Italy; and wage dispersion increased modestly—if at all—in Australia, Canada, Japan, and Sweden.

In all of these capitalist countries, intensified global competition and technological innovation pushed the distribution of earnings and income toward greater inequality. Structural protection against this onslaught was

greater in countries that did not follow the Reagan-Thatcher road to full-scale deregulation and laissez-faire trade policies.

True, the flexibility of the U.S. market may be partly responsible for lower overall unemployment rates compared with these other countries, but the price of this flexibility seems to be much higher levels of economic polarization and social inequality. Moreover, recent research by Rebecca Blank, a labor economist at Northwestern University, suggests there is little empirical evidence that social protection programs substantially affect labor market flexibility. Expansive social protection problems, then, are not the most important factor behind the high rate of unemployment in Europe, as many others suggest. Blank goes on to show that cutting back on social protection policies does not automatically reduce unemployment or increase the speed of labor market adjustment. Instead she finds that by enhancing worker well-being, social protection policies may actually permit flexibility that would not otherwise be possible. All of which means that the U.S. can adopt policies to directly redress income inequality without raising the specter of double-digit unemployment.

So can we avoid fulfilling Michael Young's prophecy for 2034? Can a society with high- and low-skill workers have a reasonably equitable distribution of income? The answer is a qualified "yes," but it requires that we focus on equal outcome, not just equal opportunity. There is a fundamental distinction separating progressives from neoconservatives and neoliberals, and it turns largely on this point: Progressives are willing to consider a broader and more balanced array of public policies to keep the free market from perpetrating and then perpetuating socially destructive levels of inequality.

Works Discussed in This Essay

Mickey Kaus, *The End of Equality.* Basic-Books, 1992.

Paul R. Krugman and Robert Z. Lawrence, "Trade, Jobs and Wages" *Scientific American,* April 1994.

Edward E. Leamer, "Wage Effects of the U.S.–Mexico Free Trade Agreement," in Peter M. Garber, ed., *The Mexico–U.S. Free Trade Agreement.* MIT Press, 1993.

Frank Levy and Richard Murnane, "U.S. Earnings Levels and Earnings Inequality: A Review of Recent Trends and Proposed Explanations," *Journal of Economic Literature,* September 1992.

Lawrence R. Mishel and Jared Bernstein, *The State of Working America.* Economic Policy Institute, 1993. Lawrence R. Mishel and Jared Bernstein, "Is The Technology Black Box Empty? An Empirical Examination of the Impact of Technology on Wage Inequality and the Employment Structure," Economic Policy Institute, April 1994.

Michael D. Young, *The Rise of the Meritocracy, 1870–2033.* Thames and Hudson, 1958.

Money, Banking, and Monetary Policy

Money works, but it doesn't work miracles. (Paul Samuelson, 1970 Nobel Laureate in Economics)

Compared to fiscal policy, monetary policy—the deliberate control of the money supply for the purpose of achieving macroeconomic goals—receives less attention in political debates and the media. Part of its apparent obscurity may be traced to differences in the manner in which the two policies are conducted: fiscal policy decisions are made by elected representatives in Congress following sometimes lengthy public debates, while monetary policies are determined by a small handful of Federal Reserve (Fed) officials meeting in closed session. In addition, the role of money in an economy is itself a fairly obscure topic for the average person; the effect of changes in the nation's money supply is generally less understood than, say, a tax cut, the effect of which can be felt immediately in a person's pockets. Nevertheless, monetary policy can have a powerful impact on a nation's economy.

The importance of monetary policy as a stabilizing instrument has increased significantly in recent years, as a ballooning federal deficit has complicated the use of its major alternative, fiscal policy. The implementation of monetary policy requires the Federal Reserve to adjust what are known as "intermediate targets" (such as the money supply or short-term interest rates). These targets stand intermediate between certain ultimate objectives (such as high employment, low inflation, and so forth) and the instruments of monetary policy (including open market operations, discount rate policy, and reserve requirement changes). The intermediate targets are of interest not for their own sake, but for the close relationship they may bear to the ultimate goal of stabilizing the economy.

The unit begins with an article in which Tom Stark and Herb Taylor discuss the potential role that an activist monetary policy might play in countering recessions; they remind us that the effectiveness of such policy will ultimately depend on which of two lines of reasoning—New Keynesian or New Classical—is employed.

Dimitri Papadimitriou and L. Randall Wray provide an assessment of recent Federal Reserve policy in "The Fed: Wrong Turn in Risky Traffic." They assert that the Fed has made a series of destabilizing policy changes that have disrupted financial markets and have adversely affected employment and investment decisions. In their view, it is far more important at present for the Fed to focus on full employment than on inflation.

Next, Harvey Rosenblum investigates proposals that would fundamentally change the way the Federal Reserve conducts monetary policy and remove the Fed's role in bank supervision and regulation. Rosenblum believes that these reforms would seriously reduce the Fed's effectiveness in carrying out its mission.

Edward Hill and Roger Vaughan survey trends in the U.S. commercial banking industry. They maintain that the United States currently has two banking systems: one is healthy and competitive, while the other is under-capitalized and dying. The future of U.S. banking as a whole depends on how quickly politicians and regulators deal with the latter.

In "Should the Feds Have Greater Control over State Banks?" Lee Adams, Carter McDowell, and Doyle Bartlett examine the pros and cons of the "dual banking system," under which banks and other depository institutions may be chartered and regulated by either the federal government or an individual state. This is followed by an article in which Kelly Holland and Amy Cortese consider what the development of "E-cash" (or electronic money) might mean for the future of banking and the U.S. monetary system.

The unit concludes with an examination of recent changes in access to banking services. Historically, U.S. financial institutions maintained a commitment to the promotion of savings among lower-income Americans. Louis Jacobson shows how, with the emergence of automated teller machines, there has been an erosion of savings institutions for the poor.

Looking Ahead: Challenge Questions

How is monetary policy used for the purpose of achieving national macroeconomic goals?

Is monetary policy making subject to political influences? What might be done about this problem?

How are deregulation and technological changes affecting the financial system?

Unit 4

Activist Monetary Policy for Good or Evil?

The New Keynesians vs. the New Classicals

Tom Stark and Herb Taylor

Tom Stark, Research Associate, and Herb Taylor, Assistant Vice-President and chief of the Macroeconomics Section, both work in the Research Department of the Federal Reserve Bank of Philadelphia.

Economic analysts and policy practitioners argue endlessly about how long it takes for monetary policy actions to affect output or employment, how long the effects will last, or how large they will be. But underneath it all, the truth is that economists cannot agree on how monetary policy affects the real economy in the first place. Theoreticians are offering two different explanations, each with its own implications for the way monetary policy ought to be conducted.

Perhaps the most popular explanation for money's impact was first proposed about 15 years ago by a group of economists now known as the New Classicals. These economists see episodes of money affecting economic activity as temporary aberrations that occur only when monetary policy actions happen to catch the public by surprise. Because they see these episodes as harmful, the New Classical economists think that central banks should avoid such surprises. They think that a central bank should just announce a simple money growth plan and stick to it. Such a policy, they say, would minimize economic disruptions and make inflation predictable.

In the last few years a group of economists labeled the New Keynesians has begun mounting a challenge to the New Classical view. The New Keynesians claim that under the right circumstances even widely publicized monetary policy actions can have a sustained impact on output and employment. And they claim that this impact can be used to help counteract what they see as the economy's tendencies toward excessive volatility and unemployment. So the New Keynesians think that a good central bank conducts an activist monetary policy—it actively manages the supply of money and credit to keep the economy close to full employment.

Which side is right? Is an activist monetary policy good or evil? Neither side has all the answers, but both command serious attention in a very important policy debate.

THE NEW CLASSICALS' CASE AGAINST ACTIVIST POLICY

Like the great Classical economists of the last century, the New Classicals see the market system naturally bringing the economy to its peak level of efficiency. They see markets as a network of competitive auctions in which prices respond quickly and completely to changes in economic conditions. Basing their decisions on these market prices, households and firms automatically deploy the economy's real resources—its labor, raw materials, factories, and equipment—fully and efficiently. Activist monetary policy has no place in this world. Policy actions designed to alter the pattern of economic activity are ineffective and unnecessary.

Competition among many small households and firms makes the Classical economy efficient. In the Classical system, overall supply and demand conditions determine the prices people pay and the wages they earn. No business or individual is big enough to manipulate market conditions to its own advantage. Any firm that tried to charge above-market prices for its product would lose all of its customers to competing producers. Any worker that held out for above-market wages would lose his or her job to competing workers.

This environment may sound harsh, but it gives firms the incentive to perform at peak efficiency. Given the wage-price structure, each firm faces just one basic decision: how much to produce. And in its quest for profits, the firm will automatically choose a production level that balances consumer preferences with resource availability.

Consider the typical firm. For each unit it produces, it gets the market price. It also incurs costs equal to the price of the requisite labor and materials. The more it produces, the more it is prone to operating inefficiencies that push

From *Business Review*, published by the Federal Reserve Bank of Philadelphia, March/April 1991, pp. 17-25. Reprinted by permission.

up per-unit production costs. At some point, the cost of producing another unit would exceed the product's market price. Expansion beyond that point would cut into profits, so the firm expands no further. Following this strategy not only maximizes the firm's own profits, it promotes overall economic efficiency as well. The product's market price measures its worth to the consumer. Wages and other input prices measure workers' and resource suppliers' valuation of their time and materials. So, in effect, the firm is producing only the units whose benefits to the consumer justify the burden their production imposes on workers and other resources.

Of course, economic conditions are constantly changing. Consumers' preferences shift away from one product and toward another; a new production technology comes along and displaces an old one. But in the Classical view, market prices and wages adjust quickly to changes in supply and demand, providing firms with the incentives to keep the economy's resources fully and efficiently employed. With the market system allocating resources so effectively, there is no reason to use monetary policy to alter the level of economic activity. But it's just as well. Because in the Classical world, any attempt at activist policy would fail.

The Classical economists developed the theory that money has no effect on economic activity. Clearly, prices are crucial to people's economic decisions in the Classical system. And usually we think of prices being quoted in terms of money. Yet the Classical economists maintained that changing the money supply would have no impact on output or employment. How can this be?

The Classicals claimed that when the money supply changed, all prices and wages would change in equal proportion, leaving the relationships among them unchanged. Consequently, households and firms would stick by their original employment and production decisions, leaving the real economy unaffected.[1]

Suppose, for instance, that the central bank pumps up the money supply. This increases the overall demand for goods and services, pushing up market prices. But workers recognize that higher prices erode the purchasing power of their wages. So they are willing to work the same hours and expend the same effort only if they get wage increases commensurate with the increase in market prices. Firms, competing for workers, agree to pay for the raises out of their inflated sales revenues, and

they maintain their original level of employment and output. All that remains of the money supply increase are higher prices and wages.

The Classical economists recognized that, as a practical matter, these adjustments to a change in the money supply would not always proceed as smoothly as their theoretical analysis might suggest. But their message comes through clearly enough: the money supply ultimately affects the level of prices, not the level of economic activity.

The New Classical economists reinvigorated the Classical argument that monetary policy is generally ineffective. The Classical perspective on money's role in the economy was among the casualties of the Great Depression. The Keynesian Revolution swept through the economics profession and gave birth to the activist monetary policies of the postwar period. But in the early 1970s, some economists resurrected the Classical viewpoint. In fact, by combining parts of the Classical tradition with the notion of "rational expectations," these New Classical economists emerged with an even stronger position: monetary policy cannot systematically affect the real economy. Instances in which monetary policy actions alter employment or output levels are occasional, random events.

The New Classical analysis of money's impact on the economy is a variation on the old adage "knowledge is power." In keeping with their Classical tradition, the New Classicals maintain that markets are competitive enough to drive the economy to full employment, and responsive enough to keep it there in the face of shifting economic conditions. To this they simply add that a key element in markets' responsiveness is market participants acting upon rational expectations about where the economy is headed. The New Classicals assume that market participants understand the underlying structure of the economy and use the available data on current economic conditions to formulate accurate forecasts about future economic performance. Presumably, participants' actions in the marketplace today reflect those rational expectations.

The New Classicals go on to argue that market participants pretty much know what to expect from the monetary authority. Competitive market prices and wages automatically reflect those expectations, thus neutralizing the impact of any anticipated policy actions on output and employment. Admittedly, policy actions that take people by surprise can affect

economic activity. But, the New Classicals point out, such "surprises" must, by definition, be occasional and without pattern. So the monetary authority cannot systematically influence the level of output or employment.

The New Classicals emphasize that even when a monetary policy action does take people by surprise, its impact is temporary. It lasts only as long as it takes for the markets to find out what the central bank has done and respond. And in the interim, people—particularly workers—are not necessarily better off.[2]

Textbook versions of the New Classical view assume that product prices respond to sudden shifts in economic conditions more quickly than wages do. For one thing, wage agreements, whether formal or informal, may cover several months, a year, or even several years—all periods much longer than it takes for product prices to change. Even where wages are set more frequently, workers usually agree to a certain wage without the benefit of complete information on the prices of the products they intend to buy. Consequently, when an unexpected monetary expansion comes along and pushes up product prices, firms find they can retain, and perhaps even expand, their work force without raising wages very much. And they make the most of the opportunity. They pay a slightly higher wage, hire more workers, produce more output, and sell it at the new, higher prices. Hence the expansionary monetary policy boosts aggregate employment and output.[3]

Of course, the workers eventually catch on. They shop. They see the higher product prices. And the next time they negotiate a wage, they demand compensation for their loss in purchasing power. Once wages rise as much as prices have, firms revert to their original hiring and production patterns. So money is, in the last analysis, neutral.

Overall, the New Classical analysis of money's impact on the economy casts activist monetary policy in a very dim light. First of all, the New Classicals see the economy exhibiting a strong tendency toward full employment that makes it unnecessary for the monetary authority to focus on the level of economic activity. But even beyond that, attempts to conduct an activist policy do more harm than good. An expansionary policy anticipated by the public simply creates instant inflation. If, as occasionally happens, the policy is not anticipated by the public, it affects output and employment essentially by tricking people into producing at a pace they would not have chosen if they were fully informed.

Given this perspective, the New Classicals' advice to policymakers is straightforward: do not try any surprise moves. Choose a simple money growth plan consistent with your inflation goals. Announce the plan far enough in advance to allow markets to react. Then just follow the plan.[4]

THE NEW KEYNESIANS' CASE FOR AN ACTIVIST POLICY

The New Keynesians don't see things quite the way the New Classicals do. The New Keynesians see an economy in which firms face only limited competition. These imperfectly competitive firms restrict their output to keep prices high and respond only partially to shifting demand conditions. As a result, the economy shows the tendencies toward underemployment and price "stickiness" that are very much a part of the traditional Keynesian perspective. The New Keynesians believe that in this world, regardless of how people form their expectations, monetary policy can and should be used to expand the level of economic activity.

Without strict market discipline, firms are less likely to achieve maximum economic efficiency. The difference between the Classical competitive firm and the imperfectly competitive firm is simple: the competitive firm must take the market price of its product as a given, whereas the imperfect competitor has the power to set price to its own advantage. And the right price structure for the imperfect competitor is not necessarily best for the overall economy.

In the competitive market, each firm is small and its output is nothing special. So its decision about how much to supply has no appreciable impact on the market price. If Farmer Jones decided to withhold some of his wheat from the market, how far could he drive up the price of wheat? If he tried to charge extra for Farmer Jones Wheat, who would pay the premium? No one.

Imperfect competitors have larger operations. Their product may have some special characteristic—real or imagined—that differentiates it in the mind of consumers. For these firms, size or special niche gives them some power over the price of their products. If General Mills were willing to cut its supply of breakfast cereal, cereal prices would rise. And if it decides to increase the price of Wheaties® , some people would be willing to pay the premium.

In short, the imperfectly competitive firm has some advantage that frees its pricing structure from the strict discipline of the market. Of course, the firm is still subject to the Law of Demand: the higher the price it sets, the fewer

units it will sell. So it must choose between setting a high price and selling to a limited number of customers, or setting a low price and grabbing the lion's share of the market. But one thing is for sure: it will not set as low a price as a Classical competitive market would establish. It will always find it profitable to set a higher price and maintain it by keeping output below competitive levels.

Exercising market power may make individual firms more profitable, but it imposes costs on society as a whole. From the social standpoint, imperfect competitors' prices are too high and their production is too low. Society would be better off if these firms would cut their prices to levels more consistent with resource costs. This would expand sales, production, and employment to more socially desirable levels.

Neither the notion of imperfect competition nor its impact on social welfare are original to the New Keynesians.[5] But the analysis offers them a rationale for their belief that the economy tends to underemployment. And it offers them something more—a jumping-off point for a new theory of how monetary policy can help alleviate the problem.

The New Keynesians believe monetary policy can work on imperfect competitors. Traditional theories of imperfect competition can explain underemployment, but they cannot explain why monetary policy should be effective in combating it. As long as prices and wages respond flexibly, the monetary authority is still powerless to affect firms' output and employment decisions. But the New Keynesians add a new wrinkle to the theory of imperfect competition: imperfectly competitive firms' prices are not as flexible as competitively established market prices. So real activity may respond to monetary policy actions.

In the Classical world, competitive markets adjust prices quickly and completely to every shift in economic conditions. In a world of imperfect competition, firms must set prices. When demand shifts are relatively small, these firms may not find changing prices worthwhile. It may be more profitable to maintain current prices and adjust production accordingly.

Economists have labeled the costs firms bear when they change their product prices "menu costs." That name captures the most obvious cost of repricing: printing new menus and catalogs and changing price tags and signs. But there are other costs as well. To find the new profit-maximizing price, the firm must esti-

mate the likely nature, magnitude, and duration of the shift in customer demand. That kind of research and analysis uses up resources. In addition, frequent price changes may alienate customers and cost the firm some of its good will.

It's difficult to say how large menu costs are. It may seem that, as a practical matter, the cost of changing prices ought to be relatively small. But the New Keynesians emphasize that the benefits to changing prices can be small for imperfect competitors, too. So even small menu costs can thwart a price change.

When the demand for an imperfect competitor's product increases, the firm can respond in any number of ways. At one extreme, it can take the opportunity to raise its prices without losing sales. At the other extreme, it can hold the line on prices and take the opportunity to pick up sales volume. If the demand shift that the firm is experiencing is large, then choosing the right strategy can have a substantial impact on profits. But if the demand shift is relatively small, there is little advantage to choosing one over the other. A firm that simply maintains its original prices will not get as much as it could on each unit, but it will sell more units. So its profits will not be substantially compromised.[6] Once menu costs—even small ones—enter the equation, they can tip the scales in favor of maintaining current prices. Thus the profit-maximizing imperfect competitor may choose to accommodate a small demand shift without changing the price of its product.

This tendency for prices to be sticky in an imperfectly competitive environment affords the central bank some opportunity to influence overall output and employment. Suppose the central bank increases the money supply and thereby boosts overall demand for goods and services. Further suppose that individual firms decide that the demand increase is too small to make a price adjustment profitable. Instead, they decide to hold the line on prices and fully accommodate the increased demand for their products. In order to increase their output, they begin to hire more workers. So both output and employment pick up. Meanwhile, since product prices are not rising, workers are not demanding an inflation adjustment to their wages, so both wages and prices remain relatively constant.[7]

The New Keynesians recognize that the central bank's ability to raise output and employment in this way is circumscribed. If monetary policy actions create too large a demand shift, firms are more likely to raise prices than in-

crease output. Furthermore, every firm faces different demand conditions and menu costs. Some will have lower thresholds for changing prices than others. So almost any policy action is likely to affect aggregate prices as well as aggregate output. In short, the New Keynesians acknowledge that a central bank cannot engineer dramatic or persistent increases in output and employment without driving up prices and wages. Nonetheless, New Keynesian analysis suggests that an activist policy can be successful, if used judiciously.

Overall, the New Keynesians see the potential for an activist monetary policy to improve the performance of an imperfectly competitive economy. Monetary policy may not be a cure-all, but it can help offset what New Keynesians see as the economy's chronic bias toward underproduction and underemployment in modern, imperfectly competitive economies.

Add to this underlying bias the fact that the economy is subject to sudden shifts in overall demand, and the New Keynesians' case for an activist monetary policy seems even stronger. For if price stickiness accentuates the impact of monetary policy on economic activity, it also accentuates the impact of other demand shifts as well. Thus a sudden decline in overall demand could drop the economy well below its potential level of performance. This suggests that monetary policymakers should be alert to these shifts and stand ready to offset them.[8]

WHO'S RIGHT?

Both the New Classicals and the New Keynesians offer explanations for monetary policy's impact on the economy. But the New Keynesian approach certainly casts activist monetary policy in a more positive light. Which explanation should we believe? One way to evaluate competing theories is to "let the data decide." But at this point, empirical tests do not provide a clear answer.

The New Classical theory has been around longer and been subjected to more empirical study. The results are not favorable to the hard-line New Classical view that only unexpected policy actions affect real activity. Statistical analyses seem to show output and employment responding to anticipated policy actions too. But, ironically enough, these kinds of results have prompted some New Classicals to support a theory that attributes even less potency to monetary policy actions: the *real business cycle* theory. According to this theory, monetary policy never causes fluctuations in

economic activity. Rather, anticipated fluctuations in the economy cause the public to increase or decrease their demand for money. The central bank and the financial system simply accommodate these demand fluctuations.[9]

The New Keynesian theory is relatively new, and empirical evidence is scantier. There is some supportive evidence, however. In countries where inflation is relatively low, which would suggest that expansionary monetary policies have not been pursued too aggressively, policy shifts seem to have more impact on real activity—as the New Keynesians would predict. But tests of the New Keynesian model are really in too early a stage to provide a convincing case one way or another.[10]

Empirical issues aside, there are unsettling aspects to both the New Classical and the New Keynesian models. Perhaps the most unsettling theoretical aspects have to do with the functioning of the labor market. Both groups admit they have trouble explaining why monetary policy actions that affect output have such a large effect on employment and such a small effect on wages. According to the New Classical theory, an unexpected increase in product demand induces firms to produce more because it pushes the product price up before wages have had a chance to rise in response. But firms need more workers in order to expand production. Won't that increased demand for labor itself push up wages?

The New Classicals' answer: some, but not much. True to their Classical perspective, they maintain that labor markets are competitive. They simply assume that labor supply is very sensitive to wage changes. Thus when labor demand increases, it evokes many more hours of work at only a slightly higher wage. The problem is that, as a practical matter, willingness to work does not seem to be all that sensitive to wage changes.

New Keynesians face a similar conundrum. According to them, when firms face a small increase in product demand, they hold the line on prices and expand output. Again, to expand output, firms need more workers. Granted, product prices are not increasing, so there is no inflation pressure on wages. But won't firms have to raise the wage they pay in order to induce more people to work? The New Keynesians' answer is no. True to the Keynesian tradition, they claim that there is a pool of involuntarily unemployed workers from which firms can always draw workers at the going wage. But to explain the involuntary unemployment, they must resort to some unconven-

tional theories of the labor market.

Imperfectly competitive firms charge high prices, which restricts both output and employment. Nonetheless, the New Keynesians claim, these firms tend to pay the people they do employ relatively high wages. Different economists offer different reasons for this tendency. Proponents of the "efficiency wage" theory emphasize that by paying workers more than they would expect to earn if they had to go look elsewhere for a new job, the firm gives the worker the incentive to perform more effectively. Proponents of the "insider/outsider" theory emphasize that employees whose experience on the job is valuable to the firm can exact wage concessions from the firm. In either case, with wages high and employment opportunities limited, there is routinely a pool of willing workers unable to get jobs. Whenever firms want to expand output, they can tap this pool for workers without increasing the wage they pay.[11]

In short, both the New Classicals and the New Keynesians have a long way to go before either can proclaim their approach to be theoretically complete.

THE ACTIVIST
POLICY DEBATE RENEWED

When the New Classical economics came on the scene in the early 1970s, it jolted academic economists and policymakers as well. The New Classicals were trying to explain precisely why monetary policy actions affect real activity. They concluded that money temporarily affects output and employment by tricking people into deviating from their preferred activity levels. This conclusion hardly cast activist monetary policy in the most favorable light, but there was little theoreticians could offer in rebuttal.

Now the New Keynesian school is offering an alternative explanation for money's impact on economic activity. That analysis, based on theories of imperfect competition, looks more favorably on activist monetary policy. The New Keynesians conclude that the economy tends toward underemployment and that an activist policy can help overcome the problem.

The New Keynesians can hardly claim to have overcome the New Classical paradigm. But they have reinvigorated the battle over the efficacy of an activist monetary policy.

──────────── **NOTES**

[1]To see this, suppose that initially bread costs $1 and workers earn $6 an hour, making a loaf of bread worth 10 minutes' work. If both prices and wages double, bread goes to $2 and wages go to $12, but a loaf of bread still trades for 10 minutes' work.

[2]Thomas Sargent and Neil Wallace, in their article " 'Rational' Expectations, the Optimal Monetary Instrument and the Optimal Money Supply Rule," *Journal of Political Economy* (April 1975) pp. 241-54, present a clear statement of the New Classical notion that expected monetary policy actions have no effect on economic activity.

[3]Analyses stressing the role of wage contracts in limiting short-run wage flexibility can be found in Stanley Fischer's "Long-Term Contracts, Rational Expectations, and the Optimal Money Supply Rule," *Journal of Political Economy* (February 1977) pp. 191-205, and John Taylor's "Aggregate Dynamics and Staggered Contracts," *Journal of Political Economy* (1980) pp. 1-24. The idea that wages adjust imperfectly because workers are not completely aware of current product prices is more consistent with the original New Classical formulation by Robert Lucas in "Some International Evidence on Output-Inflation Tradeoffs," *American Economic Review* (June 1973) pp. 326-34.

[4]The New Classical argument for this approach to monetary policy has most recently been articulated by Bennett McCallum in *Monetary Economics: Theory and Policy* (Macmillan, 1989).

[5]The term "imperfect competition" is used here as a convenient expression for "monopolistic competition," a market model that can be traced back to the work of E.H. Chamberlin in the 1930s. Texts such as Paul Samuelson's *Economics* (McGraw-Hill) provide readable discussions of this market type.

[6]This idea is sometimes called the PAYM insight because it emerged from the work of economists Michael Parkin, George Akerlof, Janet Yellen, and N. Gregory Mankiw. Specific references are to Parkin's "The Output-Inflation Tradeoff When Prices Are Costly to Change," *Journal of Political Economy* (1986) pp. 200-24; Akerlof and Yellen's "Can Small Deviations From Rationality Make Significant Differences to Economic Equilibria?" *American Economic Review* (September 1985) pp. 708-21; and Mankiw's "Small Menu Costs and Large Business Cycles: A Macroeconomic Model of Monopoly," *Quarterly Journal of Economics* (May 1985) pp. 529-37.

[7]Olivier Blanchard and Nobuhiro Kiyotaki develop this argument formally in "Monopolistic Competition and the Effects of Aggregate Demand," *American Economic Review* (September 1987) pp. 647-66.

[8]Prospects for this kind of policy get some theoretical support in Lars Svensson's "Sticky Goods Prices, Flexible Asset Prices, Monopolistic Competition, and Monetary Policy," *Review of Economic Studies* (1986) pp. 385-405.

[9]Frederic Mishkin provides a more complete discussion of the evidence on the New Classical hypothesis in *A Rational Expectations Approach to Macroeconometrics* (University of Chicago Press, 1983). For a good discussion of the real business cycle view and its monetary policy implications, see "Monetary Policy with a New View of Potential GNP," by John Boschen and Leonard Mills, this *Business Review* (June/July 1990) pp. 3-10.

[10]This New Keynesian result is presented by Laurence Ball, N. Gregory Mankiw, and David Romer in "The New Keynesian Economics and the Output-Inflation Trade-Off," *Brookings Papers on Economic Activity* (1988:1) pp. 1-65. For an up-to-date discussion of the empirical evidence on the New Keynesian economics, as well as a good evaluation of its theoretical underpinnings, see Robert Gordon, "What Is New Keynesian Economics?" *Journal of Economic Literature* (September 1990) pp. 1115-71.

[11]Lawrence Katz provides an excellent overview of these modern labor market theories in "Some Recent Developments in Labor Economics and Their Implications for Macroeconomics," *Journal of Money, Credit, and Banking* (August 1988, Part 2) pp. 507-30.

The Fed: Wrong Turn in Risky Traffic

Dimitri B. Papadimitriou and L. Randall Wray

DIMITRI B. PAPADIMITRIOU is Executive Director of the Jerome Levy Economics Institute of Bard College. L. RANDALL WRAY is Research Associate at the same institute and Associate Professor of Economics at the University of Denver.

The moderate inflation achieved recently does not entail significant costs. Indeed, the benefits to be gained by eliminating this inflation cannot be expected to exceed the costs that would be engendered by higher unemployment, greater uncertainty, and lost output. Given the current state of the economy, it is far more important to focus on full employment than on inflation.

In the past decade and a half, U.S. monetary policy has deviated radically from that of the postwar period. It has embarked on a series of policy experiments that is focused almost exclusively on price stability. Beginning in 1979, under Chairman Volcker, the Fed pushed interest rates above 20 percent and unemployment above 10 percent. That resulted in the deepest recession since the Great Depression. Similarly, under Alan Greenspan, the Fed pushed interest rates to nearly 11 percent in the first quarter of 1989 (when inflation was less than 5 percent) and contributed to a long recession. More recently, the Fed has tightened six times in ten months to fight perceived inflationary pressures. In our view, the pursuit of stable prices by the Fed since 1979 has contributed to high levels of unemployment, low productivity growth, and reduced economic growth—all of which was experienced by the U.S. economy during the 1980s and 1990s.

In the summer of 1993, Chairman Greenspan announced that the Fed would drop monetary aggregates as targets of monetary policy and would, instead, target a real interest rate.

This announcement was met with nearly universal surprise and was rejected by most economists as unworkable. In later testimony, Greenspan advocated inflation expectations as the target of monetary policy. During the past year, the radical shift in policy announced by

> **Unstable interest rates, uncertainty over actions to be taken at the Federal Open Market Committee (FOMC) meetings, and unstable exchange rates generated by rudderless central bank policy have all reduced stability, confidence, and the ability to engage in long-run planning.**

Chairman Greenspan in four separate testimonies, as well as the six occasions on which the Fed raised short-term interest rates, violated the goals of monetary policy as laid out by the Chairman himself in June 1994. At that time, he said:

From *Challenge*, January/February 1995, pp. 15-21. © 1995 by M. E. Sharpe, Inc., Armonk, NY 10504. Reprinted by permission.

Figure 1   **Actual and Expected Inflation Growth**

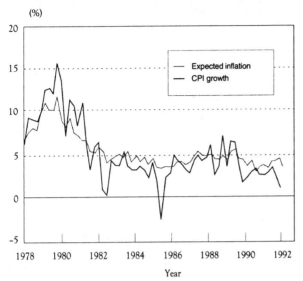

Note: The figure represents the inflation rate as measured by quarterly changes in the consumer price index and expected inflation as measured by the University of Michigan's expected inflation series one-year foreward forecast.
Source: The Forecasting Center of The Jerome Levy Economics Institute.

Figure 2   **Real *Ex Ante* and Real *Ex Post* Interest Rates**

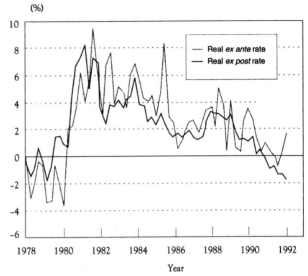

Source: National Income and Product Account and the Forecasting Center of The Jerome Levy Economics Institute.

"Most importantly, we can reinforce ongoing trends in the private sector that enhance our productive potential by helping to create a stable environment for sustainable noninflationary economic growth. Stability in economic conditions boosts confidence and makes long-range planning by businesses and households much easier."

Unstable interest rates, uncertainty over actions to be taken at the Federal Open Market Committee (FOMC) meetings, and unstable exchange rates generated by rudderless central bank policy have all reduced stability, confidence, and the ability to engage in long-run planning. Finally, there is, so far, no evidence that the Fed's moves since February 1994 have

lowered inflation expectations. The policy has caused investors to shun the long-term end of the market. The yield curve will remain steep, because high long-term rates are required to compensate holders of long-term bonds for the capital losses they would suffer when the Fed tightened further.

WOULD RANDOM POLICY BE BETTER?

While the Fed's policy clearly failed by Chairman Greenspan's own test, we analyzed the data since 1959 to determine how well Chairman Greenspan's

Table 1   **Chairman Greenspan's Scorecard: Inflation**

Period	Number of Quarters with STr > 1.5%	Number of Quarters with Inflation > 4.7%	Number of Quarters with Inflation < 4.7%	Number of Quarters Followed by Accelerating Inflation	Chairman Greenspan Adopts Wrong Policy (%)
1959.2–1971.1	23	2	21	22	96
1971.2–1983.1	12	8	4	6	50
1983.2–1993.3	30	4	26	20	66

Period	Number of Quarters with STr < 1.5%	Number of Quarters with Inflation > 4.7%	Number of Quarters with Inflation < 4.7%	Number of Quarters Followed by Accelerating Inflation	Chairman Greenspan Adopts Wrong Policy (%)
1959.2–1971.1	25	8	17	10	60
1971.2–1983.1	36	28	8	26	28
1983.2–1993.3	12	4	8	0	100

Note: STr is the real short-term interest rate as measured by subtracting the inflation rate (as measured by the rate of increase of the consumer price index) from the three-month Treasury bill rate. Owing to data limitations, it was assumed that the inflation rate will not rise above 2.3 percent within four quarters following 1993.3. Inflation is measured as the quarterly rate of change in the consumer price index.
Source: Authors' calculations based on National Income and Product Account and The Levy Economics Institute Forecasting Center.

Table 2   **Chairman Greenspan's Scorecard: Capacity Utilization**

Period	Number of Quarters with STr > 1.5%	Number of Quarters with Capacity Utilization > 82%	Number of Quarters with Capacity Utilization < 82%	Number of Quarters Followed by Falling Capacity Utilization	Chairman Greenspan Adopts Wrong Policy (%)
1959.2–1971.1	23	16	7	9	61
1971.2–1983.1	12	0	12	7	42
1983.2–1993.3	30	9	21	3	90

Period	Number of Quarters with STr < 1.5%	Number of Quarters with Capacity Utilization > 82%	Number of Quarters with Capacity Utilization < 82%	Number of Quarters Followed by Falling Capacity Utilization	Chairman Greenspan Adopts Wrong Policy (%)
1959.2–1971.1	25	15	10	8	68
1971.2–1983.1	36	22	14	19	47
1983.2–1993.3	12	0	12	4	67

Note: STr is the real short-term interest rate as measured by subtracting the inflation rate (as measured by the rate of increase of the consumer price index) from the three-month Treasury bill rate. Owing to data limitations, it was assumed that capacity utilization will not fall below 78.8 percent or rise above 82.8 percent within four quarters following 1993.3.

proposals would have fared, had they been adopted in the past (see *Figure 1*).

If the Fed had adopted a real interest rate target in the past, how often would it have correctly read economic conditions? Over the entire examined period, the real *ex post* short-term interest rate averaged just less than 1.5 percent, with a maximum of nearly 9.5 percent and a minimum of -5.5 percent (see *Figure 2*). Assuming that the average real rate of 1.5 percent is a proxy for Chairman Greenspan's "equilibrium" real rate, then a real rate above this should indicate an economy facing disinflationary pressures. And a rate below this should presage dangers of accelerating inflation.

Table 1 is a "scorecard" for Chairman Greenspan's proposed policy. Assume that he plans to implement tight policy when the real interest rate drops below

---

In most cases, relatively high real interest rates did not foretell falling capacity-utilization rates.

1.5 percent to fight inflationary pressures and to implement easy policy when the real interest rate is above 1.5 percent. As this table shows, there were sixty-five quarters in which Greenspan would have adopted easy policy. However, forty-eight of these quarters were followed by accelerating inflation (defined as a rise of inflation by one percentage point or more within the following four quarters). Chairman Greenspan's policy would have been *mistaken* 74 percent of the time. Indeed, as the table shows, he would have adopted the incorrect policy 96 percent of the time between 1959.2 and 1971.1, 50 percent of the time between 1971.1 and 1983.1, and 66 percent of the time between 1983.2 and 1993.3. There were sev-

enty-three quarters in which the real rate fell below 1.5 percent. This suggested to Greenspan that tight money policy would be required. However, thirty-seven of these quarters were followed by declining inflation. This policy would have been incorrect 100 percent of the time between 1983.2 and 1993.3, 28 percent of the time between 1971.2 and 1983.1, and 60 percent of the time between 1959.2 and 1971.1— for an overall score of incorrect policy responses 51 percent of the time.

In addition, the real interest rate often misinterprets the "tightness" of the economy as measured by the capacity utilization rate (see *Table 2*). Chairman Greenspan claims that when the real short-term interest rate is below "equilibrium," bottlenecks will follow as capacity-utilization rises, thereby generating inflation. In other words, when the short-term interest rate is below 1.5 percent, capacity utilization is expected to rise, generating inflationary pressures that can be lessened if the Fed adopts tight policy. Similarly, when the real interest rate is above 1.5 percent, capacity utilization is expected to fall. We examined the four-quarter period following each real interest-rate observation to see whether a real rate below 1.5 percent predicts rising capacity-utilization rates and whether a real rate above 1.5 percent indicates falling capacity-utilization rates. We defined a rise or fall as an increase or decrease of capacity utilization by two percentage points or more over any quarter within four quarters of the period under observation.

As Table 2 shows, when the real rate was above 1.5 percent, the Chairman would have chosen the wrong policy 61 percent of the time between 1959.2 and 1971.1, 42 percent of the time between 1971.2 and 1983.1, and 90 percent of the time between 1983.2 and 1993.3—for an overall average of 71 percent incorrect policy choices. In other words, in most

cases, relatively high real interest rates did not foretell falling capacity-utilization rates, so that easy policy was not indicated. On the other hand, when the real rate was below 1.5 percent, the Chairman would have chosen the incorrect policy 68 percent of the time between 1959.2 and 1971.1, 47 percent of the time between 1971.2 and 1983.1, and 67 percent of the time between 1983.2 and 1993.3—for an overall average of 58 percent incorrect policy responses. These tests, then, lead us to conclude that real interest rates do not correctly predict future capacity utilization rates and cannot be used to guide monetary policy designed to affect capacity utilization with a lag of up to a year.

However, our tests assume the Fed did not actually adopt the "correct" (that is, Chairman Greenspan's) policy. For example, if the Fed adopted tight policy each time the real rate fell below 1.5 percent, this would (according to Chairman Greenspan's theory) prevent inflation so that Table 1 would report a policy error (because the low real interest rate would not be followed by inflation). If the Fed actually (perhaps unknowingly) followed Chairman Greenspan's rule, then Table 1 might report a score of 100 percent wrong policy responses. If the Fed had actually adopted perverse policy (that is, the opposite of Chairman Greenspan's rule), then Table 1 could report no policy errors. But, through close examination of actual Fed

---

Expected inflation seems to be the only guide analyzed by the Chairman that has yet to be dismissed. But commentators have noted that expected inflation is frequently not a good predictor of future inflation.

---

discount rate policy, we found that the Fed has, in the past, adopted "perverse" policy a bit more than 40 percent of the time and "correct" policy a bit less than 30 percent of the time. This indicates that the incorrect policy responses of Tables 1 and 2 cannot be attributed to the Fed's unknowing adoption of Chairman Greenspan's policy, because the Fed's past policy appears to be nearly random with respect to Greenspan's prescription.

Greenspan has also claimed that expected inflation is a good predictor of future inflation. Indeed, expected inflation seems to be the only guide analyzed by the Chairman that has yet to be dismissed. But commentators have noted that expected inflation is fre-

Table 3		Volatile Interest Rates		
Period	Mean	Stand. Dev.	Max.	Min.
1959.2–1993.3				
Long-term governments (composite)	7.25	2.61	14.00	3.00
3-month T-bills	6.18	2.80	15.09	2.32
1959.2–1965.4				
Long-term governments (composite)	4.04	0.14	4.35	3.80
3-month T-bills	3.18	0.61	4.30	2.32
1966.1–1977.4				
Long-term governments (composite)	6.08	0.84	7.27	4.44
3-month T-bills	5.59	1.27	8.39	3.43
1978.1–1993.3				
Long-term governments (composite)	9.51	1.87	13.60	6.15
3-month T-bills	7.91	2.96	15.09	2.98

Sources: The Levy Economics Institute Forecasting Center; National Income and Product Account.

quently not a good predictor of future inflation. In 1980, respondents to surveys predicted inflation would average 9 percent over the next decade. Actual inflation turned out to be only half of that. Any policy based on longer-term inflation expectations during the 1980s would have seriously overestimated inflationary pressures. Indeed, the evidence suggests that, rather than expected inflation predicting inflation, inflation expectations are adaptively formed on the basis of current inflation along with past inflation. At best, expected inflation is a good predictor only over the very short run (see Figure 1).

To determine whether expected inflation would serve as a useful target for monetary policy, we looked at data since 1978 on expected inflation, actual inflation, and Fed policy to see whether an increase in inflation expectations could be used as the basis of policy actions to be taken in advance of accelerating inflation. We examined whether an increase in inflation expectations had, in the past, correctly anticipated future inflation. We next examined whether the Fed had knowingly or unknowingly followed this policy in the past. We found that instances of accelerating actual inflation were predicted by rising expected inflation (within the previous four quarters) only 24 percent of the time. In most cases, expected inflation did not cor-

rectly anticipate inflation. We also found that, in the majority of cases where the expected inflation guide does not predict the accelerating inflation that actually occurs, the acceleration of inflation cannot be attributed to easy-money policy.

ALTERNATIVE APPROACH TO MONETARY POLICY

The period from World War II to the late 1960s or early 1970s has frequently been called the "golden age" of U.S. economic history. It is beyond the scope of this article to review in detail all the factors that contributed to the superior economic performance. We will focus, instead, only on the Fed's aggregate monetary policy. The key difference between the early post-

The recent tightening has occurred while government deficits have been falling and after the President and Congress reached agreements that will substantially reduce fiscal stimulus.

war period and the late postwar period is the degree of commitment of the Fed to stable, and generally low, interest rates. In 1951, the Fed abandoned the interest rate peg and gradually abrogated its commitment to low and stable interest rates over time. Still, until 1966, the Fed maintained the discount rate below 4 percent and the three-month Treasury bill rate well below 5 percent. In 1966, the Fed (apparently due to fear of forthcoming inflation) pushed the discount rate to 4.5 percent and the Treasury bill rate above 5 percent. That resulted in the first postwar financial crisis. After 1966, the Fed embarked on a series of attempts to "fine-tune" the economy through the use of tight-money policy each time there was fear that inflation would accelerate. In late 1969, from 1973 to 1974, from 1978 to 1985, and from 1988 to 1990, the Fed pushed short-term rates higher. In each case financial crises and/or recessions ensued.

The transition to attempts at fine-tuning has led to much greater interest-rate instability (see *Table 3*). From mid-1959 to 1966, the standard deviation of the three-month Treasury-bill rate was 0.61, while that of long-term government securities was only 0.14. For the Treasury bills, the standard deviation increased to

1.27 for 1966 to 1978, and to 2.96 for 1978 to 1993. For long-term securities, the standard deviation rose to 0.84 and 1.87 for these periods. While Chairman Greenspan refers to the costs of uncertainty generated by inflation, we believe that the costs generated by unstable interest rates (and exchange rates) may be as important, if not more important. Indeed, the explosion of the derivatives market, which entails substantial costs and risks, is evidence that markets believe interest-rate instability is costly.

We emphasize our belief that active Fed policy is sometimes warranted. We agree that the Fed must retain some discretionary power to take aggressive action when it becomes necessary. But the escalation of its intervention into the economy that has occurred under the leadership of Chairmen Volcker and Greenspan has raised uncertainty, increased instability in domestic financial markets, contributed to instability of the dollar in foreign-exchange markets, generated costs of hedging, and increased interest rate and default risk. It certainly has had deleterious consequences for economic growth. A comparison of the results of Fed policy before and after 1966 suggests that policy directed at stabilizing interest rates more successfully accomplishes the goals outlined in the 1946 Employment Act and the 1978 Full Employment and Balanced Growth Act.

Previous to Chairman Volcker's experiment, the Fed employed tight-money policy to fight perceived inflationary pressures, usually in response to expansionary fiscal policy. For example, the Fed's move to tight policy in 1966 was in the context of a high-employment economy with rising government defense expenditures during the Vietnam War. Tight policy during the early 1980s was frequently justified as necessary to reduce inflationary pressures thought to result from the large and rising government deficits. But the recent tightening has occurred while government deficits have been falling and after the President and Congress reached agreements that will substantially reduce fiscal stimulus. Thus, unlike previous periods in which tight-money policy could be justified on the basis of fiscal policy being excessively stimulative, the current tightening comes while fiscal policy is widely believed to be moving to reduce the stimulus.

The evidence also suggests that Chairman Greenspan's proposed targets (whether real interest rates or expected inflation) would have led to incorrect policy much of the time in the past. There is no reason to expect these will perform any better in the future. By Chairman Greenspan's own admission:

• Our understanding of the economy is imperfect and the measurement of important variables like inflation is imprecise;

• no observable variables are sufficiently well-correlated with inflation to allow their use in policy formation;

• the impact of monetary policy on the economy is subject to long, uncertain, and variable lags;

• economic theory does not provide unambiguous guidance for the formation of monetary policy;

• there is no consensus regarding how the Fed can stabilize prices even if, as Chairman Greenspan claims, there is growing consensus that central-bank policy should stabilize prices.

However, we do not agree that this should be the sole goal of monetary policy. Nor does Congress agree. It has twice directed the Fed also to pursue full employment.

The Fed has moved to tighten policy this year while citing a variety of arguments to justify its actions. But recent statements have suggested that Fed policy is based on hunches rather than on any specific indicators. Governor LaWare admitted to Keith Bradsher of the *New York Times*, "I get a feel

---

The tighter monetary policy was a mistake, and it would be an even greater mistake to tighten further.

---

for what I think is going on based on the information—not only the anecdotal information in the press and the statistical information assembled and compiled by the staff here, but also from the general tone of the markets. I'm probably least sensitive to the money figures because I don't know what they mean anymore."

Noted monetarist Jerry L. Jordan admits: "In the last thirty years, economists have uncovered little additional information about how monetary policy works, except for the finding that expectations of future policy are vitally important in the process." David Jones, a long-time Fed watcher, says that "policy has become more intuitive over the last year." Bradsher reports that "Fed officials in effect rely on educated hunches of what they should do, rather than following the dictates of computer models or a couple of key indicators." And finally, Governor Lindsey's statement to Bradsher summarizes the problem faced by the Fed: "I came on believing what I had been taught—and taught as a professor—which was M_2. I

don't think I can use it anymore. [Instead] we look at a whole raft of variables. We ignore nothing and focus on nothing."

The Fed's stance from mid-1992 to February 1994 was the correct policy. By holding the discount rate at 3 percent, the Fed allowed short-term rates to fall quickly, and long-term rates gradually declined. The economy began to recover from a prolonged recession. Firms and households were able to refinance at lower interest rates. They reduced debt loads, thereby allowing them to undertake new spending. Unemployment fell. The government interest burden declined and the federal budget deficit was reduced. Financial institutions and markets recovered. And the dollar held steady in foreign-exchange markets (although it fell against the yen, which is exactly what it should have done given the large U.S. trade deficit with Japan). The experience since February 1994 stands in stark contrast to the relative tranquility of that period. The tighter monetary policy was a mistake, and it would be an even greater mistake to tighten further.

VAIN PURSUIT OF ZERO INFLATION

The experiment of targeting monetary aggregates has been a failure. Chairman Greenspan has proposed replacing monetary aggregates with either real interest rate or expected inflation targets. We have cast some doubt on Chairman Greenspan's choice of either a real interest rate or expected inflation target for monetary policy. We have also argued that, had the Chairman adopted such targets in the past, this would not have helped to stabilize the economy. We also cast doubt on the use of expected inflation data series as the basis of policy formulation. Chairman Greenspan has argued that current conditions indicate inflation will soon accelerate, and will impose intolerable costs on society. It is apparent that the only justification for frequent changes of policy is, to a great extent, the Fed's intuition regarding what will lower inflation expectations and the Fed's hypothesis that lower inflation expectations are necessary to prevent a future acceleration of inflation. We see little evidence that inflation is likely to accelerate. Globally, manufacturing is operating far below capacity. Real wages are falling in the United States and in other developed economies. Labor productivity has risen rapidly in the United States. Many Eastern European countries are set to increase exports. Unemployment rates are high among most OECD nations. And low-wage, high-unemploy-

ment countries in the developing world can increase exports to meet any rise of world demand. Most important, we do not agree that the moderate inflation achieved recently entails significant costs. Indeed, the benefits to be gained by eliminating this inflation cannot be expected to exceed the costs that would be engendered by higher unemployment, greater uncer-

---

> ## *Fed policy should be refocused on providing a stable financial sector (through lender-of-last-resort policy and maintenance of low interest rates).*

---

tainty, and lost output. Until economists obtain a clearer estimate of the costs of inflation, of policies that can be used successfully to fight inflation, and of the costs of fighting inflation, pursuit of zero inflation as the ultimate goal of monetary policy must be seen as an insupportable, risky, and excessively radical proposition.

What is most apparent from recent policy statements is that the Fed's policy has become increasingly rudderless. The Fed appears to be "flying blind." It has chosen target variables that reflect "hunches" that inflation will rise. The result is a series of destabilizing policy changes that disrupt financial markets and have negative impacts on the "real" sector (that is, on employment and investment decisions). Rather than watching inflation or other economic variables, Wall Street is watching the Fed. It is trying to guess what the Fed might do next. Even the noted monetarist, William Poole, argues: "It's a very dangerous game to play, to drag out whatever indicator is pointing in the right direction."

Inflation has been, is, and is likely to be, well within acceptable limits. Fed policy should be refocused on providing a stable financial sector (through lender-of-last-resort policy and maintenance of low interest rates). This will help to provide an environment in which employment can rise. Given the current state of the economy, it is far more important to focus on full employment than on inflation.

For Further Reading

The following books and articles may be of interest to readers who would like to explore the topics in this issue more fully.

ROBERT A. BRUSCA, "The Economy Squeezed: Between a Rock and a Hard Place," *Challenge,* September–October 1993.

STEVEN M. FAZZARI and HYMAN P. MINSKY, "Domestic Monetary Policy: If Not Monetarism, What?" *Journal of Economic Issues,* March 1984.

MILTON FRIEDMAN, "Lessons from the 1979–82 Monetary Policy Experiment," *American Economic Review,* May 1984.

JAMES K. GALBRAITH, "Self-Fulfilling Prophets: Inflated Zeal at the Federal Reserve," *The American Prospect,* Summer 1994.

WILLIAM GREIDER, *The Trouble With Money: A Prescription for America's Financial Fever,* Whittle Direct Books, 1989.

HENRY KAUFMAN, "Opportunities and Challenges Confronting Monetary Policy," *Challenge,* September–October 1993.

HYMAN P. MINSKY, *Stabilizing an Unstable Economy,* Yale University Press, 1986.

WALLACE PETERSON, *The Silent Depression: The Fate of the American Dream,* Norton, 1994.

PAUL A. SAMUELSON, "Leaning Against What Inflationary Wind?" *Challenge,* September–October 1993.

MARTIN WOLFSON, *Financial Crises,* M. E. Sharpe. 1986.

It's Not Broke: So Don't Fix It: Why The Federal Reserve Should Not Be Reformed

Harvey Rosenblum

Harvey Rosenblum is Senior Vice President and Director of Research, Federal Reserve Bank of Dallas, TX. The original version of this paper was presented at the Annual Economic Policy Meeting of the National Association of Business Economists, Washington, DC, February 23, 1994. The views expressed are the author's and do not necessarily reflect the opinions of the Federal Reserve System.

> *Several proposals have been made that would fundamentally change the way the Federal Reserve conducts monetary policy and remove the Fed's role in bank supervision and regulation. These reforms would seriously reduce the Fed's effectiveness in carrying out is mission. In particular, the exquisite set of checks and balances between the public and private sector organization aspects of the Fed would be removed, thereby subjecting the Fed to direct political control. This would reduce even further the Fed's ability to pursue price stability and sustainable economic growth.*

DURING THE PAST FEW YEARS, proposals have been made that would reform the Federal Reserve System (the Fed) in at least five areas: (1) the conduct of monetary policy; (2) the Fed's role in bank regulation; (3) the degree of Fed independence, particularly the amount of openness vs. secrecy accorded to monetary policy; (4) the Fed's role in dealing with systemic risk; and (5) privatizing the Fed's role in the payments system. Altering the Fed's role in any single one of these areas would seriously reduce the Fed's ability to respond appropriately to changing economic and financial conditions. Any combination of these proposed reforms would likely render the Fed impotent in dealing with a financial crisis. Given the Fed's strong and competent performance in all of its operational areas, it would appear that efforts to reform the Fed are either misguided or based upon criteria that have little to do with the Fed's performance against congressionally established goals.

THE FED'S MISSION, GOALS AND ORGANIZATIONAL STRUCTURE

The Fed's mission is to protect the integrity of our nation's money by providing a healthy banking and financial system that is consistent with, and that can support, price stability and sustainable economic growth. These are the purposes and functions that the Fed was created to achieve; this basic mission has not changed for eighty years.

The economic, financial, and social environment has changed over time, and the Fed has evolved by transforming itself, and the way it does business, in response to this changing environment. The Fed is now a market-driven and customer-driven entity. The textbooks refer to the Fed as "a quasi-government institution," i.e., the Fed has elements of both the public and private sector in its form, functions, and operations. The Fed's primary mandate is public policy; for this reason it was created by an act of Congress rather than by the private sector. In this context, the Fed can be thought of as a government instrumentality (or bureaucracy) that runs on private sector rhetoric.

Given this environment, the Fed's operational goal is to maximize the return and value of the Fed to its shareholders. The shareholders are the roughly 260 million U.S. citizens. The Fed's outside directors and governance board are the U.S. Congress and the Administration. Like a private sector board of directors, they choose the Fed's chief executive officer, the Chairman of the Federal Reserve Board. And like the board of directors of many not-for-profit institutions, the President and Congress select many of the members of the Fed's most senior management ranks, namely, the six governors on the Federal Reserve Board. The Congress, like any governance board, sets the Fed's goals and broad policy guidelines, and then monitors the conformance and performance against these goals and guidelines.

From *Business Economics*, October 1994, pp. 37-42. © 1994 by the National Association of Business Economists. Reprinted by permission.

4. MONEY, BANKING, AND MONETARY POLICY

To carry out its mission and mandates, the Fed has organized itself into three seemingly separate but, in reality, three *inseparable* business divisions: (1) monetary and economic policy; (2) supervision and regulation of the banking and financial system; and (3) the provision of payments system services to the financial system and the U.S. Treasury. These are *not* separate subsidiaries on an organization chart. They work as a coordinated unit, especially during times of financial stress in an effort to minimize systemic risk. Even during periods of economic and financial "normalcy," these units work closely together to minimize payments system risk and to monitor developments in the banking and financial system for early warning signs of changes in economic conditions.

The Fed is an adaptive, market-driven institution. Nowhere is this clearer than in the provision of payments services (check clearing, wire transfer, ACH, and cash/coin services). The Monetary Control Act of 1980 mandated the Fed to charge explicit prices for these services and to exit the business if it could not compete successfully with the private sector. To the surprise of its detractors, the Fed successfully met that challenge. What is not recognized is that the same management principles that guided the Fed to meet the challenge of competing in the provision of payments services — such as cost cutting, efficiency, customer satisfaction, quality, and market responsiveness — have spilled over to and permeated the management and employees throughout the rest of the Fed organization.

If, in the name of reform or reinventing government, the Fed were divided into separate entities or merged into other parts of government, the market-driven imperative to be "lean and mean" would be lost throughout all the splintered parts of the previous Fed organization. If one wants to reinvent or reform government, the Fed is the likely standard or role model that other parts of government should aspire to emulate. The Fed's not perfect — after all, it is run by humans — but it has adapted itself to be a learning organization that responds to changes in its external environment and does a generally fine to outstanding job of balancing a number of complex and oftentimes conflicting goals. The Fed must internalize several tradeoffs, such as bank safety and soundness, economic growth, price stability, and an efficient yet leading edge payments system. In judging the need to reform the Fed, the standard of comparison should be other institutions that must balance complex and conflicting mandates, not entities that pursue a single mandate with tunnel vision.

The word "reform" means a major change in the mission, goals, purpose and structure of an institution. Such a reformation might be necessitated by the failure of the institution to perform its mission, or a failure to adapt the way it carries out its mission to a changing external environment. As mentioned above, the Fed has not failed to perform its mission and has adapted well to a changing economic and financial landscape. Thus, the motives for reforming the Fed likely have little to do with the Fed's accomplishment of its mission.

THE CONDUCT OF MONETARY POLICY

Discussions about reforming the Fed in the monetary policy arena have centered around two questions: (1) whether monetary policy has been too easy or too tight or, more importantly, whether there has been a persistent bias toward excessive ease or tightness; and, (2) whether there is constitutional legitimacy for Federal Reserve Bank presidents serving on the FOMC?

The Appropriate Stance For Monetary Policy

Achieving a consensus from the economics profession on the appropriate direction for monetary policy has never been an easy task. In recent times, op-ed articles have appeared in the *Wall Street Journal* written by leading economists who argue that monetary policy has been either too tight or too easy. In recent times, articles by Milton Friedman and by James Buchanan, both Nobel Laureates, concluded that monetary policy has been too tight.[1] The basis for their view is that M2 growth has been at the low end or below the bottom end of the Fed's target range for M2. More recently, Allan Meltzer concluded that monetary policy was too easy.[2] The basis for Meltzer's conclusion is that narrow measures of money, such as M1 and the monetary base, have been growing well above their historical averages over the past few years.

If the leading monetarists of our day cannot agree whether monetary policy is too tight or too easy, imagine the difficulty the Fed faces in setting its monetary growth targets. The need to set money growth targets is established by law in the Full Employment and Balanced Growth Act of 1978, otherwise known as the Humphrey-Hawkins Act. Thus, the Fed is required by statute to follow monetarist principles.

The problem with being a monetarist these days is finding a measure of money that has all the right properties: (1) a stable velocity, i.e., a measure of money that bears a predictable relationship to nominal income; (2) a measure of money whose growth rate correlates well with *future* rates of inflation; and (3) a measure of money that is subject to some degree of control, or at least predictable influence, by the Fed. Unfortunately, finding a single monetary aggregate that simultaneously has all three of these properties has been difficult, if not impossible, thus far in the 1990s decade.

---

[1] See footnotes at end of text.

To deal with these problems, several Federal Reserve economists have developed experimental measures of money that overcome some of the shortcomings of M2. The Dallas Fed has developed a broader measure of M2 that includes bond funds.[3] This bond fund-adjusted M2 has a more stable velocity than M2 and correlates much better with future inflation than M2. However, the Fed has even less influence on bond fund-adjusted M2 than conventional M2, i.e., hardly any control at all. Some economists at the Board of Governors have been experimenting with a bond and stock mutual fund-adjusted measure of M2 that also exhibits a stable relationship with nominal income and future inflation, but suffers even more with respect to the controllability issue.[4]

The key point is that the Fed has demonstrated considerable flexibility and adaptability regarding the "guiding light" (or indicator or information variable) it uses in the conduct of monetary policy. The Fed's focus has been on the economy, not on hitting a particular monetary aggregate target for its own sake. This is an especially important distinction because, as mentioned earlier, the relationship between the Fed's conventional measures of money and the ultimate policy goals, such as nominal income and future inflation, has broken down.

The breakdown in the relationship between money and economic performance in the 1990s is not unprecedented; it happened around 1973-75 and again in the early 1980s. Changes in regulations, advances in technology and financial innovation have altered the competitive structure of the banking and financial system and thereby undermined the paradigm on which previous econometric understanding of monetary relationships rested. In reaction to these shifting paradigms, the FOMC shifted its monetary focus from M1 in the late 1970s and early 1980s, to M2 in the late 1980s, to ever-reduced emphasis on M2 in the early 1990s. If the experimental measures of M2 that are broadened to include bond and/or stock mutual funds should turn out to have the set of desirable properties one wants in a target variable, then the FOMC will shift its monetary focus once again. In a dynamic, free enterprise economy where markets are allowed to work, it should be expected that relationships between monetary indicators and the economy will continue to change over time. The best that can be achieved under these circumstances is to shift from one monetary indicator to another in an effort to splice these changing paradigms together.[5]

Even if the economy and the financial system did not evolve over time, it would still be difficult for the Fed to stick with and exploit any stable relationship between a single measure of money and economic performance. The Fed has long understood Goodhart's Law (that any observed statistical regularity will tend

to collapse once pressure is placed on it for control purpose) and has adapted its monetary policy accordingly.

If one wanted to reform the Fed for reasons having to do with monetary policy shortcomings, it should be based on the Fed's *not* having adapted to changing monetary relationships, rather than the other way around. The Fed has done a good job on conducting monetary policy in an environment where economic relationships have been plagued by a high degree of uncertainty. In short, don't reform what's working well.

This discussion highlights the dangers of a monetary rule. In a fixed institutional environment, monetary growth rules may have some merit. But during an era of shifting paradigms, as has been the experience of the past twenty-five years or so, a monetary rule would, more often than not, have been counterproductive. Reforming the Fed by introducing a monetary rule would not be reforming the Fed; rather, it would be a disaster for the economy and would destroy the Fed at the same time. This raises questions about the underlying agenda of those who would have the Fed follow a monetary rule.

FED Presidents On The FOMC

Over the past two years, two bills have been introduced that would alter the membership of the FOMC, thereby reforming the Fed in a material way. One bill sponsored by Senator Sarbanes would remove the presidents of the twelve Federal Reserve Banks from the FOMC.[6] The Sarbanes bill would create, instead, a Federal Open Market Advisory Committee consisting of the twelve Fed presidents that would meet at least four times a year and advise the Board of Governors on monetary policy and open market operations.

What would be the impact of the Sarbanes bill? Anybody who has been in Washington recognizes that advice without a vote is the same thing as having no input at all. It would eliminate the diversity of views, research, and regional input that are so critical in the making of monetary policy. It would be analogous to the Congress having to rely solely on the Administration's economic forecasts and budget projections without being allowed independent analysis of its own.

In a bill introduced by Congressman Henry B. Gonzalez, the Fed presidents would be appointed by the U.S. President and would be confirmed by the Senate.[7] Under the Gonzalez bill, the governance role of the quasi-private sector board of directors of the Reserve Banks would be diminished in that they would no longer choose the chief executive officer of each Reserve Bank. The motive behind this reform seems

to be that, in the minds of its sponsors, such a reform would be more in keeping with *their* interpretation of the U.S. Constitution.

Three concerns with the Gonzalez bill are worth noting:

1. A long series of court challenges have been made of the constitutional legitimacy of the Fed presidents serving as voting members of the FOMC. These challenges have gone all the way to the U.S. Supreme Court, but all of the court decisions that have been handed down have been in favor of the status quo. In one District Court[8] decision that is worth mentioning, Judge Harold H. Greene noted that the "exquisite balance" of political compromises that has sought to blend public and private interests would be destroyed by altering the appointments process for Fed presidents, and that "while the composition of the Federal Open Market Committee may be unusual, it is not unconstitutional."

2. The current appointments process for Fed presidents is based on a long historical precedent in that the present day structure of the Federal Reserve System is modeled after the First Bank of the United States, particularly with regard to the role and appointment process for the chief executives of the branches of the Fed. Many of the same people who wrote the U.S. Constitution participated in writing or approving the legislation that founded the First Bank of the United States. If this private-public blend was deemed to be constitutionally correct in the eyes of our Founding Fathers, why should we doubt the constitutional legitimacy of the Fed president appointment process two centuries later?

3. The Gonzalez bill would largely disenfranchise the boards of directors of the Federal Reserve Banks. By removing the ability to appoint, reappoint, and influence the salary and managerial direction of the Fed presidents, the Gonzalez bill would reduce the role of directors to acting as an advisory committee, whose advice and counsel could be largely ignored by a political appointee whose agenda may have little to do with the economic and financial needs of the Federal Reserve district. This could reduce the quality and effectiveness of the private sector input received by the Fed. By diminishing the influence of directors, this reform could reduce the willingness of potential directors, including women and minorities, to serve on Reserve Bank boards.

REGULATORY REFORM

The U.S. Treasury has proposed that the regulatory and supervisory functions of the Fed, and the three other federal banking agencies — the Office of the Comptroller of the Currency (OCC), the Federal Deposit Insurance Corporation (FDIC), and the Office of Thrift Supervision (OTS) — be consolidated into a single Federal Banking Commission.[9] This consolidation, it is argued, would streamline the regulatory process and reduce the costs of bank regulation for the industry and the taxpayers. Whether these goals would be achieved by consolidation is another matter. Robert Glauber, former Undersecretary of the Treasury for Finance, has argued that this new Treasury proposal would replace the present regulatory system, imperfect though it may be, with "the Blob — a monolithic, centralized, plodding regulator almost certain to be less innovative and more costly."[10]

The Fed has issued its own regulatory reform counterproposal.[11] The Fed proposal would reduce the number of federal regulators from four to two by consolidating the OCC and OTS, relegate the FDIC to being an insurer, and make the Fed the federal regulator over state chartered banks, and bank holding companies whose lead bank is state chartered. This would result in having one supervisory agency per banking organization. The exception would be the very largest banking organizations that pose systemic risk issues to the financial system. They and their nonbank subsidiaries would be supervised by the Fed, while their bank subs would be supervised by the primary regulator of their lead bank. One of the primary benefits of the Fed proposal, particularly from the viewpoint of banks, is that it retains some degree of choice for banks in selecting their federal supervisory agency.

Much has been written over the years about the pros and cons of bank regulatory reform. A few points not covered elsewhere are worthy of mention. First, most advocates of regulatory reform generally point out that in most other countries, the central bank generally has little or no superviosry authority over the banking system. What is generally *not* pointed out, however, is that *no* other country has a banking structure like that in the United States. It is easy to have direct contact with and influence over the CEOs of most banks in a country when there is only a handful or at most a couple dozen banks. It is quite another matter to have an on-going, working relationship with the banking community that can be depended upon in a financial crisis when there are more than eleven thousand banks, as happens to be the case in the United States. Furthermore, while many central banks have no formal *statutory* role in bank regulation, they do have an important informal role, especially during a crisis when their lender of last resort function must be exercised. Again, it is easier to serve the *informal* regulatory role when there are only a few banks to deal with.

In discussing the need to maintain a hands-on bank supervision role, many in the Fed have suggested that bank supervision enhances its ability to conduct monetary policy. While this argument is correct, an even stronger argument can be made the other way around. Namely, monetary policy duties enhance bank supervision. As mentioned earlier, the Fed's mandate calls

for it to balance the goals of economic growth, bank safety and soundness, price stability, and financial system stability in a holistic way.

The OCC and FDIC are accountable for safety and soundness only. Given the Fed's broader set of responsibilities, it was no surprise that the Fed was the first regulatory agency to voice concern over and admit the existence of the credit crunch of 1990-92. Were it not for its monetary policy role and the responsibilities that it entailed, the Fed might have acted like the OCC and FDIC, pursuing the safety and soundness goal irrespective of the economic consequences. However, and this is the key point, the Fed, OCC, and FDIC compete for client institutions, with the result that some of the Fed's need to internalize these goal trade-offs spills over to the actions of the other regulators. Take the Fed out of bank supervision, however, and *no* regulatory agency will focus on the broader set of goals that is necessary for a healthy economy as well as a healthy banking and financial system. People often lose sight of the fact that, under the Treasury's proposal, banks would operate in a world in which there is a monopoly regulator that pursues only bank safety and soundness, and not a world like there is now where having one regulator pursuing a broader set of goals is tantamount to having all regulators, to some degree, acting as if they shared this broader goal set.

The last concern with regulatory restructuring is the motives behind it. If consolidating the regulatory agencies is supposed to benefit the banks by reducing their costs of compliance, why is it that there has been no ground swell of bank support for the Treasury's proposal? To the extent there has been overt support for regulatory reform, the banking system seems to be behind the Fed's proposal. If government is to be reinvented, it should be done for the benefit of constituents, not for its own sake or for the sake of consolidating political power.

FED INDEPENDENCE AND OPENNESS

With the exception of the United States, there has been a noticeable trend around the world toward making central banks *more independent*, not less independent. Canada, Mexico, Great Britain, New Zealand, France, and Argentina have all taken measures to strengthen the independence of their central banks. Many of the recent attempts to reform the Fed would undermine the Fed's independence in subtle, and perhaps, unintentional ways. In a country like the United States, which suffers from a $4 trillion level of federal debt, one of the few bulwarks against rising inflation is Fed credibility. The financial markets understand this very well, and they react warily whenever the Fed's independence is threatened. Rising inflationary expectations, and its corollary, high interest rates, will come back if the firewall between the Fed and the rest of government continues to be undermined.

In this context, it is useful to discuss another attempt to reform the Fed by requiring the videotaping of FOMC meetings. Such an attempt to increase the openness of Fed policy deliberations by statute seems to be an over-reaction to the perceived lack of openness, and would constitute a major reform of the Fed's way of doing business. It would reduce the Fed's independence by making every member of Congress, in effect, an ex-officio member of the FOMC.

Most economists, including the author, favor more immediate release of FOMC policy *decisions*. This is a separate issue from videotaping the FOMC meetings. Videotaping would destroy the deliberative process, undermine the collegial consensus building that is an essential element in the determination and formulation of monetary policy, and result in FOMC meetings becoming a series of bland or politically motivated statements aimed to please and appease the folks back home.

The FOMC already divulges a great deal of information about its activities, probably as much as most government agencies. If Congress desires more timely information about FOMC decisions and activities, standards for timely release of information can be negotiated with the FOMC. This is more like turning a dial slightly in the direction of more timely release. There is a substantial difference between a slight nudge of the dial and the big, sudden twisting of the dial that would be entailed by proposed legislation on videotaping monetary policy deliberations. Turning the dial toward shedding a little more light on FOMC *decisions*, and seeing if this works as intended, would seem to be a necessary first step before jerking the dial all the way toward full disclosure.

SYSTEMIC RISK

As the lender of last resort, the Fed stands ready to deal with financial crises that have the potential to disrupt the economy, whether such crises originate with banks regulated by the Fed or whether they originate elsewhere in the banking or financial system. Clearly, the Treasury's proposal to remove the Fed from bank supervision would reduce the Fed's effectiveness in dealing with any financial disruption, let alone a financial crisis that could escalate into a systemic disaster.

One other proposal to reform the Fed has important, but not well understood, implications of systemic risk. This reform proposal would remove the Fed from the payments system by privatizing its payment system operations. In doing so, it would remove the possibility of the Fed acting as the check clearer (or payments system provider) of last resort.

4. MONEY, BANKING, AND MONETARY POLICY

The importance of having a check clearer of last resort is illustrated by the experience of the Dallas Fed during the Texas banking crisis of 1986-89 and by the Boston Fed during the New England banking crisis of 1990-91. When one or more major regional correspondent banks encounter financial difficulties, their respondent banks tend to utilize the Fed's check clearing arrangements because of the difficulty of finding another safe correspondent. Similarly, whenever smaller respondent banks get in financial trouble, all corespondent banks tend to shut them out of the check clearing network at the first hint of trouble, thus hastening their demise. Had the Fed not taken on the added check volume during the era of increased bank failures, it is possible that the economic ramifications of those bank failures would have been much more serious for the communities involved. The lesson to be learned is that the Fed is designed to deal with these types of market failures in the payments system. If the Fed were removed from the payments system, there would be no *public* entity that could step in at a moment's notice to prevent a banking crisis from becoming a payment system crisis and economic crisis next time around.

SUMMARY

It is ironic that there are so many proposals to reform the Fed at a time when the U.S. economy is performing quite well on an absolute basis and relative to other industrial nations, and when the banking and financial system are as healthy as they have been in quite some time. While many of these reforms appear to be well intentioned, virtually all of the reforms reviewed in this article would be detrimental to the economy and the banking and financial system, and would seriously diminish the Fed's ability to intervene to minimize the effects of an incipient financial crisis. In short, "It's not broke, so don't fix it."

FOOTNOTES

[1] Milton Friedman, "Too Tight for Strong Recovery," *Wall Street Journal*, October 23, 1992; and James Buchanan and David Fand, "Monetary Policy: Malpractice at the Fed," *Wall Street Journal*, December 21, 1992.

[2] Alan Meltzer, "Still Too Easy," *Wall Street Journal*, February 9, 1994.

[3] John Duca, "Monitoring Money: Should Bond Funds be Added to M2?" *Southwest Economy*, Federal Reserve Bank of Dallas, Special Edition, June 1993.

[4] Work done at the Federal Reserve Board is summarized in two papers presented at a St. Louis Fed Symposium on March 24, 1994. See Athanasios Orphanides, Brian Reid, and David Small, "The Empirical Properties of a Monetary Aggregate that Adds Bond and Stock Mutual Funds to M2;" and Sean Collins and Cheryl Edwards, "Issues in Measuring a Monetary Aggregate Containing Bond and Equity Mutual Funds."

[5] Havey Rosenblum, "The Impact of Banking Reform on Monetary Policy," unpublished paper presented at the Western Economic Association Annual Conference, June 21, 1993.

[6] S. 219, "Monetary Policy Reform Act of 1993," sponsored by Senator Paul Sarbanes, et.al.

[7] H.R. 28, "The Federal Reserve Accountability Act of 1993," introduced by Congressman Henry B. Gonzalez.

[8] Melcher v. Federal Open Market Committee, 644 F. Supp. (D.D.C. 1986), p. 510-524. (Quotes from p. 524.)

[9] On March 1, 1994, Treasury Secretary Lloyd Bentsen introduced proposed legislation for the Treasury Department's single regulator plan, S. 1895, the "Regulatory Consolidation Act of 1994."

[10] Robert R. Glauber, "The Blob that Killed Bank Reform," *Wall Street Journal*, December 13, 1993.

[11] John LaWare, "Comment: LaWare Finds Flaws in Regulatory Reform," *American Banker*, January 4, 1994.

Banking: Real Risks Require Real Reforms

Mounting problems in the banking industry loom. Can we avert them?

EDWARD W. HILL AND
ROGER J. VAUGHAN

Edward W. Hill is an associate professor and economist at the Levin College of Urban Affairs at Cleveland State University, and Roger J. Vaughan is an economic consultant based in Santa Fe, N.M. They are the authors of Banking on the Brink: The Troubled Future of American Finance, *published by Washington Post Company Briefing Books.*

America currently has two banking industries: one, with about 10,000 members, is healthy, profitable and competitive; the other, with fewer than 2,000 members, is undercapitalized, unprofitable and dying. The future of American banking as a whole depends on how quickly politicians and regulators deal with the latter.

Unfortunately for healthy banks and taxpayers, Washington—and the banking industry itself—seem to be suffering from chronic denial that a massive problem exists.

Federal banking regulators continue to minimize the number of banks that must be closed, pinning their hopes on a much delayed economic recovery or upon the magical powers of deregulation, and eerily replaying the behavior of savings-and-loan regulators a decade ago.

Yet, regulators are not alone in repeating the steps taken in the savings-and-loan minuet. The banking lobby itself is closing ranks around its weaker members, sacrificing the interests of its larger constituency—healthy bank holding companies—in a vain and doomed attempt to prolong the lives of the industry's crippled giants.

We called our recently published book *Banking on the Brink* not only because we identified nearly 2,000 banks on the brink of failure, restructuring or merger, but also because we believe that *the industry stands on the brink of radical change*. It is being transformed by both fierce competition from non-banks and the technological revolution sweeping through the world's capital markets.

Dramatic change coming

The industry is poised to shrink dramatically, with its survivors falling into one of three categories: retail banks, merchant banks, and loan boutiques.

Even more significant is that this transformation will restructure the geography of banking. *The all-purpose financial supermarket that many of New York's money-center banks tried to become is quickly fading*, and with it the overwhelming influence of New York, Chicago and Los Angeles as banking centers. These cities will continue to house merchant banks, arranging complex financial transactions for large corporate customers in global markets and earning their income from fees instead of loans. Because these merchant banks do not need deposits to fund their operations, they will be unwilling to submit to high insurance premiums and inconvenient regulations. In fact, many merchant banks already are contemplating turning in their bank charters, choosing instead to operate as financial corporations. These institutions could offer money-market mutual funds rather than checking accounts and could borrow on the commercial paper market instead of using brokered certificates of deposits.

So, who will meet America's day-to-day banking needs? It will be the *new breed of retail banks*, emerging from a group of successful super-regional banks. These retail banks will live on their ability to mass-market banking services—from checking accounts and ATMs to credit cards, home mortgages and home equity loans. The winners in this category will be those banks that keep costs low, are well-capitalized, and take advantage of scale economies in advertising, marketing and credit scoring.

Retail banks now have more in common with Wal-Mart than than they do with J.P. Morgan, and their continued expansion will likely resemble the hub-

and-spoke strategy used by airlines. Retail giants are currently, or soon will be, located in so-called second- and third-tier cities often in the heart of the Rust Belt, where costs are much lower than in yesterday's financial centers. They can be found in Albany (KeyCorp), Pittsburgh (Mellon Bank Corp. and PNC Financial Corp.), Cleveland (Society Corp. and National City Corp.), Columbus (Banc One Corp. and Huntington Bancshares, Inc.), Detroit (Comerica Inc. and N.B.D. Bancorp Inc.), Minneapolis (First Bank System Inc. and Norwest), and, possibly, St. Louis (Boatmen's Bancshares Inc.).

Other major headquarters cities include Charlotte (NCNB Corp. and First Wachovia Corp.), and San Francisco (BankAmerica Corp.). Although Cincinnati has two excellent retail banks in Fifth Third Bancorp and Star Banc Corp., both are currently too small to be considered giants. The endangered banking species are smaller regionals lacking either a large market or large market share, or those banks that attempt to combine retail and merchant banking within the same corporate structure.

Bank management, as recent events have shown, cannot control a fully diversified supermarket-type institution. Merchant banks and super-regionals can't serve everyone. Smaller businesses will need their own loan boutiques—small lending institutions familiar with their industry or local community. Loan boutiques, such as Commerce Exchange Bank in Beachwood, Ohio and Chicago's South Shore Bank, will operate as a small-business analogy to consumer finance corporations.

Evolution requires extinction

There is little question that the banking industry will continue to shrink over the decade. It already plays a much smaller role in the financial system than it did two decades ago, with growing international financial markets replacing many of the traditional functions of banks. This shrinkage will generate a fierce public-policy debate over the banking industry in terms both arcane and confusing. Fortunately, the lay person needs only to remember two simple questions to keep his or her bearings in the coming storm of verbiage: How will the banking industry shrink? Will healthy banks be able to retain their current international competitive strength, or will the burden of supporting their weaker competitors drag them down as well?

If what you hear in the upcoming discussion about banks and banking does not ring true when you con-

sider these questions, hold on to your wallet. The great banking debate, if it is to have any meaning, should be about how to shrink the industry at the least cost to the taxpayer. Keeping crippled banking giants alive neither shrinks the industry nor minimizes taxpayer cost.

Despite what you may hear, *there is a mounting problem in commercial banking*, resulting largely from bankers' overindulgence in commercial real estate during the 1980s. But if we act promptly, the problem may be less of a shock to taxpayers and to healthy banks than if we deny and delay.

According to our analysis in *Banking on the Brink*, there are now roughly 2,000 troubled banks and 300 troubled bank holding companies, with combined book assets of more than $1 trillion. Perhaps 1,200 or so of these banks are likely to either fail, become victims of forced mergers, or reorganize themselves. This is not a radical estimate; the FDIC has roughly 1,000 banks on its own secret list of "problem banks," and it publicly admits that between one-quarter and one-half of these banks will fail within two to three years.

And yet, banking industry spokesmen blandly insist that all is well, pointing to this year's record profits as proof. Unfortunately, the very basis of these profits is creating future problems. Why? Because most of the earnings of weak banks are the result of the industry's plunge into government securities. Banks are able to profit from the difference (or spread) between the low rates they pay to depositors and the higher rates they earn on "riskless" government securities in the face of weak borrowing demand.

No sensible observer thinks that these interest-rate spreads can continue indefinitely. The bond markets are already making allowances for a rise in short-term interest rates; so, weak commercial bankers may soon be caught in the same vise that crushed thrift executives a decade ago.

As spreads narrow (and they must), bank earnings will plummet. When this happens, weak banks' true problems—the reduced valuations that should have been assigned to commercial real estate loans—will become painfully obvious. At the same time, confident assurances from bankers that the government securities they hold will be easy and profitable to sell will ring hollow.

In a market suddenly flooded with bank-held securities that have lost value, ask this question: Who will buy and at how much of a loss to the selling banks? This mismatch is most apparent in weak commercial

banks eager to book quick earnings to offset their defective commercial real estate loans.

Of these banks, Boston College's Edward Kane has said, "This is not only the same road that the thrifts traveled, it is the same rut in the road." As Federal Reserve Chairman Alan Greenspan recently told a Japanese audience, America is bogged down in the worst recession since World War II. The principal culprit is a continuing slide in asset prices. Nowhere is this slide more apparent than in the commercial real estate market, in which even the "appraised" values—to which banks mark down non-performing real estate loans—often are well above realistic market values. The U.S. Comptroller of the Currency reported in October that banks were receiving 50 cents on the dollar of the appraised value of real estate they owned.

Given time, the overwhelming majority of banks will work through this problem, as they did earlier problems with other forms of high-risk lending. But weak banks with weak managers face insolvency.

The cost of delay

The core of the banking crisis lies in 54 bank holding companies, *14 with more than $10 billion apiece in assets and another 40 with assets between $1 billion and $10 billion each.*

If the portfolios of each of these holding companies had been given honest market valuations, it is likely that none could have demonstrated a positive net worth at the end of 1991. Several are too poor to write off their bad loans, too weak to survive without deposit insurance, and too large to be swallowed by even the most gluttonous competitor.

Yet, over the course of the past year, *industry analysts have claimed that these banks were staging a turnaround. This is almost certainly wrong.* The improvement that has occurred in bank stock prices, and the ease with which even relatively weak banks raised new equity, is largely the result of three external factors: the Federal Reserve's decision to lower reserve requirements, the FDIC's decision to bail out sick banks before they became truly insolvent, and falling interest rates allowing banks to cut their cost of funds even more rapidly than their loan rates.

None of this changes the underlying problems facing weaker banks. This year's record bank profits, applauded by the industry's cheerleaders, have done little or nothing for sick banks. Strong banks have grown stronger and weak banks weaker.

Congress and the administration must decide when and how these crippled giants will be liquidated, restructured, or merged with healthy and willing partners. And the longer Washington delays, the higher the ultimate bill. Had Washington acted to resolve the banking crisis at the start of 1992, for instance, it would have cost the Bank Insurance Fund (BIF) about $50 billion, most of which could probably have been covered by the fund's resources.

The cost and consequences of this delay will be tremendous. The banking problem can easily grow to $75 billion. Weak multibank holding companies are likely to transfer their remaining profitable assets (for example, credit card operations, or leasing businesses) from sick to healthy affiliates. They would then be in a position to approach regulators and demand a suspension of the cross-guarantees that require them to back their sick affiliated banks with all their capital.

Regulators would then face a real nightmare. Either they bail out investors in the holding company along with depositors in the sick bank, or they force the entire bank, sick and healthy affiliates alike, into receivership.

Delay might also drive strong banks, such as J.P. Morgan or Bankers Trust, to abandon their banking charters altogether and operate instead as non-bank financial institutions. Why should they tolerate steep fees and unpredictable special levies for insurance they do not really need? After all, their sound credit ratings allow them to raise funds directly in the commercial paper market at competitive prices, without paying FDIC premiums or submitting to the burden of outdated regulations.

Or, more frightening still, what if healthy banks were to engage in risky lending behavior in reaction to higher insurance fees? After all, they are charged as if they are wild-eyed risk-takers. Why shouldn't they behave that way and get their money's worth? Stockholders of healthy banks should wonder why they must subsidize their less competent competitors at the behest of federal regulators.

In either case, if healthy banks give up their charters or become large risk-takers, the outlook for the bank insurance fund and taxpayers is bleak. If many banks start opting out of the federal insurance system, the FDIC will be forced to increase fees on the remaining weaker banks, further hindering their ability to recover while encouraging still more banks to return their charters. Or, if healthy banks begin taking larger risks, the fund will eventually face larger and larger losses. Either is a nightmare scenario, and neither is inconceivable.

Reverse Triage

Now that we have weathered the "December surprise" that Ross Perot referred to during his presidential campaign, it may yet be called the "December Dud." Because of the small number of banks closed, the temptation will be to sit back and relax, and to listen to the blandishments of industry spokesmen and regulators that all is under control and that the worst is past. Unfortunately, the December closings will mark not the end of "the banking problem" but the continuation of a slowly rising tide of bank failures. These failures will be precipitated by the FDIC's new and tougher capital standards, but their underlying cause remains the long-postponed recognition of massive real estate losses. As the economy recovers, the inevitable rise in interest rates will ensnare desperate bankers who have both invested heavily in long-term Treasury bonds and have not written down their problem real estate.

In the months since the publication of *Banking on the Brink,* regulators, trade association, industry lobbyists and even key staffers of Senate committees have savagely attacked our conclusions. Many in the press have focused only on our worst-case projections, ignoring our most likely range of estimates. Beyond these quibbles over accounting techniques and estimation methods, however, is a more basic question, namely: What is commercial real estate worth in today's market?

Our answer is that it is worth not nearly as much as bankers and regulators would have us believe. Given the faint hopes for a short- or mid-term turnaround in commercial real estate values, or a sudden and sharp rise in economic activity (miraculously unaccompanied by a rise in interest rates) this ugly fact threatens the viability of poorly capitalized banks.

It is true that the vast majority of American banks are quite healthy. But they are being systematically bled by regulators determined to prop up weak banks so as to maintain a system with fundamental flaws. These same regulators backed away from attempts to create a real system of risk-related FDIC insurance premiums in 1992, under a full-court industry lobbying effort. The result is that income is being transferred between banks, with weak banks paying too little for their insurance and well-managed banks paying too much. Taking from the rich and giving to the poor hurts not only healthy banks but the economy as well.

Congress, the White House and regulators are searching, with increasing desperation, for a miracle cure that imposes neither a direct cost to the taxpayer nor an increase of the deficit. They hope, for example, that by relaxing antitrust laws, two sick banks can merge their way back to health. Unfortunately, this policy is more likely to create crippled giants that can survive only by hiding behind the FDIC's doctrine of too-big-to-fail.

The best U.S. bankers recognize this, calling instead for the banking system to winnow out its lesser members, rather than waiting for the FDIC to finally act when a bank's losses become too big to ignore.

Another much-touted cure is to require banks to carry deeper reserves. But rational private investors will not provide sufficient funds to shore up weakly capitalized banks. Why? Because investors not only recognize that these banks have paid dismal dividends for more than a decade, they also know that bank accounting practices make it impossible to measure the true value of bank capital. This makes the enforcement of meaningful capital standards extremely difficult.

What to do?

So far, Congress and the White House have placed their full faith in further deregulation. But while the expansion of banking powers—interstate banking, the sale of non-bank products such as insurance, and the ownership of banks by non-banking companies—is laudable, it must take a back seat to three more urgent actions.

• *They must close problem banks.* Given sufficient time, some troubled banks might recover. But for each that does, others will fall into even deeper trouble. It is preferable to err on the side of caution by closing, restructuring, or merging all banks that fail to meet strict, market-based standards of net worth.

• *They must improve bank accounting.* Murky but legal bank accounting procedures allow banks to disguise large asset losses. Our study highlights the enormous discrepancy between conventional bookkeeping and the actual market value of bank assets. Adopting market-value accounting will allow regulators to close banks as soon as they are insolvent. It will also allow bankers to manage operations, and to enter into mergers and acquisitions more efficiently.

• *They must narrow deposit insurance.* Because depositors have no reason to care whether their bank is well-managed, bad banks are free to keep repeat-

ing their mistakes. We recommend that depositors with a total of more than $100,000 in a bank (including certificates of deposits, brokered deposits regardless of size, payroll accounts and inter-bank deposits) be required to purchase private deposit insurance. Once a vigorous private insurance market develops, this statutory amount could be lowered to $80,000 or even $60,000.

Private insurers will charge depositors in different banks varying premiums based on the bank's capitalization, portfolio diversity, and strength of management. As these premiums begin to affect the real interest rates earned by depositors, money will begin to flow out of weak and badly-managed banks and into good banks without harming small depositors. After all, that was the original purpose of public deposit insurance. Although it may be preferable for banks to purchase this private insurance, thereby saving on transaction costs, who purchases the insurance has no impact on the economics of the proposal; this is a "Coasian" problem. What does make a difference is that private insurance is purchased and that markets are at the core of risk assessment and rate setting.

The premiums charged by private insurers also should be used to run the FDIC's insurance program on a sound actuarial basis (for the first time). FDIC premiums should be automatically linked to private market rates, not rates negotiated by highly paid lobbyists or through political pressure. Needless to say, this cannot be done in the halls of Congress or in the boardroom of the FDIC. Weak banks will fight these proposals down to the last dollar in their lobbying budgets.

Still, while many powerful economic arguments can be leveled against deposit insurance, it remains a political fact of life. The question is how to live with it.

Politicians must recognize that bank failure is an inherent part of the financial system, and that no regulation can alter that fact. This means redesigning deposit insurance so that when failures occur they can be readily absorbed without a direct spillover to the taxpayer. It also means designing a deposit insurance system that does not prolong the life of inefficient banks.

For the public, the challenge lies in admitting that the deposit insurance system cannot be kept in its present form without incurring enormous costs. Banks have tripped four times since the mid-1970s and they will assuredly stumble again without real reform. That means learning to live with coverage limits as well as a system that rewards strong banks and punishes poorly managed ones.

For bankers, it means learning to live without the heavy subsidy that federal insurance provides for their deposits, while accepting new restrictions on risk-taking, at least at insured depository institutions.

For stockholders, it means forgoing the subsidies provided by the federal government through the too-big-to-fail doctrine, deposit insurance and various accounting gimmicks devised by the Fed and the FDIC.

For regulators, it means forcing banks to finally come clean about the condition of their portfolios.

The truth may not set them free, or spare the taxpayer the final bill for the banking mess, but it's a start.

Should the feds have greater control over state banks?

Point ►►►►►►►►►►

Lee S. Adams and Carter K. McDowell

Lee S. Adams is deputy general counsel for Banc One Corp. Carter K. McDowell is senior attorney.

I magine what major league baseball would be like if each state had its own baseball commissioner and teams played according to a combination of state and national rules.

The federal government might set rules regarding the size of the ball and the shape of the playing field. New York and Georgia might require that all teams playing within their borders use a designated hitter.

Ohio and California might require that batters be given four strikes before they were called out. Illinois might forbid night games; and Minnesota might require that all games played there be in a domed stadium.

Welcome to the world of major league banking.

Instead of a single national league with a single set of rules and a single regulator, banks and bank holding companies in the United States operate within the "dual banking system," a system under which banks and other depository institutions may be chartered and regulated by either the federal government or state. As a result, the dual banking system is actually composed of one federal and 50 state systems. The result can best be described as two interdependent systems in which various federal laws and regulations apply to state-chartered banks, and various state laws and regulations are applicable to federally charted banks.

In theory, the dual banking system gives states the flexibility to tailor their banking laws to local needs, encourages experimentation and innovation, and operates as a system of checks and balances among the various state and federal agencies regulating the banking industry.

In reality, however, the states and federal government often pursue different agendas with the result that no uniformity emerges from the experimentation and innovation the system encourages.

This lack of uniformity was less of a problem when banks operated within a single city or state. However, as a national, and increasingly international, market has developed for bank products and services, this lack of uniformity has begun to hamper competition and harm the safety and soundness of the banking system.

◄◄◄◄◄◄◄ Counterpoint

Doyle C. Bartlett

Doyle C. Bartlett is vice president and director of Legislative Services for the Conference of State Bank Supervisors, the professional association of state officials who charter and regulate banks.

B ank reform. The two words evoke strong emotions among those inside the Capital Beltway, and those fortunate or wise enough to live outside it.

Inside Washington, the emotional reaction varies among the players. For most senators and congressmen, the main emotion is dread. Bank reform means voting for extremely unpopular issues, such as spending billions of taxpayer dollars to fill black holes of debt. Worst of all, the money doesn't buy one single slab of pork: No roads. No ships. No new jobs. Only angry taxpayers.

If you can't make the taxpayers happy, congressional logic goes, make a special interest group happy. No luck here either. Banking reform pits the biggest, richest and most vocal groups against one another.

For lobbyists, bank reform means at least an extra 15 pounds from wining and dining legislators and staff. Many enter a bank reform fight with visions of personal gain dancing in their heads. Their hourly fees could mean expensive cars, African safaris, Ivy League tuition for their children. Most finish with expanded waistlines and deflated dreams.

The administration enters the bank reform fight with an overpowering sense of frustration. Many in the administration have fought this battle before — in 1984, in 1986 and in 1988. Their slogan: "This time it will be different."

The president is making it a priority. The Treasury and the federal banking agencies are all on board. They have new arguments; they polish up the old ones.

How should states view bank reform? Just as anyone outside the Beltway should — with skepticism and caution.

In Washington, the players' emotions too often obscure the point of reform. Any reform effort must start with the questions: How will this reform affect us? What will the outcome be? What will it cost our citizens? How will it change our economy? How will it meet our needs?

In the area of bank reform, states and the federal government may come up with different answers. True reform must be separated from false reform.

Point

Counterpoint

For example, as late as 1985, Banc One Corp. was authorized by state law to operate banks only within Ohio. Since then, many states, including Ohio, have enacted interstate banking statutes.

As a result, as this article is being written, Banc One operates banks in seven states and competes with numerous banks and other financial service providers, such as mutual funds, insurance companies and finance companies, from around the world.

By requiring banks and bank holding companies that operate on a multistate basis to comply with varying federal and state laws, banks and bank holding companies are precluded from establishing a company or industrywide policy or standard for the products and services they offer.

The result is that compliance with redundant laws becomes complex, time-consuming and expensive.

In areas where a national market has developed or a national consensus has emerged among the states and the federal government or among consumers, the dual banking system should serve customer needs, not the local or regional interests of a particular state or group of states.

The dual banking system can operate efficiently only by encouraging competition, efficiency and the development of new products and discouraging the regulatory gridlock and industry paralysis that inevitably result when too many agencies regulate an industry.

To achieve this evolution the federal government should act like the baseball commissioner and ensure uniform, understandable and fair results from the experimentation encouraged by the dual banking system.

The federal government must assume this role because it is the only party in the system with the authority to establish and enforce a national standard and, when necessary, pre-empt state laws.

Credit card disclosure, and most other forms of consumer credit disclosure, represents an area where the federal government has established a uniform national standard following a period of state experimentation.

With the use of 800 telephone numbers and national advertising campaigns, a national market for bank credit cards, such as Visa and MasterCard, has developed, and consumers routinely shop across state lines for the best interest rate and terms. Before the passage in 1980 of the Truth in Lending Simplification and Reform Act and the revision of Regulation Z by the Federal

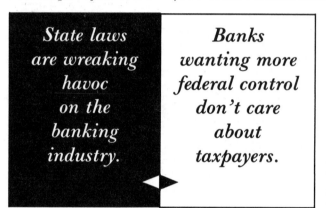

State laws are wreaking havoc on the banking industry.

Banks wanting more federal control don't care about taxpayers.

From the states' point of view, some federal reforms pass muster and are necessary. These are true reforms because they reduce the taxpayers' exposure to losses from bank failures.

These reforms also improve banks' ability to serve their communities and provide the funds necessary for economic growth.

Fortunately, many of these reforms were included in the bank reform legislation passed by Congress late last year. These reforms include charging banks deposit insurance premiums based on risk, better standards for bank accounting and supervision, and a renewed emphasis on bank safety and soundness. These are reforms best enacted at the federal level.

Several proposed federal reforms were rejected, which also is fortunate. One of these proposals, a federal mandate for nationwide interstate branch banking, is an example of a reform that should not be made at the federal level.

Interstate branching addresses the fundamental question of who should decide where a bank can do business. Under current law, banking companies that operate in more than one state must have a separate charter in each state. This system, which evolved at the state level, lets banks expand but ensures local accountability. A state can decide whether and under what conditions a banking company may operate within its borders.

The administration calls this system, which has worked well, inefficient and anti-competitive. Its proposal, which certainly will be offered again, would allow banks to have branches anywhere, regardless of state law.

The administration argues that its proposal would boost banks' efficiency and create banks large enough to compete in international markets. The administration says this is reason enough to trade the American tradition of local control over banking for a centralized system.

From a state perspective, this proposal is not true reform. It would not reduce the risk of bank failures or offer better services to communities.

Unchecked, government-sponsored concentration would put too many eggs in one basket — a fragile basket that would leave the taxpayer liable. With this proposal, the federal government is making a judgment that big banks are better for the nation's economy. Better for whom?

Point

Reserve Board, federal law and a host of different state laws and regulations governed credit card disclosures and other forms of consumer credit disclosures.

This scheme forced banks to prepare a separate disclosure statement for each state where they issued credit cards or made consumer loans. While the type of information disclosed was generally the same, the format was different.

These differences frustrated the purpose of the disclosure statement, namely to describe the costs and features of the credit card in a manner that gave consumers a basis for comparing similar cards issued by various competitors. The Truth in Lending Simplification and Reform Act and the revision of Regulation Z eliminated this confusing practice and established a national standard.

Interstate banking is an area where state experimentation has run its course and where the federal government should step in to create a uniform standard.

Compliance with state laws becomes complex, time-consuming and expensive.

Until the mid-1980s, state and federal law, with certain historical exceptions, prohibited banks from operating on an interstate basis. This prohibition developed out of a fear that economic power would become concentrated in the hands of a few financial institutions, primarily New York money-center banks, and that credit would not be allocated fairly throughout the country.

Beginning in the mid-1980s, as competition intensified and banks and thrifts began to fail in numbers not seen since the Depression, states worried less about economic concentrations of power and more about the safety and soundness of the banking system.

In response to this shift in priorities, states began allowing banks and bank holding companies to diversify their assets and, to a lesser extent, their deposits by expanding geographically.

Geographic expansion began with the formation of regional interstate banking compacts that fostered regional consolidation and excluded the large New York and California banks. Now a majority of states have authorized nationwide interstate banking.

The problem with this progression is that the progress has not been uniform and in many cases frustrates the stated purpose of interstate banking statutes.

Even in the states that authorize interstate banking, the law often imposes restrictions on how banks and bank holding companies can avail themselves of these provisions.

Counterpoint

The Congressional Budget Office has said the administration's interstate branching proposal would actually cause an increase in bank failures. Studies in communities with interstate banks show that lending to small business falls, and fees for consumer services rise.

To the states, the administration's proposal means states could no longer control the entry of banks into their markets. Furthermore, revenue would drop along with states' ability to tax the activities of banks within their borders.

Only state-based reform will allow each state the flexibility to meet local needs.

This is not to say that interstate branch banking is altogether bad. Certainly it may offer some advantages to customers as well as to banks, particularly in metropolitan areas that cross state lines. Some communities might see a broader range of services as a result of interstate branching.

Interstate branching reforms, however, should originate at the state level. Only state-based reform will allow each state the flexibility to meet local needs by deciding the terms and conditions of interstate branching. Furthermore, states need time and flexibility to adapt their tax systems to banking across state borders.

The states have shown that they are able to enact bank reform in a rational, measured way. Interstate banking — the acquisition of banks by out-of-state bank holding companies — has been a state-driven reform during the past 10 years.

In adopting interstate banking laws, states balanced the needs of local marketplaces against the needs of large financial institutions. States' success with interstate banking is only the most recent example of the strength of our locally controlled, decentralized banking system.

The bank reform bandwagon will keep rolling in Washington. We can expect to see major campaigns about once every two years. The faces, the names, the slogans may change, but states' response should be the same: Keep your money in your pocket and your hands on the reins. ■

Crossing borders

Nationwide interstate banking is allowed by 34 states. Another 14 states, largely in the South and Midwest, allow regional interstate banking. Hawaii permits reciprocal banking with some Pacific Island groups. Only Montana doesn't allow banking across its borders. States have controlled interstate branch banking since 1864.

Point

The result is a patchwork of state laws that protects local banks but often fails to accomplish its stated purpose: geographic expansion and asset diversification.

President Bush has recognized the need for a national standard, and during its last session, Congress debated this issue, although legislation has yet to be adopted. But nationwide interstate banking is likely to be one of the key banking issues debated during the next session of Congress.

The federal Community Reinvestment Act represents an area where the federal government and the states continue to experiment.

The act requires banks to define the market area they serve, to describe in an annual statement the products and services they offer, and to monitor whether they are meeting the credit needs of the communities they serve, including low- and moderate-income neighborhoods.

Several states have adopted similar statutes and regulations. The purpose is to ensure that banks meet the credit needs of all segments of their market.

But problems arise over what it means to serve the credit needs of a community, what data should be collected and how this data should be reported. When every state, county, city and neighborhood group requests different data to support pet projects or objectives, the burden on banks of data collection and reporting becomes onerous.

To prevent this the federal government probably will have to impose some discipline by establishing a national standard.

Without a federal umpire, the theory of the dual banking system gives way to regulatory deadlock and paralysis for the banking industry.

The rules of major league baseball are intended to permit those that play the game best, wherever they call home, to win. If the Minnesota Twins could not come to Georgia to compete, the players, the spectators, and the game itself, would suffer. These rules forge strength through fair competition. The dual banking system should strive for nothing less. ■

The Future of Money

E-Cash Could Transform the World's Financial Life

In his pinstriped suit and wire-rimmed glasses, Timothy L. Jones looks every bit the traditional British banker. Sure enough, he has spent a dozen years at National Westminster Bank PLC. But ask Jones what he is doing now, and he responds with an intensity worthy of a Silicon Valley entrepreneur. Leaning across a table, he waxes eloquent about his new enterprise, Mondex, and the future of the product he's selling: a new kind of electronic money.

Mondex, which was launched by NatWest, is not alone: a raft of companies are developing their own forms of electronic money, known as E-cash. E-cash is money that moves along multiple channels largely outside the established network of banks, checks, and paper currency overseen by the Federal Reserve. These channels enable consumers and businesses to send money to each other more cheaply, conveniently, and quickly than through the banking system.

Some of the E-cash players are faceless, dubious outfits that exist in cyberspace and can be traced only to a post-office box—in the physical world. But there are plenty of others, ranging from techno-savvy startups with names such as DigiCash and CyberCash, to corporate icons including Microsoft, Xerox, and Visa. Citicorp is even developing what it calls the Electronic Monetary System, an entire infrastructure for using electronic money to be issued by Citi and other banks.

These companies are part of a mass experiment that could transform the way we think about money. In the process, it could change consumers' financial lives and shake the foundation of global financial systems and even governments.

Digital money is the ultimate—and inevitable—medium of exchange for an increasingly wired world. With E-cash, you'll no longer need to carry a wad of bills in your pocket or fumble for exact change. Instead, you might carry a credit-card-size piece of plastic with an embedded microchip that you will "load" up with E-money you buy with traditional currency. Or, you might store your digital coins and dollars—downloaded over phone lines from your bank or other issuer of E-money—on your PC or in an electronic "wallet," a palm-size device used to store and transmit E-money.

This digital money will let you shop online, zapping money to a merchant over the Internet, or perhaps paying for a movie on demand over an interactive-TV network. It also has the potential to replace cash and checks for everyday purchases—in stores, restaurants, or taxis that accept E-cash. Businesses could also keep a stash of E-cash on hand for buying office supplies, or use it to transact directly with each other instead of going through banks and electronic funds transfers.

THE START OF A REVOLUTION. In many ways, E-cash, which can be backed by any currency or other asset, represents the biggest revolution in currency since gold replaced cowrie shells. Its diversity and pluralism is perfectly suited to the anarchic culture of the Internet and the evolving web of networks known as the Information Su-perhighway. "Electronic commerce will literally change the way business is done worldwide," says James G. Cosgrove, vice-president and general manager for business multimedia services at AT&T. "We're about to see another revolution similar to the Industrial Revolution." Adds Richard K. Crone, senior manager in the financial-services group at KPMG Peat Marwick: "We're in the beginning stages of the cash-replacement cycle."

But the advent of E-cash raises all sorts of questions, most of which remain unanswered: Who should be allowed to issue E-cash, and who will regulate those issuers? How will taxes be applied in cyberspace, which transcends physical boundaries? Who will set the standards? How do you ensure that payments made over the Net will be secure? How will consumers be protected? How will regulators police money laundering and counterfeiting on private networks?

While regulators wrestle with these questions, technology is remaking the monetary system. That's what Microsoft CEO William H. Gates III had in mind when he bid for personal-finance software maker Intuit Inc. He saw programs such as Intuit's as the gateway that would draw millions of consumers onto his online network where they could pay bills, get financial advice, or shop, perhaps paying him for access. But the Justice Dept. worried about Microsoft's reach, and he abandoned the deal on May 20.

Tough break, but it will hardly slow Gates down. Microsoft is working with Visa on a system for securing credit-

Early Money

Seashells, odd rough-hewn coins—the first money was flexible, highly distinctive, and exchanged in multifarious ways. Objects were gradually replaced by standardized commodities such as gold and silver, and these in turn by paper money. Yet even early currency was at first issued by private banks, local governments, and others—usually backed by gold and silver. Diversity abounded.

card transactions over the Net. But that's just one piece of a much bigger problem Microsoft is trying to solve. Gates has dozens of programmers busy devising a sweeping system, Microsoft Network, to help people do business safely in cyberspace—or more specifically, in Mocrosoft's own network and interactive-TV systems—using a range of payment options. Microsoft won't reveal much about its E-cash plans, but, says Nathan P. Myhrvold, Microsoft's top advanced-technology expert, "we're very interested in the area."

They should be. The stakes are enormous. Seamus McMahon, a vice-president at Booz, Allen, and Ham-

Bank Money

The current money system is largely monolithic. Nearly all major countries have a single system of national currencies and bank checks. Most have elaborate infrastructures built around commercial banks and a central governing body such as the Federal Reserve Board. That entity is usually the only facility allowed to issue money. Perhaps because of their monopoly structures, money systems tend to resist change and innovation. Traders can move millions of dollars around the globe at the touch of a button. But the small check-based transactions of consumers can take days to clear. And chartered airplanes physically transport billions of checks around the country every workday.

ilton, sees as much as 20% of total household expenditures taking place on the I-way just 10 years from now. If any operation, whether Citicorp or a startup such as Mondex, gained control of a new medium for even part of those exchanges, it would have the opportunity to charge royalties or fees for its use and earn interest on the E-money sitting in its accounts. Even a tiny charge, when applied to millions of transactions, would be highly lucrative.

E-cash could also create a competitive free-for-all. Because the Internet knows no boundaries, a company offering E-money can gain direct access to millions of consumers and businesses—no matter what state or country they are in. "The retail banking market will collapse and give way to global competition," says Eric Hughes, president of Open Financial Networks, a Berkeley (Calif.) consulting firm. "Those [regional] separations don't work on the Internet."

WINNING CONSUMERS' TRUST. Governments' and central banks' control of money flows has already been loosened, as shown by recent currency and market crises in Mexico and elsewhere. But with the growth of E-cash, money could flow in and out of countries at lightning speed without being traced, weakening governments' ability to monitor and tax. "Over the long haul, this is going to lead to the separation of economy and state," declares Bill A. Frezza, president of Wireless Computing Associates and co-founder of the advocacy group DigitaLiberty.

The growth of E-money could also be bad news for banks. If other companies successfully offer their own brand of digital cash, they could bypass banks as primary providers of consumer financial services. The companies, not the banks, might be consumers' first contact when they wanted to obtain some digital money. "Banking is essential to the modern economy, but banks are not," says J. Richard Fredericks, senior managing director at Montgomery Securities.

E-Cash

E-cash may be technologically light-years ahead of early money. But in many ways, it is closer to seashells than greenbacks. E-cash is digital money that moves through a multiplicity of networks instead of the current bank system. It comes in lots of guises, is created by lots of individual parties, and is backed by anything constituents demand as an accepted medium of exchange: gold, dollars, yen, whatever. It is the ultimate, and inevitable, currency for the wired world. Competition is intense, producing rapid innovations. Using money downloaded to your PC or a palm-size electronic "wallet," you'll be able to zap money to merchants on the Net—or buy a newspaper faster than you can grab a greenback. If you're a business owner, you can bypass banks and move E-cash directly to customers and suppliers. The advantages: convenience, speed, cost savings. The technology is complex, but to the user, E-cash is as easy as pushing a button.

Commercial banks are, of course, entrusted with the creation of money through the fractional reserve system. They lend out more than they have on deposit, and they are the only companies authorized to do so. If each unit of E-cash had to be backed by a corresponding unit of traditional currency, that would mean that lending out E-cash wouldn't create new money. But if non-bank money suppliers started backing just a fraction of their digital cash with traditional money—just as commercial banks today keep on hand only a fraction of the deposits on their books—nonbanks, which are largely unregulated, could create money just as commercial banks do now.

Bankers must move fast to keep up. Ronald A. Braco, head of electronic banking at Chemical Bank, estimates that banks have less than five years to come up with viable E-money products before other players carve out the big-

The New World of E-Cash

THE GOOD

• E-cash is more convenient and flexible than traditional money. It can be used by consumers and businesses, and for everything from buying wares on the Internet to lending a pal five bucks.

• Banks that issue E-cash could find it much cheaper than handling checks and the paper records that accompany traditional money.

• Consumers doing business on the Internet will find some forms of electronic money afford much greater privacy than using ordinary credit cards.

THE BAD

• Uncontrolled growth of E-cash systems could undermine bank- and government-controlled money systems, giving rise to a confusing and inefficient Babel of competing systems.

• E-cash may be less secure than bank money: Money stored on a PC could be lost forever if the system crashes.
E-cash could foster a have and have-not society: Those with PCs would have ready access to the stuff, while those without, many of them low-income consumers, would not.

AND THE UGLY

• Money laundering and tax evasion could proliferate in stateless E-money systems as criminals use untraceable cyberdollars to hide assets offshore.

• Counterfeiters could create their own personal mints of E-cash that would be indistinguishable from real money.

• If computer hackers or other criminals were to break into E-cash systems, they could instantaneously filch the electronic wealth of thousands or even millions of innocent consumers.

DATA: BUSINESSWEEK

---

gest chunks of the market for themselves. "No question, it's for real," says Richard M. Rosenberg, chairman and CEO of BankAmerica Corp. In a couple of years, "it will take off fairly dramatically." The issues now: winning consumers' trust and

This could be bad news for banks. What if phone companies offered their own brand of E-money?

getting them to change their buying habits.

The first step in that direction could be to get consumers used to using credit cards for purchases on the Internet. Once that happens, the thinking goes, they may be willing to start using E-cash systems.

One of the first purveyors of a Net credit-card system is First Virtual Holdings, run by onetime celebrity manager Lee Stein. Stein has launched a relatively simple system using E-mail that lets consumers use credit cards on the Internet without fear that their account numbers will be misappropriated. The card numbers are stored away on a protected computer system and never pass over the network. Instead, consumers register with First Virtual by phone and receive I.D. numbers in exchange for their card numbers. When they want to buy

something electronically, they simply supply their I.D. number to the merchant.

First Virtual, which became the first secure payment system on the Net when it handled its first transaction last October, is growing fast. Stein won't disclose activity levels, but he says volumes are increasing by 16% a week. "If you make it simple and safe, people will use it," he says. First Virtual has enlisted such merchants as Apple Computer, Reuters, and National Public Radio—which sells transcripts of programs.

Most electronic extensions of the credit-card system, though, are built around encryption—scrambling card numbers so they can pass safely on electronic networks. For example, CyberCash Inc., a Reston (Va.) startup, is cutting its teeth on a deal with Wells Fargo & Co. for encrypted credit-card transactions over the Internet.

Visa and MasterCard, not surprisingly, are also working to make credit cards usable on the I-way. Visa is, among other things, developing with Microsoft a system using encryption technology that they hope will become an industry model. "We want to be sure that the industry as a whole has certain standards," says Carl F. Pascarella, president and CEO of Visa USA. Meanwhile, MasterCard has teamed with Netscape Inc., a maker of security and browsing software for the Internet, to pursue a similar goal.

WILTSHIRE EXPERIMENT.
Credit-card-based systems have the advantage of seeming familiar to consumers. But the card systems don't do everything cash can: They're not anonymous, they do not work person-to-person, and they have credit limits. They're also not suited for the grass-roots economy the Internet makes possible, where any outfit or individual can sell its wares, whether a newsletter or a stock tip.

That's where E-cash comes in. But E-cash needs to be just as secure as credit cards for people to use it. David Chaum, CEO of pioneer DigiCash in Amsterdam, has done the most to solve this problem. He had devised a clever system that uses so-called public-key cryptography that, like encryption, makes it possible to send sensitive information over the Net. But Chaum's big breakthrough was "blinding" technology, which lets the issuing bank certify an electronic note without tracing whom it was issued to. The result: Your E-cash, unlike an encrypted credit-card transaction, is as anonymous as paper cash.

Chaum has yet to announce firm deals with companies to issue his E-money. But in a pilot, some 5,000 consumers are part of a DigiCash marketplace, using the equivalent of $1 million in E-money to do business with 50 companies, from Encyclopaedia Britannica Inc. to Ricky's Junk Shop. Chaum's technology is also at the

heart of CAFE, a European Commission-sponsored project to develop an electronic wallet for pan-European use.

CAFE's setup is similar to Jones's Mondex system. "Imagine it's the same as physical money, and you won't be far off," says Jones. Mondex money will be created initially by NatWest and a partner, Midland Bank PLC, which will then "sell" it to customers. The E-money is loaded onto credit-card-size "smart" cards with embedded microchips. The cards can be used in point-of-sale terminals or fit into electronic wallets that can transmit money to merchants or—just as with traditional cash but not with credit cards—to other consumers. Mondex money is still in pilot form, but the company has signed up 40,000 consumers and over 1,000 retailers in the Wiltshire town of Swindon to test Mondex money beginning in July.

CyberCash, too, is experimenting with E-cash in addition to its credit-card-based system. In the E-cash system, consumers will set up E-money accounts at their banks. Then, using proprietary software provided free of charge by CyberCash, they can go about their business on the Net. At the end of the day, CyberCash will clear all the E-money transactions and convert E-cash balances back to dollars.

No matter who develops the best E-cash, consumers and businesses alike stand to reap sizable benefits. No longer will consumers have to wait for

change or scurry to automated teller machines for cash—out of sight, they hope, of the nearest mugger. E-cash will let businesses carry out transactions around the world without transferring bank funds—and they will be better able to reach a large population of technologically savvy, often affluent consumers.

Moreover, because E-money is basically software, it can be programmed to do things that paper money could never do. Microsoft's Myhrvold explains that electronic money could be earmarked for special purposes, with conditions on where it can be spent. For example, a business could have electronic version of petty cash to be used for supplies at an Office Depot—but not a beer at a local tavern. Or parents would wire to a college student E-money that is designated for rent or books. "There will be new forms of smart money and payment systems that can only be done online," says Myhrvold.

Along with the opportunities, though, comes huge uncertainty. Existing monetary regulations don't cover all the potential uses of E-cash. Nathaniel S. Borenstein, a computer scientist and co-founder of First Virtual, says: "One of the hardest questions merchants ask us is, 'When do we owe taxes?' " That's not a trivial question: With E-money, the merchant could be in Guam and the buyer in Canada, while First Virtual's

computers are located in Ohio. So whose sales tax do you pay? Borenstein's advice to merchants: "I tell them to consult a lawyer."

There's also a major potential for crime (see box on page 125). E-money can be easily sent in and out of a country undetected, facilitating money laundering on a grand scale. Tax evasion could become a matter of pushing a button. And without foolproof cryptography, counterfeiters could replicate the series of digits that constitutes E-money. Governments would be hard pressed to monitor or control stateless E-money. "Digital cash is a threat to every government on the planet that wants to manage its currency," says David E. Saxton, executive vice-president of Net1, a startup that has developed a secure way to send electronic checks across the Internet.

BATTLE OF THE LOGOS. Even law-abiding citizens and companies using E-money could be victims of sophisticated hacker attacks. Says Colin Crook, senior technology officer for Citicorp: "We have to assume electronic money will be the subject of sustained attack from all kinds of people."

Another open question—and a large one—is the role of banks in the new electronic world. "E-cash will be offered by both banks and nonbanks," says Chaum. Sure enough, DigiCash or CyberCash could join forces with

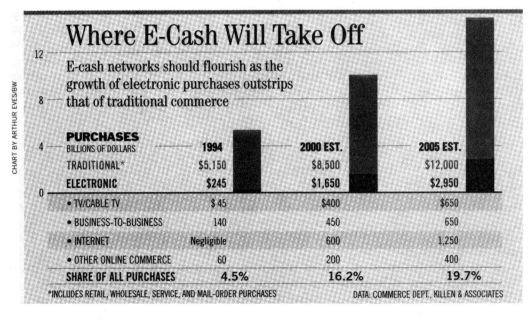

Where E-Cash Will Take Off

E-cash networks should flourish as the growth of electronic purchases outstrips that of traditional commerce

CHART BY ARTHUR EVES/BW

PURCHASES BILLIONS OF DOLLARS	1994	2000 EST.	2005 EST.
TRADITIONAL*	$5,150	$8,500	$12,000
ELECTRONIC	**$245**	**$1,650**	**$2,950**
• TV/CABLE TV	$45	$400	$650
• BUSINESS-TO-BUSINESS	140	450	650
• INTERNET	Negligible	600	1,250
• OTHER ONLINE COMMERCE	60	200	400
SHARE OF ALL PURCHASES	**4.5%**	**16.2%**	**19.7%**

*INCLUDES RETAIL, WHOLESALE, SERVICE, AND MAIL-ORDER PURCHASES   DATA: COMMERCE DEPT., KILLEN & ASSOCIATES

Call It E-Money Management

It's a Saturday morning sometime in the not-too-distant future, and you sit down at your PC to do a little end-of-the-month planning. First, you call up the balances from your various accounts—credit-card, checking, savings, and E-cash—and break down your spending by category. Oops, better cut down on those pricey dinners.

Your investments are offsetting some of those expensive habits—at least you hope so. Finding out is as easy as a few clicks of a mouse button, as you call up your investment portfolio. Hmmm, it may be time to get into a more aggressive mutual fund. So you quickly dispatch a software "agent" to rustle up profiles for the top-performing funds. By filling out an online form, you transfer some of your holdings into a hot overseas fund.

Just as technology is revolutionizing money, it is also set to transform the way we manage our money. "Complexity has gotten beyond the level that people can deal with," says Scott D. Cook, the founder and chairman of Intuit Inc. With programs like Quicken, Intuit's best-selling personal-finance software, Cook aims to make that complexity easier to deal with.

"Automatic Agents." Indeed, today's programs for personal-finance management and home banking are giving consumers unprecedented control over their financial life. But this is just the beginning. Gradually, programs are linking users to banks, electronic bill-paying services, and a broad array of vendors of financial advice that is starting to be offered online. Colin Crook, head of technology at Citibank, says software programs will be constantly at work for you, for instance, using information gleaned on the Net to optimize your portfolio. "You're going to hand off your personal affairs in cyberspace to automatic agents who represent you," says Crook.

The competition to supply these services will be heated. Microsoft Corp.'s Bill Gates saw the potential—one reason why he was willing to shell out $2 billion for Intuit. With that deal blocked by the Justice Dept., Microsoft is throwing its considerable resources behind Microsoft Money, a home-grown personal-finance package already offered by Chase Manhattan and others. From Money, Microsoft expects to link customers to a variety of online financial services, including electronic bill-paying. Bank of America and Nations Bank recently paid $35 million for Meca Software, which makes Managing Your Money. And Intuit, for its part, has just released new programs for selecting mutual funds and planning for retirement and children's college education.

Expect banks to jump into the fray. They are sitting on a gold mine of valuable data: their customers' payment information. The statements they send out, though, typically offer little value, and consumers' credit-card, checking and savings, and investment accounts are handled separately. "There is an opportunity to consolidate that," says Richard K. Crone, a banking consultant at KPMG Peat Marwick.

With so much available to help you manage your financial affairs, someday you may be able to bag those Saturday mornings at the computer and instead just take a long weekend.

By Amy Cortese in New York

AT&T or Microsoft just as easily as with Citibank. Having one of those companies dispensing E-cash directly to consumers could do serious damage to banks' main link with their customers.

Even if banks are involved, they could find other players taking center stage. Early entrants to the E-money business could set the operating standards for digital cash. And the nonbanks could even devise systems that would make their logos the first thing people see. William M. Randle, senior vice-president at Huntington Bancshares, warns that banks could become "buttons on a network operated by other entities."

Improbable? Not really. Take a look at credit-card processing. Twenty years ago, banks owned the car-transaction-processing business. Now, close to 80% of card transactions are processed by nonbanks such as First Data Resources Inc., says KPMG's Crone.

A similar erosion has occurred in wholesale banking, where banks have ceded to such outfits as General Electric Information Services and Electronic Data Systems Corp. nearly the entire market for transferring payment data to corporations, leaving themselves the mundane, low-margin service of transferring money between corporations. Today, says banking consultant Edward E. Furash, although the situation is improving, fewer than 100 banks offer full-service electronic data interchange, as the data part of payments transmission is known. "We should do more of that," says Richard Matteis, head of Chemical Banking Corp.'s Geoserve unit.

Banks have one key advantage: a near lock on consumers' trust when it comes to depositing money. For that reason, many bankers tend to dismiss the threat implicit in E-money. "The reason financial institutions are going to win in the long run is trust," says Kawika Daguio, the American Bankers Assn.'s federal representative on operations and banking. Indeed, many E-cash makers are choosing to partner with banks because of that consumer trust. "We've positioned ourselves to work with the banking industry and make sure that if there are heroes in this, it is the banks," says William N. Melton, CEO of CyberCash.

But Microsoft's bid for Intuit last fall gave bankers a collective scare. And even though the deal did not work out, banks worry that Microsoft could hood its 70 million Windows customers into the electronic-commerce networks that it is developing—with or without banks' help. If Microsoft becomes a utility, "it will take a lot of

business from the banks." says Montgomery's Fredericks.

Now several of the biggest banks are pushing hard to develop E-money. Citibank's Electronic Monetary System is one of the most advanced bank offerings, although officials there stress that it is still in development. It would allow retail and business customers of Citi—or any other bank that paid to use Citi's system—to convert money in their accounts to electronic cash. Citi customers would also have access to a credit line they could draw down in E-money, just as they would use a credit card. Banks "should be experimenting," says Sholom Rosen, vice-president for electronic commerce at Citi. "That's what we're doing."

Beside NatWest and Midland, Bankers Trust Co. has a group dedicated to electronic commerce. And even some regional banks see opportunities. There is Wells Fargo's work with CyberCash. First Union Corp., based in Charlotte, N.C., has created an electronic mall for Internet transactions. Even Cardinal Bankshares Inc., a $607 million Lexington (Ky.) bank, on May 24 formed a new subsidiary, Security First Network Bank, which aims to grow into a full-service interactive bank on the Internet. "We'll be a one-branch bank in Kentucky with potential customers all over the U.S.," says CEO James S. Mahan III.

While it's not clear who the players will be 10 or even 5 years from now, it is inevitable that much E-money will originate outside the purview of central banks such as the Federal Reserve or the Bank of England, which are largely responsible for traditional monetary regulation. And that has major policy implications.

To begin with, consumers using the stuff could be extremely vulnerable. When consumers lose their credit cards, they are only liable for the first $50 of charges on the card. But for now at least, if a consumer misplaced, say, a Mondex card, it would be like losing cash. Similarly, if your digital coins are stored on the hard drive of the PC, a system crash could wipe out your electronic savings.

Electronic money also creates vast opportunities for tax evasion, money laundering, and other financial crime. "There is an imaginable potential for a serious challenge to the whole political and social order," says First Virtual's Borenstein. "I am not all that sanguine that the government has the control they think they do." For people trying to avoid paying taxes to a national government, the lure of a stateless currency would be powerful indeed. Already, "virtual currencies" serving electronic communities of people are springing up on the Internet.

Patrolling the Black Holes of Cyberspace

At first glance, the offer sounded legitimate. First Bank of the Internet began advertising to Net browsers in March, offering a new way to pay for goods over the Net. By sending First Bank a check for at least $20, cybershoppers would get a Visa automated teller machine card "loaded" with their money—less a hefty 5% commission—which they could then use to obtain cash or pay for their cyberwares.

First Bank got numerous inquiries—but it also drew some unwanted scrutiny. State banking regulators warned that it couldn't call itself a bank. The Office of the Comptroller of the Currency sent an advisory to banks and regulators warning them about FBOI. First Bank CEO Vinn K. Beigh, a 34-year-old computer technician in Des Plaines, Ill., says he will soon pull his Net listing. But he is still looking for a way to cash in on the wave of electronic commerce. "There is quite an interest in buying on the Internet," he insists.

He's got that right. First Bank isn't the only upstart trying to cash in on the demand. Consider World Trade Clearinghouse Ltd., which offers a gold-backed cybercurrency with cashlike anonymity that offers "protection from bureaucratic snoops, nasty ex-spouses, and lawsuit-hungry lawyers." And officially opening this month is the Internet Online Offshore Casino, run out of the Turks and Caicos Islands, which says it will accept all manner of E-money and pay customers 10% annual interest on the balances they leave in an offshore bank the company recently bought.

These enterprises may never draw in a meaningful number of customers. And many raise red flags to regulators. But the government is also a long way from getting a good fix on the activities of the much larger number of ostensibly legitimate E-money players.

Money Launderers. The regulatory gaps are sizable. For example, Stanley E. Morris, director of the Treasury Dept.'s Financial Crimes Enforcement Network (FinCEN), points out that there are no laws that limit the balance of electronic currency that can be loaded into an E-cash card. That could create a major opportunity for money launderers. And no one has determined how to define whose tax laws apply to transactions in cyberspace. Says John H. Gibbons, assistant to the President for science and technology: "If you go to a cashless society, it makes it very difficult tracking cash income or reportable income.

Right now, regulators are simply trying to understand the new technology and how the market is evolving. Last April, the Federal Trade Commission held a conference to examine the impact of electronic commerce on consumer protection. FinCEN is organizing a colloquium on electronic currency to be held later this fall. "We are nowhere near the issue of regulating it," warns FinCEN's Morris. "We're one step back." Given the speed with which the market is advancing, regulators don't have much time to close that gap.

By Amy Barrett in Washington

Then there's the issue of the volatility of money. The effects of high-speed electronic trading have been painfully apparent in market crises over the past several years. Market swings could be magnified if consumers and businesses could send their money around the globe with the touch of a button on a PC.

The monitoring of national money supplies will also change. While some regulators dismiss the issue, arguing that E-money will inevitably convert back to traditional money and get counted, other experts disagree. Martin Mayer, a guest scholar at the Brookings Institution, says that he expects the Fed to lose control of a significant portion of the money supply.

One of the most pitched debates is likely to be over privacy. As a society, we have relied on a system that allows us to keep some transactions private by using cash, while others, such as big-ticket purchases, are entrusted to a credit-card company or a bank. Competing forms of E-cash offer wildly differing degrees of privacy: DigiCash's E-money offers virtually complete anonymity, while every dollar you spend using the credit-card-based systems would leave a trail. The problem will be balancing individuals' rights to privacy with government's need to monitor money flow and trace criminal activity.

BREAKING INTO THE E-MINT.
More dire is the possibility of major break-ins to E-money systems—the electronic equivalent of penetrating the U.S. Mint. If someone were to crack the sophisticated code of, say, the DigiCash system, he could start minting unlimited amounts of his own DigiCash money.

That's why it is all the more alarming that some regulators and even some central bankers still seem unconcerned with the advent of E-cash. After a breakfast speech to several hundred business leaders in San Francisco last March, Fed Vice-Chairman Alan Blinder was asked whether the Fed is studying the regulatory issues surrounding digital cash. His answer: "Digital what?" Then, after pausing a moment, he added: "It's literally at the thinking stage."

Slowly, though, some regulators are beginning to explore the concept of E-money so they can set policies. The Federal Reserve's payment-systems committee is meeting with Chaum of DigiCash and other E-money pioneers. State tax collectors are looking at the issue of taxing electronic commerce. The Financial Crimes Enforcement Network is also weighing in. Even the White House technology office is taking a big interest.

It's not a moment too soon. "There's no going back," says Digita-Liberty's Frezza. "The genie's out of the bottle. The Internet doesn't have an off switch." And no amount of wishing by regulators will change that.
By Kelley Holland and Amy Cortese in New York, with bureau reports

Bank Failure

The Financial Marginalization of the Poor

Louis Jacobson

Louis Jacobson is associate editor at National Journal *magazine in Washington, D.C.*

As Ross Perot might say, there's a great sucking sound coming from America's poor neighborhoods these days—the sound of large chunks of paychecks and benefit checks flowing into the pockets of check-cashers, at five times what it would cost a typical bank to provide similar services.

Thanks in part to deregulation, bank branches have closed in low-income communities since the early 1980s, and check-cashing outlets have often taken their place. Meanwhile, another institution that more affluent Americans know from old movies and short stories—the pawnshop—has made a big comeback among the poor. The flight of the banks not only means that the poor must now pay more for financial services; it also means their communities are losing the institutions that promote personal savings. It is an irony of the recent era of economic policy: While commentators regularly preach sermons on Americans' low rate of savings, public policy has contributed to the erosion of savings institutions for the poor.

The replacement of regular banks by check-cashers and pawnshops, or "fringe bankers" as they are known, ought to trouble people across the political spectrum. Whatever their other differences, liberals and conservatives generally agree that saving is a good thing and that public policy ought to encourage it. The historical development of many of America's financial institutions, from mutual savings banks to credit unions, reflects a long commitment to the promotion of savings among lower-income Americans.

Since the 1980s, however, progress in incorporating the poor into the banking mainstream has ground to a halt. Indeed, we may well be going backwards. Surveys sponsored by the Federal Reserve Bank show that between 1977 and 1989, the percentage of households holding a deposit account changed little among the four highest income bands, but in the fifth—the poorest—account ownership dropped more than 11 percentage points. And while the rates for whites hardly varied during that time, the proportion of minority households with a bank account dipped almost six percentage points.

Reasonable people differ about what or who (if anybody) is to blame for this decline. The primary cause is probably the decline in real incomes among the poor; adequate evidence to resolve questions about causation isn't available. But it cannot help that poor communities are losing access to banks. The rise of fringe banking, says Allen Fishbein, general counsel for the Center for Community Change, an advocacy group for low-income neighborhoods, "underlines the decline of the universal banking system."

Up From Under the Mattress

Early in the nation's history, commercial banks catered to the rich; everyone else stored what little extra money they had in the proverbial mattress. But, as Swarthmore economist John P. Caskey explains, in the 1820s and 1830s wealthy Americans with a sense of civic duty began to create a new kind of institution, the mutual savings bank, to target the growing middle class. Mutuals were cooperative savings banks that shared profits among depositors, hoping they would be so inspired by the

exhortations in their passbooks ("a penny saved is a penny earned") to graduate to more traditional banks.

By the early twentieth century, visionary businessmen such as Edward Filene, of Basement fame, sought to widen the community of savers even further. They borrowed an idea from Germany that became known in America as the credit union—a nonprofit institution owned by lower- and middle-income depositors who shared the same occupation. Credit unions, with restricted lending opportunities but certain legal advantages over banks, continue to flourish today.

Also in the early part of this century, the government loosened regulations on finance companies. Finance companies, which today include such familiar names as Home Finance Corporation and the Money Store, lent money to lower-income customers whom commercial banks considered too risky. Meanwhile, borrowing another European idea, some civic-minded Americans opened non-profit pawnshops.

The most radical plan was the postal savings system, a simple savings and payment scheme operated, for most of this century, from post office counters. The system reached its apex before the Great Depression, when it offered just about the only federally insured deposit accounts. But after federal insurance was extended to commercial banks during the New Deal, the postal banks withered away until they were finally abolished in 1966.

In the years since, there have been further attempts to bring lower-income Americans into the banking system, from the advent of savings and loans to the Community Reinvestment Act of 1977 (and its strengthened revisions of 1989), which pushed banks to serve lower-income customers. Despite their many limitations, these efforts have, on the whole, succeeded in their central objective: banking and saving are far more common for most Americans today than they were when their grandparents were young.

The Banks' Getaway

With financial deregulation in the 1980s, the historical movement to include the poor in the financial mainstream came to an end. Deregulation changed the business of banking in lower-income neighborhoods in two ways. Banks have always had an incen-

tive to close unprofitable branches, but the competition stimulated by deregulation pushed many banks to act on those incentives. With deregulation, they no longer needed approval for branch closings. Regulators also began to welcome policies favoring locations in affluent areas because they helped raise bank profitability. In addition, per-check fees and minimum deposit levels, once nonexistent, rose dramatically. Few doubt that this helped push away some lower-income depositors who once used banks regularly, despite the widespread offers of "no-frills" bank accounts.

With the traditional banks gone, fringe banking took off. The dimensions and sources of their growth have been laid out by Caskey in a new book, *Fringe Banking: Check-Cashing Outlets, Pawnshops, and the Poor*, published by the Russell Sage Foundation. Caskey found that telephone listings of pawnshops increased 80 percent in the five years leading to 1992 and that check-cashers doubled over four years in that period. According to the National Check Cashers Association, cashers now process 150 million checks a year worth $45 billion, generating about $790 million in fees. The few states that lack interest ceilings or have the highest ceilings, where pawnbrokers often charge 240 percent interest a year, are home to the majority of such shops. Caskey emphasizes that the profile touted by press reports—gritty, inner-city locations that serve a predominantly African-American clientele—is only accurate in the Northeast. Elsewhere, such outlets also operate in working- and middle-class neighborhoods, often suburban, and serve mostly whites.

A recent report on check-cashers wryly calls them "one of the few growth industries in lower-income communities." The report, by veteran consumer activist Mark Green, shows that despite population increases, since 1978 Brooklyn has lost 14.3 percent of its bank branches and the Bronx has lost 19.9 percent. Green, who is now the elected public advocate for the city of New York, reports that "in both boroughs, bank closings disproportionately affected the poorest neighborhoods." Check-cashing outlets, which were hardly new (and benefited from loosened rules on their locations), filled the void. From 353 establishments operating in New York State in

1981, such outlets increased by 44.5 percent by the early 1990s.

The disparity in access to banking services is apparent from another local study, sponsored by the Los Angeles city council. The council found that in a 40-square-mile region of South Central Los Angeles, 133 check-cashers and only 19 banks served 587,000 people in 1991. Nearby Gardena boasted 21 banks for 49,800 residents.

There is nothing new, of course, about reduced access and higher prices for services in poor communities. David Caplovitz described the phenomenon in a 1963 book *The Poor Pay More*, which focused on installment credit. Financial deregulation in the 1980s allowed banking services to follow the same pattern. Caskey estimates that a family of four earning $10,000 would today spend $211 using check-cashers for a year; at $16,500, a family would spend $325 a year and at $24,000 a year it would spend $456. Pawnshops take even bigger bite. By comparison, if the same families used banks, they would spend about $60.

But if they cost more, why are check-cashers and pawnbrokers booming? For one thing, fringe bankers have their finger on the pulse of low-income communities. Surveys suggest that customers are satisfied with the services they receive from check-cashers, which include convenient locations, flexible hours, short lines, ancillary services such as bus passes and lottery tickets, and, perhaps most important, immediate cash without waiting for a check to clear. Allen Fishbein, who works to convince traditional banks to return to low-income areas, admits that check-cashers were one of the few businesses to return to Los Angeles immediately after the 1992 riots. (They operated from the back of trucks.) Pawnshops, too, have long been willing to overlook a client's lack of creditworthiness when lending.

As a result, although surveys differ, at least a sizable minority of check-cashing customers also have deposit accounts. The problem is with the others, who too often have been robbed of the chance to own a convenient deposit account because of bank flight.

Defenders of the banks argue, correctly, that automated teller machines in low-income neighborhoods have filled in some of the banking-services gap. However, ATMs cannot compete with the range of services that check-cashers provide, nor can they serve the traditional educational functions of banks, such as teaching customers about different saving and borrowing options. Given the absence of marketing outreach by the banks in poor areas, it's hardly surprising that the check-cashers' customers—whom studies show to be not only poorer but also less educated than average—are unaware of the price advantages banks can offer.

Compounding the gulf between banks and the urban poor is a divergence in banking needs. Recent immigrants who send funds to their families abroad—a growing sector of the check-casher clientele—have less need for a savings account than for convenient wire transfers. Language barriers (combined with a lack of education and a dearth of banking experience) complicate attempts to explain consumer choices, so non-English speakers are tempted to stick with the easiest option, even if it is expensive. For all their convenience, ATMs can hardly handle such questions.

Substituting check-cashers for banks generates some indirect costs to the poor, beyond the higher prices for services. For one, patrons of check-cashing outlets only receive signals to spend, not to save (right down to the lottery machines). They are also prime targets for thieves: Green's report highlights a growing trend of robberies near check-cashing outlets. And the absence of local bank branches makes it difficult for many residents to get loans or other services a bank might provide. This not only worsens the historical problem of redlining—that is, when banks avoid loaning money to residents and businesses in low-income areas—but also creates a vacuum that fosters the growth of occasionally unscrupulous and often usurious mortgage brokers that satisfy the lending demand.

The larger worry in all this is the financial marginalization of the poor. A bank account symbolizes economic participation. It's also vital for building a credit rating, for example. The growing detachment of the poor from the culture of banking and saving threatens to push them even further from the middle class. It is unclear whether a general cultural shift de-emphasizing thrift may have contributed to the

decline in account-holding by the poor. Even if it has, however, the flight of banks from low-income neighborhoods can only reinforce the declining sway of traditional economic virtues.

Back to Banks?

What can be done to make banks more accessible and to limit the cost of financial services to the poor? It is not necessary to repeal banking deregulation altogether, only to use some policy creativity. One limited response, already made by at least 11 states, is to set ceilings on check-cashing fees. A majority of states also regulate the interest rates offered by pawnshops. As long as states do not set limits so low as to prevent these businesses from operating—if they did, Caskey suggests, it would wreak havoc on low-income money management—replicating these rules elsewhere and strengthening enforcement could help eliminate exploiters and rogues from the business. Another idea is to require check-cashers and pawnshops to post the cost of their services in a clear and standard way.

These rules, however, would not necessarily promote better access to banks. One way to do that is to encourage local check-cashers to become de facto bank branches by offering no-frills accounts on behalf of a traditional bank. Participating banks would gain customers, check-cashers would retain their customer base, and the customers would gain security. Another idea is to get better mileage out of the federal Community Reinvestment Act, which was designed (not very stringently) to withhold government approval from banks unless they made an effort to serve all communities in the region where they did business. Regulators might mandate that laggard banks join in a consortium that would operate branches in low-income neighborhoods under a single name. This would be less onerous than requiring each bank to serve poor neighborhoods, and it would create a bank network experienced with the specialized needs of low-income customers.

Since many residents of low-income communities receive some form of government assistance, government checks provide another appealing means for reconnecting banks with the poor. A bill offered by Senator Howard Metzenbaum, Demo-

crat of Ohio, in 1991 would have required banks to cash government checks for non-depositors. Critics point out, however, that this approach could weaken many of the small and marginally profitable banks already serving poor neighborhoods. A better alternative would be to expand the system of electronic benefit transfers—that is, bypassing checks altogether and offering benefits such as unemployment, Social Security, welfare, and veterans payouts by wire directly into deposit accounts. Currently, about half of Social Security and veterans' benefits are paid out electronically. The Clinton administration has released a plan to create an integrated electronic benefit distribution system and hopes to have it in place nationwide by 1999. Early feedback from Maryland's electronic benefits program, now about a year old, shows that four of every five users are satisfied.

Mark Ragan, deputy director of a federal task force on electronic benefit transfers, says the proposal was designed to reduce fraud, lost checks, and crime. As written, the proposal helps recipients gain experience with ATM machines, reducing their dependence on check-cashers and the need to hold on to large amounts of cash for weeks at a time. But the plan could easily include incentives for low-income recipients to open a savings or checking account—something that almost no other reform can promise.

Private-sector efforts can also help. New non-profit credit unions, which would enjoy flexibility from banking requirements in exchange for a commitment to small depositors in the inner city, are a good idea. So too is the Clintonesque vision of new community development banks that would focus on commercial lending. Above all, banks need to recapture the momentum from check-cashers, filling the vacuum with their own brand of inventive and creatively marketed institutions. A useful model is offered by First Community Bank, a bank-within-a-bank operated by Bank of Boston.

Jeff Zinsmeyer, a director of the bank, says the idea sprung from the "not very novel notion that we should treat the low-income community as a separate business, just as we separate high-tech or transportation lending, or over-50 banking or private banking." The Bank of Boston opened the

doors to its subsidiary in 1989 and, says Zinsmeyer, has been successful ever since.

A key move was to avoid what Zinsmeyer calls the "United Way" approach to banking—a charitable paternalism that annoys customers and saps management talent. "Who wants to be the guy who makes bad loans?" he asks. Rather, the bank saw the inner city as a business opportunity. New immigrants are one target market. Despite language barriers and low incomes, Zinsmeyer sees their market as stable, reliable, and set for growth. "If you were told that the market was growing at 10, 20, 30 percent, you'd want to be in," he says. Public-private partnership funds for community development have made it easier for the bank to make loans no other bank would touch.

To be sure, this kind of endeavor isn't for every bank, Zinsmeyer says. Rather, he suggests that legislative sticks might be less beneficial than carrots. And Zinsmeyer admits that there are limits to banks' usefulness. Because a single failed $100,000 loan can only be recouped, at present profit margins, by the successful repayment of 20 to 30 others, some loans really are too risky to make, he says. Rather than wait to build new institutions from scratch, he says, why not help endangered communities benefit sooner from the knowledge and infrastructure of experienced banks?

Creative coalition-building could help promote this kind of change. Jack Kemp, for example, has been building bridges with liberals on policies that give the poor an ownership stake in the economy. Chris Jacobs, who is policy director of the Kemp-affiliated Empowerment Network Founda-tion, says banking services are as central to their vision of community empowerment as it is for community activists. With a little luck and a lot of hard work, the next wave of low-income banking reform has the potential to be a bipartisan affair.

Recent news reports have noted that the popularity of ATMs and of banking by phone has made bank branches in affluent suburbs almost superfluous, putting these branches, for the first time, on the same closure lists long inhabited by branches in poor neighborhoods. This need not be a bad omen for the customers, and potential customers, in low-income areas. The chief advantage of ATMs is that they are both inexpensive and cost-effective. Thanks to ATMs, banks may now cheaply enter geographical niches that were once seen as unprofitable—and, once there, the machines' long-term cost-effectiveness will make banks more likely to stay put.

But ATMSs should not be seen as a quick technological fix. Just plopping teller machines in poor neighborhoods will hardly attract droves of new customers. Serious outreach is needed; a good start would be to plow a small portion of the savings from closed suburban branches into marketing efforts in poor areas. Moreover, the government must continue its regulatory pressures to insure that the precious few existing branches in low-income areas are not now closed. If banks decide to pursue this new market with a little creativity—using either the consortium model or the First Community Bank model—the time may be surprisingly ripe for a rebirth of private sector low-income banking.

Unemployment, Inflation, and the Business Cycle

We mustn't have it too good. Too much growth—too little unemployment—is a bad thing. These are not the idle thoughts of economic nail-biters; they are the economic policy of the United States. (Robert Eisner, *The American Prospect*, Spring 1995)

Business cycles are a key feature of all market-based, capitalist economies. While no two cycles are identical (either in terms of their intensity or duration), they all share a common characteristic: a wave of recession (or falling real Gross Domestic Product [GDP]) is always followed by a period of recovery (when real GDP rises)—which leads in turn to another recession. In discussions of the business cycle, these terms are sometimes imprecise. For one thing, politicians (particularly those in positions of power) are generally reluctant to admit that a recession could ever occur under their watch (preferring instead to lay blame for this development at the doorstep of the rival party). For another, the terms "recession" and "depression" (a large and prolonged recession) are sometimes confused. In fact, only just recently have economists generally shown a willingness to use the latter term at all. And, finally, while it is usually possible to determine when a recession has come to an end, there is no guarantee that the recession will always be followed by a recovery vigorous enough to ensure that the economy is finally "out of the woods." The pause between recession and recovery (sometimes referred to as a "soft landing," a "rolling adjustment," or something equally vague) often confounds forecasters and frustrates politicians.

There can be little doubt, however, that business cycles exert a powerful influence on modern economies. As real output falls, recessions can displace tens of thousands of workers from their jobs, cause businesses (both large and small) to fail, and oust politicians from office. Even recoveries are not risk free; if they prove to be too vigorous, inflationary pressures can develop as the economy's output approaches capacity. Those workers and businesses unable to stay ahead of inflation may eventually experience an erosion of the purchasing power of their income.

This unit begins with Robert Eisner's article, "Our NAIRU Limit: The Governing Myth of Economic Policy."

Eisner examines a concept which has become a powerful influence on U.S. macroeconomic policy, the "nonaccelerating-inflation-rate of unemployment" (or NAIRU). According to this view, too much growth or too little unemployment automatically result in inflation. Eisner pinpoints flaws in the NAIRU concept.

Recent studies indicate that technology, especially information technology, is responsible for destroying millions of jobs. The hope is that it will ultimately create more jobs than it destroys. "Technology and Unemployment: A World without Jobs" investigates the evidence.

Since the early 1970s the rate of part-time, temporary, and subcontracted employment (otherwise known as "contingent employment") has grown far faster than the rate for full-time work. In the next article, Virginia duRivage considers possible implications of this development for public policy.

Next, "The Real Un(der)employment Rate," by Marc Breslow and Matthew Howard, asserts that present methods for tabulating unemployment significantly understate the true extent of joblessness. When allowance is made for discouraged workers and those who have gone from full- to part-time work, the overall rate of unemployment jumps from 6 percent to more than 10 percent.

Does a rising stock market help make the economy safe from recession? Sylvia Nasar finds that, compared with other forces at work in the economy, the impact of fatter stock portfolios is relatively modest.

The article "Has Our Living Standard Stalled?" asks why, if inflationary trends have moderated, so many Americans feel worse off today than in the past. The answer may lie in how the Consumer Price Index tracks inflation. In "As Parties Skirmish over Budget, Greenspan Offers a Painless Cure," Adam Clymer notes that recent findings indicate that the actual rate of inflation is at least one percentage point less than officially recorded. Clymer considers what this might mean for the conduct of macroeconomic policy.

Finally, Thomas Synnott III draws on the study of long wave cycles in economics to explain trends in inflation and interest rates in the U.S. economy. Synnott maintains that long wave analysis provides a better explanation than does traditional business cycle analysis for why low inter-

est rates have not done more to stimulate the economy, and for why job growth has been so slow during the current expansion.

Looking Ahead: Challenge Questions

What is the present outlook for unemployment, inflation, and economic growth in the U.S. economy?

What is meant by the term "nonaccelerating-inflation rate of unemployment"? What role does this concept play in macroeconomic policy?

Why has contingent employment grown so fast? Have American living standards stalled?

What is "long wave analysis," and how might it be applied to the U.S. economy?

OUR NAIRU LIMIT
THE GOVERNING MYTH OF ECONOMIC POLICY

ROBERT EISNER

Robert Eisner, the William R. Kenan Professor Emeritus in the economics department of Northwestern University, is a past president of the American Economic Association. His recent book, The Misunderstood Economy: What Counts and how to Count it, *is published by McGraw-Hill (1994). Professor Eisner's article is the first in a series on inequality, poverty, and the changing economy, supported by a grant from the John D. and Catherine T. MacArthur Foundation.*

We mustn't have it too good. Too much growth—too little unemployment—is a bad thing. These are not the idle thoughts of economic nail-biters; they are the economic policy of the United States. After real growth of gross domestic product (GDP) hit 4.5 percent in the last quarter of 1994 and unemployment dipped to 5.4 percent in December, the Federal Reserve moved on February 1 to raise interest rates for the seventh time in less than a year. Why? To slow our too rapid rate of growth and stop or reverse the fall in unemployment. Why do that? To fight inflation.

Ordinary people may wonder. Overall inflation, as measured by the GDP implicit price deflator, was down to 2.1 percent, its lowest in three decades. The Consumer Price Index rose only 2.7 percent in 1994 and knowledgeable analysts, including the Fed's chairman, Alan Greenspan, recognize that this measure overstates the rise in consumer costs, perhaps by as much as two percentage points.

Hard-nosed economic analysts and business leaders are also raising questions. They point to technological advances and downsizing in U.S. industry and suggest that productivity and output potential may well be rising more rapidly than the 2.5 percent long-term growth rate that Greenspan and others think marks the outer limit for the economy. Furthermore, as people lose old, high-paying jobs and look desperately even for lower-paying employment, there is slack in the labor force. Perhaps most important, increasing globalization and world competition may limit the ability of American firms to raise prices and workers to push for higher wages.

These heretical observations have so far failed to dent the dominant dogma haunting economic policy. The central tenet of that dogma is a concept familiarly known among economists as the NAIRU—the "nonaccelerating-inflation-rate of unemployment." While unknown to the general public, the NAIRU has become one of the most powerful influences on economic policy this century. My recent work, however, shows that even on the basis of a conventional model used to estimate the NAIRU, there is no basis for the conclusion that low unemployment rates threaten permanently accelerating inflation. And, according to an alternative model more consistent with the data, inflation might actually be lower at unemployment levels than we are experiencing today.

THE NAIRU FRAMEWORK

The basic proposition of the NAIRU is simple: Policymakers cannot use deficit spending or an increase in the money supply to reduce unemployment below some "equilibrium" rate, except at the cost of accelerating inflation. This is a sharp departure from the Keynesian view that inflation poses a danger only when increased spending or demand presses against full or near-full employment.

The concept of the NAIRU, derived from Milton Friedman's notion of a "natural rate of unemployment," rejects the assumed trade-off between unemployment and inflation described by the Phillips Curve, named after A.W. Phillips, an innovative economist from New Zealand. The Phillips Curve suggests that maintaining lower unemployment does produce higher inflation, but the inflation is constant. In the NAIRU view, the Phillips Curve is only a short-run relation. Trying to reduce unemployment by increasing spending or aggregate demand may work for a while, but then the higher inflation will cancel out the effects of the stimulus. Increased actual inflation will raise expectations of future inflation; only the excess of

 Reprinted with permission from *The American Prospect*, Spring 1995, pp. 58-63.

actual inflation over what workers, employers, borrowers, and lenders expect will stimulate the economy. At each round, higher spending and inflation will be necessary to maintain the original reduction in unemployment.

Thus, according to the NAIRU, fiscal or monetary policies aimed at reducing unemployment would leave us like a dog chasing its tail. If policy were aimed at keeping total spending sufficiently high to keep unemployment below its "natural rate," inflation would rise more and more rapidly. Ultimately, policymakers would give up in the face of runaway prices. Unemployment would then be back at its natural rate and inflation would stop accelerating, but it would stay at its new, higher level until unemployment rose above the natural rate and the process was painfully reversed.

In this view, the only way to reduce unemployment, except possibly in the short run, is to change conditions affecting the supply of labor—for example, by cutting the minimum wage, reducing or eliminating unemployment benefits, or upgrading the skills of workers. If the NAIRU is taken seriously, supply-side measures are the only ways to get unemployment down and keep it down. And if unemployment is at or close to the NAIRU, the monetary authority must take prompt anti-inflationary action to prevent the economy from "overheating." Otherwise, inflation will not only be higher but will be launched on its accelerating course, from which it can be diverted only by the medicine of excess unemployment—that is, unemployment above the NAIRU.

This is the view that underlies the otherwise inexplicable policy of the Federal Reserve. Most of our central bankers believe that we are at the natural rate of unemployment or below it, and we need more unemployment before it is too late. The main difference among macroeconomists today is that conservatives tend to put the NAIRU higher, at say 6-plus or 7 percent, while liberals put it at 6 or perhaps 5-plus percent. A few brave souls suggest that since our estimates of the NAIRU are imprecise, we should cautiously try to bring down unemployment until we have signs of inflation. But others say by then it will be too late.

Few economists have challenged the basic concept of the NAIRU. Keynes observed six decades ago that economists could stubbornly stick to their assumptions in the face of crushing reality, as when they argued in the depths of the Great Depression that there could be no

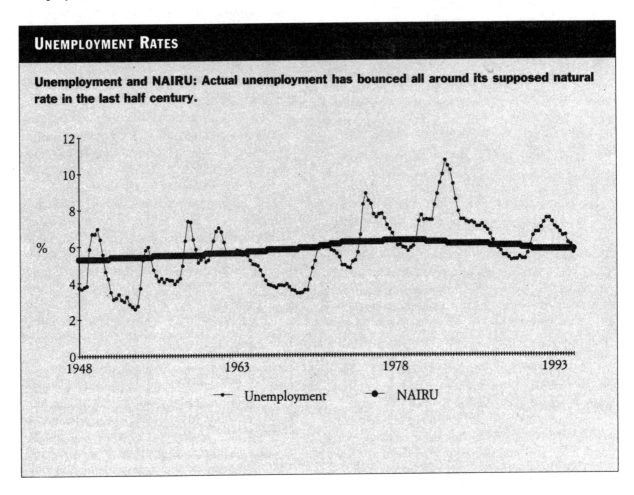

UNEMPLOYMENT RATES

Unemployment and NAIRU: Actual unemployment has bounced all around its supposed natural rate in the last half century.

involuntary unemployment. Another such episode of professional obstinacy may well be unfolding. Business leaders report, and national statistics confirm, that despite unemployment falling below the conventional NAIRU, accelerating inflation is nowhere in sight. But many economists are unmoved by mere evidence.

> The premises of the Fed's anti-inflation policy are now in doubt.

The available data do not, in fact, show that the NAIRU has much to do with historical levels of unemployment. In the United States, as shown in the figure on page 135, actual unemployment has bounced all around a NAIRU that was altered only slightly to keep up with it. Why, for example, did unemployment dip well below the NAIRU through most of the 1960s? The theory does not tell us why it was possible then but impossible now.

The conventional model could simply be ignoring many factors affecting inflation or the interaction of unemployment and inflation. These factors may also have a different impact when unemployment is high and when it is low. When unemployment is high, workers may indeed hesitate to press for higher wages because they are worried about losing their jobs. Still higher unemployment and falling demand may lead to more competition for limited markets, which may further check inflation.

But when unemployment is low, inflation may also be held in check. Low unemployment is usually associated with more efficient use of all resources. Persistent low unemployment rates that might lead to higher wages may encourage the substitution of capital for labor and raise anticipated future productivity, which would curb inflation. And with profits high and overhead costs spread broadly, firms may keep down prices to discourage others from entering their markets. Firms that are flush with profits may consider moving into new areas. Firms already there may well hesitate to raise prices and thus offer greater invitation to would-be interlopers.

This is, of course, just a sketch of why low unemployment and the high profits usually associated with it may inhibit inflation. Thus, the relationship may be different from what is usually assumed. It may be true that high

unemployment reduces inflation, while it is false that low unemployment raises inflation.

THE CONVENTIONAL FORMULATION

Two crucial assumptions are necessary to arrive at the usual concept of the NAIRU. The first is that, left to itself, any given rate of inflation is self-perpetuating; the second, that unemployment is a key factor in changing inflation rates—specifically, that higher unemployment lowers inflation, and lower unemployment raises inflation.

There has been something of a cottage industry in estimating the NAIRU over the years. An exemplary case is the formulation by the Congressional Budget Office (CBO) in its August 1994 *Economic and Budget Outlook: An Update*, which is similar to influential work a decade earlier by Robert Gordon. The general idea is that inflation is a function of a number of variables such as presumably independent food and energy price movements, changes in productivity, the imposition and removal of price controls, and, most important, past inflation and current and past unemployment. The idea that inflation is self-perpetuating is embodied in the assumption that past inflation enters the equations with a coefficient of one. The formulation then has an estimated constant term—which is positive, pushing inflation up—and negative coefficients of unemployment to hold inflation down. The size of those negative coefficients determines how much unemployment will be necessary to keep inflation from increasing. The rate of unemployment just sufficient to do this is the NAIRU.

I have replicated the CBO estimates and have confirmed the agency's results using its own model. The sum of the past inflation coefficients is at or above that crucial value of unity necessary for inflation to be self-perpetuating unless stopped. The constant terms are positive and the sums of the unemployment coefficients negative. My estimates yield a NAIRU at just about CBO's figure of 5.8 percent. (The measure of unemployment used by the CBO is the unemployment rate for married men, which it then adjusts to estimate the general rate of unemployment.)

> We have no basis for deliberately raising unemployment.

However, even this model does not support some of the implications usually drawn for policymaking. Many economists argue that we must never let the

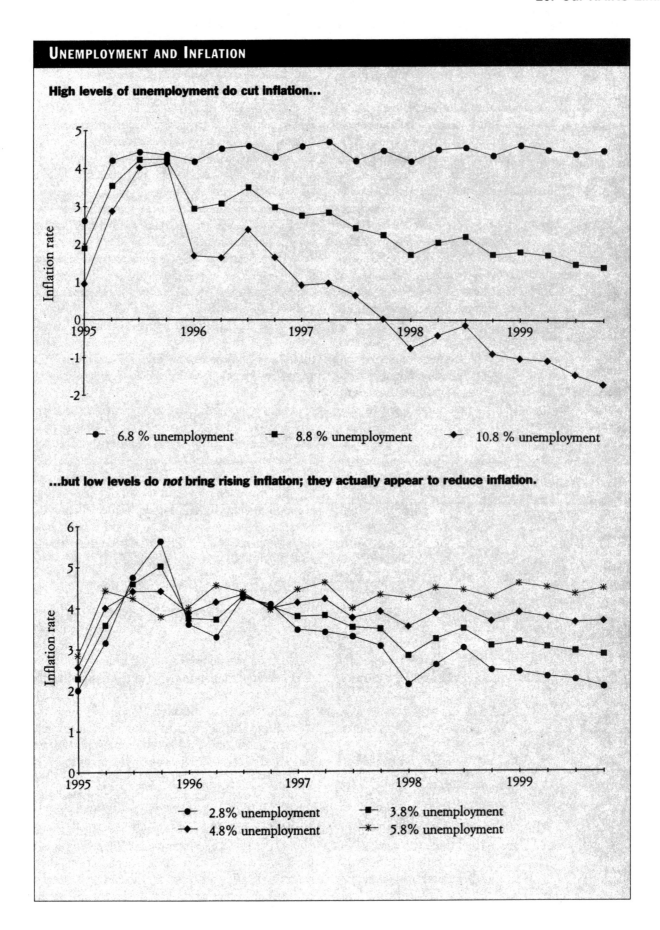

UNEMPLOYMENT AND INFLATION

High levels of unemployment do cut inflation...

● 6.8 % unemployment   ■ 8.8 % unemployment   ◆ 10.8 % unemployment

...but low levels do *not* bring rising inflation; they actually appear to reduce inflation.

● 2.8% unemployment   ■ 3.8% unemployment
◆ 4.8% unemployment   ✳ 5.8% unemployment

genie of inflation out of the bag because even a brief, inflation-accelerating experience of low unemployment will be disastrous and difficult to correct. Testing that proposition, I found that a one percentage point reduction in the married-male unemployment rate to 2.55 percent (one percentage point below the CBO estimate of the married-male NAIRU) generates a sharp increase and fluctuation in CPI inflation for several quarters, which subsides quickly if unemployment goes back up to the NAIRU. Even permanent unemployment of 2.55 percent does not, after five years, get inflation past 7 percent.

These results are based on the conventional formulation, but that is only the beginning of the story. The conventional model constrains the unemployment and inflation parameters in ways that are in fundamental conflict with the data. Freeing the model from those constraints leads to dramatically different conclusions; this calls into question the use of the NAIRU as a justification for blocking fiscal and monetary policies that might bring "full employment," or distinctly lower unemployment than what is now widely viewed as acceptable.

AN ALTERNATIVE MODEL

My reformulation of the conventional model suggests that the effect of unemployment on inflation is different when unemployment is low compared to when it is high. The key question, then, is what happens to the estimated values of the unemployment coefficients when unemployment is low. Do they differ consistently from the coefficients when unemployment is high?

First, estimates of separate relations for high and low unemployment show that differences between the unemployment coefficients are clearly statistically significant.

Second, the unemployment coefficients in the low-unemployment regressions are generally positive, though usually modest in size. This suggests that, whatever the effect on inflation of unemployment below the NAIRU, once below the NAIRU, lowering unemployment further may reduce inflation.

Third, under low unemployment, the sums of inflation coefficients were below unity, contradicting a critical assumption underlying the NAIRU. Inflation left to itself would not be self-perpetuating, and low unemployment would not cause accelerating inflation. Even if unemployment below the NAIRU did raise inflation, it would raise it by a finite amount—the old Phillips-Curve relation, not permanently accelerating inflation.

SIMULATIONS AND FORECASTS

One way to reveal the effects of the various interacting coefficients is to simulate or forecast ahead. I show results based on a single equation for inflation in the consumer price index. The high-unemployment inflation paths in the figure on page 137 fit the conventional view. Unemployment above the NAIRU drives inflation down, although the implicit NAIRU is closer to 6.8 percent in my simulations based only on high-unemployment observations. It takes still higher unemployment to break the back of inflation. But high enough unemployment does eventually turn inflation negative; that is, it drives prices down.

The low-unemployment paths shown, however, offer quite a different picture. At 5.8 percent unemployment, contrary to Alan Greenspan's fears, there is no accelerating inflation. By the end of the century, inflation settles at about 4.4 percent. Strikingly, at lower unemployment rates, inflation is no higher. At 4.8 percent unemployment, the simulation shows inflation coming down to 3.6 percent. At 3.8 percent unemployment, inflation comes down to 2.9 percent. At 2.8 percent unemployment, inflation at the end of 1999 is down to 2.1 percent.

NAIRU ESCAPE?

I would not bet the family farm or the nation's economy on any set of econometric estimates, even my own. But promoters, defenders, and practitioners of the conventional NAIRU have done exactly that, with increasingly dogmatic assertion. They have paralyzed macroeconomic policy that should be aimed at the "high" and "full" employment targets set by the Employment Act of 1946 and the Humphrey-Hawkins Full Employment and Balanced Growth Act of 1978.

If accelerating inflation is not our fate, some might think a few extra percentage points of constant inflation might offer a pretty good bargain. Lower unemployment would generate large increases in output. According to the robust Okun's Law, named after Arthur Okun, the late Yale economist, each percentage point of unemployment costs at least two percentage points of output. That would amount to more than $130 billion of GDP this year.

Those committed to the concept of a NAIRU cannot easily dismiss the evidence of asymmetry that I have presented. I am not proposing a new dogma that lowering unemployment will reduce inflation.

Even if my formulation is right, my standard errors are often too high—as, I should add, are those of practitioners of the conventional model— to permit any precise conclusions. There may be no stable, universal relation among unemployment and all the various factors contributing to inflation.

But the results reported here should clearly show the lack of empirical support for the NAIRU and the policies based upon it. They suggest that we have no sound basis for deliberately raising unemployment.

On the contrary, we ought to be trying to reduce it, not only by supply-side measures, but by ensuring that the economy is not starved for adequate aggregate demand or productivity-increasing public investment. These measures should aim at reducing both underlying structural unemployment and the unemployment caused by misguided anti-inflation policy. The fight against inflation can then be focused where it should be—on promoting the greatest measure of domestic and international competition.

TECHNOLOGY AND UNEMPLOYMENT

A world without jobs?

Technology, especially information technology, is destroying millions of jobs. The hope is that it will create more than it destroys. Will it?

SINCE the beginning of the industrial revolution people have predicted that machines would destroy jobs. In the early 19th century the Luddites responded by destroying the looms and jennies that threatened their livelihood. Marx said that, by investing in machinery, factory owners would create a vast army of unemployed. And in the late 1940s Norbert Weiner, a pioneer of computing, forecast that this new technology would destroy enough jobs to make the depression of the 1930s look like a picnic.

Fear of what machines will do to men at work waxes and wanes. Right now, the fear is growing strongly. Typical of the new wave of pessimistic forecasts is a book, "The End of Work" (G.P. Putnam's Sons), by Jeremy Rifkin, an American technophobe whose previous target was the biotechnology industry. Within the next century, he predicts, the world's rich economies will have virtually no need of workers. Predictions such as this reinforce a growing fear in the middle classes that technology, having eliminated much of the work previously done by manual workers, is about to cut a swathe through white-collar ranks as well.

Are such fears justified? In one way, yes. Millions of jobs have indeed been destroyed by technology. A decade ago, the words you are now reading would have reached you from two sets of hands: those of a journalist and those of a typesetter. Thanks to computers, the typesetter no longer has a job. But cheer up—a bit, anyway. Although the typesetter no longer has *that* job, he may well have a different one. John Kennedy put it well in the 1960s: "If men have the talent to invent new machines that put men out of work, they have the talent to put those men back to work." That is as true now as it was then, and earlier.

In the past 200 years millions of manual workers have been replaced by machines. Over the same period, the number of jobs has grown almost continuously, as have the real incomes of most people in the industrial world. Furthermore, this growth and enrichment have come about not in spite of technological change but because of it.

The idea that technology is capable of creating more jobs than it destroys, and will do so again, would not surprise an economist. Later, this article will describe the mechanism that explains why you would expect it to be the case. But first it is necessary to look at a big claim made by people like Mr Rifkin and other modern-day Luddites. They argue that the wave of technological change now under way is different in pace and nature from any of its predecessors. If they were right, the reassuring lesson of the past—the evidence that technology has created jobs faster than it has destroyed them—would be a lot less comforting.

This time it will really hurt!

The claim that information technology (IT) is different from spinning jennies is based on three observations:

• Although inventions such as the mechanised loom and the spinning jenny threw people out of work, their impact was confined to a fairly small part of the economy. Even truly enormous changes, such as the advent of electricity or the assembly line, mainly affected manufacturing, which has never accounted for much more than 40% of the jobs in anybody's economy. By contrast, IT (computers, software and advanced telecoms) is all-pervasive. It seems to have the potential to displace workers not only in manufacturing industry but in service jobs too—and not just the humble desk worker, but more highly skilled people.

Mr Rifkin notes that, in the past, when new technologies replaced workers, a new sector always emerged to absorb those who had lost their jobs. When farm labourers were replaced by ploughs and tractors, manufacturing became a big employer. When much factory work was automated, the service sector took over. For half a century, services have accounted for almost all the net new jobs created in the so-called industrial economies. But now service jobs are being automated too. Telephone operators are being replaced by voice-recognising computers, postal workers by address-reading machines, bank tellers by cash-dispensing machines that can handle ten times as many transactions in a day.

And all this is only the beginning, says Mr Rifkin. He estimates that three out of every four workers in industrial countries perform simple repetitive tasks that could be automated. Even the skilled are at risk. Already, clever computer programs can diagnose some illnesses just as well as doctors can. A robot that will perform hip replacements is under development in California. Some American companies are using Resumix, a computerised hiring system, to screen job applicants. In 1993, a "computer-generated" novel was deemed no worse than hundreds of humanly crafted love stories published each year.

• As well as being more pervasive, IT is being introduced much faster than earlier new technologies were. This means that societies have less time to replace the jobs that are lost and to train people for the new jobs that might be created. Although the pace of technological change is not easy to measure, the speed at which the price of computer power has fallen lends some weight to the claim. This is also part of the answer to those who ask why, since computers have been around since the 1950s, they have not already caused mass unemployment. Only recently have prices fallen to the point where a vast amount of computer power can be placed cheaply on every desk.

• IT makes work more portable. In some services physical contact with customers becomes unnecessary. Tele-working enables firms to move jobs overseas, so that low-paid workers in India, say, end up writing software programs or preparing tax returns for multinationals. In this sense, new technology not only reduces the demand for labour; it also increases its supply.

The reasons for resisting despair

All this sounds plausible. And, since it is mainly speculation about the future, it is hard to say with certainty that it is wrong. Yet such evidence as does exist bears out few of the doomsters' claims. There is also a strong theoretical reason for doubting them.

First, some anecdotal evidence. Despite a huge investment in computing and so on over the past decade, unemployment in the United States, at around 5½%, is currently no higher than it was in the early 1960s. In Western Europe, where the investment has been smaller (see chart 1), 11% of workers are jobless. This is hardly a persuasive sign that IT is a big cause of unemployment. Some of the new jobs in America have been disparaged as McJobs—hamburger flipping and the like. But such jobs do not seem to make up a big share of the total.

Next, some theory. A new machine helps you make more stuff with fewer people. But the assumption that this results in fewer jobs rather than more output (and hence more goods, and more job-stimulating demand, in a beautifully virtuous circle) is based on an economic fallacy known as the "lump of labour": the notion that there is only a fixed amount of output (and hence work) to go round. This is clearly wrong. Technology creates new demand, either by increasing productivity and hence real incomes, or by creating new goods.

For example, as demand for black-and-white televisions was becoming satiated in most rich industrial countries, colour TVs were introduced, and then video-cassette recorders. Microwave ovens, video games and soft contact lenses are among the many goods that did not exist in 1970. New things go on getting invented. If output expands, productivity growth can march in step with rising employment.

From an individual firm's point of view, process innovation (making things more ef-ficiently) as opposed to product innovation (making new things) may indeed reduce employment. But the economy as a whole will enjoy compensating effects. If a new machine reduces the amount of labour needed, and so cuts costs, one of three things can happen. The price of the good or service will fall; wages will rise; or profits (and hence investment income) will increase.

All three of these things imply a rise in consumer purchasing power, and so an increase in demand (and thus in output and jobs, too), either for that particular good or for other goods or services. So even if IT destroys more jobs than previous technical innovations, its pervasiveness also means that the compensating demand-generating effects will be stronger, with enormous invest-ment and growth opportunities for the economy as a whole.

It is of course impossible to predict exactly where the new jobs will emerge over the next 25 years. Many jobs listed in the vacancy columns of today's newspapers—such as aerobics teachers, software engineers and derivatives specialists—did not exist in 1970. There are some clues, however, about where the expansion might come.

• In America in the past ten years, employment in the computer-software industry has almost trebled. The Bureau of Labour Statistics forecasts that between 1992 and 2005 the number of jobs for computer systems analysts and programmers will more than double—the fastest-growing occupations after home-health workers, who tend the sick in their own beds (see chart 2).

• The number of elderly people in the population is growing, and they are a lot richer than elderly people were 50 or 100 years ago. They will create jobs in—for instance—health care, home help, financial advice and the holiday industry.

• Rapid technological change increases the need for workers to train themselves for new sorts of work when the old sort gets done by machines. So there will be a growing demand for training, and teachers to do it.

• There is scope for a big expansion of the entertainment and information services. "Virtual reality" experiences, such as pretending to be a jet pilot for a couple of hours in a session with a sophisticated simulator, could become as popular as going to the cinema. If it does, it could create quite a lot of jobs.

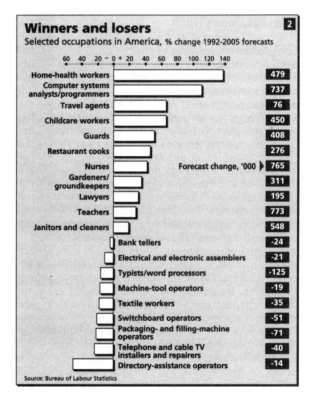

Winners and losers 2
Selected occupations in America, % change 1992-2005 forecasts

Occupation	Forecast change, '000
Home-health workers	479
Computer systems analysts/programmers	737
Travel agents	76
Childcare workers	450
Guards	408
Restaurant cooks	276
Nurses	765
Gardeners/groundkeepers	311
Lawyers	195
Teachers	773
Janitors and cleaners	548
Bank tellers	-24
Electrical and electronic assemblers	-21
Typists/word processors	-125
Machine-tool operators	-19
Textile workers	-35
Switchboard operators	-51
Packaging- and filling-machine operators	-71
Telephone and cable TV installers and repairers	-40
Directory-assistance operators	-14

Source: Bureau of Labour Statistics

The first shoots of optimism

The notion that technology creates more jobs than it destroys is borne out in a review of various economic studies published last year in the OECD's "Jobs Study"*. Admittedly, such studies have their limitations, including a habit of examining yesterday's technology rather than the most up-to-date machines. It is also easier to quantify the direct labour-saving effects of technology—the number of jobs replaced by robots in the car industry, say—than the compensating demand effects, which may occur at a different time and in a different place. This makes it hard to estimate the net impact on employment. Nonetheless, the OECD found little support for the view that technological change is to blame for high unemployment.

The modern abacus 1
Computers per 100 people, 1993

	0	5	10	15	20	25	30
United States							
Australia							
Canada							
Britain							
Sweden							
Switzerland							
Holland							
France							
Germany							
Belgium/Luxembourg							
Japan							
Spain							
Italy							

Sources: IMD; World Economic Forum

If anything, says the OECD, the current wave of technological change has been modestly beneficial for jobs. The demand-boosting effects have more than offset the job-destroying ones. Indeed, the countries that have been most successful in creating jobs—America and Japan—have also seen the fastest shift in their industrial structure towards a high-tech, knowledge-based economy (see chart 3). Japan, for example, has more industrial robots per worker than any other big economy but also has the lowest unemployment rate. A survey of European employers in 1988 found that, far from reducing the number of jobs available, IT had helped to create work. Nearly 40% of employees affected by IT in the sample were newly recruited, more than twice as many as had been made redundant by IT.

To be sure, there are reasons to hesitate before concluding that everything is all right. One difficulty with estimating the impact of technology on productivity and jobs is that it is hard to measure productivity in services. Robert Solow, an American Nobel laureate in economics, gave birth to what is known as "the Solow paradox".

He observed that the huge investment which service industries had made in computing had made little measurable difference to productivity in the service sector. During the 1980s, when service industries consumed about 85% of the $1 trillion invested in IT in the United States, productivity growth averaged a niggardly 0.8% a year. Services have actually invested proportionately more in IT than manufacturing has. In six important services (air transport, telecommunications, retailing, health care, banking and insurance), investment in IT was equivalent to 5.6% of their output, compared with only 2.6% in manufacturing.

The apparent failure of IT to boost productivity in services may in part be due to measurement problems. New technology tends to boost the quality of services, which conventional measures of output do not capture. And it can take a long time for firms to learn how to use new technology properly. When computers first appeared in offices in the late 1970s, they were used like superior typewriters, mainly by secretaries. Now they are becoming tools for managers at every level. According to the OECD, obsolete management structures inherited from the past have also hindered the efficient use of technology in many organisations.

But there is now some evidence that even in services IT has started to have its effect. Official statistics show that productivity growth in America's services has picked up in the 1990s, to an annual average of almost 2%. As deregulation has exposed previously sheltered services to competition, firms have had to slim themselves down in

search of higher productivity. A few companies have eliminated entire layers of middle-managers ("delayered", in the ghastly jargon). These are people who, thanks to computers and telecommunications, are no longer needed to co-ordinate the flow of information up and down the corporate ladder. Although the number of jobs disappearing in this way has been exaggerated, more may go in future: maybe a lot more.

A vulnerable generation

Both theory and evidence suggest that in the long run new technology should create more jobs than it destroys. But the long run can take a long time. In the next decade or so, things depend on how quickly demand expands to match increases in productive capacity. Unfortunately, there may be prolonged lags between job losses and the creation of new jobs. And the new jobs may anyway be inappropriate for the displaced workers. Not every redundant steel worker

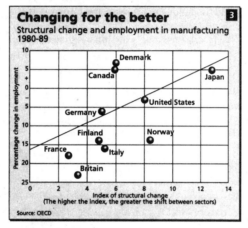

Changing for the better ③
Structural change and employment in manufacturing
1980-89

Source: OECD

in Scotland will be able to work as an aerobics teacher in London.

How can this problem of mismatch be alleviated? The familiar but nonetheless correct answer from the OECD is that compensating demand effects are likely to come through more quickly when general economic growth is strong, and when the markets for both labour and products are flexible. Governments can therefore help by making workers more adaptable through improvements in education and training, and by removing obstacles to free markets in labour and in goods and services.

Experience suggests that the worst thing governments can do about new technology is to try to slow down the period of adjust-

....

* "The OECD Jobs Study: Evidence and Explanations". See also: "The OECD Science and Technology Review", No. 15 (forthcoming).
† "Employment Performance", McKinsey Global Institute.
** "Past and Prospective Causes of High Unemployment", Paul Krugman, Economic Symposium of the Federal Reserve Bank of Kansas City at Jackson Hole, August 1994.

ment by using subsidies, protectionist barriers or strict regulation. A study by McKinsey†, a management consultancy, concludes that product-market restrictions may be more important than labour-market rigidities in explaining unemployment. In America, although automated teller machines and telephone banking have caused many traditional jobs in banks to disappear, jobs in the financial services industry as a whole have grown rapidly over the past decade, thanks to the growth of new products. In many continental European countries, by contrast, just as many jobs were lost, but stricter regulations have hindered the creation of new products and jobs.

Upstairs, downstairs

In sum, there are good reasons for believing that new technology will in the end have little effect on the level of employment. It will, however, have an impact on the composition of jobs and the pattern of wages. Over the past decade or so technology has mainly displaced low-skilled workers. Combined with stronger competition from low-wage developing countries, this has in America put downward pressure on the pay of low-skilled workers compared with that of highly-skilled ones. In most of Europe, where wages are less flexible, unemployment has risen among the low-skilled.

However, according to Paul Krugman** of Stanford University, it does not follow that technological change must always have the effect of widening the wage gap between the haves and the have-nots. The industrial revolution in the 19th century shifted income from workers to capitalists; yet, from the 1920s to the 1970s, technological change (plus trade unions) helped to improve the lot of blue-collar workers, and level out the distribution of wages. It is only since the 1970s that the wage gap has widened.

Mr Krugman speculates that in the long run it may be easier for computers to replace people in many jobs now thought "skilled" than in more ordinary work. Gardening, for instance, may be uncomputerisable. Lawyers and accountants, he suggests, could be today's counterparts of early-19th-century weavers, whose incomes soared after the mechanisation of spinning only to crash when the technological revolution reached their own craft. Marvin Minsky, a big name in artificial intelligence, points out that it has been easier for computers to solve hard problems in mathematics than to perform "common-sense" functions like arranging toy building blocks in simple towers.

It is not always the least-educated who are most at risk from new technology. But it is they who, if they do lose their jobs, may find it hardest to get new ones.

*F*lexibility Trap
The Proliferation of Marginal Jobs

Virginia L. duRivage

*F*ull-time, career employment is fast becoming an anachronism in today's changing economy. Since 1973, the rate of part-time, temporary, and subcontracted employment—what labor market analysts call "contingent" employment—has grown far faster than the rate of full-time work. Nearly one in five workers today works part-time while the temporary help industry is one of the fastest growing sectors in the economy. Close to 30 million people—over a quarter of the U.S. labor force—are working in jobs outside the regular full-time work force. And while a significant number are well-paid freelancers, most contingent workers are women and minorities clustered in low-wage jobs with no benefits or opportunities for advancement.

The expansion of contingent employment is evidence of a fundamental transformation of work. These changes are driven, in part, by business's need for flexibility in a changing, competitive economy. But while the

word "flexibility" connotes more creative adaptation and a sensible strategy of shifting workers to new tasks, locations, and skills, the reality is grubbier. Mainly it has to do with business's desire to trim short-run costs. By classifying workers as "part-time," "temporary," or "independent contractor," employers can shift the burden of fringe benefits and job transition to individual workers and their families. They can pay workers lower hourly wages, exclude them from better-compensated permanent jobs, save on health and pension costs, weaken labor unions, and, in the case of independent contractors, avoid payroll and unemployment insurance taxes.

At the same time, a growing number of workers welcome shorter working hours, as a strategy for combining paid work and family responsibilites, or for mixing work and school, or for phasing in retirement. But

there is a mismatch between what workers want and what available jobs offer. There are more part-time and temporary jobs than people who want them, yet workers who prefer to work less than full time are severely limited in their job choices and in the benefits offered. Under the guise of "flexibility," workers are being trapped into accepting lower standards of employment.

*T*he real issue is not labor market flexibility—we all want that—but rather who will bear its costs, and how we can reconcile job flexibility with the lives of employees and the productivity of society. Employers do need flexibility to adjust the shape and size of their work force to meet changes in product demand and necessary employee skills, just as workers need flexibility to reconcile home and work. U.S. employment policies that hurt contin-

gent workers are undergirded by three major assumptions which no longer describe today's labor market realities:

- Public and private employment policies presume full-time workers with one life-long employer—a prototype clearly out of date with today's workforce.

- Federal and state labor laws exclude from protection or treat poorly the women and minority groups who predominate among contingent workers on the assumption that they are marginal or peripheral to the primary labor force.

- Basic social welfare needs in the United States—health care, paid time off, and pensions—are tied to the employer-employee relationship rather than citizenship, on the assumption that employers will continue fulfilling those responsiblities.

The full-time archetype still dominates virtually every institution governing work life in the U.S., beginning with how workers are counted, how much they are paid, what fringe benefits they receive, and what benefits they are entitled to when they lose their jobs or retire. But it leaves out tens of millions of workers who are the fastest-growing category of employee.

Contingent work, in short, is no longer just a marginal phenomenon. It has emerged as a permanent strategy for cheapening the workforce and weakening the bargaining power of labor. It threatens the economic security of all workers by dragging down wages and increasing wage-income inequality. It weakens the public purse through lost tax revenues and higher public welfare costs for contingent workers who are more likely to depend upon public assistance. It increases the burden on good employers who are forced to subsidize the poor employment practices of others. And, finally, contingent employment threatens to undermine the productivity and efficiency of the U.S. economy.

As public consciousness of the economic costs of "short-termism" increases, the damage done by the contingent work approach ought to be at the center of the debate. To maximize productivity, the economy needs highly skilled workers, with a commitment to their jobs. That, in turn, requires employers to view workers as long-term partners, worthy of investment in skills training and long-term career development. But contingent work is the antithesis of that model.

Who Is a Contingent Worker?

Contingent workers are often missed in official counts of the U.S. labor force. Part-time workers, the most numerous among this group, are the best documented. Today, nearly one in five U.S. workers is employed part-time—defined as working in a job less than thirty-five hours a week—but labor market analysts agree the real number is probably higher. Surveys only ask workers how many hours they work in a week, not how many jobs. The dramatic growth in moonlighting or multiple job-holding in recent years suggests that many workers who look like full-timers when their hours are counted may in fact hold two or more part-time jobs. Over seven million workers now have more than one job.

It is a myth that most part-time workers, especially women, prefer to work part-time. In recent years, the sharpest increase in part-time employment has been due to the jump in the involuntary part-time labor force—workers who want full-time hours but cannot get them. Women predominate in this category, accounting for over half of the five million involuntary part-time jobs in 1990. Women are also more likely than men to work part-time routinely. What looks voluntary, however, often obscures the fact that many women prefer full-time work or nearly full-time work that offers full-time benefits, but feel constrained by a lack of adequate child care—information that is not recorded in official tallies of why people work part-time.

The motivation for temporary employment is also misconstrued. Contrary to popular belief, women—who make up two-thirds of the temporary labor force—do not opt for temporary employment as a way to balance work and family needs. Research by the Institute for Women's Policy Research has shown that married women with children are no more likely to prefer temporary employment than are unmarried women in these jobs. In reality, most temporary workers are looking for permanent full-time jobs.

Official estimates of the size of the temporary work force are also understated. The temporary work force includes individuals hired out by a temporary employment agency such as Kelly Services as well as temporary workers who are hired directly by an employer. The federal government, however, only counts workers employed by temporary help agencies. Since 1982, this category has grown nearly three times as fast as overall employment. During the course of one year, over six million persons perform some work through a temporary help agency. Private surveys of firms who hire temporary workers directly suggest that the total use of all types of temporary work is probably twice as large as the official count.

In recent years there has been a surge of black men into blue-collar temporary employment. Low-skilled manual work now makes up the second-largest category of work in the temporary help supply industry, employing roughly one in five temporary workers. This is the fastest-growing and the poorest-paying segment of the official temporary labor force—and nearly all would prefer full time and permanent employment.

Contract work—subcontracting by another firm or by an individual—is the third leg of the contingent work force. Many contingent workers employed by a firm contracted to perform specific services such as cleaning or food preparation are counted as part-time or temporary workers. But individuals who identify themselves as self-employed or as independent contractors have grown during the 1980s from 6.2 million to 9.5 million. Some of these workers are well-paid entrepreneurs providing medical, legal, or financial services to multiple clients. A significant number, however, work illegally for only one "client"—their real employer—who lists them as contractors to save payroll taxes, fringe benefits, and paperwork.

Trade unionists in the construction industry have documented the practices of unscrupulous employers who fire regular workers and rehire them as "independent contractors." The Internal Revenue Service estimates that as many as 38 percent of employers deliberately misclassify their employees as "independent contractors" to avoid paying unemployment compensa-

When employers fail to pay decent wages, not only do contingent workers get poorer, the rest of us get squeezed.

tion taxes as well as Social Security and workers' compensation.

The diffused nature of contingent employment has yielded a range of estimates, from 27 million to 37 million—about one-third of the total U.S. work force. The emergence of contingent employment mainly signals the economy's failure to create adequate employment for individuals who need full-time work. And it has consigned these workers—especially women and male members of minority groups—to a marginal existence of low wages, no benefits, and uncertain futures.

The Problem of How to Pay

As noted, employers hire contingent workers to cut labor costs. Part-time workers earn about 60 percent of the hourly wages of full-time workers, while temporary agency workers take in about 70 percent of the hourly earnings of all workers. Much of this wage gap can be explained by the concentration of these workers in the lower-paid retail trade and services industries and the disproportionate number of women, teens, and elders who make up this labor force. Yet even when workers are matched by industry, occupation, sex, and age, a substantial wage difference (about 15 percent) persists between full- and part-time workers.

Minimum-wage policy reinforces the failure to pay contingent workers wages more comparable to those of full-timers. Part-time workers are six times more likely than full-timers to work for the minimum wage. Yet despite long-delayed recent increases, the minimum wage has continued to drop below its real value in 1981, pushing more of these workers into poverty. During the debate on raising the minimum wage, many opponents argued that an increase was unnecessary because more than three-quarters of minimum-wage workers hold jobs that are not essential to family well-being. Yet the majority of the people counted as nonessential are working wives.

As long as women's earnings are deemed peripheral to family income, policy makers will continue to ignore the critical importance of raising the minimum. Small business is currently lobbying Congress to legislate a permanent small-business exemption to the minimum wage—a move that would do further harm to the contingent workers who make up the bulk of the work force in small firms. Business costs are an important consideration in evaluating proposals to increase the minimum wage. But an equally important consideration is the weakening effect of an inadequate national pay standard upon the entire wage structure. In fact, according to University of Massachusetts economist Chris Tilly, 42 percent of the growth of wage inequality in recent years can be attributed to the growth of part-time work and the widening gap between the earnings of part-time and full-time workers.

When employers fail to pay decent wages, not only do contingent workers get poorer, the rest of us get squeezed. According to research by Sar Levitan and Elizabeth Conway, one in six part-timers and one in five involuntary part-timers have family incomes below poverty compared with only one in thirty-seven regular full-time workers. Involuntary part-time workers are almost twice as likely as all other workers to depend upon public subsidies. The pressure to liberalize the earned income tax credit, at taxpayer expense, arises primarily because not enough work pays a wage that families can live on.

An important strategy for boosting the pay of contingent workers is wage parity. In the U.S., we have laws requiring that blacks and whites or men and women doing identical jobs receive equal pay, but no equal hourly pay laws. There is no federal labor standard assuring that a part-time telephone operator who performs work identical to the full-time operator sitting in the next chair will receive the same hourly pay. Ignoring the equal-pay rights of part-time workers underscores the low status accorded them in public and private employment policy. On the other hand, in much of Western Europe official labor standards and collective bargaining agreements, as well as proposals to the Social Charter governing labor standards under a united Europe, recognize equal pay guidelines for part-time and many temporary workers. Fairer pay standards for contingent workers—including wage parity and a more adequate minimum wage—would boost the wages of contingent workers and restrain employers from exploiting this labor force.

Contingent Work: Bad for Your Health

Contingent workers have become a major weapon in the employer's fight against escalating health care costs. Part-time and temporary workers are three times less likely than full-time workers to receive health insurance coverage through their employers. More private insurers are simply refusing to underwrite employer coverage for part-time workers. Employers and policy makers alike assume that these workers receive health insurance through their spouses, yet dependent coverage is an item employers are dropping from employee health benefits packages. In addition, the growing number of single-parent families weakens the notion that contingent workers can count on a spouse for health insurance.

In today's market, the costs of buying individual health insurance are prohibitive for most contingent and other low-wage workers. Tax policy is also stacked against the contingent worker. Tax laws permit employers to exclude certain classes of workers from their company health care plans and, not surprisingly, contingent workers get excluded most often. In addition, employers can fully deduct the cost of health care premiums. The self-employed, on the other hand, can deduct only 25 percent of the cost of their insurance. Working families can only deduct medical costs if their expenses exceed a certain level—which keeps rising—so that, in practical terms, low-income working families get no tax breaks for their health care costs. And contingent workers are ineligible for most public health insurance programs like Medicaid. One of the few attempts by Congress to fill in the gaps in employee health coverage by offering extended coverage to laid-off workers excludes part-time workers from coverage. As a result, the vast majority of part-time and contingent workers simply go without health insurance.

Happily, the question of universal health care is back on the table, and even the administration has

proposed remedying some of the inequities. One way to evaluate the proposals currently flooding Congress is to examine how each one treats contingent workers.

For instance, mandating employers to provide health benefits may only induce employers to create more worker categories to avoid their obligations to this workforce. It provides some protection for part-time workers (meeting a minimum work-hours requirement), but overlooks workers who are deliberately misclassified as short-term hires, temporary employees, or independent contractors. A better approach would be to sever the workplace tie entirely, and opt for a more inclusive system that provides equal access to health care conditioned by residence or citizenship and not by relationship to a particular employer.

Vanishing Pensions

Contingent workers are also the have-nots in the U.S. public and private pension systems. Only one in six part-time workers is covered under an employer's pension plan compared with one in two full-time workers. And where part-timers are covered, their shorter job stays virtually ensure they will not be able to vest their pensions, get back their contributions, or carry their pension credits with them to another job. Public policy often sanctions this discrimination. For instance, federal law allows companies to exclude from their pension plans workers employed fewer than twenty hours a week or 1,000 hours a year, or workers who fall into certain work classifications including part-time and temporary employment.

Pension reform in the 1980s did strengthen benefits for temporary and leased employees by requiring employers who hire these workers for more than a year to include them in company pension plans. Current proposals, however, would take back some of these protections.

Once a contingent worker gets over the hurdle of pension coverage, she or he must confront policies that make it difficult to vest in a pension plan or carry pension credits over to a new job. Most workers stay on the job for less than five years, while the job stays of part-time workers average only three years.

Economic downturns and family responsibilities increase the likelihood that such workers will fail to vest and thus forfeit

As workers largely outside the "core" of regular employment, contingent workers get none of the benefits that accrue to permanent workers.

pension benefits. Congress has changed the vesting requirement from ten years to five years for companies with single-employer pension plans and has adopted three-year vesting for many small companies.

These reforms, however, still leave many workers without a realistic chance of vesting. One solution would be to standardize vesting requirements across all employers using a more realistic measure of job tenure; an even better solution would be to make an earnings-related pension a fully portable citizenship right, as many European nations do.

Contingent workers change jobs frequently yet to date there is no federal mechanism that allows workers to carry their pension credits with them from job to job. Proposals to enact pension portability have been repeatedly rejected by Congress yet in some employment sectors, such as university teaching, professors freely move from school to school carrying their pension credits with them. This is a good model to follow in fashioning pension reform that fits the real experiences of today's workers.

Obviously, universal pension plans offer the best protection for contingent workers. In Western Europe, national schemes of employer-sponsored pensions coexist with Social Security. In both France and Finland, special private pension plans have been developed for seasonal workers and the self-employed. During the early 1980s, Congress considered a minimum universal pension system (MUPS) that would have permitted immediate vesting and pension portability. A universal pension system would benefit contingent workers more than the current policy favorite, Individualized Retirement Accounts (IRAs), which rely solely on workers' contributions. Any new proposals for a MUPS-type system must include protections for part-time workers—a group left out of earlier proposals.

When contingent workers cannot get pensions it increases their dependence upon Social Security—a system designed to supplement, not supplant, other retirement

> *Policy makers must begin to challenge management's version of flexibility and create the kind of flexibility workers genuinely need.*

income. The varying work schedules of part-time and other low-wage workers bring lower earnings and thus lower Social Security benefits. Family members who reduce their number of paid work hours to care for children or sick relatives end up with fewer Social Security credits and lower benefits in contrast to care-givers in other advanced economies, such as England, who receive Social Security credits for their work at home. Similarly, persons who are laid off or forced into a contingent work schedule suffer losses in Social Security credits during their time away from the labor force.

When the economy is unable to provide workers who need full-time jobs with adequate work, or when women reduce their paid work time to resolve work-family conflicts that are ignored in the workplace, these same workers should not be condemned to poverty in old age. Such workers could be granted Social Security credits for their reduced participation in the work force as a way to boost retirement income and curb old-age poverty earnings.

Outside the Unemployment Insurance System

If you work part-time and lose your job, don't expect to get unemployment insurance (UI) benefits. States' eligibility standards and employer practices effectively eliminate most contingent workers. Some categories of workers, including the self-employed, independent contractors, and casual or seasonal workers, are excluded outright. In addition, an unemployed worker must meet a minimum earnings test to qualify for benefits. But in half the states, the average part-time worker does not earn enough to pass the test. In recent years, to save money, several states have tightened UI eligibility standards, a move that has hurt part-time and low-wage workers the most.

Unemployment insurance policies that disadvantage contingent workers are another reflection of the archetype of full-time, permanent employment. They can also reflect the gender discrimination built into the unemployment compensation system. For example, if you regularly work full time but your employer cuts your hours in half, you and your dependents can still receive benefits for the work hours you have lost. However, if you choose to work part time to accommodate family care responsibilities, you are likely to be considered "not available" for work and you will lose your benefits.

Ironically, a woman who forgoes paid employment to care for family members is more likely to receive a "dependent allowance" as the wife of a laid-off husband than as an unemployed worker looking for a part-time work job. Such inequities have produced a profile of the insured unemployed that is grossly out of sync with the real unemployed. Policy makers could help by fashioning a federal standard for UI eligibility that strengthens the ties among contingent workers, employers, and the state and respects the changing work lives of family care-givers.

Parents who seek part-time work hours to care for children are no less deserving of unemployment insurance benefits when they lose their part-time jobs than a full-time worker forced to work part-time as a result of economic conditions. Policy makers should also consider how the method of unemployment insurance financing encourages employers to misclassify employees and manipulate work hours. Employers pay a tax based on how many "regular" employees are laid off and workers who are not defined as "regular"—such as contingent workers— escape these counts. Western European countries have addressed this problem by guaranteeing to all workers a minimum UI benefit guaranteed augmented by a privately financed scheme.

Better Jobs

As workers largely outside the "core" of regular employment, contingent workers get none of the benefits that accrue to permanent workers, including most rights

based on seniority. Contingent workers seldom enjoy the right to bid for a full-time job. As a result, the contingent strategy reinforces the invisible barriers between what economists call the primary and secondary labor market. And it reinforces gender and race divisions at work by preventing these workers from moving into better jobs. For example, employers can avoid compliance with federal equal employment opportunity laws by reducing their core or "regular" workforce to just below the legal trigger for affirmative action and hiring contingent workers—whom they are not obliged to protect—to pick up the slack.

The growth of contingent work signals declining employer commitment to career development. Internal labor markets, which provided avenues to career advancement in the large firm, have contracted in the wake of corporate downsizing and are practically nonexistent in the smaller firm. And public employment and training programs, like the federal Jobs Training Partnership Act, constrained by shrinking budgets and eligibility rules that exclude working persons, are unlikely to fill the void.

In the short run, the contingent work strategy saves business money, but over the long term, workers who are unfamiliar with company practices and products, have no loyalty to the firm, and leave as soon as they can find a better job, undermine efficiency and drag down productivity.

Who Speaks for the Contingent Work Force?

Labor unions remain the most effective tool for curbing the worst abuses of contingent employment. Unions do this both by representing workers, and by serving as a political constituency for higher-quality jobs generally. However, rotating work schedules and shifting job sites make it difficult to organize the contingent work force. At the same time, U.S. labor law, by ignoring changing employer practices, has hindered the ability of labor unions to represent part-time and temporary workers. Consequently, only 8 percent of part-time workers belong to labor unions compared with nearly 22 percent of full-time workers. And even unionization of full-time workers is decreasing.

Contingent workers are more likely to be organized in workplaces where less than full-time work or irregular work is the norm and in industries where labor unions have traditionally been strong such as the building trades, entertainment, and retail food. In the manufacturing sector, unions have been successful in restricting or prohibiting the use of part-time and contingent employees. In the public sector, unions representing service workers have successfully bargained for restrictions on the use of part-time and contingent labor, hourly pay parity, seniority rights, pro-rated and full benefits, and opportunities for more permanent employment.

Organizing drives to represent contingent workers in non-union shops have been more difficult. In fact, many employers have used the contingent work strategy to undercut union organizing drives or to exact concessions during contract negotiations. Much of this difficulty derives from the complex employee classification schemes employers develop to thwart union organizing efforts as well as the failure of labor law to protect contract workers.

The National Labor Relations Board (NLRB) plays the major role in determining "appropriate bargaining units" and has been inconsistent in deciding whether contingent workers should vote along with full-time workers in union elections. Under the original National Labor Relations Act (Wagner Act), the NLRB was instructed to determine bargaining units according to "employees' preferences." However, later reforms under the more business-friendly Taft-Hartley Act outlawed this practice.

Another stumbling block to representing contingent workers, especially contract workers, is the increasingly complex nature of the employment relationship today. Workers often have more than one supervisor. Taft-Hartley's ban on secondary boycotts makes it difficult for sub-contracted employees, such as janitors or food service workers, to protest collectively the practices of the leasing employer.

The Wagner Act guaranteed to workers the right to collective bargaining. Yet the failure of labor law to keep up with changes in the employment contract challenges the very foundations of collective bargaining in the United States. The public sector, with its own set of labor laws and with less vehement opposition to unions, provides a more congenial environment for organizing contingent workers.

In reforming labor law, policy makers should also examine how the NLRA regulates external labor markets operating in such industries as construction and entertainment. In these sectors, unionized workers, like continent workers, work intermittently and are often not attached to a particular employer yet the NLRA preserves their right to collective bargaining.

The decline in union representation in the U.S. and the difficulty in organizing part-time and contingent workers suggest the need for new strategies to ensure their representation. One approach would be to introduce works councils or workers committees into the U.S. workplace. Works councils operate in Canada and parts of Western Europe, playing a role in a variety of workplace decisions involving occupational safety and health, layoffs, and technological change and often pave the way for union representation.

Works councils also serve as a permanent constituency for a definition of jobs that is more friendly to workers. One proposal in this spirit would amend the Occupational Health and Safety Act to require a selection of a safety steward to monitor the health and safety of all workers. Labor law reform could include similar forms of representation on workplace issues beyond health and safety, including the determination of work hours and job contracts.

Policy Directions

Policy makers must begin to challenge management's version of flexibility and create the kind of flexibility workers genuinely need. Involuntary part-time jobs, long-term temporary assignments, and the growing numbers of women in two part-time jobs are poor options for people who need and want full-time work. And for men and women who choose to work less than full-time—to raise children, go to school, or semi-retire—society needs part-time jobs that dignify workers instead of penalizing them. We also need public and private policies designed to combat the gender and race basis of many of these inequities.

Reform should take place on three fronts. First, there are work-specific issues, such as how to shift contingent workers into regular employment, or how to boost hourly pay. These goals require reforms specifically targeted to changing the rules of the workplace. Second, there are structural concerns, such as how to generate more full-time jobs or how to meet the short-term hiring needs of employers. Those issues demand broader economic reforms such as shortening the work week, or creating publicly owned employment services that hire out temporary workers while ensuring these workers adequate pay, hours, and benefits.

And finally, there are social welfare issues, such as health care, pension coverage, unemployment insurance, sick leave, vacations, and family leave that do not require employer-specific solutions. Most advanced democracies regard these benefits as universal rights rather than as privileges of employment. If we continue to view the employer as the key provider of social welfare, we run the risk of creating incentives for employers to marginalize more workers, and of generating policy solutions that perpetuate rather than ameliorate this marginalization—and then hand the bill to U.S. taxpayers.

The proposed Family and Medical Leave Act, which was vetoed last year by President Bush, is a case in point. In Western Europe, subsidized family leaves are available to all workers—regardless of regular work hours— through the Unemployment Compensation system.

In the U.S., by contrast, this reform legislation has been tied to private employers. Consequently, the debate has focused upon restricting the number of workers considered eligible for a family or medical leave in order to garner business's support. An amendment to the latest bill approved by Congress raised the minimum work requirement from twenty hours to twenty-five hours per week, a cut-off point that effectively excludes most part-time workers from coverage. Benefits such as family and medical leave, health care, pension coverage, and unemployment insurance are basic needs that, at a minimum, should not be exposed to the pressures of the marketplace or the whims of an employer. Rather, they must be protected as social guarantees critical to the growth of a healthy economy.

While western European policies vary, these basic social provisions are largely extended as rights, rather than a privilege of employment. That reality has cushioned

the impact of economic restructuring in western Europe, and thus facilitated it. Similarly, policies implemented at the national level in the U.S., particularly universal health insurance, pension portability, and wage parity, can act as buffers against a volatile economy and ensure that "flexibility" in the marketplace benefits workers as well as managers.

An administration committed to restoring a labor market made up primarily of good, "core" jobs and lifelong career ladders would have to proceed on multiple fronts. These include shifting job-related fringe benefits to citizenship entitlements; insisting on either broader pension coverage through social insurance or full pension portability; and regulating the conditions of part-time work to require the same wages and benefits as comparable full-time work.

Finally, and perhaps most important, the contribution of the labor movement toward defending and improving the quality of working life must be reinforced. Unions offer the best private remedy for bringing equity to part-time and other contingent workers. Labor law reform, including reinstating workers preferences to determine the scope of a bargaining unit, allowing greater rights for contract workers, as well as restoring the effective right to unionize in the first place, can open up opportunities for unions to represent contingent workers. Workplace committees, in union and non-union shops, would also increase employee bargaining power over work schedules and job design. As a nation, we need to give far higher priority to this reclamation of tens of millions of marginal jobs. At issue is not just the well-being of workers, but the productivity of society.

THE REAL UN(DER)EMPLOYMENT RATE

An average of eight million people were unemployed in 1994, yielding an unemployment rate of 6.4%. But the rate would jump to at least 9.2% if the Bureau of Labor Statistics (BLS), the government agency that tracks unemployment, counted everyone who wanted to work but couldn't. And these averages do not show the consistently higher unemployment rates of African Americans, Latinos, and teenagers.

The BLS calculates unemployment rates from a monthly random telephone sampling of about 60,000 households. BLS surveyors ask all members of the household over the age of 16 a series of questions about their work activities, then classify the respondents as employed, unemployed, or not in the labor force.

The BLS counts you as employed if you work full- or part-time for pay, work 15 hours or more without pay in a family business, or are on unpaid leave because of illness, a labor dispute, or personal reasons. You are considered unemployed if you were jobless during the survey week but were available for work and had made specific efforts to find work sometime during the past month — answering want ads, contacting an employment agency, and so on. The BLS categorizes students, retirees, people at home because of long-term ill health or disabilities, homemakers, those "voluntarily idle," and "discouraged workers" as being out of the labor force.

The BLS undercounts the unemployed in several ways, understating the economic distress of millions of people. The most glaring exclusion is the category of "discouraged workers" — people who are available for work and have looked for a job within the past year, but have stopped searching. The BLS counted an average of 500,000 such "discouraged workers" in 1994.

Also omitted by the BLS were 1.3 million people who said they were available to work but were not currently looking due to family responsibilities, time taken up by school or training, or health problems.

Another 4.3 million workers told the BLS they were working part-time, either because they could only find part-time work, or because business was slack. We can incorporate these workers into the unemployment count by assuming they work on average half-time, and counting half of them as unemployed.

Adding together the discouraged workers, those who are available to work but are unable to search for a job at present, half of the involuntary part-timers, and those the BLS lists as unemployed, the number of unemployed people rises to 11.9 million, a rate of 9.2%.

It is also important to consider the "underemployment rate" — which includes all people who have less hours of work than they desire. This statistic counts all those who are working part-time but would prefer full-time work (instead of only half of them), yielding an underemployment rate of 10.9%.

Even this figure counts only those people who searched for work in the previous year. Another 6.2 million people said they wanted a job, but had not looked for one within the past 12 months. Even if only a small fraction of them were truly available for work, this would add more than a million people to the unemployment rolls, increasing the true underemployment rate to around 12%.

These "real unemployment" and "real underemployment" rates better measure our economy's ability to provide paid work to all those willing to do it. With at least every tenth person unemployed or underemployed, the economy is failing far more people than official statistics suggest.

— *Marc Breslow and Matthew Howard*

Sources: Monthly Labor Review, February 1995; *Employment and Earnings*, January 1995; both from the Bureau of Labor Statistics, U.S. Department of Labor.

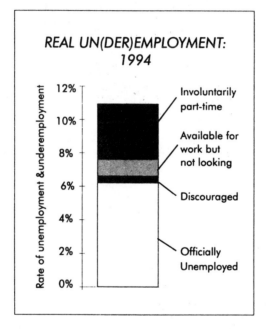

REAL UN(DER)EMPLOYMENT: 1994

Rate of unemployment & underemployment

- 12%
- 10%
- 8%
- 6%
- 4%
- 2%
- 0%

Involuntarily part-time
Available for work but not looking
Discouraged
Officially Unemployed

Only a Paper Boon

Consumers Aren't Spending Their Profits From Surging Stocks

Sylvia Nasar

With blue-chip stocks up 16 percent since January, many Americans are a lot richer today than they were on New Year's Day. This year's bull market, the strongest surge since late 1990, has been powered by lower interest rates and rising corporate profits. It has already added more than twice as much to the wealth of America's households as all the money families painstakingly salted away in savings last year.

So now that signs of an economic slowdown are multiplying, the Federal Reserve chairman, Alan Greenspan, is acknowledging the possibility of a brief downturn this summer, and anxiety is starting to well up, shouldn't all that freshly minted wealth help make the economy safe from recession?

Maybe, but don't count on it. When it comes to the fortune of someone like William H. Gates, the chairman of Microsoft, or the outlook for specific companies, the stock market is a powerful force. But when it comes to determining the course of the overall economy, it is still just a bit player.

"People might feel better if the market's up," said Edward Yardeni, chief economist at C. J. Lawrence, a Wall Street investment house, "but are they really checking their balance sheets?"

By one estimate, a rise in the stock market of the current magnitude—if it is sustained for a year or so—could mean a boost to spending of about $22 billion. That is worthwhile, but

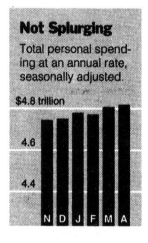

Not Splurging
Total personal spending at an annual rate, seasonally adjusted.

$4.8 trillion

4.6

4.4

N D J F M A

not enough to make a big difference in an economy that is expected to produce almost $7 trillion in goods and services this year.

Shares are more likely to be owned by savers, not big spenders.

Rising prices for assets like stocks, bonds and real estate do deliver a very real impact—called the wealth effect by economists—that shows up in a variety of ways. Higher stock prices increase the financial wealth of shareholders, who might be able to afford more, whether a Cadillac instead of a Chevrolet or an Ivy League education for the children versus State U. The most common reaction to a fatter portfolio is to save less from current income, since the

market helps build extra savings without sacrifice.

Higher stock prices also enhance the purchasing power of companies. Corporations whose stock is rising face a lower cost of capital and thus have extra resources to invest in new technology or expansion. Wall Street firms, where salaries and bonuses are closely tied to the issuing of new stocks and bonds, turn more open-handed.

Indeed, if the wealth effect is visible anywhere, it is in and around the nation's major financial centers, like New York, Boston, Los Angeles, San Francisco and Chicago. And those are the same places where there are also heavy concentrations of affluent families with lots of investments in the market.

New York is typical. While the underlying economy in the metropolitan area remains tepid, there are plenty of signs of extra spending money among the upper crust in the crowded aisles at Barneys, hefty sales of luxury cars and expensive four-wheel-drive vehicles at local dealers, and the tighter summer rental market in some trendy beach communities.

"There are a lot of people looking at the higher end, over $1 million," said Patricia Patrillo, a broker at Sotheby's International Realty in Southampton, L.I. "The buyers are ready, willing and able."

And Karen Houghton, an interior designer in Nyack, N.Y., a suburb of New York City, said she saw evi-

dence of the wealth effect in her own business. "Two of my clients who work for I.B.M. have been talking about putting extensions on their homes for five years," she said. "Now that I.B.M.'s stock is recovering, they're moving forward."

Trouble is, relative to the national economy, the impact of these kinds of case-by-case decisions is not enough to be decisive. Compared with other forces at work in the economy, from consumer confidence to changes in personal income to swings in business inventories, the impact of fatter stock portfolios is relatively modest.

How much does all this add up to? Laurence H. Meyer, president of a forecasting firm in St. Louis that bears his name, recently sent a note to clients predicting that the higher market—provided it does not give back too much of the recent gains—should inject roughly $22 billion in extra spending power into the economy this year. But while expressing confidence that the economy will avoid a recession, he nonetheless scaled back his estimates of future consumer outlays because of the weak job market.

"The economy would be weaker if not for the stock market," Mr. Meyer said. "But the bigger effect comes from lower interest rates," which are just beginning to work their way through the pipeline.

Economists at the Federal Reserve have developed a similar guideline, estimating that about 4 cents of every dollar in sustainable extra wealth eventually shows up in spending by consumers and business.

Many economists, starting in the 1950's with Milton Friedman, the winner of the Nobel Memorial Prize in Economic Science, once thought the wealth effect carried a bigger wallop. But the stock market crash of 1987 changed all that. After a trillion dollars of wealth evaporated overnight, a lot of economists—particularly those close to the epicenter on Wall Street—predicted a sharp slowdown in consumer spending, if not an outright recession.

Instead, in part because the Federal Reserve moved quickly to counter the effects of the stock market crash by lowering interest rates, spending kept right on growing, and 1988 turned out to be a banner year in the long 1980's economic expansion.

In response to that event, many forecasters threw their wealth equations out the window or significantly scaled back their estimates of the impact on consumer spending from changes in the stock market.

"Traditionally, we had wealth variables in our models," said David Kelly, an economist at Lehman Brothers in Boston. "But the wealth effect was put to a very significant test in 1987 and failed miserably."

Why doesn't all that new-found wealth prompt more spending? Economists now point to three big reasons.

First, while a majority of Americans may hold stock through their pensions and other indirect means, four out of five households do not own any stock directly. For all the bullishness among investors, consumer confidence readings have been falling this year because most Americans are more affected by their own expectations about jobs and incomes than by reports of riches being reaped on Wall Street.

Second, many households that do own stock do not change their behavior much in response to changes in the value of their portfolios, particularly because they are aware that what goes up can also go down. Most stock is owned by the relatively affluent—two-thirds of stock and mutual fund shares are owned by the top one-fifth of households— who already tend to be high savers and do not alter their spending patterns simply because their accountants tell them they are worth more.

Finally, more and more stock is now held in various restricted ways, through individual retirement accounts, 401(k) plans and the like. The added wealth in those accounts cannot usually be tapped until retirement, unless the owner is prepared to pay a stiff penalty for the privilege.

In contrast to the relatively modest effect from stock market changes, rises and falls in real estate values appear to have a stronger impact. In the 1980's, real estate values and stock prices rose in tandem; that is much less true today.

"The effect of changes in equity prices is less than half the effect of a change in house prices," said Roger Brinner, chief economist at Data Resources/McGraw-Hill in Lexington, Mass. "If your house appreciates, you know it and you can borrow against it. If your debt goes up, you know it and you tighten your belt."

For all the current anxiety about the economy, however, there are factors other than the buoyant stock market that offer reassurance. After all, unemployment is still relatively low, income growth remains decent if unexciting, and long-term interest rates have fallen back to levels not seen in more than a year.

"Other things may save us," said Mr. Kelly of Lehman Brothers, "but I'm not sure it will be the wealth effect. Other forces are more important in reviving consumer spending than the gains you see in the stock market."

HAS OUR LIVING STANDARD STALLED?

If you pay any attention to the monthly announcements of changes in the Consumer Price Index, you may have heard that inflation has been running at a relatively modest pace in recent years. In 1991, according to the CPI, prices went up a mere 3.1 percent.

Yet many Americans think they're worse off, that they can afford less than they had expected. In poll after poll, they lament a decline in their standard of living, saying that many of the essentials of a middle-class lifestyle, such as home ownership and higher education, seem to be sliding ever farther out of reach.

The Consumer Price Index is an accurate enough measure of the things it measures. But because it underestimates the impact of certain major costs on the households that must bear them, and because it doesn't relate prices to wages, the CPI is also an imperfect mirror of economic reality.

The table on the next page illustrates that point. Using average hourly wage rates for 1962, 1972, 1982, and today, it shows how long the typical American had to work to buy a particular item. Our selective sample of things consumers buy demonstrates that many goods with smaller price tags—the ones we measured in minutes of labor—are actually less expensive in terms of purchasing power than they used to be. In other words, you don't have to work as

long on average to buy them. It's the big things—the ones measured in days of labor—that cost more. In some cases, a lot more.

Inside the CPI

The Consumer Price Index, put out once a month by the U.S. Bureau of Labor Statistics, tracks the average change in prices of a basket of goods and services in 91 urban areas. Data collectors visit 25,000 stores and other places of business to record prices.

Those prices fall into seven categories—food, housing, clothing, transportation, health services, entertainment, and a mixed bag called "other goods and services"—everything that a typical American family supposedly buys. Each category is assigned a weight. Food, for example, is assumed to represent 17.6 percent of the total; transportation, 17 percent; entertainment, 4.3 percent.

According to the CPI, prices overall have gone up by 31.4 percent since 1983. But here's the rub: A number of items essential to a better-than-subsistence lifestyle have defied the laws of economic gravity. Health care, college tuition, and child care, for example. Health care is up 82 percent since 1983, according to the CPI. College costs are up over 100 percent. Child care, over 40 percent.

The CPI includes those expenses on its list, but it assigns them a weight that may dramatically under-

state the impact they have on families that face them. For example, the CPI figures health-care costs at 6.6 percent of the "average" consumer's budget, college costs at 1.1 percent, and day-care costs at less than 1 percent. Of course, try telling that to anyone who actually pays those bills.

Another problem with the CPI concerns what it counts as a price increase. Consider new cars. They've shot up 68 percent in price since 1982, according to the Motor Vehicle Manufacturer's Association. But the CPI says auto prices rose only about 24 percent in that same period. The reason for the discrepancy? When automakers tack on options that add to the price of a car, the CPI counts that as an improvement in quality, not a price increase.

Pay's role

Of course, prices are only half of the equation. Wages are the other half. After a long post-World War II period of rising "real wages" (wages compared to prices), wages began to stall around 1973. There has been little real gain since that time.

Back in 1948, as economists Frank S. Levy of the University of Maryland and Richard C. Michel of the Urban Institute point out, an average 50-year-old man working full time had an income of $16,702 (in 1989 dollars). By 1973, a 50-year-old worker's income would have almost doubled, to $31,862, after adjusting

FROM OUT-OF-POCKET TO OUT OF REACH

While many of the little things are cheaper now...

MINUTES of labor

1962 1972 1982 1992

...And midpriced goods are less costly, too...

HOURS of labor

1962 1972 1982 1992

...High-priced items have just kept climbing.

DAYS of labor

1962 1972 1982 1992

Data derived from the table on following page.

for inflation. In other words, a 1973 worker could buy nearly twice as much as a 1948 worker. But 15 years later, in 1988, the worker's real wage would have risen just slightly, to $32,701.

The average U.S. household has maintained its living standard largely because families are working more hours. Millions of women entered the work force in the past 25 years. In 1970, about 21 million women worked full time. Now that figure is over 36 million. That has helped to keep family buying power fairly stable. But for many families, it now represents the labor of two earners rather than one.

The U.S. says the cost of living has risen only modestly in recent years. Why do many Americans feel so much worse off?

This table shows how long the average American had to work, before taxes, to earn enough to purchase the goods and services listed. For our calculations, we used the actual prices of items in 1962, 1972, 1982, and 1992 and the average hourly wages in each of those years. For simplicity's sake, we show the inexpensive items in the top third of the list in minutes of work, the more costly goods and services in hours, and the big-ticket items at the bottom in days.

	1962	1972	1982	1992
Small items	**Minutes of work**			
Postage (first class, 1 oz.)	1.1	1.6	1.7	1.6
Newspaper (New York Times, daily)	1.4	2.4	2.3	2.8
Long-distance phone call (3 min., N.Y. to L.A.)	60.8	23.5	13.4	4.3
Apples (Red Delicious, 1 lb.)	3.1	2.9	3.3	4.7
Gasoline (1 gal.)	7.5	5.2	9.1	6.4
Chicken (whole, cut, 1 lb.)	13.5	8.7	7.4	7.4
Milk (½ gal.)	12.5	9.6	8.8	7.8
Ground beef (chuck, 1 lb.)	15.3	13.9	13.0	11.1
Film (Kodak, 35mm, color prints)	60.0	37.9	27.7	27.2
Barbie doll	81.1	60.8	33.2	31.3
Medium items	**Hours of work**			
Record album	1.8	2.2	1.2	[1] 1.6
Consumer Reports (1-yr. subscription)	2.7	2.2	1.8	2.1
Timex watch (men's Mercury model)	3.1	2.1	2.2	2.4
Electricity (500 kwh)	4.6	3.3	4.2	3.9
Theater ticket (Broadway, best seat)	3.4	4.1	5.2	5.7
Television (RCA, 19-in.)	85.1	121.6	42.6	21.7
Dishwasher (GE, midpriced model)	112.2	64.9	55.3	35.5
Washing machine (Sears, midpriced model)	92.3	52.7	58.3	37.8
Refrigerator (Frigidaire, top-freezer)	168.0	99.2	83.7	59.8
Mattress (Simmons, with box spring)	71.6	59.5	44.0	60.7
Large items	**Days of work**			
Auto insurance [2]	7.1	7.8	7.3	11.3
Income taxes (Federal) [3]	50.0	48.3	63.8	49.0
Child delivery [4]	15.5	37.2	33.3	62.2
College (public) [5]	61.7	64.1	68.9	99.2
Car (average, new)	203.1	131.0	161.0	197.8
College (private) [6]	129.5	140.4	144.0	251.4
House (3-bedroom ranch, Matawan, N.J.)	1125.5	1330.7	1530.0	1777.3

[1] Compact disc.
[2] National average.
[3] Includes Social Security.
[4] Normal delivery (hospital and doctor fees).
[5] University of Michigan (room, board, tuition; 1 yr.).
[6] Colgate (room, board, tuition; 1 yr.).

As Parties Skirmish Over Budget, Greenspan Offers a Painless Cure

Adam Clymer

Special to The New York Times

WASHINGTON, Jan. 10—As Democrats kept demanding that Republicans spell out their plans for cutting the budget, the head of the Federal Reserve Board offered them an initially painless way to do it: changing the way the Government calculates inflation.

Alan Greenspan told a joint meeting of the House and Senate Budget Committees that the Consumer Price Index now exaggerates annual inflation by 0.5 to 1.5 percentage points. That leads to higher payments for Social Security and government pensions and lower revenues from those taxes that are pegged to inflation.

Mr. Greenspan said correcting those estimates could save the Federal Government $150 billion over five years, which could be used for tax cuts or spending without increasing the deficit.

A change in calculating the Consumer Price Index could cost typical Social Security recipients $3.49 to $10.47 a month. Phil Gambino, a spokesman for the Social Security Administration, said today that the current average monthly benefit is $698. One and a half percent of that, the high range of overestimating cited by Mr. Greenspan is $10.47, while 0.5 percent of it, his low estimate, is $3.49.

It would also affect pensions tied to the rate of inflation and union contracts with automatic adjustments based on inflation. The index is calculated by the Bureau of Labor Statistics, and it would be politically difficult for the Labor Department in a Democratic Administration to move directly to change those estimates.

Republicans welcomed his suggestion, even though it could bring attacks from the Social Security lobby, one of the nation's strongest. It also failed to distract Democrats from keeping up a drumbeat of demands that Republicans "show us the fine print," of their budget balancing plans as Representative Richard A. Gephardt of Missouri, the minority leader, put it.

Mr. Gephardt, testifying first before the House Budget committee and then before the Ways and Means Committee, argued that a constitutional amendment to require a balanced Federal budget should be approved only if supporters would first spell out the cuts they would make to reach that goal. He said he would introduce an "honest budget bill" to require such accounting.

Orrin G. Hatch, chairman of the Senate Judiciary Committee, said supporters of any proposal like Mr. Gephardt's were "not serious about a balanced budget amendment because they know that kills it."

His committee today put off a vote on the proposed amendment for a week, and opponents began to speak hopefully of their chances of defeating it in the Senate. It would take 34 votes to deny the measure the two-thirds majority required for a constitutional amendment, and 33 of last year's 37 opponents are still in office. They hope the "honest budget" argument can win them a few more critical votes. The House Judiciary Committee plans to vote on the amendment Wednesday.

Another House committee actually began the process of cutting spending. The Appropriations Committee began looking for ways to take back money that has already been committed for spending in the current fiscal year. Representative Robert L. Livingston of Louisiana, the chairman, said "we are looking for billions" in cuts.

Mr. Gephardt also told the Ways and Means Committee that Democrats were working on a tax plan with fewer tax breaks and fewer tax brackets. He said he would not go as far as many Republicans who favor a "flat tax," with only one rate for all taxpayers. But he said he could back a "flatter tax," under which most Americans except those with very high incomes would pay only about 10 or 11 percent.

He said he ultimately favored this approach because most efforts to change social policy through tax incentives had failed. "I don't think you can micromanage society through the tax code," he said. But in the short run, he urged a tax cut for workers earning less than $75,000 a year.

The Greenspan proposal was an unusual departure for the Fed chair-

man, who habitually declines to advise Congress on budget matters. Mr. Greenspan volunteered that changes in the index would cut spending and increase tax revenues and thus help reduce the deficit.

That would help solve the Republican problem of trying to balance the budget without formally raising taxes.

Representative John R. Kasich, the Ohio Republican who heads the House Budget Committee, initially said after hearing Mr. Greenspan's that the Government's calculations of the Consumer Price Index should be adjusted. He said he had already discussed the idea with Representative Bill Archer, the Texan who heads the Ways and Means Committee.

"We will attempt to incorporate accurate C.P.I. estimates," he said. Later, during a break in the hearing, he was more cautious in speaking to reporters. "Clearly the fact that we may have been overstating the C.P.I. and may have been having more entitle-ment spending than mandated under the law is something we are going to look at very, very carefully."

The idea that the C.P.I. overstates annual inflation is not original with Mr. Greenspan. The Congressional Budget Office estimated late last year that it exaggerated inflation by from 0.2 to 0.8 percentage point. Top Labor Department officials have also acknowledged that the index is an exaggeration.

It is calculated by the Bureau of Labor Statistics and adjusted about once each decade, so that it fails to capture fully such changes as suddenly successful inventions like television sets in the early 1950's or the introduction of more sophisticated computers, which reduce prices and enhance efficiency.

Mr. Greenspan based his $150 billion estimate on a one percentage point reduction in the Federal Government's inflation estimates. "If the annual inflation adjustments in the indexed programs and taxes were reduced by one percentage point," he said, "and making the admittedly strong assumption that there are no other changes in the economy—the annual level of the deficit will be lower by about $55 billion after five years, with cumulative five-year savings, I might add, of about $150 billion."

The Bureau of Labor Statistics is now working on a regular revision of the price index, a process likely to take another year or two to complete.

A more direct approach, one Mr. Greenspan suggested as a possibility today, would be for Congress to pass a law providing that current laws that adjust benefits based on the Consumer Price Index be amended so that the adjustment would be lower by a percentage point, or half a percentage point.

Such an approach would be almost certain to invite opposition from groups representing Social Security recipients, who are probably the nation's most effective lobby.

The Long Wave in Inflation and Real Interest Rates

Thomas W. Synnott III

Thomas W. Synnott III is Senior Vice President and Chief Economist, United States Trust Co., New York, NY.

The purpose of this paper is to look at the present situation in the U.S. from a broader perspective than traditional business cycle analysis and see if the long-wave concept can be helpful in understanding why (1) very low interest rates haven't done more to stimulate the economy, and (2) job growth has been so slow during this expansion.

ALTHOUGH THE U.S. economy is perceived, more and more widely, to be on a sustainable growth path, there is not much cheering about it. Media articles continue to focus on the loss of the American dream and the lack of growth in "high-quality" jobs. As the debate over NAFTA revealed, there is a lot of zero-sum thinking around. Indeed, a prominent economist's book, *The Zero Sum Society*, became a best seller in its field. All in all, there seems to be considerable self-doubt on the part of government policymakers, businessmen and the general public about long-term U.S. economic prospects. This attitude reinforces other forces pointing toward slower growth.

The striking parallels between our current economic setting and that of the last quarter of the nineteenth century suggest that a review of the economic history of that period can make an important contribution. Then, as now, new industrial competitors were emerging on the world scene (the U.S. was one of them), moderate real growth was accompanied by intense downward pressure on prices in established industries, and the growth of new industries — such as electric power and light — could then only be dimly foreseen.

A BRIEF HISTORY OF LONG WAVE ANALYSIS

Economists have long been fascinated by fluctuations in economic activity and by apparent repeating patterns in prices and interest rates. By the latter part of the nineteenth century, the ordinary business cycle was pretty well understood to be the result of an interaction between monetary conditions and business inventories. Work done at the National Bureau of Economic Research (1920-46) by Wesley C. Mitchell and Arthur F. Burns resulted in a thorough description of this three- to four-year cycle and how it operates.

However, even in the early years of business cycle analysis, some economists saw cycles of a longer duration in the historical economic data. According to Joseph Schumpeter (*History of Economic Analysis*, Oxford University Press, 1954), Clement Juglar in 1862 "was the first to use time series material systematically with the clear purpose in mind of analyzing a definite phenomenon." He identified a cycle of roughly ten years duration containing phases with the very modern labels of upgrade, explosion, liquidation, and depression. His famous statement that "the only cause of depression is prosperity" implies that both prosperity and depression are natural consequences of the same economic system. Some nineteenth century economists saw the cause of this Juglar cycle in changing weather patterns.

Since then, however, many economists have come to believe that there is a capital investment cycle of seven to eleven years duration and that low points in this cycle are associated with severe recessions. In the United States in the past twenty-five years several major cycles have occurred in commercial real estate investment, while business investment in plant and equipment has been less volatile. In Japan, however, a high rate of investment in plant and equipment as well as in office buildings during the "bubble-economy" era created a substantial excess capital stock. It will take

Figure 1
The Building Cycle (1960-1993)
Private Residential and Nonresidential Investment as Percent of Real GDP (Quarterly Average)

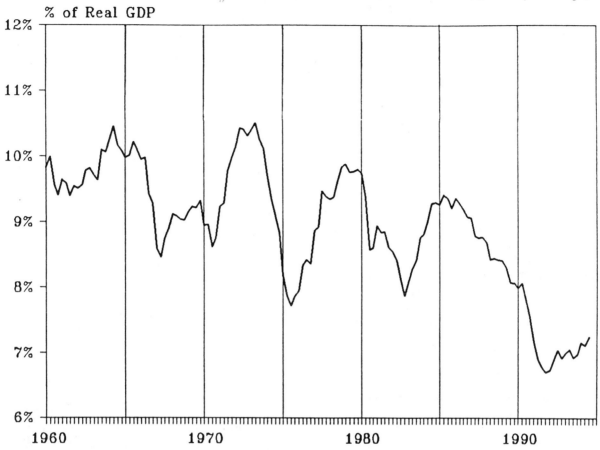

a long time to absorb this excess capacity. The medium-term cycle basically rests on the fact that office buildings and major factory expansions take a considerable period of time to plan and execute.

Furthermore, the decision to invest or not depends on expectations about future prices and costs as well as on current interest rates. In addition, investment has a self-reinforcing aspect. At one point during the recent office building boom, it was estimated that one-third of the demand for new office space was coming from the architects, engineers and contractors who were planning new office space!

Early Long Wave Analysis

The severity of the Great Depression of the 1930s sparked a good deal of interest in theories of long cycles, because it was observed that the most severe depressions were separated by fifty-year intervals. One such theory stemmed from the work of the Russian economist-statistician, Nicolai D. Kondratieff, in the 1920s. In what must have been a major statistical effort in the precomputer age, he eliminated both secular trends and regular business cycles from an extensive set of time series covering various types of data in different countries. The result was a long wave of about fifty years duration.

Schumpeter took the idea seriously, although there were significant differences between his and Kondratieff's dating of long waves in series such as production and consumption, which have strong secular trends. William Fellner in his *Trends and Cycles in Economic Activity* (Henry Holt, 1956) felt that the case for long waves was more clearly established for prices and interest rates than for production. While he did not believe long waves could be extrapolated into the future with any precision, he felt that the concept was useful in explaining why some business downturns are more severe than others and why the corresponding upturns are weaker.

Recent Long-Wave Studies

The severe recession of 1974-75 and the following period of accelerating inflation resulted in a number of articles and books built around a supercycle concept. This literature continued during the 1980s, perhaps in recognition of the fiftieth anniversary of the Great Depression. Much of it was entertaining but did little more than catalog similarities between that era and the present.

However, the economic slowing and renewed disinflation that began in late 1984 led some economists to postulate that more was at work than a simple business cycle. One interesting treatment of the long wave concept was Albert Sommers' November 1985 article *The (Ugh) Kondratieff Idea: A Long Wave Hypothesis for the United States*. He concluded that, while there was "no logical case for a *periodic* systematically generated long wave," there was a strong case for a particular long wave in the United States that began with the end of World War II. After that, Sommers, an insightful and widely read proponent of business-cycle analysis, returned again and again to long-term themes. His piece *The Schumpeter Vision*, December 3, 1993, focused on the paradox that the developed countries have now carried Keynesian short-term stabilization policies to the point where high debt-to-GDP ratios mean that virtually none of them has the fiscal freedom to pursue Keynesian policies any further. It is clear that many European countries have found that the social and economic policies that had their origin in the Great Depression can no longer energize their economies, and they now must find other ways of coping with (apparently) permanently high unemployment. In effect, even socialist governments have been forced to rely on private investment, just as in the pre-Keynesian world of sixty years ago.

Jay Forrester, the father of complex dynamic models, has turned his talents to determining the causes of long waves. In his article, "The Next Decade in the Economy," *CFA Readings*, March 1987, he concludes that economic long waves primarily result from major shifts in the construction of physical capital and in the prices of physical capital. He also stresses the importance of real interest rates and financial policies that "take two or three generations to complete." Indeed, his models can easily generate long waves from apparently simple information-feedback and time-delay functions.

Finally, the work of W.W. Rostow in the 1970s emphasizes changes in the relative price of commodities. His insight was that the long-wave force shows up most clearly in the prices of certain basic commodities, such as wheat and oil. After a long period of price stability, rising demand overtakes slowly expanding supply. Prices rise more quickly, perhaps abruptly, making it profitable to undertake large-scale investments with a long gestation period. When the investment is completed, the price of the commodity falls back, making new investments unprofitable. But the excess supplies persist, leading to stable or declining prices for the commodity in question. The recent major cycle in the relative price of oil is a case in point. It took the jump in prices from the first oil shock to make it profitable to exploit Alaskan and North Sea oil. Similarly, in the latter part of the nineteenth century the high price of wheat in Europe spurred major railroad developments in the U.S., Canada and Australia. Other examples come to mind: the waves of office building construction in the 1920s and nuclear power plants in the 1970s.

THE LONG WAVE

While the evidence of long waves in overall economic activity is ambiguous, there have clearly been extended periods of rising and falling inflation. Indeed, the curves superimposed on the wholesale price swings constitute a sine wave with a period of fifty-six years. What this chart tells us is that the average inflation rate for the nine years centered on the peak is about 10 percent above the average for the nine years centered on the trough. Because the time interval is twenty-eight years, this represents an annual acceleration in inflation of about 0.3 percent. In the short run, this figure could well be lost in the normal fluctuations in inflation during an ordinary business cycle. But cumulatively it becomes important, which is the essential point.

Causes and Characteristics

There is probably no simple or single answer to the question of what causes this rising and falling tidal force in inflation. Wars, government policy shifts and technological change all play a role. However, it is characteristic of the process that prices rise faster than costs during upgrades, and vice versa. In the upgrade phase of the long wave in inflation, prices are either high or rising relative to costs, and profitability is generally good.

This process encourages a high rate of investment, which boosts economic growth for a time and pushes inflation up further. Eventually the growth in investment leads to overcapacity and reduces profitability. As might be expected, these profitability swings lead to prolonged credit cycles.

But, as long as the profitability of investment is high relative to the cost of capital, after each setback the investment cycle will begin again, sustaining the long-term uptrend in prices. As this uptrend is more and more built into business decisions, investments become more speculative and more oriented toward real assets.

For instance, in the wake of the Civil War high commodity prices led to major investments in railroads and in the cotton textile industry. This upgrade in prices was brought to an end when the U.S. government decided in 1874 to go back on the gold standard (by 1879) and adopted a very restrictive monetary policy (i.e., it stopped issuing greenbacks that had been used to finance the Civil War). This policy led to a long period of falling prices and growing political discontent, especially on the part of farmers and debtors.

Figure 2
Wholesale Price Inflation
9 Year Centered Moving Average
(1862-1993)

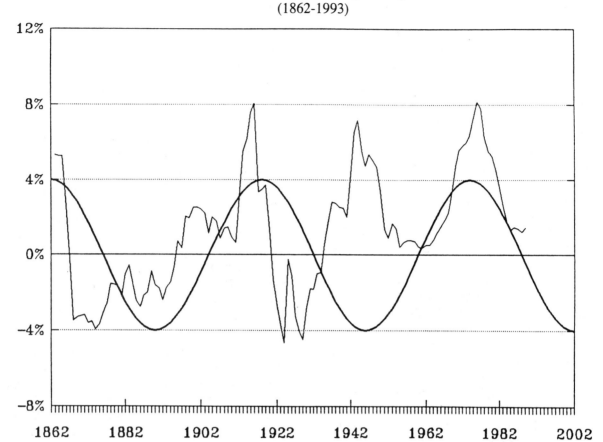

Monetary policy was not the sole factor, of course. Besides the U.S., several other industrial competitors emerged on the world scene — Germany, Japan and Russia — so that older industries were under relentless competitive pressures.

Similarly from 1966 to 1980, the U.S. experienced a series of recessions as the Federal Reserve attempted to control inflation. However, each business cycle saw progressively higher peaks and troughs for inflation. By the mid 1970s is seemed that borrowing heavily and buying real assets was the only way to come out ahead. Initially the explosion in private debt was kept under control by conservative businessmen and bankers who either remembered the 1930s themselves or, more likely, absorbed its lessons from their parents. However, eventually they passed from the scene and the growth in money and credit accelerated.

Finally, when inflation was full-blown and larger and larger constituencies were suffering from it, the government responded decisively. But this took time. It took fifteen years from the imposition of wage-price guidelines, through price controls, to Chairman Volcker's draconian monetary policy. Parenthetically, it took about the same amount of time to restore

price stability and put the U.S. back on the gold standard after the Civil War. It does seem that one important force in generating long waves in inflation is the time it takes for the body politic to forget the lessons of the past.

Real Interest Rates

The long wave in inflation leads to a long wave in real interest rates, because nominal interest rates tend to be sticky. This has a significant impact on both the economy and the social order.

The present long wave had its inflation peak in 1974 for the world economy. (Price controls on oil and gas delayed the peak in the U.S. for a few years.) It is not surprising, then, to find that real interest rates were negative during this period. When the long wave in inflation finally broke, nominal rates remained high — because of bond holders' aversion to inflation risk — and real long-term interest rates shot up to levels not seen since the 1930s (or the 1890s).

High real interest rates affect the basic economy in several ways. Obviously, they dampen truly long-term investment, both public and private, because interest

Figure 3
Trends in Wages and Prices
Deflated by CPI
(1950-1993)

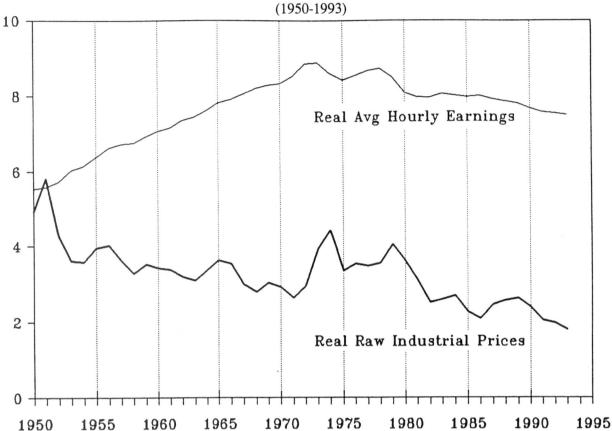

costs tend to grow faster than the economy's ability to service the debt. Furthermore, by raising the cost of all corporate capital, they depress Tobin's "Q-ratio" (the ratio of the market value of corporate assets to replacement value). This encourages successful firms to expand by acquiring existing assets rather than creating new investment. In itself, this is a force for slower economic growth. Additionally, mergers and acquisitions mean rationalization, and that reduces employment.

It seems likely that this rationalization process is part of the explanation for the downward trend in real average hourly earnings in recent years.

Persistently high real interest rates would result in significant transfers of wealth to bondholders. However, the slowing in borrowing by all sectors of the economy except the Federal government has brought real long-term rates down considerably from their peaks in the mid-1980s.

Where Are We in the Current Wave?

Figure 4 shows, in somewhat idealized form, the fifty-six year long wave suggested by Figure 1, divided

into four subperiods or phases. Whereas in earlier periods prices in general could rise and fall, now wages and the general price level almost always rise. It seems that only basic commodity prices are free to move up or down in the modern world. Thus the center line in Figure 4 should be taken as a long-run average rate of inflation. Furthermore, the high-inflation and low-inflation periods can be divided into phases when the inflation rate is rising and when it is falling. A look at the chronology of Figure 4 suggests that the U.S. and the world economy are about in the middle of the third phase.

From its peak in 1974, the inflation rate for the world economy has steadily declined. During the first period after the peak, 1974-88, the inflation rate and commodity prices remained above their long-term average. This was a period of disinflation but not low inflation. In the second period, 1988-2002, disinflation continues, but now many commodity prices and the inflation rate itself are below their long-term average. (Since 1940 consumer prices in the U.S. have increased at a 4.4 percent compound annual rate.) Schumpeter called both periods — Phases II and III in the chart — the downgrade in prices. However, it is

Figure 4
Current Long Wave Cycle
(1960-2016)

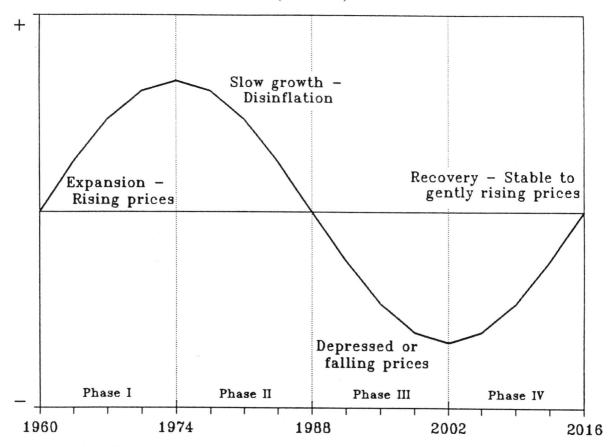

helpful to distinguish between them because each phase has different economic and financial characteristics.

Phase III, our "current condition," is in some ways a difficult time. Years of ebbing inflation have severely depressed the profitability of basic industries. Many older industries are under great financial pressure. With business in general focusing on cost reduction rather than expansion, job growth is weak. This adds to economic uncertainty and spurs a growing political reaction. The memory of the evils of high inflation is dimmed by the passage of time (except for bond investors). The perils of deflation seem more and more important.

Table 1 lists some of the characteristics of "third phase" periods. There are many similarities between the late nineteenth century period and the present.

The emergence of new industrial powers has already been cited. But the shifting of domestic manufacturing to Mexico and Southeast Asia in our era had its parallel in the movement of the cotton textile industry (at that time the largest manufacturing industry in the United States) from New England to the South. Innovation in that industry was relentlessly directed toward cost saving and productivity improve-

ment. This was in stark contrast to the inflationary period of the 1860s and early 1870s when the key decisions were where to build a new mill and what type of cloth to produce.

Large businesses dealt with the profitability problem through mergers and consolidations, both to reduce excess capacity and to have better control over markets. This was the era of the great trusts — steel, oil, and sugar for example — many of them constructed with the aid of the House of Morgan, and financed with the high-risk securities of the day — common stocks.

Economic pressures brought forth the modern labor movement that had its birth in the Knights of Labor. The Progressive Movement drew on the support of farmers and small business. The great debates over the free coinage of silver (bimetallism) pitted the miners of the West against the "sound-money" crowd of Eastern bankers. Later, as real long-term interest rates continued to decline, there was a new wave of railroad expansion.

One other characteristic of that era that seems to be true today is that business cycle downturns lasted longer and the upturns were weaker than in the periods of rising inflation.

Table 1
**Characteristics of Third Phase of Long Wave in
Inflation**
1876-1890; 1932-1946; 1988-2002

Downward pressure on prices:
- Many commodity prices below cost of production
- Corporate restructuring and mergers
- Commercial real estate – declining rents and values

Intense credit pressures:
- Bank loan losses
- Rising debt burdens

Political tensions:
- Zero-sum thinking
- Income redistribution and other socialist measures
- Depression of spirit
- Protectionism

Emergence of new engines of growth:
- New products and industries
- Major infrastructure projects

CONCLUSIONS AND OBSERVATIONS

The long wave concept forces us to look at our current situation in the context of economic history. While the economic environment is continually evolving and is never quite the same as in earlier periods, the basic mechanism underlying the long wave in inflation seems timeless. This is the principle that high prices for basic commodities eventually lead to low prices and vice versa. The long lags in this process seem due as much to human memories and thought processes as to the naturally long gestation period for large-scale projects like the Alaskan pipeline. Thus the long-wave concept may well give us some insights into the economic environment we face during the balance of this decade.

First, although disinflation as a force appears to be ebbing, with many basic commodity prices bottoming out, inflation will stay relatively low. While some economists fear that the past two years of high growth in the monetary base will lead to high 6+ percent inflation by 1995, long-wave analysis suggests that inflation will respond less to economic growth and

monetary stimulus than in the 1970s. At the next business cycle peak it is likely to be well below 1990's 6 percent level, probably in the 4 to 5 percent range.

Second, political pressures mean that monetary policy is unlikely to become really tight as measured by a real Federal funds rate over 2-1/2 percent during the next several years. If so, short-term interest rates will be less volatile and the uncertainty premium in real long-term rates could decline further. This suggests that the next peak in interest rates will be well below that in March 1989 when the Federal funds rate was 9.85 percent.

Third, U.S. government economic policy in the years ahead has a crucial role to play in restoring the long-term strength of the U.S. economy. With the prospect of an extended period of low real interest rates, the federal government has an opportunity to shift spending toward long-term investment — both public and private — increasing the economy's capacity to grow and thereby reducing the federal deficit. Furthermore, a policy mix of generally easy money and tight fiscal policy would tend to reduce the U.S. balance of payments deficit and strengthen the dollar. In turn, a strong dollar would allow the U.S. to play the role of world banker as Britain did 100 years ago. This would certainly benefit the U.S. financial services industry.

Finally, the period ahead is likely to see increased political turmoil in the industrialized world as restive electorates strive to find political solutions to high unemployment. We should not be surprised to see more election outcomes like that in Canada, where a major political party is obliterated at the polls. In such an environment, protectionism will be a constant threat as the U.S. and foreign governments strive to protect their special interests.

In conclusion, we should recognize that the long wave in inflation is a global phenomenon. We may find that the clearest evidence of this downgrade period is to be found not in the United States but abroad — in Japan, for example, where asset price deflation has been most severe. Also, we should not forget that the huge changes in relative prices that are occurring in this phase of the long wave create not only problems for old industries but also opportunities for new ones. As for the depression of spirit that is weighing on many of the developed economies, history teaches us that this too shall pass.

International Economics

One of the most critical challenges presented by the current worldwide economic revolution (is): How will we be able to maintain and expand the multilateral trade system, integrating the many new players who want their share of the pie while also preserving the standard of living of the industrialized countries so as to prevent a possibly violent backlash? (Klaus Schwab and Claude Smadja, *Harvard Business Review,* November/December 1994)

Up to this point, the readings in this book have primarily focused on issues involving the U.S. domestic economy. However, many of the world's most pressing economic problems are international in scope, involving the complex web of the trading and financial arrangements that link all countries in a global network. The world economy is in a period of rapid change. Over the last decade we have witnessed a series of unforeseen events: an end to the cold war; ambitious market reforms in what were formerly centrally planned economies; an acceleration of the process of economic integration in the Americas, Western Europe, and the Pacific Rim; and increased use of protectionist measures by most major traders. How the United States responds to these challenges may well influence events in the world economy for many years to come.

The U.S. economy is extraordinarily resilient. Historically, it has consistently demonstrated an ability to adjust to change, to adapt new technologies, and to create new jobs. In absolute terms, the United States is presently the world's most important international trader: total U.S. exports and imports each exceed $700 billion annually. In addition, the United States has for many years been able to enjoy the advantages of remaining relatively self-sufficient; whereas Canada and most Western European countries derive roughly a quarter of their national income from trade, the United States obtains just over 10 percent of all income from this source.

However, it is increasingly apparent that an important shift in power has occurred: the United States, once the world's predominant economic power, must now share the spotlight with Western Europe and East Asia. In this new multipolar world, America still appears to be the first among equals. But it no longer has the economic leverage or moral authority to dictate the course of world events. Evidence of the constraints that the United States faces include fierce competition from foreign businesses, continuing trade deficits, and an apparent decline in its ability to meet major commitments both at home and abroad.

This unit begins with "Consolidating Capitalism," in which Jeffrey Sachs tries to put globalization of the world economy in historical context and to identify the policies needed to consolidate a new international economic system. He shows that the world has much to gain from the emerging system and much to lose if action is not taken to put it in place.

Next, Klaus Schwab and Claude Smadja show how during the 1990s the world embarked on a radically different "post–Bretton Woods" era, in which industrialized nations must confront the cumulative impact of both cyclical crisis and structural change. They assert that, if present trends continue, East Asia should be poised to claim preeminence over North America and Western Europe before the turn of the century. In "Global Growth Is on a Tear," Louis Richman provides a detail of trends in specific countries to show how developing economies are driving a global expansion. Richman discusses what this might mean for the industrialized world.

This is followed by "From GATT to WTO: The Institutionalization of World Trade," the article in which Salil Pitroda offers a brief history of trade. He traces the evolution of the World Trade Organization and assesses its prospects.

The U.S. trade policy after the cold war is addressed by Kimberly Ann Elliot. She foresees that trade disputes and other disagreements over economic policy may become more antagonistic and disruptive in the future. In her view, trade policy is less important to U.S. competitiveness than reforming macroeconomic policies, which have priced U.S. exports out of international markets. Richard Boltuck and Robert Litan assess the effectiveness of U.S. unfair trade laws as a device to counter dumping by foreign rivals. In "U.S. Trade Deficits and International Competitiveness," Robert Parry investigates the role that U.S. trade deficits play in international competitiveness. Susan Dentzer shows how a recent change in the way the U.S.

Commerce Department tracks trade could change the size of the trade deficit. Then, Sylvia Nasar examines data on U.S. productivity in individual industries and uncovers a number of areas in which the United States presently enjoys a comparative advantage over her trading partners.

The unit concludes with three articles that offer perspectives on other countries. Francisco Valdés-Ugalde examines the changing relationship between the state and the economy in Mexico and finds that state reform cannot be limited to economic matters. John Hall and Udo Ludwig examine major sources of current problems in the East German economy. Finally, can a socialist republic find happiness trading in a capitalist world? David James focuses on China and Vietnam, which have recently turned to foreign investment and export-led international

trade as a means of building economic strength in a world of capitalist economies.

Looking Ahead: Challenge Questions

How should America respond to the challenges of global competition?

Where does the U.S. enjoy a comparative advantage over her trading partners? What are the major causes of the U.S. trade deficit? What role do "unfair trade laws" play in world trade?

What is the World Trade Organization, and how does it work?

What role do the developing nations of Asia, Central Europe, and Latin America play in global economic growth? Characterize recent economic developments in Mexico, East Germany, and China.

Consolidating Capitalism

Jeffrey D. Sachs

Jeffrey D. Sachs is the Galen L. Stone professor of international trade at Harvard University. He has served as an economic adviser to Bolivia, Estonia, Mongolia, Poland, and the Russian Federation, among other countries.

The 1990s is one of the great watershed decades in economic history. The postwar division of the world economy into the First, Second, and Third Worlds has ended. Not only has communism collapsed, but other ideologies of state-led development that were prevalent in the Third World for decades have fallen into disrepute. If the United States and the other industrial democracies act with wisdom, they have a chance to consolidate a global capitalist world system, with profound benefits for both the rich and the poor countries. But the greatest foreign policy misjudgment of our time would be to assume that such a system will automatically fall into place. Weak U.S. leadership and fractious relations among the industrial democracies are already putting at risk the unprecedented opportunity to create a law-bound and prosperous international system.

The overarching benefits of the emerging world capitalist system, if it takes hold, will lie as much in global security as in economics. With a few notable exceptions, the market revolution has gone hand in hand with a democratic revolution. That is true in virtually all of Latin America, Central Europe, and the former Soviet Union, and also in parts of East Asia (South Korea and Taiwan) and Africa. The spread of democracy by itself almost surely reduces the risks of war, as do the increased economic links among countries. Careful scholarly work has bolstered rather than weakened the old claim that democracies do not wage war on each other, as Yale political scientist Bruce Russett has recently demonstrated in *Grasping the Democratic Peace*. It has been instructive, and no accident, that Russia's *elected* Duma has become the most ardent voice for peaceful rather than military solutions to the deepening conflicts among Russia's diverse regions.

While globalization may seem to be a well-worn theme, it remains poorly understood, which helps to account for the weak international leadership at the moment. Moreover, policies to promote global integration, such as the new General Agreement on Tariffs and Trade (GATT) accord, are becoming highly contentious in the advanced economies. The half-century commitment of the United States to open international trade is under unprecedented attack from various ideologies on the Left and Right. Free trade is even more strongly under attack in parts of Europe, such as France. And key tools to promote the new international system, such as foreign aid, are similarly under unprecedented attack.

This essay aims to put the recent globalization in historical context and to identify the policies needed to consolidate a new international economic system. The world has much to gain from the emerging system, and much to lose if we fail to act decisively to put it in place.

As a result of developments of the past decade, a global capitalist economy is within view for the first time, though it has not yet arrived. Countries with a combined population of roughly 3.5 billion people have undertaken radical economic reforms to adopt the institutions of the capitalist system. These core reforms include six common points: (1) open international trade; (2) currency convertibility; (3) private ownership as the main engine of economic growth; (4) corporate ownership as the dominant organizational form for large enterprises; (5) openness to foreign investment; and (6) membership in key international economic institutions, including the International Monetary Fund (IMF), the World Bank, and the GATT, which is now superseded by the new World Trade Organization (WTO). The revolution is remarkable in two dimensions: the "extensive" margin (the worldwide scope of the policy changes), and the "intensive" margin (the depth and complexity of the new economic links among countries).

While specific forms of advanced capitalism in the United States, Western Europe, and East Asia certainly differ, they all share the six basic characteristics just enumerated. There are two main dimensions of difference among the alternative "models" of capitalism: the extent of the social welfare state and the nature of corporate ownership. On the first, Western Europe has by far the most extensive social welfare system in the capitalist

Reprinted with permission from *Foreign Policy,* Number 98, Spring 1995, pp. 50–64. © 1995 by the Carnegie Endowment for International Peace.

world, followed by the United States, and then East Asia. With regard to corporate governance, Western Europe and Japan have more extensive cross-holdings of equity ownership by non-financial corporations (that is, enterprises holding shares in each other), and more bank ownership of enterprises, while the U.S. and British economies have traditionally relied more heavily on public ownership via traded shares in stock exchanges. There are of course also differences in the role of industrial policy, state ownership, and openness of the economies, but those differences tend to be exaggerated by some analysts. Note that even the most market-oriented economies are not strictly laissez-faire. Capable public administration is surely needed to guide infrastructure, enforce laws, protect the environment, and promote public health and education.

Weak U.S. leadership and fractious relations among the industrial democracies are already putting at risk the unprecedented opportunity to create a law-bound and prosperous international system.

Much is written about the relative merits of the alternative models, but in terms of globalization, the overriding similarities of the advanced capitalist economies are more important than the differences. For a developing country rejoining the world system, the fact that the advanced economies all share certain key features—openness, private ownership, corporate governance—offers a relatively straightforward set of guideposts for the most fundamental reforms. Moreover, increasing internationalization of the advanced economies seems to be eroding the structural differences among them. The welfare state in Western Europe is likely to be trimmed in coming years, while stock market ownership seems to be gaining importance relative to corporate cross-holdings in Europe and Japan.

It is important to remember that as recently as the late 1970s, only around one-fourth of the globe—the First World—operated according to the core capitalist institutions. The socialist world included around 26 countries, with a combined population in 1986 of 1.7 billion people, or 34 per cent of the world system. The dozens of non-socialist developing countries were mainly pursuing models of "state-led industrialization," in which the state aimed to lead the industrialization process through state ownership of industry and extensive trade restrictions to protect so-called infant industries (which all too often were already senescent industries). In fact, only a handful of developing countries, mainly in East Asia, adopted institutions that were recognizably "capitalist" in orientation.

Those that did were a lucky few. If there is one overriding lesson from the comparative growth experience of the past 50 years, it is that capitalism "pays." If we consider countries that maintained the main precepts of capitalism—open trade, currency convertibility, and the private sector as the engine of growth—throughout the 1970s and 1980s, there is apparently not a single development failure among them. *All* countries that played by the rules throughout this entire 20-year span experienced increases in per capita income, with the poorer countries tending to grow more rapidly than the richer ones, and therefore tending to "converge" in living standards. Of course, the outward-oriented economies of East Asia (Hong Kong, Singapore, Taiwan, and South Korea) are the prime exemplars, but there are success stories as well among the poorer countries in all regions of the world. Many countries that behaved badly until recently and have only now adopted the core capitalist institutions are stuck in a transition crisis.

TRIUMPH OF CAPITALISM

If capitalist economic performance has been so dominating, how can we account for the fact that the vast majority of developing countries chose anticapitalist policies until recently, policies that left them in poverty and often in financial bankruptcy? Answering that crucial question will help us to understand the risks that we still face in consolidating the emerging international system.

The sharp divisions of the capitalist and non-capitalist world date back around 150 years, to the 1840s. Before the nineteenth century, there was, of course, no modern capitalist economy anywhere. While many aspects of modern capitalism predate the nineteenth century (especially the mechanisms of international trade, contract law, commercial banking, and even rudimentary capital markets), the modern capitalist system really emerged at the start of that century, with the development of the factory system, the modern corporate form for company organization, central banking, the final elimination of servile obligations in Western Europe, and the easing or elimination of mercantilist trade practices. These characteristics of the modern capitalist world emerged first in England and its colonies, and then spread to Western Europe (some carried by Napoleon's armies, others by imitation in the face of the evident superiority of English or French examples).

By the 1840s, the profound economic superiority of capitalist institutions was apparent to keen observers no less than Karl Marx and Friedrich Engels, who rightly predicted in *The Communist Manifesto* that capitalism would undermine traditional societies:

> The bourgeoisie, by the rapid improvement of all instruments of production, by the immensely facilitated means of communication, draws all, even the most barbarian, nations into civilisation. The cheap prices of its commodities are the heavy artillery with which it batters down all Chinese walls, with which it forces the barbarians' intensely obstinate hatred of foreigners to capitulate. It

compels all nations, on pain of extinction, to adopt the bourgeois mode of production; it compels them to introduce what it calls civilisation in their midst, *i.e.*, to become bourgeois themselves. In one word, it creates a world after its own image.

This proposition was put to the test from the 1840s onward, and has been nearly vindicated, but only after 150 years of wrenching confrontations between capitalism and traditional societies. The puzzle is not that capitalism triumphed, but that it took so long. China was the first to feel the onslaught, in the Opium War of 1839–42, which gave the British a foothold on the Chinese mainland. Russia was confronted with the stark evidence of its relative industrial backwardness in its stunning loss to Great Britain in the Crimean War of 1854–56. Japan was shocked out of complacent isolation by the arrival of Commodore Matthew Perry's Black Ships in Edo Bay in 1853. India was finally swallowed whole by the British in 1858, after more than a century of encroaching control by the British East India Company. The Ottoman empire was dismantled piece by piece, beginning with the British occupation of Aden (1839) and the French conquest of Algeria (completed in 1847).

The traditional empires (excepting colonized India) attempted at least some partial modernizing reforms in the face of the Western onslaught. For example, in Russia, the 1860s were an era of significant reforms under Alexander II, with the emancipation of the serfs (1861), the introduction of an independent judiciary (1864), and the start of local self-government (1864). But by the 1870s, these partial reforms had stalled, and with Czar Alexander's assassination in 1881, a wave of reaction followed. Further reforms under Count Sergei Witte (1890s) and Prime Minister Pyotr Stolypin (1900s) left Russia financially fragile and therefore prone to collapse in World War I. The Bolshevik Revolution, far from inevitable, filled the vacuum of the financial chaos of 1917.

In China, reforms were delayed until the first decade of this century, after China's imperial rulers were stunned by their loss in the war with Japan in 1895. As in Russia, when the Ching dynasty eventually collapsed in 1911, the financial rot was so far advanced that it proved impossible to consolidate a new, modernizing regime. China fell prey to warlordism and then to the Japanese invasion of 1931.

Only Japan met the capitalist challenge by a systematic adoption of Western institutions, in what became history's first case of "shock therapy" economic reforms. Between 1868, the start of the Meiji Restoration, and 1885, the new Japanese leadership systematically put in place the new capitalist institutions copied from the West. Japan eliminated feudal institutions, introduced taxation in money rather than in kind, initiated a private market in land, created a stable currency, opened the economy to international trade (under the strictures of the "unequal treaties" imposed by the Western powers), introduced commercial law (much of it copied from German commercial law), reorganized the government on cabinet lines, and so on. Those reforms ushered

in a century of remarkable economic growth that carried Japan to the number two position in the world economy.

Japan remained the only significant non-European power to make the transition to modern capitalism until after World War II. If we examine the fitful process of reforms in Russia, China, the Ottoman Empire, and elsewhere, we note that those countries too might have eventually made a successful transition—more gradually and less boldly than in Japan—were it not for the upheavals of World War I, the consequent financial turmoil of the 1920s, and the collapse of the international economy in the Great Depression of the 1930s. By the time World War II ended in 1945, there was no international trading system; no convertible currencies except the American dollar; and no moral attraction in the developing world to a capitalist system that had led to imperialist plunder, depression, and two world wars in 30 years.

After 1945, the world divided into the proverbial First, Second, and Third Worlds, and the division remained mostly intact until the 1980s. The First World was reconstructed under U.S. auspices, starting with the Bretton Woods institutions, the GATT, the Marshall Plan, and the European Economic Community. A few developing countries, particularly in East Asia (South Korea and Taiwan), joined the system, mostly to reinforce their place under the U.S. security umbrella. The Stalinist model was imposed in the Second World, including on the formerly capitalist economies of Czechoslovakia, Hungary, and Poland.

The nationalist leaders of the newly independent states of the Third World, such as Jawaharlal Nehru, Sukarno, and Kwame Nkrumah, made a thoroughly understandable, if deeply flawed, economic choice in the late 1940s to try to protect their hard-won independence through autarkic policies and forced industrialization promoted by the state. After all, independence had been won on the Gandhian rallying cry of "self-sufficiency." Moreover, few economists in the leading countries demurred at these choices. Following John Maynard Keynes, the capitalist world was "known" to be unstable (witness the Great Depression). The state became the great stabilizer. In any event, there was barely a "world economy" to join, following the disasters of the Great Depression and World War II.

REVOLUTION IN THE 1990S

The Capitalist Revolution of the 1990s is the unraveling of the tripartite world system that emerged after World War II. There is, of course, one overriding reason for the revolution: The alternatives proffered by the Second and Third worlds did not work. At the same time, the countries that joined the First World experienced an economic boom of unprecedented magnitude, and they included the handful of poor countries in the world that happened to land on the right mixture of economic policies.

It is interesting to note that the collapse of the Second and Third World models of state-led, autarkic development proceeded according to a common pattern. There were, in most

cases, three steps on the way to collapse. The first stage of the state-led strategy actually worked reasonably well in most of the countries. It turned out that certain kinds of heavy industry—such as steel mills and coal mines—were enough like bureaucratic units, with standardized inputs, outputs, and technology, that they could be run effectively as state enterprises. It is these heavy industrial sectors that were the first, and generally only, successes of state-led industrialization. State-led industrialization was also particularly effective when poorer countries could draw on reserves of low-productivity agricultural workers for low-wage employment in the new factories.

The second stage was the onset of economic stagnation, already beginning in the early 1960s. While state-led industrialization could spur heavy industry, it could not succeed in the next stage of spurring consumer goods industries, services, or product and process innovation. Also, large reserves of low-skilled agricultural labor diminished as industrialization and urbanization proceeded. Countries found themselves saddled with hothouse industries, protected by tariff and quota barriers, and kept alive by subsidies, but with little use of their outputs. In Latin America, this became known as the crisis of "the second-stage of import substitution." It was universally agreed that the second-stage of import substitution was much more difficult than the first. Yet there were still relatively few calls to abandon the strategy altogether.

In the socialist countries, the problems of stagnation were also becoming evident in the early 1960s, prompting Nikita Khrushchev to authorize the experimentation with market incentives under the so-called Liberman reforms, which were aborted when Khrushchev fell from power. In Poland, economic stagnation led to the ouster of one party secretary and his replacement by another who promised to speed economic growth by importing modern technologies from abroad. The regime embarked on a borrowing spree that raised the country's foreign debt to more than $42 billion in 1987, which equaled 70 per cent of the country's gross national product. The only significant result of that borrowing spree was to drive the Polish government into bankruptcy at the end of the 1970s.

The pattern of stagnation leading to foreign borrowing was replayed dozens of times throughout the socialist and developing countries. Foreign borrowing, in short, became the illusory way to "fix" a more fundamental problem of economic policy. It failed to work, of course, leaving much of the Second and Third Worlds in financial distress by the 1980s. Virtually every Latin American government was in default on foreign loans by 1983; Hungary and Yugoslavia fell into acute financial crises by the mid-1980s, and Bulgaria defaulted on its foreign debts at the end of the 1980s. Of course, external shocks (such as swings in oil prices and spikes in world interest rates in the early 1980s) sometimes played a role in the onset of state bankruptcy, but it is clear that poor policies rather than external shocks were really decisive. Strikingly, Mexico, Nigeria, and other profligate oil exporters went bank-

rupt in the early 1980s in the midst of an unprecedented oil export boom, as a result of incredible government waste, inefficiency, and corruption attendant upon a state-led strategy for industrial development.

Remarkably, Mikhail Gorbachev replayed the foreign debt disaster 15 years after Poland's debacle by the decision to jump-start the Soviet economy through foreign-financed modernization in the second half of the 1980s. The Soviet Union's foreign indebtedness grew from $28 billion in 1985 to $67 billion in 1991. With no increased export capacity in sight, the creditors finally pulled the plug, ceasing new lending and demanding a repayment on earlier credits. The Soviet government went into default in late 1991, just as the Soviet Union itself collapsed.

RISKS TO THE SYSTEM

The most remarkable story of the past 150 years is not that successful economic institutions inexorably replace unsuccessful ones, but that unsuccessful ones can persist so long, often at the cost of unimaginable human suffering. Russia and China delayed reforms in the nineteenth century until their teetering empires suffered utter fiscal and military collapse. Other countries finally succumbed to foreign conquest. Economic weakness, especially in the face of foreign challenges, has often led to extreme militarism rather than economic reform. Retrograde economic institutions can even be imposed on successful countries through military conquest, as with the Soviet destruction of Central Europe's more prosperous capitalist economies after World War II.

There are only a handful of countries in the world today that are aggressively shunning participation in the emerging global economy. Even Cuba, North Korea, and Iran are trying, if unconvincingly, to court foreign investors. Nonetheless, Russia and China remain with one foot rather tentatively in the global economy, and both face monumental problems of consolidating their opening to the world. At the same time, much of Africa is collapsing from social and economic disorder before basic reforms can be put into place.

The most important strategic problems of international economic policymaking in the next few years will involve the consolidation of market reforms in Russia, China, and Africa. Beyond that, there is the need to avoid backsliding on international commitments made by the developed countries, which are themselves experiencing intense domestic protectionist pressures. Finally, there is the need to deepen the international system of law to better govern the emerging global economy.

Without doubt, the Western neglect of the current Russian economic crisis is the greatest foreign policy failing in decades. Since 1991, Russia has been within reach of successful market reform. Yet, delay in successful economic stabilization in Russia has deeply undermined public support for reforms and added great strength to

extremist and military forces within the Russian body politic. The main reformers are now gone from the government, having been defeated at the polls. Not only the Russian economy, but also Russian democracy, has been put recklessly at risk by Western neglect.

The Western effort has failed at three levels. First, there was no intellectual understanding among Western leaders of what to do. The Marshall Plan architects had one brilliant insight that is missing today: The purpose of economic assistance is *political*, to support fragile democratic regimes attempting to implement more basic reforms. As George Marshall put it in his famous 1947 speech, the aim of aid is to stabilize economic conditions "so as to permit the emergence of political and social conditions in which free institutions can exist." In recent years, by contrast, the little aid that has been provided has been apportioned almost entirely by economic bureaucrats, whose main concern has been the avoidance of "waste," rather than the fate of Russian democracy. Second, the sums have been derisory. In fiscal year 1995, Russia will receive roughly $380 million in U.S. aid, or about one-sixth of the aid to Egypt. U.S. aid to Russia will amount to roughly .005 per cent of U.S. gross domestic product (GDP), compared with Marshall Plan commitments to Europe in fiscal year 1949 of 2 per cent of GDP. Russia may or may not receive a few billion dollars of IMF support, years later than the money should have arrived from that institution.

Third, the Bush and Clinton administrations failed almost entirely in leading a coordinated Western effort to aid Russia. Virtually all Western "aid" has come in the form of export credits to Russian enterprises, with short periods for repayment, rather than in the form of grants and long-term loans to the Russian budget (almost all of the Marshall Plan support was in the form of grants). Repayments of these loans are already straining the Russian budget. Overall support from Western governments for the Russian budget, vitally needed for stabilization, has been essentially nil. Moreover, despite several hasty announcements of Group of Seven aid packages ($24 billion announced in 1992, and $28 billion announced in 1993), very little coordination was ever undertaken to bring those packages to fruition. In 1994, there was essentially a complete collapse in U.S. attempts to mobilize international assistance from governments on behalf of Russian reform. Now, the IMF and the World Bank are the only real games in town, and they have proved to be hugely insufficient.

The case for foreign aid is the strongest in decades, but the public support is surely at its lowest ebb since the war. Though a democratizing Africa will desperately need support, the new Republican leaders in the Congress have discussed zeroing out Africa in the fiscal year 1996 budget. That position comes from a complete misunderstanding of the role of aid. Yes, free-market Republican critics of aid are correct that foreign assistance cannot substitute for market reforms in producing economic prosperity. On the other hand, they fail to recognize that

fragile regimes are likely to collapse before they can implement needed market reforms if aid is not present as a *temporary* support.

The most remarkable story of the past 150 years is not that successful economic institutions inexorably replace unsuccessful ones, but that unsuccessful ones can persist so long, often at the cost of unimaginable human suffering.

A new public consensus on aid is vitally needed for Russia, Africa, and other reforming countries. In accordance with economic logic and U.S. long-term strategic goals, economic assistance should be guided by the following principles. First, it should go only to countries pursuing market reforms. Second, it should go only to democracies or countries in the process of democratization. Third, it should be limited in time to no more than five consecutive years for a particular recipient, since the goal is to bolster fragile governments, *not* to finance economic development. Fourth, it should be mobilized as part of a combined effort of Western democracies, based on agreement on underlying principles.

Would temporary aid really be sufficient? There will of course be individual cases of backsliding even after five years of aid and reform, but the postwar experience suggests that most countries that make it through the treacherous first several years of reform arrive on the other side with positive economic growth and are unlikely to reverse course fundamentally in the future. Of course, economies may stumble—with recessions or new outbreaks of inflation—but governments that have navigated a liberalization of the economy and then held it for several years very rarely adopt highly protectionist or statist strategies once again. New social forces, especially newly arisen exporters and the strengthened private sector, add important countervailing pressures. Admittedly, some cases where serious reversals occur may merit throwing in another aid lifeline, if a new reformist government takes power at a later date.

For China, Russia, the other successor states of the former Soviet Union, and several countries in Africa, accession to the new WTO will be a crucial step toward joining the world system. The United States rightly resisted allowing China to enter the WTO during 1994 without further Chinese reforms. The American goal is to induce countries to join a system, not merely a club. And yet, the organizational work to bring in China and these other countries has been inadequate. For most of the former Soviet Union, active negotiations are not yet even underway on accession. The Russian negotiations have been desultory, and are more than a year behind sched-

ule. As with financial aid, delays not only hinder Russian economic recovery, but also put the entire reform at risk by giving time for militarists and extremists to undermine the reforms.

The second enormous risk to the emerging system lies in the developed economies. At the moment of fruition of 50 years of steadfast foreign policy support for an open and law-bound international economic system, international trade is under unprecedented attack. There is little doubt that the increased trade and financial flows between developed and developing countries have created losers as well as winners in the advanced economies. The key is to recognize that the winners vastly outnumber the losers. In the United States, for example, perhaps one-fourth of manufacturing jobs in the most labor-intensive sectors—such as apparel, footwear, and leather goods—have been lost to low-wage competition from abroad; yet manufacturing as a whole accounts for only 17 per cent of total employment, and the workers exposed to low-wage competition are perhaps one-fourth of all manufacturing workers. For that basic reason, a free-trade coalition (of suburban service-sector workers and high-tech manufacturing exporters) has continued to muster majorities against an increasingly strident protectionist bloc. Of course, the economy will continue to be hit by technological shocks as well as trade shocks. The technological shocks are also very important in provoking shifts in income distribution and patterns of employment, even if such shocks are often harder to identify or quantify.

There is a political and economic case for meliorative measures in response to intensified trade pressures, including further adjustment assistance, enhanced job training programs, and a shift of tax burdens from low-wage labor to other sources of income. And yet, we should be realistic that these measures by themselves will not accomplish all that much. Market inducements will play a much larger role in redirecting job training, shifting patterns of employment across industries and regions, and changing decisions about schooling. In the United States, such adjustments occur relatively rapidly, over the course of five to ten years, not over generations.

The much greater protectionist risks will come from Western Europe rather than the United States. The European Union (EU) labors under a much more extensive, rigid, and expensive social-welfare system than the United States. EU social welfare provisions have slowed the adjustment to low-wage competition, meaning that Europe still has considerably more downsizing ahead than does the United States. Moreover, high levels of European taxation continue to chase European capital abroad or into the grey economy, pushing up official unemployment rates to more than 11 per cent for the EU as a whole. Dangerously, the unease in Western Europe has undermined political support for quickly absorbing Eastern Europe into the EU, with the inadvertent result of undermining Eastern Europe's highly charged and complex economic transition to the market.

The cement that will ultimately hold the world system together is not markets per se, but the international rule of law. The world has already had one brief episode of global market integration at the end of the nineteenth century, under the domination of Western powers, but it collapsed in an orgy of imperialism, lawlessness, and, eventually, war among the leading states of Europe. The weaker countries are now signing on to the world system and joining the global institutions, not only because they recognize the advantages of capitalism, but because they see the hope of joining a system that protects their national sovereignty while operating on the basis of an agreed upon international rule of law.

The public's recognition of and support for international law are both shallow and subject to populistic manipulation. In last year's congressional debate over a new GATT treaty, the leading charge against it was that the international rules of the WTO, especially its new binding dispute settlement process, would deprive the United States of sovereignty. It was essentially the assertion that the "freedom" of international lawlessness would serve U.S. interests better than the binding constraints of mutually negotiated international law. It is the same sentiment that fuels the U.S. reliance on "tough" unilateral actions against Japan, rather than the reliance on an international system of trade rules. These views remarkably fly in the face of the deepest wisdom of the U.S. system, which is based not on liberty alone, but on "ordered liberty" under the constraints of law.

However fragile are American commitments to the international law, they are more fragile almost everywhere else. If the United States undermines its greatest gift to the world community, the commitment to constitutional government, by circumventing rules and looking for short-term trade advantages over its competitors, Americans will find themselves quickly descending into a swamp of mercantilism and trade conflict as other countries abandon the agreements of the international trading system. On the other hand, if the United States can manage to stick with its abiding principles that have brought it to the brink of an integrated, law-bound world system, and if Americans in conjunction with the other advanced democracies can deliver aid with generosity and farsighted self-interest, this generation has the possibility to usher in an unprecedented period of peace and prosperity.

Strategic economic parity among Western Europe, North America, and East Asia demands a new modus operandi.

Power and Policy: The New Economic World Order

Klaus Schwab and Claude Smadja

Klaus Schwab is president of the World Economic Forum and a professor at the University of Geneva. Claude Smadja is senior adviser to the World Economic Forum.

In the last three years, we have been told again and again that the industrialized world is undergoing a crisis—its worst one since 1945. Traditional recipes for boosting economic activity have failed to work, and every new forecast of economic growth in the Organization for Economic Cooperation and Development's *Economic Outlook* has brought a downward revision of the preceding one. (The only exception is the forecast in the latest semiannual issue, published in July, which was readjusted upward). Even now, as the long-awaited recovery finally begins to gather strength and momentum, it is failing to make itself felt in the most critical domain: employment. In fact, the OECD's *Economic Outlook* has confirmed what everybody knew already: that unemployment in Europe can be expected to continue increasing, presumably until the end of 1995.

What we actually have been going through is not merely a crisis but a worldwide economic revolution, which has been making itself felt at the same time that we have been hit by a cyclical crisis. In other words, for the last three years, the industrialized world has been confronted with the cumulative impact of *two* distinct phenomena.

Let us deal first with the purely cyclical crisis. There has, of course, been an economic turnaround in the United States, and the economies of Europe are moving in the right direction as well. The recovery is gradually, if to varying degrees, taking hold

> **What we actually have been going through for the last three years is not merely a crisis but a worldwide economic revolution.**

in all the industrialized countries, lifting the industrialized world out of the worst recession it has faced in the last two decades. The United States is currently on a solid growth path (with a 4% growth rate expected this year), and the same can be said for Canada and the United Kingdom. Elsewhere in Europe – where Germany and France have been showing stronger than expected re-

sults since the second quarter – and in Japan, indications are that the lowest point of the downturn has already been reached.

However, the failure of the current economic recovery to translate into a significant improvement in employment is evidence that more than a mere cyclical crisis has been at work. Observers have been speaking of a "jobless recovery" or a "recovery on crutches" because neither present nor projected growth rates are sufficient for creating jobs on a large scale. The hard truth is that growth in the industrialized countries will have to be greater than the 2.6% annual average of the last two decades for these nations to achieve a substantial reduction in their unemployment levels. But because the necessary growth rates are difficult for mature economies to sustain, unemployment will remain a critical issue in the industrialized world for the next few years, and political and economic leaders will have no instant solutions to offer anxious citizens.

In fact, the weakness of the current recovery – its failure to deliver

jobs – is only one of several manifestations of the worldwide economic revolution that is now under way. The many structural changes brought about by this revolution are creating new rules of the game and necessitating a new modus operandi for all the primary players in the world economy.

Perhaps the most spectacular component of the current revolution is the shift in the world economy's center of gravity to Asia. The extraordinary process of fast and steady growth in East Asia since the end of the 1960s has led to an overall redistribution of the world's economic power, the impact and implications of which are just beginning to be felt. In 1960, East Asia accounted for just 4% of world economic output. Today its share amounts to 25%. While GNP in Europe and the United States has grown at an average of 2.5% to 3% per year over the past 25 years, many East Asian countries have managed an annual average of 6.5% to 7.5% – a trend that is expected to continue beyond the turn of the century. Between 1992 and the year 2000, 40% of all the new purchasing power created in the world will be in East Asia, and the region will absorb between 35% and 40% of the global increase in imports. East Asian central banks now hold close to 45% of the world's foreign reserves, and while the United States and the major European countries keep piling up foreign debt, Japan, Taiwan, Singapore, and Hong Kong are in the remarkable position of not having any.

All those developments mean that we are already, economically speaking, in a fully tripolar world, with the three centers of power – Western Europe, North America, and East Asia – in a position of strategic economic parity. Indeed, if present trends continue (as they probably will, barring some unforeseen regional upheaval), East Asia should be poised to claim preeminence over its two counterparts before the turn of the century.

The shift of economic power in the direction of Asia has been made possible by, and in turn has helped accelerate, a number of other developments that are dramatically altering global economic arrangements. Now that national or regional barriers restricting financial flows no longer exist, and neither technology nor management and marketing techniques observe any boundaries, the key prerequisites of economic success are increasingly transferable from one country to another. At the same time, the failure of Communism and the general spread of economic liberalization have brought previously isolated countries—the most spectacular examples being China, India, and Vietnam—into the world economy. This development has resulted in fierce competition for foreign investment among countries previously hostile to it, as well as the sudden entry of 2.5 billion people into the global marketplace.

All these conditions, in the meantime, have helped bring about what is now a worldwide delocalization of industrial production. That phenomenon lies at the very core of the worldwide economic revolution and is gathering momentum. Countries that only 10 years ago were confined to low-tech, labor-intensive economic activity are now able to produce, at low cost, goods and services that were previously monopolies of the advanced industrialized nations. One especially notable example is Malaysia, which over the past 20 years has shed its dependence on commodities to become the world's leading producer of semiconductors, and which now discourages labor-intensive industry.

Not so long ago, Japan was the only major industrial power able to take full advantage of cheap production bases in its own region. Yet today, Western Europe and the United States, along with the new economic powers of East Asia, also enjoy opportunities for delocalization within their own regions. The collapse of the Soviet empire in Central and Eastern Europe now offers manufacturers within the European Union the advantage of low-cost production bases in countries such as Poland, Hungary, and the Czech Republic. Meanwhile, the North American Free Trade Agreement has provided the United States with similar opportunities in Mexico.

As these developments in Europe and North America illustrate most clearly, the whole phenomenon of delocalization has broken the linkage that previously existed among high technology, high productivity, high quality, and high wages. It was this linkage that once appeared to guarantee ever-improving standards of living in the industrialized countries. Today, however, it is possible to have high technology, high productivity, high quality, and *low* wages. Of course, as the economies of the industrializing and newly industrialized nations mature, we can expect that current wage differentials (taking skill levels and productivity into account) will eventually narrow. Yet for now, the factor of low wages in these countries will remain paramount in corporate decision making, especially for transnational corporations.

The most spectacular component of the current revolution is the shift in the world economy's center of gravity to Asia.

The delocalization option is one that no corporation can resist in view of the intense competition all companies are facing. In fact, it has become a matter of life and death for corporations to take advantage of such opportunities in the face of what can truly be termed megacompetition – yet another crucial aspect of the global economic revolution. Corporations and countries must now compete not only against rivals in their own league but also against a continual stream of newcomers, while at the same time playing catch-up with competitors claiming to have made the latest breakthroughs. These competitive realities are creating intense pressure to rationalize production, cut internal costs, and search for the least expensive production base.

That no country today is immune to this pressure is shown by two surprising examples: Taiwan and South Korea. These countries, which only ten years ago were themselves very low-cost production bases, must now transfer most labor-intensive activities to still cheaper production bases, such as China, Indonesia, and Vietnam. Meanwhile, the percentage of Japanese industrial production

transferred to other countries in East Asia has multiplied three times since 1980. (Matsushita is planning to have a full 50% of its foreign sales come from delocalized production by March 1997 – up from 38% at present.) In Europe, we now see a pattern of companies diverting investment from the former East Germany—already considered too expensive—to the Czech Republic or Hungary. (The average cost for a worker in the Volkswagen-Škoda factory in the Czech Republic is approximately ten times less than for a worker in the company's plants in Germany, but productivity in the Czech plant is 60% that of its German-based counterparts and increasing rapidly.)

It will take years of effort in the area of education to overcome the problem of inadequately prepared workers.

The pressures created by the new megacompetition, as well as by the impact of delocalization in the industrializing and newly industrialized countries, are being compounded by a further development in the industrialized world. The burst of technological innovation in the last two decades, and the productivity gains registered as those innovations have been integrated into production processes, are severely cutting employment in industry. In this case, one example tells the whole story: between 1970 and 1993, manufacturing output doubled in the United States while industrial employment actually declined by as much as 10%, according to some estimates. The situation in Western Europe, although less striking, is much the same. Not coincidentally, we have long witnessed an opposite trend in most East Asian countries with respect to the percentage of manufacturing employees in the total labor force. From 1961 to 1991, while the share of manufacturing employment declined by one-third in the United States, one-quarter in France, and about 15% in Germany and Italy, it multiplied five times in South Korea, three times in

Malaysia, and two times in Taiwan and in Singapore.

There would be nothing wrong with those opposite trends if the service sector in the industrialized countries were able to absorb the workers displaced by manufacturing, and at roughly comparable wages. But one development of the last few years has been a decrease in the rate of job creation in the service sector, compounding the problem of structural unemployment in the industrialized world. Of course, new sectors of economic activity – some of them unheard of only ten years ago – are emerging and will create new jobs, and the current recovery is boosting the creation of new jobs in the traditional service sector. Yet it remains to be seen whether that sector will be able to create the kind of high-wage jobs that manufacturing once provided to highly skilled workers. The new jobs will not necessarily pay as much as industry did in the past, and the better-paying ones will require education and training that many of the currently unemployed do not possess. (Workers caught in this gap account for a large proportion of the long-term unemployed in continental Europe.)

As the process of economic restructuring in the industrialized world continues and gathers momentum, it will take many years of effort in the area of education and training to overcome the problem of inadequately prepared workers. Meanwhile, many observers have noted that while the United States – with an ever-increasing reliance on the service sector – has fared much better than Europe in creating jobs and holding down unemployment, the other side of the coin has been a near stagnation of real living standards in the last 12 years. This fact raises the possibility of the end of another linkage, that between high employment and high wages, which has until now guaranteed ever-increasing living standards in the industrialized countries.

Much has been written about the widening gap between rich and poor in the United States during the 1980s – a phenomenon often attributed to the policies of the Reagan administration. In fact, that development seems to have had much more

to do with the ongoing structural evolution of the U.S. economy in its shift from industry to services. So far, that same evolution – with its perceived consequences for wages and social welfare benefits – is meeting with strong opposition in Europe, where the welfare state is much more developed and solidly entrenched than in the United States. The broader and more generous social safety net, especially with respect to unemployment benefits, makes it easier for people to refuse lower-paying jobs when they are the only alternative to unemployment. One result is what happened in France last spring, when strong popular opposition forced the government of Prime Minister Edouard Balladur to renounce its project of scaling back the minimum wage for young people in their first jobs – a plan that had been designed to alleviate high unemployment rates among youth.

The issue must be faced directly: there is no way that the Western European nations will be able to ease their enduring unemployment problems without dealing with the structural rigidities in their labor systems, even though such an undertaking will require a kind of cultural revolution for Europeans accustomed to the notion of an ever-expanding welfare state. The European systems have so far proved more adept at caring for the unemployed than at creating employment. And European trade unions have seemed more interested in maintaining benefits for the employed than in helping the unemployed get back to work. Consequently, as the financial burden of the safety net grows to levels that may soon become unbearable, the very survival of the European systems will come into question.

Given the worldwide economic situation, the issues of job creation and job protection are sure to be paramount on the agendas of political leaders throughout the industrialized world for the next few years. As a result, we will also witness a complete modification of the international trade picture. From now on, the most important criterion in trade issues will be not the nationality of a product or a service – a notion

that has, in any case, already become blurred – but rather where and to whom it provides jobs. This development was already manifest last summer when the Clinton administration broke with a long-standing U.S. tradition of protecting the interests of U.S. corporations without regard to their location. A new order of priorities set by the administration put U.S. corporations located in the United States first in line for protection, foreign corporations located in the United States second, and U.S. corporations operating outside the country a mere third. The clear emphasis on job protection for U.S. workers is being echoed in Europe with assertions of a similar order of priorities.

In this world of higher stakes, with many governments both struggling for their own survival and attempting to maintain the fundamental social and political stability of their countries, there is no risk in predicting a toughening of stances on international trade issues and an increase in international trade tensions. It is indeed quite revealing that both the European Union and the United States have adopted tougher trade postures even while assenting to the Uruguay Round Agreement. In Europe, as a price for agreeing to the deal on agricultural exports to which it had objected, France got from its partners a commitment to even tougher enforcement of antidumping regulations (measures that the Europeans have already used arbitrarily, in many cases, to penalize overly efficient competitors). Similarly, even as it was preparing to sign the Uruguay Round Agreement, the Clinton administration resuscitated Super 301, which provides for mandatory sanctions to coerce other countries into opening their markets. Moreover, in preparing to present the Uruguay Round Agreement to Congress for ratification, the Clinton administration has condoned a protectionist interpretation of the agreement's antidumping provisions – a reading that would grant the United States more leeway to act against competitors.

Of course, the Uruguay Round Agreement is, in itself, a considerable step forward, covering as it does

such increasingly important domains as agricultural exports, services, investment, and intellectual property rights (none of which were previously covered by the General Agreement on Tariffs and Trade). It also creates what should become the key mechanism for policing world trade, the World Trade Organization. Yet the most immediate advantage of the agreement lies not in the $300 billion to $400 billion it should add to the current $3.6 trillion annual volume of world trade. The advantage lies, rather, in the prospect of a significant containment of trade tensions and the prevention of outright trade wars.

Taking these trade issues into account, one of the most critical challenges presented by the current worldwide economic revolution can be summarized by the following question: How will we be able to maintain and expand the multilateral trade system, integrating the many new players who want their share of the pie while also preserving the standard of living of the industrialized countries so as to prevent a possibly violent backlash? For most of its existence, the multilateral trade system has functioned with a large but homogeneous group of players. It now must operate under quite different conditions, with the number of players, for one thing, having increased dramatically in a short span of time and especially rapidly in the last few years. The field has also now become very heterogeneous, with countries operating under widely different standards of living, social traditions, and political conditions.

This situation is obviously creating severe tensions. For example, confronted with competition from low-wage countries that are attracting more and more new industrial activities while also entering fields previously dominated by the more advanced countries, Europe and the United States have launched an offensive against so-called social dumping. There has been a concerted and sometimes very vocal effort on the part of Western nations to link trade issues to workers' and human rights, social conditions, and environmental standards. Yet the newly industrialized and industrializing coun-

tries perceive those moves as a manifestation of bad faith—a case of the industrialized countries utilizing whatever pretexts lie at hand to rob the developing world of its few competitive advantages. There is, moreover, some justification for their position. If the industrialized countries freely take advantage of their technological lead and mastery of management, marketing, and financial techniques, on what grounds do they try to prevent the newcomers from taking advantage of *their* cheap labor and natural resources?

How can the multilateral trade system be expanded to integrate the many new players who want their share of the pie?

Indeed, in many quarters of Asia, there is today a lingering suspicion that behind whatever arguments North Americans or Europeans use in trade negotiations lies an unspoken reluctance to acknowledge the end of Western supremacy and to share economic power. For Europeans, however, what the competition from East Asia means above all is that the vaunted European social model is now under assault, its very essence being called into question. With so much at stake, it is not surprising that trade discussions are acquiring such an emotional tone, even more so when a cultural element is added. For example, there have been some disquieting attempts lately by Europeans, notably at the top levels of the French government, to enlist the United States in a kind of holy alliance against the East Asian countries, which the Europeans accuse of playing by different rules and flouting Western-established "universal values." As those attempts make clear, there is now a distinct risk that trade frictions will fuel cultural ones, thereby creating a dangerous spiral of tension and confrontation that would be to no one's benefit.

These emerging tensions, if well managed, could prove a passing phenomenon as the world adjusts to the shift of economic power and to the new strategic economic parity among East Asia, North America, and Western Eu-

rope. The problem is that even if most Europeans and North Americans have by now intellectually grasped the magnitude of that trend, many of them have yet to adjust to its implications. One obvious consequence of the new parity is that the West can no longer hope to dictate the rules of the game. Another is that existing international economic institutions that do not yet reflect the new realities (for example, a G7 process that includes no East Asian countries except Japan) will have to be reevaluated. The necessary adjustments will take time. And that time lag creates the danger of an escalation of tensions.

One consequence of the new parity is that the West can no longer hope to dictate the rules of the game.

As the world economy continues both to globalize and to organize itself around the three regional centers, we are witnessing another revolutionary development that may actually help to contain interregional tensions: a desynchronizing of economic cycles in the three regions. East Asia, for example, has been booming despite the accelerating decline in the Japanese economy from 1991 to the beginning of 1994, while Europe and the United States have been stuck in one of the most severe recessions in contemporary history. And although the U.S. economy would receive an additional boost from a recovery in Europe, it has been able to climb out of the recession while Europe is still struggling to do so.

The process of regionalization and the desynchronization of regions in the world economy are, in fact, linked. Six years ago, Japan exported one-third more to the United States than it did to the rest of East Asia. Today the situation is reversed. East Asia's intraregional trade now constitutes about 43% of the region's total, compared with 33% in 1980. Meanwhile, East Asia's intraregional investment and financial flows represent the fastest growing share of the region's exchanges: from 1986

to 1992, almost 70% of all investment in East Asia came from within the region, while 10.3% came from Europe and 10.9% came from the United States.

These developments are creating a pattern in East Asia that is increasingly similar to the one that already exists in Western Europe (where intraregional trade accounts for almost 70% of the total) and that will come about in North America with the implementation of NAFTA. Under these conditions, each region is becoming less and less vulnerable to fluctuations that may occur within the others. In other words, desynchronization means that if the United States sneezes, the rest of the world will no longer automatically get the flu.

Yet for the process of regionalization to run its full course in East Asia, Japan will have to assume responsibilities to its regional neighbors more commensurate with its economic weight, particularly by opening its markets to many more East Asian exports. Doing so would be critical not only to reducing the growing trade deficit between Japan and the other East Asian countries but also to containing emerging interregional tensions created by dramatic increases in East Asian exports to Western Europe and North America. If, on the other hand, Japan continues to fail to bring its domestic consumption as a percentage of GNP to a level more in line with that in Western Europe and the United States (around 65% of GNP), then the other East Asian countries will be even more compelled to push their exports toward Western Europe and North America, if only to finance their own growing trade deficits with Japan. Thus a further opening of the Japanese market and a gradual normalization of Japan's trade and current-accounts situations are necessary for the emerging tripolar economic world order to function without frictions reaching a crisis level.

In this new context, where national and regional economies remain vitally interconnected but no one player is in a position to impose its will on the rest of the world, one crucial issue will be the management of the bilateral, regional, and multi-

lateral dimensions of international trade so that they do not conflict with one another. The need for such management will become even more critical as the trend toward economic regionalization picks up momentum. (There are today more than one hundred regional pacts in existence.) On the bilateral front, disputes such as those still brewing between the United States and Japan, and between the United States and China, can at any moment affect the stability of the multilateral trade system because of initiatives that one or the other protagonist may feel compelled to take. For instance, when the United States periodically attempts to impose managed trade agreements on Japan and to set mandatory market shares for U.S. products or services, it contradicts the very basis of the multilateral trade framework.

The new economic world order will also increasingly result, as it has already, in variable, ad hoc alliances on the international trade scene. Europe, for example, now suffers from a huge trade deficit with Japan and voices the same complaints that the United States does about barriers to the Japanese market. Yet Europe refuses to follow Washington in its efforts to set numerical objectives, because doing so could backfire in its own disputes with the United States. However, at the same time, Europe *is* cooperating with the United States in its attempts to link international trade rules with issues such as social and labor rights.

In short, the revolution in the world economy – with the requirements that it puts on both countries and corporations – means that traditional trade policies are becoming more and more inadequate and may even prove harmful in their capacity to set off chain reactions that can rapidly burst out of control. Today, as countries face the challenge of establishing comprehensive economic strategies integrating fiscal, monetary, and education and training goals, they must do so in accordance with basic guidelines and rules about which the key protagonists on the world trade scene will have to reach a consensus.

Of course, the most immediate requirement for the Western industrialized nations is to take full advantage of the present recovery from the cyclical crisis so they can be in a better position to address the structural issues that confront them. Those issues include the restoration of flexibility to the European labor market in order to stimulate the creation of new jobs; an increased focus on key technologies of the future through which the industrialized countries can still hope to claim a competitive advantage; and the adjustment of education and training systems to create a supply of human resources able to generate higher and higher added value in economic activity.

Trade policies are becoming more and more inadequate and may even prove harmful in their capacity to set off chain reactions.

As this process of restructuring evolves in Western Europe and North America, it will be complemented by three factors now at work in the industrializing and newly industrialized countries of East Asia. The first is the creation, through the process of economic growth in the region, of a widening consumer base: Singapore, Malaysia, Thailand, Indonesia, Taiwan, and South Korea can already claim spectacular increases in domestic consumption, thanks to the emergence of a middle class with both rising expectations and the rapidly increasing means of fulfilling them. Between 1992 and the end of the decade, the number of automobiles put in service in East Asia will grow from 3 million to 7 million per year, according to World Bank estimates. The nascent development of domestic consumption in southern China is another promising indication of things to come.

The second factor in East Asian economic development with important implications for Western restructuring is the exploding infra-

structure and energy needs of the still emerging industrial countries of the region. This growing demand will offer unprecedented opportunities in areas such as energy, telecommunications, and transportation. (It is expected that the share of GNP devoted to infrastructure in East Asia will increase from its current 4% to 7% by the year 2000.) In the same vein, the growing concern with environmental protection and the need for clean technologies will provide new opportunities for corporations able to furnish the required technologies and services.

A third and final factor in East Asian development that holds out promise for the West is the accelerating liberalization now taking place in the region's industrializing and newly industrialized countries. South Korea and Taiwan, for example, have recently made strides in privatization, while rapid growth in regional financial markets and telecommunications will also provide new opportunities for European and U.S. corporations.

From 1980 to 1990, total imports in the industrializing and newly industrialized countries of East Asia increased by almost 250%, and the 1990s should see even more growth. Despite the increase in East Asian intraregional trade, European and U.S. corporations can hope to get their share of these markets if they adjust their strategies to the new realities of the tripolar world order, setting the right priorities and making the necessary commitments.

Uncertainty, tension, and the potential for conflict are part of any period of change, especially when the change approaches the magnitude of the one now occurring in the world economy. If the current worldwide economic revolution is to lead to a new phase of widespread and steady growth, the strongest emphasis will have to be placed on three priorities:

□ The international institutions required to sustain, monitor, and supervise the new global economic order will need to be established or revamped as soon as possible. The creation of the World Trade Organization is one important step in this

respect. Another is the ongoing debate about the role of the World Bank and the IMF in view of the entry of so many new countries into the world market.

□ The whole modus operandi of the international economy will have to be reviewed in light of the new strategic parity among North America, Western Europe, and East Asia. As previously noted, the G7 process (on which so many expectations were placed in the 1980s) will have to undergo a fundamental reevaluation. As the trend toward regionalization gains momentum, the key element will be support for whatever policies and initiatives sustain and expand the notion of open regionalization.

□ A kind of "cultural revolution" will need to be instigated in the developed countries of the West in order to bring about the required adjustment, at the corporate and national levels, to the shift in economic power toward East Asia. The loss of the benefits that these countries once derived from their preeminent position in the world economy need not lead to a long-term decline in living standards, provided that, by adopting the requisite attitudes and policies, these nations can learn to utilize their remaining competitive advantages. At the same time, the newly industrialized countries must show, by their attitudes and initiatives in international economic forums, that they are ready to assume the new responsibilities resulting from their emerging power and status in the global arena.

In recent commemorations of the end of World War II and of the establishment of the subsequent global economic arrangements, much has been said about the merits of the Bretton Woods institutions in creating the conditions for postwar growth and prosperity. Today we can say, in the aftermath of the Cold War and in the midst of a worldwide economic revolution, that we are entering the post-Bretton Woods period. There is no reason to think that in this phase we cannot bring about even greater and more widespread prosperity.

GLOBAL GROWTH IS ON A TEAR

Developing economies are driving the expansion. If they're smart, companies in the U.S., Japan, and Europe will climb aboard.

Louis S. Richman

Nearly lost in all the dire headlines—MEXICAN PESO COLLAPSES! ECONOMIC AFTERSHOCKS OF JAPAN QUAKE! U.S.-CHINA TRADE WAR LOOMS!—is 1995's Big Event: the beginnings of a global expansion of breathtaking proportions where developing countries, not the usual elite club of rich nations, head the charge. As the chart shows, the 16 largest such economies will average an estimated 6% annual growth in GDP through 1996, more than double the rate of the mature economies of North America, Japan, and Europe. Says economist Miron Mushkat of Lehman Brothers in Hong Kong: "The developing economies are beginning to assume a leadership role as a driver of global growth."

Even more epochal, this enormous shift is taking place in a post–Cold War world where the players compete in economic contests rather than ideological ones. For mature economies, the big opportunity is in riding these winds of change. By becoming more competitive, they can boost exports, create more jobs for themselves, and assure a prosperous future. The U.S. economic rally, an early arrival at the planetary growth party, could even surpass the record expansion of the 1980s.

Risks abound, of course. International investors are understandably nervous of developing economies, particularly after Mexico. And central bankers dread inflation and have their hand perpetually poised over the lever that hikes interest rates. But for all this, the worldwide boom is likely to prove exceptionally durable. For one thing, previous ex-

pansions have seen nations advance—and then tumble—in lock step. This time around, the world's business cycles are more independent of one another. Witness the unilateral timetables that the U.S., Europe, and Japan have followed out of their most recent recessions. Now watch how countries in Asia, East Europe, and Latin America—many of them embracing free markets for the first time—compete as scrappy individuals that can win or lose regardless of other economies.

All this vibrant, self-sustaining growth could keep the more mature economies cooking with increased demand for their products, just as the U.S. benefited from the reconstruction of war-wrecked Europe and Japan in the 1950s and 1960s. But the timing of the 1990s boom catches the traditionally elite waist-deep in sweeping technological and organizational change. The challenge in these countries, says Robert Hormats, vice chairman of Goldman Sachs (International), will be to preserve their competitive edge amid a frenzy unleashed by the worldwide ratcheting up of both supply and demand.

Call it the Restructuring Recovery. New rivals surfacing from every point of the compass are putting heat on manufacturers throughout the U.S., Europe, and Japan to step up investment in their search for efficiencies. In the U.S., for example, gross capital spending on new plant, equipment, and office technologies increased at a near-record rate of 12.5% in 1993 and in 1994. The Organization for Economic Cooperation and Development (OECD), the economic research agency in Paris, forecasts that such investment will continue to increase in 1995 and yet again, for an unprecedented fifth consecutive year, in 1996. In the European Community, capital spending

REPORTER ASSOCIATES *Patty de Llosa and Kimberly Seals McDonald*

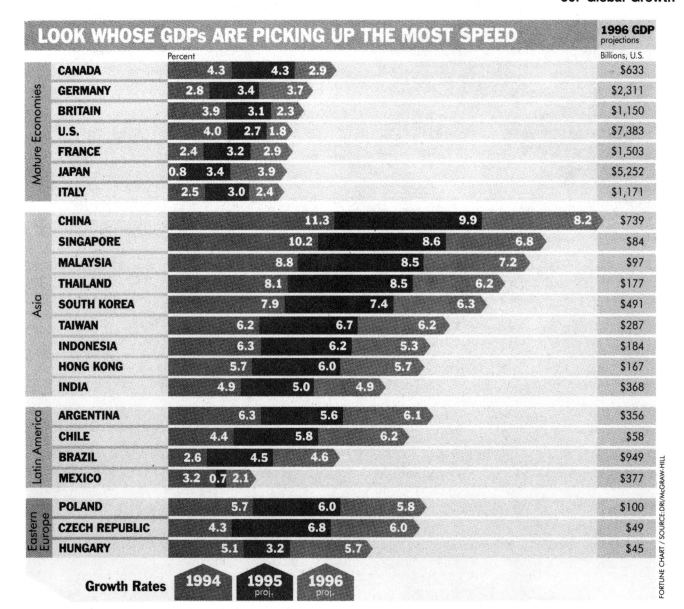

LOOK WHOSE GDPs ARE PICKING UP THE MOST SPEED

1996 GDP projections

	Growth Rates (Percent)			1996 GDP projections (Billions, U.S.)
	1994	**1995** proj.	**1996** proj.	
Mature Economies				
CANADA	4.3	4.3	2.9	$633
GERMANY	2.8	3.4	3.7	$2,311
BRITAIN	3.9	3.1	2.3	$1,150
U.S.	4.0	2.7	1.8	$7,383
FRANCE	2.4	3.2	2.9	$1,503
JAPAN	0.8	3.4	3.9	$5,252
ITALY	2.5	3.0	2.4	$1,171
Asia				
CHINA	11.3	9.9	8.2	$739
SINGAPORE	10.2	8.6	6.8	$84
MALAYSIA	8.8	8.5	7.2	$97
THAILAND	8.1	8.5	6.2	$177
SOUTH KOREA	7.9	7.4	6.3	$491
TAIWAN	6.2	6.7	6.2	$287
INDONESIA	6.3	6.2	5.3	$184
HONG KONG	5.7	6.0	5.7	$167
INDIA	4.9	5.0	4.9	$368
Latin America				
ARGENTINA	6.3	5.6	6.1	$356
CHILE	4.4	5.8	6.2	$58
BRAZIL	2.6	4.5	4.6	$949
MEXICO	3.2	0.7	2.1	$377
Eastern Europe				
POLAND	5.7	6.0	5.8	$100
CZECH REPUBLIC	4.3	6.8	6.0	$49
HUNGARY	5.1	3.2	5.7	$45

FORTUNE CHART / SOURCE:DRI/McGRAW-HILL

will rise some 6% in 1995 and 8% in 1996 as manufacturers try to close a widening competitiveness gap with the U.S. and Japan. The estimated $60 billion repair bill for the Kobe quake is sure to increase Japan's spending over the previously forecast 1.4% in 1995 and 4.1% in 1996.

Soaring investment is already yielding hefty dividends. Flexible automation equipment that improves quality and efficiency in U.S. factories is boosting productivity and helping to fuel profits. Similar benefits are showing up elsewhere. In Germany, for example, labor productivity in manufacturing jumped 7.5% during 1994, while unit labor costs should nudge up this year by a mere 0.1%.

Also paying off bigtime: capital spending for computerized inventory-tracking technology and the just-in-time management techniques it makes possible. Manufacturers around the world are reducing dramatically the costly stockpiling of raw materials

and intermediate products. This contrasts with the early phases of past recoveries, when inventory building accounted for as much as half of total GDP growth. In their race to acquire the materials they'd need to fill anticipated orders, producers would bid up prices and thus light the fuse that ignited inflation.

But now that pattern appears to be ending. A recent OECD study has found that inventory accumulation in Germany accounted for about 22% of the total growth that brought the country out of its recession trough last year, compared with some 44% in the recovery of the early 1980s. In Japan's nascent recovery, stock building is adding just over 6% to total growth, vs. 15% in the 1983 upswing. And in the U.S., manufacturers reduced inventories by some 14% in early 1992. This compares with an inventory accumulation that accounted for more than 43% of total growth coming out of the 1982 recession. In the current expansion, these tighter

disciplines have partly quelled the war between growth and inflation. Says Woody Brock, who heads the Strategic Economic Decisions consulting firm in Menlo Park, California: "Instead of 2.5% growth and 4% inflation, we're seeing 4% growth and 2.7% inflation."

Continued steady, low-inflation expansion should be all the more sustainable because of the degree to which the global recoveries are out of sync. In the four preceding business cycles, says Victor Zarnowitz, director of the Center for International Business Cycle Research at Columbia University, the economies of all the eight largest industrial nations, including those of the U.S., Germany, and Japan, fell and rose in tandem. But, that lock-step bust-and-boom tradition was shattered in the latest downturn. The U.S. slid into its recession in the summer of 1990. But the economies of Europe and Japan didn't even dip until mid-1992, nearly a year after the U.S. had begun its upswing. The decoupling, says John Lipsky, chief international economist for Salomon Brothers in New York City, should slow the buildup of potential excesses that set off inflation—and that invite central banks to increase interest rates, dousing growth.

An unusual dampener for U.S. inflation last year was its $200 billion trade deficit. Lipsky estimates that this import surplus knocked about half a percentage point off GDP growth, holding it to a less inflationary 4% rate while helping to reignite recoveries abroad among the country's trading partners. Now, as U.S. growth slows and demand for imports cools, the accelerating expansions of Europe and Japan will stimulate demand for American goods.

Meanwhile, the prospect of an extended period of balanced growth in which exports play a more prominent role is giving major cyclical U.S. industries a chance to strut their regained competitiveness. Chemical manufacturers, America's largest exporters, put themselves through a decade of painful downsizing, and the gradual resumption of demand abroad will lift industry profits. Paul Raman, an analyst with the New York investment firm S.G. Warburg, expects that the 20% unit-cost advantage enjoyed by U.S. chemical companies over their European and Japanese competitors should enable the Americans to gain market share.

Raman estimates that U.S. chemical producers will see a 5% increase in net profits for each 1% increase in production volumes. The industry is already looking great. It had an outstanding 1994, when profits jumped between 30% and 40% on a 7% growth in domestic sales. Raman thinks that an easing of U.S. growth in 1995 and 1996 will be more than offset by the 5% increase in demand he's forecasting from Europe. That, he says, should let chemical manufacturers maintain production capacity through 1996 at a profitably high 90%.

Growing confidence that global growth will extend the life of the current U.S. expansion is encouraging some cycle-sensitive manufacturers to stretch out their planning horizons. Case in point: Detroit's reinvigorated automakers. Steady, moderate growth, points out Chrysler's chief economist W. Van Bussmann, will minimize the dislocations of the industry's typical boom-bust cycle. This will help his company make continued progress in improving product quality while keeping employment high, he says. Ford Motor, flush with near-record profits from buoyant U.S. car and light-truck sales last year, plans to increase capital outlays and new-product development spending by some 20% over the next five years. The company is aiming for heroic leaps in productivity—by more than 100%—as it looks to double export volume from North America by the end of the decade.

THE LIKELIEST KILLER of his global boom is, of course, the usual suspect: interest rate increases, the central bankers' generic cure for inflation. Certainly inflation is an especially sinister felon because it stalks an economy so quietly before striking. The bankers are also aware of inflation's recidivist history, especially now because, with economic growth occurring in every corner of the globe, the pressure to bid up prices for scarce resources is much stronger than in past expansions.

So where do they see inflation threatening? Just about everywhere. Most commodity prices have been moving up at an accelerating rate since the end of 1993; the Commodity Research Bureau's index of spot raw material prices has advanced by nearly 18%. But it could have been worse. Manufacturers have become more sparing in their use of raw materials—they now account for just half a percentage point of GDP—and hot global competition prevents producers from passing on their higher commodity costs to consumers.

Right now potential wage inflation looks like the more serious worry. Though U.S. unemployment edged up to 5.7% in January, it is still below the 6% rate that many, including dyspeptic bond traders, consider compatible with stable inflation. This non-

accelerating inflation rate of unemployment (Nairu, as economists call it) has been rising for the past two decades. OECD labor economists say its biggest footprints have been left in Europe, where rigid labor rules and initiative-sapping unemployment benefits have caused the Nairu to soar. It was about 5% in the late 1970s and is some 9% today, the economists say.

Even though U.S. manufacturers are up against their capacity limits, there's still plenty of idle plant around in the decoupled expansions of other countries to hold prices of finished goods in check. Consumer price inflation in Europe, for example, is near a 30-year low, and Brian Mullaney, an economist with Morgan Stanley in London, forecasts that CPI growth in Europe will stay flat at 2.8% through 1995. In Japan, where the strong yen has deflated the cost of most dollar-priced commodities, economist Dick Beason of investment firm James Capel Ltd. in Tokyo estimates that a gradual recovery this year will boost consumer prices just 1%.

Still, central bankers in the mature industrialized economies and in the fast-emerging ones seem determined to err on the side of caution. Says Farid Abolfathi, an international economist at DRI/McGraw-Hill, the economic forecasting firm: "The children of Paul Volcker [the former Fed chairman and renowned inflation warrior] are everywhere. There's an almost perverse competition among them

CANADA'S ENDANGERED BACON

What rich irony. Global investors are in a sweat over the potential financial problems of emerging markets in countries where domestic saving rates are high, currency reserves are strong, and government deficits are stable—or even declining—as a percentage of GDP.

The real problem may be lurking in those same investors' back yard if, as is statistically likely, they live in an "advanced" industrial economy where savings are falling, deficits ballooning, and interest rates heading up. The $430 billion increase in public debt in the U.S., Europe, and Japan to $780 billion between 1990 and 1993 clearly dwarfs the $100 billion current account deficits the emerging markets are running.

Europe's governments are counting on the continued strengthening of their economies to help rein in their swollen budget deficits and stabilize debt. But even with moderate growth, most of them find themselves caught in a vise. They are desperate to lower taxes to foster job creation and reduce sky-high unemployment, but they are reluctant to antagonize voters by taking an ax to popular social spending. For example, Sweden's new government, facing one of Europe's highest deficits—it represents 11.2% of GDP—punted until at least 1998 on

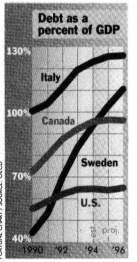

Debt as a percent of GDP

making promised spending cuts that would stabilize that social welfare state's debt burden.

The pressure on European interest rates and currencies, warns Columbia University economist Victor Zarnowitz, could bring in an economic slowdown within a year. "Europe's fiscal disorder is very, very destabilizing," he warns. Short-term interest rates in Sweden and other heavily indebted European countries like Italy and Spain are already four percentage points higher than in Germany, and the krona, lira, and peseta all fell sharply in the week following the collapse of the Mexican peso.

Canada is in a similar stew. Its deficit is 6.2% of GDP. (In the U.S., the figure is 2%.) Canada's annual interest payments on federal debt absorb 40% of all government expenditures. Short-term rates have moved up five percentage points in 1994, to 8.2%, but even that hasn't stopped currency speculators from bidding down the Canadian dollar to a near-historic low of 70 cents against the U.S. greenback. Economist Robert Fairholm with DRI in Toronto worries whether the Liberal government will deliver a new budget in February austere enough to save the Canadian bacon. Says he: "If Canada doesn't stabilize its debt, it courts a currency crisis of unprecedented proportions."

to be the first to raise rates." Volcker's scions at the Fed, including his successor, current Chairman Alan Greenspan, have led this cautionary pack, hiking short-term U.S. rates seven times in the past year, most recently to 6.5%—or back to where they were in 1991.

Because the slowing effects of rate increases don't show up until six months to a year later, the chances that the Fed's preemptive hikes will push the U.S. into a 1995 recession are remote. Even so, a sharp deceleration of U.S. growth, accompanied by rising interest rates in other countries, could stall the global expansion. Countries like Italy, Sweden, and Canada, which operate under enormous debt (see box), look particularly vulnerable.

ALSO HOBBLING global growth, if only temporarily, are the increases in U.S. interest rates, which have narrowed the spread between safe returns domestically and riskier ones overseas, and encourage investors to keep their money close to home. Says David Shulman, chief equity strategist at Salomon Brothers: "The Fed is the world's lawn sprinkler. When U.S. interest rates were low, liquidity spread to the farthest reaches of the global lawn. Now that the Fed is tightening, the capital flowing to the remoter emerging markets is drying up."

Not entirely. Scary as the plunge into Asian and Latin American currencies and bourses may look in the aftermath of Mexico's meltdown, investment in the dynamic growth economies via country funds or particular stocks will likely continue. For one thing, many investors consider the big risk to be more than outweighed by potential gains. Foreign securities still account only for 1.2% of U.S. investors' portfolios despite the fact that they have more than doubled since 1990.

Whatever its immediate problems, even Mexico hardly merits all the hyperventilating one hears. Yes, its mismanaged liquidity problems will reduce the country's short-term growth prospects and will slow demand for U.S. imports. But Christopher Probyn, a DRI economist, estimates that the drop in orders will shave U.S. exports by only 1.5% over the coming two years. After that, he says, Mexico's fundamentally sound long-term economic prospects will begin to reassert themselves.

As for those countries still in the shadow of the clouds sent up by Mexico, Lehman Brothers economist Mushkat sees two silver linings. First, a slower inflow of portfolio capital should prove easier for still immature developing economies to absorb.

Second, Mushkat expects that market regulators in those places will use the cooling of investor ardor to reform their stock and bond exchanges, the better to compete for capital once the passion returns.

Until then, emerging economies will be able to tape their own large reservoirs of domestic savings. Gross saving rates in many countries from Brazil to India exceed 20% of GDP and run as high as 45% in China and Singapore. This puts most of the West to shame. The rate in the U.S., for example, is 12%, and in Britain nearly 13%.

Even as portfolio investors hold back, increasingly open emerging markets should have little problem attracting foreign direct investment (FDI) in everything from pizza restaurants to power stations. Since 1989, worldwide FDI has nearly tripled, to more than $80 billion last year. The lure is irresistible. Among U.S. multinationals, nearly 20% of total pretax profits now come from sales by foreign affiliates. Their profit margins in the dynamic developing economies—9.5%—are more than twice those earned in North America, Europe, or Japan.

Infrastructure spending is the flywheel at the heart of the emerging nation growth engine. By some estimates, investment for power generation, transportation, telecommunications equipment, and the like could add up to $1 trillion by the end of the decade, a potential bonanza for U.S., European, and Japanese manufacturers of capital goods—and a cushion against slower growth in their home markets. This boosted demand is even giving new vitality to some sunset industries. Anticipating weakening domestic sales, for example, restructured U.S. steelmakers are plotting their first significant export push in better than a decade.

BECAUSE infrastructure investments are usually backed by the operating revenues they generate, they are far less vulnerable than portfolio investment to sudden shifts in investor sentiment. Recognizing that this spending helps break through bottlenecks that retard further development, governments of emerging nations are giving these projects top priority. Not surprisingly, foreign companies are eager to seize some of this action. Among them: the Hughes division of General Motors. In late 1994 it was awarded a license by India to install and operate the country's first private earth relay system, transmitting data via satellite for commercial users.

AT&T has reached out and put together a string of like deals. Over the past six years its Network Systems group has created seven joint ventures in China, and it counts In-

donesia, Thailand, and the Philippines among its fastest-growing international markets. In January AT&T signed a $150 million contract to provide gateway switches to the telecommunications authority in South China, the first phase of a multiyear, $500 million telephone system upgrade. Richard Brandt, a group vice president, estimates that the project, financed with conventional bank loans, will pay for itself within a year of completion. Brandt expects that the resulting communications improvement will spark additional investment as companies are drawn to the region. Says he: "The multiplier effects are absolutely staggering."

The rate of expansion among the dynamic emerging markets will, of course, eventually slow. In 1995—the Year of the Pig in the lunar calendar, by tradition a year of prosperity—growth will slow in six of 13 Asian economies, including China's, say economists at Jardine Fleming, the Hong Kong bank. But for the foreseeable future, says Keith Ferguson, an economist with Barclays de Zoete Wedd in Hong Kong, probably none of the six will experience the kind of business contractions common in the mature industrial nations. Instead, they will see some rise in unemployment against a backdrop of continued increases in GDP—characteristics of a so-called "growth recession."

This isn't such bad news. Jardine's economists forecast that these "slowing" economies will still be growing, at an average 7.2% a year. We should all celebrate the Year of the Pig with such recessions.

From GATT to WTO

The Institutionalization of World Trade

SALIL S. PITRODA

Salil S. Pitroda is a Staff Writer for the Harvard International Review.

O VER THE PAST FEW DECADES, a system of relatively open exchange, particularly in merchandise trade, has prevailed in the world under the auspices of the General Agreement on Tariffs and Trade (GATT). Today, most economists acknowledge this trading system as one of the greatest contributors to the world's rapid recovery from the desolation of the second World War, and to the phenomenal growth in world output thereafter. Through all of those years, however, GATT has served its member countries through a loose and informal structure, with all the inevitable problems that accompany a weak and ill-defined authority. With the passage of the Uruguay Round of trade talks, this trading system is poised to take on a new shape in a permanent institution known as the World Trade Organization (WTO). Although much skepticism and controversy have surrounded the birth of WTO, it is the hope of all free-traders that the new WTO will be able to amend what went amiss with GATT.

A Brief History of Trade

At the beginning of the nineteenth century, economists began to make advances in interpreting why human beings had always engaged in economic exchange. The theory of comparative advantage posited that countries specialize in those goods and services that they can produce more efficiently relative to other countries. When nations concentrate their production on commodities in which they have a comparative advantage, consumers as a whole benefit from lower prices and a greater range of consumption possibilities. Because each good is produced by the country that is best at producing it, scarce world resources are allocated efficiently. Like all economic activities, the distribution of the benefits of trade is not uniform; yet in general and in the long run, trade leads to a more optimal economic outcome with greater competition and greater productivity—a rising tide on which all boats float.

In 1947, such a view of the benefits of international cooperation inspired a group of visionaries gathered in Bretton Woods, New Hampshire, to erect a new economic world order from the ravages of the second World War. The Bretton Woods Accords, which celebrated their fiftieth anniversary last year, established the World Bank and the International Monetary Fund and led to the creation of GATT. These structures, albeit not always true to the visionary spirit in which they were founded, have formed the underpinnings of world economic development for the past half century.

GATT has become the framework for international trade in our time. The body was formed as an interim secretariat for trade negotiations after the United States, bowing to protectionist sentiment, refused to ratify the charter of the stillborn International Trade Organization, a full-fledged institution of the stature of the World Bank and the IMF. Based in Geneva and currently encompassing over 120 member nations, GATT has acted as a conduit for multilateral negotiations on a variety of international trade issues, including tariff and quota policy and trading practices. It has sponsored several rounds of protracted, though eventually fruitful, trade talks where members gathered to hammer out the details of the set of rules governing economic exchange. GATT panels make recommendations on changes in trade regulations and review complaints against member countries.

Despite GATT's success in coordinating international trade policy, it must be remembered that GATT is only an interim body without a fully defined institutional structure and with little legal enforcement power. For instance, many loopholes exist in the mechanism dealing with disputes regarding unfair trade practices. If a country complains of unfair trading practices on the part of another country and a GATT panel concurs with the complaint, the accused country can dissent from the finding, effectively vetoing it and preventing the complaining country from retaliation within the GATT framework. Another increasingly popular way of doing business in an extra-GATT environment is through the creation of regional trade blocs, such as the European Union (EU), the North American Free Trade Agreement (NAFTA) and the impending Association of Southeast Asian Nations (ASEAN) free trade agreement. These regional agreements, in effect, set their own rules of trade, encouraging cooperative exchange within a

bloc but hinting of protectionism against countries outside the region. Non-tariff trade barriers (NTBs), such as a German requirement that, for health reasons, beer sold in Germany be made with German water, are also another device for bending GATT rules. Another way of eschewing GATT policy through these regional trading arrangements is to manipulate the rules of origin stipulation. By raising the requirement of local content value, aspiring profiteers and vested interests can turn an ostensible reduction in a tariff into an actual increase by subjecting formerly tariff-exempt goods to duties, thus circumventing the GATT guideline that for any free trade agreement the new common external tariff be no higher than the average tariff of the constituent states before the accord. Without any institutional framework or legal authority, the most that GATT can do, when confronted with such adroit legerdemain with its regulations, is to urge and exhort a spirit of cooperation among member states, each of whom has an individual incentive to cater to local interests by eschewing a rule here and raising a protectionist wall there.

Seeking to address some of these problems, the Uruguay Round of negotiations was launched nearly nine years ago. Under the leadership of GATT Director-General Peter Sutherland, this latest round of trade talks has arrived at a consensus on implementing changes to the international framework that will encourage greater openness and trade integration among the world's nations. First and foremost, the Uruguay Round promises a lowering of trade barriers and a slashing of tariffs by an average of one-third. It broadens the scope of liberalization to include traditionally protected industries such as textiles and apparel. Reflecting the changing nature of world trade, the Uruguay Round will open up exchange in the previously closed but rapidly emerging areas of agriculture, services, and intellectual property. It imposes a new discipline on NTBs and government procurement and offers clarification on subsidies, dumping regulations, quota restrictions and voluntary export restraints. It also lays the foundation for further talks dealing with important trade issues including the treatment of foreign direct investment, labor and environmental concerns, and capital and currency market fluctuations. Most importantly, the Uruguay Round of accords has boldly moved the world a step closer to global free trade by calling for the establishment of the WTO to succeed the GATT secretariat.

The Birth of WTO

The WTO will be a new international institution, on par with the World Bank and the IMF, that will outline a framework for all areas of international trade and will have the legal authority to settle trade disputes. In legal terms, it represents the maturation of the GATT secretariat into a full-fledged, permanent international entity. The supreme decision-making body will be a biannual ministerial meeting, affording the organization more political clout and a higher international profile. This WTO council will then have subsidiary working bodies that specialize in areas of trade including goods, services and intellectual property. Unlike GATT, the WTO will have a clearly defined dispute settlement mechanism. Independent panel reports will automatically be adopted by the WTO council unless there is a clear consensus to reject them. Countries who are accused of engaging in unfair trade practices can appeal to a permanent appellate body, but the verdict of this body will be ultimately binding. If an offending nation fails to comply with WTO panel recommendations, its trading partners will be guaranteed the right to compensation as determined by the panel or, as a final resort, be given the right to impose countervailing sanctions. All members of the WTO will have legal access to these multilateral dispute settlement mechanisms, and all stages of WTO deliberation will be time-limited, ensuring efficiency in dispute settlement. The World Trade Organization will be akin to an International Court of Justice for world trade, with the institutional strength and legal mandate to ensure fair trade and global economic integration.

Who will be the pioneering leader of this newly constructed international organization? The ideal candidate must possess a strategic global vision of world trade while being comfortable with technical complexity. He or she must combine the finesse of a diplomat, the organizational acumen of an experienced administrator and the leadership qualities of a seasoned statesman.

Since Peter Sutherland, the incumbent Director-General of GATT has indicated his wish to stand down in favor of fresh leadership, the competition to be the head of the WTO has been opened up to three dynamic candidates. Renato Ruggiero, the favored candidate of the EU, is a former trade minister of Italy and has also been suggested in the past as a possible president of the European Commission. He has emphasized his experience as a capable administrator with international experience in Brussels, the GATT, and world economic summits. Carlos Salinas de Gortari, who during his tenure as the President of Mexico defined the paradigm for economic liberalization in developing countries, is the candidate favored by the Americas. His international stature as a head of state and his commitment to free trade—as evinced by his personal crusade for NAFTA—are Salinas's most important assets. The South Korean trade minister, Kim Chul-Su, has proven international experience and is naturally supported by countries in Asia and Australia, the fastest growing region in the world. In the end, politics will most likely decide who heads the WTO. Similar leadership positions are opening up at the Organization for Economic Cooperation and Development (OECD) and other international organizations, with political horse-trading sure to play an integral role in determining the new leaders of these organizations.

There are various other strategic issues relating to the establishment of the WTO. At least for the initial transition stage, the new organization is expected to grow by expanding on the existing GATT structure. The WTO will most probably be situated in the existing GATT building in Geneva and will require an increase in GATT's present budget and staff. Yet even with this augmentation in resources, the WTO will still remain far smaller in size than either the World Bank or the IMF.

Aside from such logistical matters, however, the precise nature of the transition between GATT and WTO remains more nebulous. Some countries, such as the United States, have already announced that they will terminate their GATT membership within sixty days of joining the WTO. Such a strict view of WTO's successor status to GATT raises interesting questions about US obligations to GATT members who have yet to ratify their entry into WTO.

Other countries envision the two organizations operating in tandem for a period of two years, with GATT still binding, to ease the transition to the WTO. There is also the question of new memberships. Will Slovenia and Croatia, for instance, who have just applied for GATT membership, be granted direct membership in the WTO? If the WTO does not completely supersede GATT immediately, where does that leave a country like the Sudan, which is not a GATT member, but has applied directly for WTO membership?

Of course, there is also the thorny problem of China, which has just been denied the opportunity of being a founding member of WTO, and Taiwan, whose competing applications will surely pose more dilemmas of politics and protocol. Certainly, careful deliberation will be needed to work

out the multitude of implementational, organizational and transitional issues.

The Foundation of the New Order

Given these birth pangs, what are the fundamental qualities upon which the WTO must lay its foundation? As Carlos Salinas de Gortari has outlined in a recent article in *The Financial Times*, the WTO must be representative, reliable and responsive. It must embrace all countries, regardless of their level of economic development, and ensure their prompt and satisfactory integration into a multilateral trading system. Reliability is a much tougher criterion to satisfy. The WTO must clarify GATT rules, broaden its mandate and improve its dispute settlement mechanisms to demonstrate to all member nations that they have a stake in abiding by a rules-based trade regime. Finally, flexibility and responsiveness to the evolving changes of the international economy will ensure that the WTO retains the political support necessary to carrying out its work.

As an organization that has ambitions of leading the global economy into the next millennium, the WTO needs to legitimize its standing in the eyes of politicians and economists wearied by decades of trade negotiations by confronting some concrete and difficult problems. One of the first tasks it might have to face is deciding whether or not it should extend the rules regulating conduct in international trade to cover national competition policies. Ideally, countries should have roughly comparable standards on anti-trust legislation so that greater competition from all-comers, whether domestic or foreign, can be welcomed. But by treading on such sensitive territories, the WTO may stray too far from the trade-related issues at the core of its mandate. The animosities which it incurs in those confrontations may permanently impair its ability to unite its membership on other, arguably even more important, issues in the long run.

One of the most crucial tasks of the WTO will be presiding over the economic and political integration of the former socialist economies. It must provide stable and expanding outlets for these countries' products to encourage the liberalization of their economies and to help them attract much needed foreign direct investment. In fact, all the newly open economies in Latin America, Africa and Asia must be nurtured by a transparent, rules-based and mutually beneficial trading system. In particular, the WTO must encourage the reversal of the growing lethargy in North-South cooperation, especially with regard to Sub-Saharan African countries, which

desperately need open international markets for their growth. The organization also has a special responsibility to bring the nearly two billion citizens of China and India, 40 percent of the planet's population, into the world trading regime as full and active members.

On a more macroscopic level, the WTO must effectively coordinate regional free trade agreements to ensure that they do not conflict in goals or create islands of protectionism, but are instead regional building blocks toward the eventual realization of global free trade which almost every economic theory praises as the ideal for future world economic relations. Pursuant to this objective of regional coordination, the institution must stiffen its regulations and their enforcement so that less and less protectionism can be veiled behind devices such as NTBs, rules of origins requirements and other technical loopholes. It must convince member nations that their greatest economic interest is to cooperate with the other nations of the world and not bow to vested interests by taking short-sighted unilateral action. The best means for guaranteeing this end is a vigorous and binding dispute settlement mechanism. In planning for the future, the organization must also proactively embrace the changing nature of the global economy from trade in manufactured goods to trade in information-intensive services and intellectual property. The technical complexity of those issues and the administrative difficulty that will inevitably accompany any rules governing them will be a challenge to WTO's energy, resourcefulness and resolve.

Finally, and very importantly, the WTO must acknowledge and deal with some of the local pains that uncompetitive industries in member nations will feel. In order to avoid the image of an elitist other-worldliness to which so many other well-intentioned international organizations have fallen prey, the WTO must ensure that the gains from trade are trickled down to the populace. Without at least some semblance of equity to compensate for the sacrifices that the working poor will be asked to make in any transition, it will be difficult for WTO to maintain the political and moral support that it needs to push through its vision of world-wide free trade. Ideally, some sort of structural adjustment fund and a common program for retraining displaced workers should be a pillar of the WTO, so that humanity and compassion, as well as hard-nosed efficiency, may be integrated into the organization's founding philosophy. There are undoubtedly a host of other important issues the new WTO should con-

sider, but careful deliberation upon the fundamentals outlined here will be a major step toward solidifying and validating a global free trade system.

Positive Sums from Cooperation

The bottom line of the emergence of the new WTO from GATT is that world trade will be institutionalized in the formal legal structure of an international organization. The more formal status of the WTO will allow it to give more focus and publicity to efforts that attempt to create greater global cooperation in international trade. The institutionalization of trade through the WTO will give some bite to the bark of a well-articulated set of trading rules and policies. With its creation, there will exist an independent political entity that can view the world trading system from a holistic perspective and to check and balance competing interests that seek to bend the trading rules in their national or sectoral favor. By paying judicious attention to the fundamental issues in international trade, the WTO has the potential of becoming a visionary organization that outlines a bold path for international trade and leads the world into a new economic renaissance.

Recent studies have released estimates of the global economic effects of the ratification of the GATT Uruguay Round and the creation of the World Trade Organization. A GATT report released in November 1994 prognosticated that implementation of the Uruguay Round will spur an increase of $510 billion a year in world income by the year 2005. This figure is a vast underestimate, for it does not account for the impact of strengthened procedures and rules in the services trade or better dispute settlement mechanisms. Breaking up the gains by region, the report predicted that by 2005 the annual income gain will be $122 billion for the United States, $164 billion for the European Union, $27 billion for Japan and $116 billion for the developing and transitional socialist economies as a group. Figures estimating the increase in volume in the goods trade range from nine to 24 percent once the liberalization of the Uruguay Round comes into effect. In 1992 dollars, this gain represents an increase in trade flows of upwards of $670 billion. The report also suggests that Uruguay Round provisions for developing and transition economies will have the intended result of encouraging rapid growth, as exports and imports from this group are likely to be 50 percent over and beyond the increase for the rest of the world as a whole. The economic impact of a well-structured and credible institutionalization of international trade is likely to be enormous.

What remains to be done is the actual construction of this economic structure. Nowhere has the debate over GATT and the WTO been more pronounced than in the world's economic leader, the United States. As is to be expected before embarking upon any bold new initiative, those who stand to suffer short-term losses are trying to stand in the way of long-term progress. Protectionist concerns and irresponsible exaggeration have been vociferously fed to the press and the deliberative bodies of the government. One example of such red herrings is a concern about a loss of US sovereignty in becoming a member of the WTO. In truth, any changes in the law of the United States or any other nation will have to be ratified by proper legislative bodies in that country, and so the practical encroachment on national sovereignty is little more than negligible. Of course, there is a germ of truth in

All nations, the US in particular, must realize that partnerships are more advantageous than going it alone.

this argument, for when any nation enters into an international treaty, it must lose some "sovereignty" to the extent that it agrees to abide by the terms of the agreement. Some kind of consensus, such as the sensitive balance that needs to be achieved by the WTO, must be reached to preserve a predictable and liberal international trade regime. To carp at the WTO for having the potential to compromise national sovereignty is little different from saying that national sovereignty is compromised because a country has to abide by any international treaty.

All nations, the US in particular, must realize that partnerships are more advantageous than going it alone, and that economic cooperation is not a zero-sum game. Free trade makes each and every nation more prosperous because it makes the entire world more prosperous. Government leaders around the world would do well to hearken to the words of Rufus Yerxa, Deputy US Trade Representative and Ambassador to GATT: "International cooperation will bring about the economic growth of the future. We cannot survive as an island in a sea of change. If we don't embrace this change, it will be our enemy rather than our friend. Cooperation is in our own self-interest."

"Trade policy is far less important to competitiveness than other issues that the United States needs desperately to address. Mismanagement of macroeconomic policy in the early 1980s severely impaired American competitiveness in the short run by leading to an overvalued dollar, which priced United States exports out of international markets, allowed foreign exporters to underprice American producers in their home market, and resulted in huge trade deficits."

United States Trade Policy after the Cold War

KIMBERLY ANN ELLIOTT

KIMBERLY ANN ELLIOTT *is a research associate at the Institute for International Economics in Washington, D.C., and the author or coauthor of several books and articles on American trade policy and economic sanctions, including* Economic Sanctions Reconsidered, rev. ed. *(Washington, D.C.: Institute for International Economics, 1990) and* Trade Protection in the United States *(Washington, D.C.: Institute for International Economics, 1986).*

What a difference a couple of decades can make. No Japanese prime minister has been called "a transistor salesman" by another foreign leader in many years. But this January, many Japanese newspapers—though not Prime Minister Kiichi Miyazawa—referred to United States President George Bush as a "car salesman" after he arrived in Tokyo with the heads of the "Big Three" American automakers and other American corporate executives seeking trade concessions. It is unlikely that the Japanese press and public would have been so vocal in their criticism of Bush's trip if they had still been dependent on the United States nuclear umbrella to protect them from an external threat like the one they had faced from the Soviet Union for more than 40 years. The tone of Bush's trip, as well as the Japanese reaction to it, illustrate the relative decline in American competitiveness and the new international economic policy challenges for the United States in the post–cold war era.

The end of the cold war presents the United States with opportunities and dangers as it develops a trade and competitiveness strategy for the rest of the decade. It raises the possibility of a "peace dividend" for the United States economy that might be used to improve American competitiveness. It also offers the prospect of substantial new markets once the economies of East-Central Europe and the Commonwealth of Independent States are stabilized.

The end of the Soviet threat, however, weakens the glue that previously held together the members of the Western alliance (defined to include Japan). Without that overriding security concern, trade disputes and other disagreements over economic policy could become more antagonistic and disruptive. For example, the European Community (EC) might have been more forthcoming in the international trade negotiations over agricultural supports (and perhaps the United States less demanding) if its leaders had feared that a breakdown in the talks could lead to a deeper rupture in trans-Atlantic relations that would compromise their national security.

The current dispute between the United States and the Community over agricultural trade could precipitate the collapse of the Uruguay Round of multilateral trade negotiations, which are being held under the auspices of the General Agreement on Tariffs and Trade. This would in turn seriously weaken GATT, which provides the framework of rules and principles governing most international trade. Conclusion of at least a modest agreement in the Uruguay Round remains at the top of the United States trade agenda, not only because of the relatively modest economic benefits that would result, but because of the important role GATT could play in containing and defusing trade disputes. Serious erosion of the system would be particularly unfortunate at a time when a new foreign policy and security environment substantially increases the importance of multilateral cooperation and the strengthening of international institutions that promote it.

The United States is also currently involved in negotiations with Mexico and Canada to create a North American Free Trade Area (NAFTA); even if these negotiations are concluded relatively quickly, the result is unlikely to be submitted to Congress for ratification until after the presidential election this November. The

usually sensitive political economy issues involved in trade negotiations are compounded in this case by the differing levels of development in the United States and Canada on the one hand, and Mexico on the other. This has raised additional questions regarding Mexico's standards on the environment, labor, and other issues that affect trade flows. The United States relationship with Japan is also under considerable strain as a result of the stubborn bilateral trade imbalance, and several proposals addressing this are pending in Congress this year.

Finally, there are many policy areas that raise security and trade issues and in which multilateral cooperation is necessary to address security concerns effectively and to avoid damage to any one country's competitive position. Revelations about Iraqi President Saddam Hussein's nuclear weapons program, for example, raise dilemmas for policymakers trying to reconcile competitiveness with export controls on strategic goods as countries tackle emerging security concerns in the "new world order."

STRATEGY SHIFTS IN THE 1980s

Trade policy is typically conducted on several levels simultaneously—multilateral, bilateral, and unilateral. Since the end of World War II, United States trade strategy has emphasized multilateral efforts through GATT to liberalize trade barriers and to contain and settle trade disputes. Although the United States was the prime initiator of the current Uruguay Round of trade talks, its own trade policy became noticeably more aggressive and unilateral in the latter half of the 1980s. This shift resulted from disillusionment with GATT, the reluctance of many United States trade partners to take steps to strengthen GATT discipline, and political pressures in the United States arising from the effects of global macroeconomic imbalances.

GATT's success led in part to this disillusionment. The organization's rules generally prohibit the use of quantitative restrictions, with limited exceptions for agriculture, textiles, and apparel, and tariffs have largely been eliminated as a significant trade barrier as a result of six earlier negotiating "rounds." Significant reductions in these traditional, highly visible barriers revealed, and in some cases promoted, a variety of other nontariff government policies that distort trade.

The Tokyo Round of multilateral trade negotiations, which lasted from 1975 through 1979, was the first to focus on nontariff barriers, including subsidies and countervailing duties, antidumping duties, technical standards, and government procurement, but it made only a dent in them. Still, the United States wanted GATT to go even further in extending GATT discipline, not only bringing in previously excluded sensitive sectors—agriculture, textiles, and apparel—but also extending its rules to new areas—services, "trade-related" investment measures, and intellectual property.

The administration of United States President Ronald Reagan originally proposed an ambitious new round of trade negotiations to address these issues at a 1982 ministerial meeting of GATT members. Frustrated by the refusal of both developed and developing country members to embrace this agenda, United States Trade Representative William Brock threatened to "go bilateral." The United States signed a bilateral free-trade agreement with Israel in 1985 and with Canada in 1988. It opened negotiations with Canada and Mexico to create NAFTA last year—primarily because of pressure from Mexico, but also to keep the fire going under the lagging multilateral round. The administration's failure to rejuvenate the multilateral system added to private-sector disillusionment with GATT because of its lengthy and often indecisive dispute-settlement process.

The trade policy difficulties posed by the faltering international system were compounded by the ill-conceived macroeconomic policies of the first Reagan administration. From 1981 through mid-1985, Reagan and his economic policy advisers largely ignored the international consequences of their domestic economic policies. Their combination of loose fiscal and tight monetary policies drove up interest rates, which—combined with tax and regulatory policy changes—attracted foreign capital to the United States market. While this capital flow ameliorated the interest rate effects of the burgeoning budget deficits, it devastated American competitiveness by driving up the value of the dollar, leading to huge trade deficits.

An increasing number of American businessmen, as well as members of Congress, also came to view GATT as not only weak but increasingly irrelevant to their concerns. As the overvalued dollar battered United States manufacturers, nontraditional export sectors like services and high technology incorporating intellectual property, which are not covered by GATT rules, gained prominence on the United States trade agenda. The rapidly expanding trade deficits also buttressed perceptions in Congress and other quarters that the American market was more open than those of United States trade partners and that the "playing field" was not level. Although even the most aggressive members of Congress usually recognized the overwhelming importance of macroeconomic factors in creating the deficits, frustration over the fiscal policy deadlock turned many of them to the politically less painful alternative of trade policy. By the summer of 1985, there were reportedly some 300 trade bills pending in Congress.

The administration finally responded in September 1985, agreeing with allies in the Group of Seven (Canada, France, Germany, Italy, the United Kingdom, and Japan) to coordinate monetary policy and intervene in foreign-exchange markets to bring the value of the dollar down. It also adopted a stronger export-oriented trade policy to head off the protectionist pressures building in Congress. Reagan tried to deflect attention from the import side of the trade balance, which tends to fos-

ter protectionist proposals, by focusing on the export side. Section 301 of the Trade Act of 1974 gives the president authority to investigate foreign trade practices that allegedly violate international agreements or are otherwise "unreasonable" or discriminatory, and to retaliate against such practices. For the first time since the act had been adopted, Reagan ordered the United States trade representative to "self-initiate" an investigation under Section 301 into various alleged "unfair" foreign trade practices, without waiting for a private-sector petition. The proportion of cases that were either self-initiated or in which the administration explicitly threatened to retaliate or imposed retaliatory duties increased from less than one-fourth of all investigations through 1984 to three-fourths of all cases from 1985 through mid-1991.

Most of the bilateral and unilateral initiatives adopted by the Reagan and Bush administrations since 1985 have been aimed primarily at supporting the multilateral system. In addition to pressuring United States trade partners to initiate the Uruguay Round, to expand the round's agenda beyond traditional topics, and then to complete it, these other trade initiatives were necessary to maintain domestic political support for liberal trade policies and the international system. The negotiations with Israel, Canada, and Mexico also had political value—they cemented relationships with strategic allies and important neighbors. The economic significance of these agreements for the United States has been minor. If the Uruguay Round is not completed, however, or if the outcome has little impact, reliance on unilateral and bilateral initiatives may come to be seen as viable alternatives, rather than complements, to the multilateral system.

THE UNITED STATES TRADE AGENDA IN THE 1990s

The Uruguay Round was initiated in Punta del Este, Uruguay, in September 1986. It was originally scheduled to conclude at the end of 1990, but instead has dribbled into 1992. The Bush administration may further delay these negotiations if the Democratic candidate for president seems hawkish on trade.

There are several possible outcomes for the Uruguay Round, including complete collapse; conclusion of a small, relatively uncontroversial reform package; and extension of the negotiations past the November elections, which might increase the chances that the political will can be summoned both inside and outside the United States to make the tough decisions necessary to extend and strengthen GATT discipline. GATT has been the favored forum for trade negotiations in the postwar era because multilateral talks typically provide more "bang for the buck" than less comprehensive negotiating efforts. Multilateral negotiations are a more efficient use of negotiating resources for two reasons: they increase the number of countries trading concessions, which maximizes the opportunities for trade creation

and minimizes the chances that an agreement will result in trade diversion (from countries that are not part of the negotiations); and they increase the number of sectors across which compromises may be made.

A recent effort to estimate the likely economic effects of two Uruguay Round outcomes—one assuming a comprehensive agreement and the other a more modest "face-saving" agreement—concluded that an agreement could generate benefits valued between 0.7 and 1.5 percent of global gross domestic product.[1] Most of the difference between the two estimates follows from the assumption that trade in services would not be liberalized in a modest agreement; liberalization of both the Multi-Fibre Arrangement, which governs trade in textiles and apparel, and agricultural policies is assumed to be about half what it would be with a comprehensive agreement. The results predicted that all regions of the world would gain on a net basis, regardless of whether the outcome is comprehensive or modest. The gains for the United States were estimated to be between 0.8 and 1.7 percent of its GDP. Thus this model suggests that even a modest, "face-saving" agreement would benefit the global economy. Moreover, those modest predicted gains are many times larger than the total anticipated gains in all Section 301 investigations. In fact, the total value of exports to targeted countries in sectors that have sought relief under Section 301 over the past 16 years is probably no more than about half that of the estimated gains from a modest Uruguay Round outcome.

The major barrier to concluding the trade talks is the inability of the United States (backed by several other major agricultural exporters) and the EC to come to a compromise on agricultural supports. The United States has been battling the EC's Common Agricultural Policy for years with little success. One-fourth of the Section 301 investigations conducted since 1975 have targeted EC agricultural policies. Although EC supports for agriculture have increased virtually without pause, American efforts may have contributed to the current pressure for CAP reform by increasing the budgetary costs borne by the Community. By consistently challenging in GATT the EC efforts to supplement the variable import levy (designed to offset the difference between world and Community prices) with various other border measures, the United States forced the EC to rely primarily on direct subsidies to producers. In the Food Security Act of 1985 Congress and the administration raised the budgetary costs to the Community by adopting their own competing export subsidies under the Export Enhancement Program.

Although the costs of its agricultural policy have increased EC interest in agricultural reform, the Community still wants the United States and other exporters to share the costs of the adjustment. The EC has demanded that "rebalancing" be part of the agricultural agreement. As a quid pro quo for reducing export subsidies, which primarily affect wheat and other grains, the

Community would be permitted to reduce its imports of oilseeds and other animal feeds by raising the tariff on those products from the zero level that had been negotiated in a previous round. Thus far, the United States and other exporters interested in agricultural reform have refused to accept the proposed compromise.

Ironically, while past American failures to force changes in EC agricultural policy unilaterally may have stiffened the resolve of United States negotiators in the multilateral trade negotiations, the relatively successful use of unilateral pressure under Section 301 appears to have weakened support in some portions of the private sector for other parts of the agreement. In recent years the American pharmaceutical and film industries have used Section 301 to push for intellectual property protection and have lobbied heavily for the issue's inclusion on the Uruguay Round agenda. They have decided, however, that the agreement as drafted does not serve their interests as well as Section 301 has, mostly because it includes a 10-year phase-in of obligations for developing countries (even longer for the least-developed countries).

Other domestic participants have opposed acceptance of the proposed dispute-settlement procedures, arguing that the agreement as drafted would preclude the use of unilateral pressure to defend United States interests. The proposed reforms were designed to address many weaknesses in the GATT dispute-settlement process that have been cited by American businesspeople and policymakers as making the aggressive use of Section 301 necessary. If the new procedures work as hoped, they should make unilateral threats and retaliation largely unnecessary, at least in areas covered by GATT rules.

Neglecting the GATT dispute-settlement process is also unwise tactically. Recent research on Section 301 suggests that use of GATT procedures contributes to effective negotiating leverage.[2] Section 301 requires a unilateral finding by the administration of "unfairness" on the part of a trade partner and unilateral action to remedy the problem if "negotiations" do not succeed in resolving the issue. However, negotiations in this context are far more likely to appear to be a zero-sum game from the perspective of the target country. Involving GATT provides political cover for the target country government by giving it an excuse for changing a policy without appearing to succumb to United States pressure. GATT support in a case also enhances negotiating leverage, since no country wants to be seen as flagrantly violating an agreement to which it has committed itself.

Overall, a modest agreement seems the most that can be hoped for and even that may not be feasible until the end of this year, depending on the tenor of the presidential campaign. For a variety of reasons, the United States has backed off from its earlier demand that GATT rules be extended to trade in services; industry opposition does not bode well for the intellectual property proposals. Only modest liberalization of the "old" issues of agriculture, textiles, and apparel seems likely at this point. Because it can probably be done without rewriting Section 301, strengthening GATT dispute-settlement procedures may be possible and could be important in containing the trade disputes that seem certain to proliferate if the outcome of the round is meager.

Some observers have concluded that GATT is dead and that the world should move toward—and in fact already is moving toward—regional trade blocs. The deepening and expansion of the EC; the North American Free Trade Agreement, purportedly to be followed by negotiations with Central and South America as part of the Enterprise for the Americas initiative; and a less well-defined Japanese-led bloc in East Asia are all cited as examples. If the Uruguay Round collapses over agricultural issues, a more likely outcome might be an inward-looking Europe and a two-bloc world: an enlarged EC and everyone else.

To date, however, the free-trade agreements the United States has negotiated have been far more important politically than economically. Even the most optimistic estimates of the potential export gains from the conclusion of NAFTA are well under one-half of one percent of GDP. Nor do free-trade agreements avoid the problems of negotiating politically sensitive issues. Early conclusion of a NAFTA draft was held up early in the year by four perennials: agriculture, textiles, apparel, and automobiles.

DEALING WITH JAPAN

No matter what else happens, Japan will continue to be at or near the top of the United States trade agenda. While the United States merchandise trade balance with the EC shifted from a deficit of nearly $25 billion in 1987 to a surplus of nearly $20 billion last year, the trade deficit with Japan has remained stuck at more than $40 billion (though that is down from a peak level of $60 billion in 1987). About 75 percent of the deficit is accounted for by automobiles and auto parts imports, which in turn accounts for the explosion of trade bills in Congress addressing that sector and the prominence of the issue on Bush's January trip to Japan.

In addition to the usual election-year shenanigans, recent trends in United States–Japan trade relations are worrisome because they suggest a much warmer embrace of "managed" trade than in the past. Through vigorous use of GATT and Section 301 procedures, the United States has succeeded in convincing the Japanese to liberalize significantly several highly visible, highly protective trade barriers. In addition, the value of the Japanese yen relative to the dollar has nearly doubled since 1985. American manufactured exports to Japan have risen rapidly in recent years, especially in sectors that have been the subject of trade liberalization negotiations, but the United States trade balance with Japan remains deeply in deficit and the perception continues

to grow that Japanese trade barriers are an important cause.[3]

With few remaining import quotas—Japan's ban on rice imports is a prominent exception—and an average tariff no higher than that of the United States, the target of market access negotiations has shifted to private and administrative practices that purportedly discourage the purchase of imported products. These include the distribution system and the *keiretsu* pattern of industrial organization, which the Japanese argue improves efficiency but which outsiders argue prevents entry. Because of the nebulous nature of these alleged barriers, there has been increasing pressure to focus on "results," measured by market shares, as a negotiating objective. So-called "voluntary" import expansions have now been tried in two cases: semiconductors since 1986, and automobiles and auto parts beginning early this year.

If one accepts the argument that "Japan is different" and believes that it will never change, then a managed trade policy for Japan might be warranted. If one believes, however, that Japan has a market economy that behaves like other market economies or that Japanese society is changing, then adopting a policy that relies on and reinforces government intervention in the economy and cooperation among large, vertically integrated firms seems short-sighted and unwise. Even in the former case, voluntary import expansions, voluntary export restraints, and other managed trade policy tools tend to be anticompetitive and costly to consumers; they would be appropriate only as a last resort.

Other policy areas are not on the trade agenda per se but have important links to international economic policy. Controlling the proliferation of chemical, biological, and nuclear weapons—and the technology to produce them—has been an international concern for years but acquired new urgency after the Persian Gulf war in early 1991. At the same time, the end of the cold war intensified pressure from high-technology firms to relax export control laws, which they argue place them at a competitive disadvantage relative to competitors from countries with far less stringent controls.

The war against Iraq suggests that elimination or even overly enthusiastic loosening of controls on sales of weapons and dual-use technologies is not a rational answer. Such policies must be coordinated multilaterally not only to avoid unfair competitive disadvantages to some countries, but also to make these policies effective. The West's Coordinating Committee for Multilateral Export Controls (CoCom) worked relatively well in denying the most critical security-related technologies to the Soviet Union. The United States and its allies now need to apply the lessons of that experience in forging a cooperative framework to prevent the proliferation of weapons of mass destruction or the technologies to develop them.

With the end of the cold war the United States must also decide how large a defense industrial base it needs to preserve domestically, to what extent the military feels comfortable relying on imported defense components, and what role foreign direct investment and technology transfer will be allowed—or required—to play.[4] Questions regarding international arms sales and the effects on defense industrial policy versus international stability and peace will have to be addressed as well. For example, a proposal under which the government would have provided export financing for commercial arms sales was largely discredited after the Gulf war. Like the pressure for relaxation of export controls, this proposal was based on the argument that it was necessary to maintain American suppliers' competitive position relative to firms in other countries whose governments provided export financing. An international accord governing arms sales and their financing would be a preferable course.

RESTORING AMERICAN COMPETITIVENESS

Although it is one factor, directly improving United States competitiveness is not the major reason for pursuing most of the initiatives that have been described here. As noted, some trade-limiting policies may be required for national security reasons even though they do not maximize American competitiveness. Trade affects America's ability to compete in international markets in two ways. First, keeping the United States market open to imports increases competition, which keeps the pressure on United States firms to innovate and to become more productive in order to stay in business. Selling abroad allows firms to expand and, if they are in a sector subject to increasing returns to scale, to become more efficient and even more competitive. Thus the main contribution of trade policy to competitiveness is in keeping markets as open as possible, both inside and outside the United States. Trade negotiations may also affect the competitiveness of particular sectors, but they are not likely to have a significant quantifiable impact on United States competitiveness generally.

Trade policy is far less important to competitiveness than other issues that the United States needs desperately to address. Mismanagement of macroeconomic policy in the early 1980s severely impaired American competitiveness in the short run by leading to an overvalued dollar, which priced United States exports out of international markets, allowed foreign exporters to underprice American producers in their home market, and resulted in huge trade deficits. The legacy of those policies has been an increase in indebtedness—for individuals, businesses, and the government—that has hampered recovery from the recession that began in 1990. While reducing government debt is one necessary component of a sound competitiveness policy (once the recession has ended), it should not be given such overwhelming priority that it prevents the adoption of microeconomic policies that are also crucial to rebuild-

ing American competitiveness. Two of the most important are improving the educational system, including retraining and adult education programs, and repairing the crumbling public infrastructure—roads, bridges, airports, and maritime ports. Tax policy is also important, both in terms of how it treats profits earned abroad and those earned in the United States by foreign investors, and in the incentives (or disincentives) it provides for savings and investment. Some shifting of government support from defense-oriented to civilian research and development, including commercialization of emerging technologies, is another area in which the end of the cold war could contribute to improved American competitiveness.

Policies like these, which directly support or encourage the efficient production of high-quality products, will have a far greater impact on American competitiveness than trade policy. However, a sound trade policy is an important component of a fully developed competitiveness policy. It is crucial to maintaining domestic political support for liberal trade, expanding the benefits

of trade by removing remaining barriers, and establishing international rules to govern trade so that disputes can be avoided and contained when they do occur.

---

[1]See Trien T. Nguyen, Carlo Perroni, and Randall Wigle, "The Value of a Uruguay Round Success," *The World Economy*, vol. 14, no. 4 (December 1991), p. 359.

[2]See Thomas O. Bayard and Kimberly Ann Elliott, "Evidence from Section 301 on the Utility of 'Aggressive Unilateralism' as a Trade Policy Tool" (Paper prepared for the National Bureau of Economic Research Conference on the Political Economy of Market Access Negotiations, Cambridge, Massachusetts, February 1992).

[3]See Peter L. Gold and Dick K. Nanto, "Japan-U.S. Trade: U.S. Exports of Negotiated Products, 1985–1990" (Washington, D.C.: Library of Congress, Congressional Research Service, November 1990).

[4]For a discussion of foreign direct investment issues linked to national security concerns, see Edward M. Graham and Paul R. Krugman, *Foreign Direct Investment in the United States*, 2d ed. (Washington, D.C.: Institute for International Economics, 1991), chapter 5.

Down in the Dumps

Administering America's "Unfair" Trade Laws

R I C H A R D   B O L T U C K

A N D

R O B E R T   E .   L I T A N

Richard Boltuck is a senior economist at the Office of Management and Budget. The views he expresses here are his own, not those of his agency. Robert E. Litan is a senior fellow in the Brookings Economic Studies program, where he heads the new Center for Law, Economics, and Politics. This article is adapted from the introductory chapter in Down in the Dumps: Administration of the Unfair Trade Laws *(Brookings, 1991), which the authors edited.*

Unfair trade. The term itself invites condemnation. Certainly many nations think so. The more than 90 signatories to the General Agreement on Tariffs and Trade allow member countries to impose import duties to counter unfair pricing ("dumping") by foreign trading partners. The Subsidies Code to the GATT, signed in 1979, authorizes similar offsetting duties against unfairly subsidized imports. On these two agreements, the United States has built a major administrative program to root out dumping and unfair subsidization and apply remedial penalties.

For years the program operated behind the scenes. Relatively obscure technicians in the International Trade Administration (ITA) within the Department of Commerce investigate charges of unfair trade. If these specialists rule that a practice is unfair, the International Trade Commission (ITC)—a six-member independent agency—decides whether it causes "material injury" to an American industry. If the ITC finds injury, offsetting duties are imposed.

The unfair practice investigations were designed to be free from politically charged trade debate. The idea is that either the imports are or are not "fairly traded" according to well-established statutory standards. Impartial government agencies make the decisions, and the consequences are automatic.

Up until about 1980 the process stayed out of the limelight. But in the subsequent decade, the ITA began to hit the headlines. It launched 451 dumping investigations and investigated 301 cases charging unfair subsidization.

Individual ITA cases triggered some of the most important trade policy decisions of the 1980s: the 1982 "voluntary restraint agreement" limiting steel imports from 18 nations, the 1986 import restraints on Canadian lumber, and the well-known 1986 semiconductor accord with Japan. Recent ITA investigations have targeted computer diskettes, cellular mobile telephones, word processors, computer display screens, and minivans.

Thus far the United States has been the world's leading prosecutor of unfair trade practices. But other nations are catching up. Australia, Canada, and the members of the European Community have been particularly active. Developing countries such as Brazil, Korea, and Mexico—in the past major *targets* of trade complaints in industrialized countries—are turning the tables by stepping up their own case filings against firms in other countries, including those headquartered here. Even here at home, foreign enterprises with U.S. manufacturing facilities are learning that they too can take advantage of the trade remedy laws. In 1991 a Japanese-owned U.S. manufacturer of typewriters brought a dumping complaint against an American-owned competitor in Southeast Asia (the case was rejected by the Commerce Department).

The way the United States administers its trade laws matters not just to manufacturers directly in-

From *The Brookings Review*, Spring 1992, pp. 42-45. © 1992 by the Brookings Institution. Reprinted by permission.

volved, but to American citizens generally. Unfairly administered trade laws can hurt both consumers, who may be forced to pay excessive prices for both imported goods and their domestically produced counterparts, and producers dependent on imported components, who may be forced to raise prices or to move their facilities offshore to obtain the cheaper inputs directly. More ominously, to the extent other nations begin copying any unfairness built into the administration of our unfair trade laws, American exporters, and thus American workers, will feel the pain.

In short, it is time to ask whether our unfair trade investigations are "fair" themselves. To what extent do they punish truly unfair trade and to what extent trade that only appears to be unfair because of procedures and computational methods that skew the outcome?

Justifying the Laws

Many economists have argued that even truly "unfair trade" should go unpunished: if firms from other nations want to sell their products cheaply in the United States, then American consumers ought to take advantage of their generosity. But most parties involved in international trade disagree. Even the GATT, which is designed to promote freer trade, recognizes that dumping and subsidization can distort international trade, harm producers in importing countries (such as the United States), and detract from global economic welfare.

Justifying laws to counter dumping and unfair subsidies, however, is still tricky. The difficulty comes in specifying exactly what distortions these laws are designed to correct.

One standard defense of antidumping laws is that they are necessary to prevent international predatory pricing. But predatory pricing makes sense only if the practitioner can later raise prices to recoup any profits lost while prices were low. And this can happen only if the firms driven out of business by predation can't return to the market when prices go up. Antitrust commentators have doubted that such conditions hold in a domestic context. The same skepticism should apply in the international case as well.

In any event, U.S. antidumping law does not direct government investigators to determine whether imports reflect a predatory pattern; if it did, dumping would be found only when import prices fell below the marginal cost of production. The dumping statute mandates a simple mathematical exercise. If home country prices are higher than those in the United States, dumping occurs. And if such price comparisons cannot be made, dumping is found when U.S. import prices are below the average cost of production, a standard that no current U.S. court accepts as the test for predatory pricing.

A newly minted justification of the antidumping law focuses on the advantages of "first-mover" firms in highly capital-intensive industries in which "learning by doing" allows firms to lower their operating costs as they expand production. When the home market of such a firm is protected from international trade competition, the firm can earn enough profits at home to allow it to exploit other markets abroad. If firms in other countries do not enjoy home market protection, they can be driven out of business and rendered unable to return because the technology has passed them by. But antidumping law in the United States (or in any other country) is neither designed nor administered to ensure that its application is limited to such instances.

Yet another argument advanced in support of laws against dumping and unfair subsidies is that while they do not promote *national* efficiency, they encourage competitive practices abroad and thus *global* efficiency. But since the unfair trade laws in the United States and in other countries as well are explicitly designed to serve domestic import-competing interests, arguments that they are *really* intended to benefit the world economy sound strained at best.

Finally, current antidumping practice has been described, but not actually defended, as a "baby 201," referring to the "escape clause" in U.S. trade law that authorizes temporary protection for domestic industries seriously injured by import competition, whether "fair" or not. In fact, domestic parties have increasingly recognized the advantages of the dumping law as a *de facto* escape clause: the injury standards are easier to meet, and when dumping is proved, relief is automatic, whereas it is discretionary with the president under section 201. That the dumping law has all but displaced section 201 as a vehicle for escape clause–type relief, however, is disturbing because the dumping remedies are most often permanent rather than temporary.

When all is said and done, about the best justification that can be made for the unfair trade statutes is that they act as a legal "safety valve" that keeps the strongest claimants for protection from trying to obtain from Congress direct forms of protection such as tariffs or quotas. Thus, the unfair trade practice program can be rationalized to the extent that it prevents more unjustified protection than it hands out.

It is not possible to determine whether the way the current unfair trade laws are administered provides net social benefits by this standard. But if the laws are to exist—and for political reasons they probably always will—they should conform to two principles. First, enforcement should be confined to practices that truly do distort international trade. And, second, remedies imposed by the laws should accurately reflect the injury that unfair practices may cause. At the moment, neither principle is followed.

Dumping

Contrary to the popular notion that the primary definition of dumping is "selling below cost," both in law and in economic theory dumping is defined as *international price discrimination*, or charging a higher price for sales in a home market than for export to another country. Only when this definition cannot be applied might export prices be compared to produc-

> The unfair trade practice program can be rationalized to the extent that it prevents more unjustified protection than it hands out.

tion costs. In making the relevant price comparisons and computing dumping margins, however, the ITA refuses to average both U.S. and foreign prices, although Congress specifically authorized it to do so in 1984. The ITA averages foreign transaction prices over a six-month period to determine a benchmark "foreign market value." It then compares that average with U.S. import prices from *individual* sales and ignores any U.S. import prices that may be above the foreign market average. Thus, ITA counts in its computation of the dumping margin only the U.S. import prices that fall below the foreign average price.

The ITA argues that it refuses to average the U.S. prices to prevent "spot" or "rifle shot" dumping. But domestic producers can, and often do, charge different prices at different times, depending on demand and supply fluctuations. Why should foreign producers selling their wares here be penalized for doing the same thing? To be sure that each and every U.S. sale is priced above the home market level, foreign producers must be sure that their average prices in the United States are above those charged in the home market. Thus, the dumping law, in effect, requires reverse dumping in order to avoid remedial duties. The result is needless harm to U.S. consumers and downstream industries.

The ITA also tends to exclude from the dumping comparisons home market sales that are below the average cost of production. The effect is to increase the home market or "fair value" price with which U.S. import prices are compared, and thus to magnify dumping margins. Although the ITA is instructed by the dumping statute to ignore below-cost sales made "in substantial quantities over an extended period of time," it has wide latitude in interpreting this provision. In effect the ITA ignores the widespread business practice of selling below average costs (but not below variable costs) for significant parts of the year or the business cycle, when demand is below normal.

When the ITA finds it cannot use home market or third-country prices as a "fair value" benchmark (because the sales volumes either do not exist or have been thrown out under the "below cost" test), it then compares U.S. import prices to an artificial "constructed value," which essentially is average cost plus fixed statutory amounts for overhead and profit. In such a circumstance, the ITA does not determine whether price discrimination exists (for pricing comparisons have been ruled out or are impossible), but instead decides whether the import prices are simply below cost. As already noted, such an inquiry makes sense only if the purpose is to discover predatory pricing, or pricing below variable cost. But predatory pricing is not the focus of the dumping statute. Thus the ITA punishes foreigners for pricing practices— selling above variable cost but below an artificially calculated average cost—that are perfectly legal for U.S. firms selling in the domestic market.

Finally, the current practice of assessing dumping duties retrospectively—that is, after the imports have already entered this country, and sometimes years later—introduces needless uncertainty into the inter-

national trade environment, which is again harmful to U.S. consumers. This problem would be easily corrected if the dumping margins determined in each annual review applied prospectively to the next year's imports.

Unfair Subsidies

Unlawful subsidization is harder to define than is dumping. Under both the GATT Subsidies Code and U.S. trade law, countervailable subsidies include direct export subsidies, production subsidies, and subsidies to factors of production, but only when they distort international trade.

When the ITA calculates duties to counter government subsidies that are not tied to the level of exports, it simply computes the benefits the subsidies confer to producers. But such subsidies can benefit firms without distorting trade or influencing the prices they can charge consumers. Accordingly, the only appropriate measure of a countervailable subsidy must reflect the trade-distorting effects caused by the subsidy. Such an approach is consistent with the GATT Subsidies Code, which *requires* any countervailing duties to be lower than the amount of any subsidy if a lesser duty is sufficient to remove the injury caused by the subsidy.

To administer the "effects" approach, the ITA must estimate the degree to which the demand and the supply of the relevant product are sensitive to price changes. Often the ITA lacks the information to make such estimates. Even when the ITA has the information, the statistical techniques commonly used to provide the estimates often entail a great deal of uncertainty. How then is the ITA to decide on a single estimate of the countervailing duty required to offset the effects of a subsidy?

The answer is that analysts make point estimates all the time in conventional economic and statistical work, recognizing that there is a band of uncertainty around those estimates. It is far more appropriate for the ITA to live with those uncertainties but at least estimate the right number than to use the wrong number—namely, the subsidy measured by the benefits approach—simply because it may be easy to compute.

Information Gathering

Another ITA practice that in many cases tilts the outcomes of its investigations toward domestic interests is its readiness to reject the data submissions of foreign respondents and to substitute "best information available" (BIA), which is usually prices and costs alleged by domestic petitioners.

The ITA maintains the BIA rule as a stick with which to threaten exporters and importers if they do not cooperate with the department's requests for information. Unfair trade investigations, however, place heavy burdens on foreign respondents, especially on smaller companies, which find it difficult and expensive (not to mention highly intrusive) to comply with the requests. Not only must they fill out long questionnaires in English (requiring them to hire

> The best chances for reform lie in multilateral GATT negotiation, if only because the United States has rarely acted unilaterally to reduce other trade restrictions.

American law firms), but also they must supply price and cost data in a computer-readable format (another hurdle for many smaller companies). Often they must use different accounting conventions from those to which they are accustomed. And they must supply all this information quickly.

Sometimes they simply can't comply. And when they don't, the ITA uses BIA. And when it does, the dumping margins are significantly higher than when it does not.

Where to from Here?

Reforming U.S. unfair trade practices is particularly hard because so many other nations are using them.

Two obvious paths to reform are open. Either the United States can change its practices unilaterally or it can persuade other countries to do likewise at the same time. Although unilateral steps to bring the administration of unfair trade laws more in line with the underlying theory of the laws—to remedy only true distortions of international trade—would actually enhance the economic welfare of the United States, it is unlikely to happen in the current political climate. Support for U.S. unfair trade laws, however, could weaken as other nations continue to copy the worst features of our practices. U.S. exporters will argue ever more forcefully that U.S. policy is causing more harm than good. Unilateral changes in the U.S. laws and their administration may well be emulated abroad as more and more developing countries implement unfair trade practices regimes.

U.S. manufacturers that rely on imported components hit unfairly or excessively with unfair trade penalties will also be in a position to help lead a movement for unilateral reform. U.S. companies have already begun to realize the risks to which they are exposed. The U.S. computer industry, for example, has felt the sting of higher semiconductor prices triggered by the 1986 dumping complaint that resulted in the U.S.-Japan semiconductor accord. The same manufacturers have been hurt by dumping penalties assessed against certain computer screen displays, prompting them to consider moving some of their U.S.-based computer assembly operations offshore.

Ultimately, however, the best chances for reform lie in multilateral GATT negotiation, if only because the United States has rarely acted unilaterally to reduce other trade restrictions. The GATT currently entertains few complaints about the enforcement of unfair trade laws, in part because it does not permit complaints to be filed by private parties, only by their governments. Governments can be strongly tempted to clothe their protectionist impulses in the convenient garb of popular "unfair trade" complaints and thus have little reason to bring complaints in this area before the GATT. If private parties could complain directly—and if the GATT tribunals were given more effective enforcement powers—then unfair trade issues could be aired in a neutral forum.

In the end, we are not so naive to think that a campaign for making our unfair trade laws "more fair" is likely to gather political strength any time soon. But as more American industries and their workers get harmed by nations that want to copy our unfair trade practice "technology," such a movement may gather political strength. In the meantime, the next time you read in the newspaper that a foreign firm has been found "guilty" of unfair trade practices, think about it.

U.S. Trade Deficits and International Competitiveness

Robert T. Parry

Robert T. Parry is President and Chief Executive Officer of The Federal Reserve Bank of San Francisco. He is a Fellow and former President of NABE and an Associate Editor of this journal. This paper was presented at the thirty-fifth Annual Meeting of NABE, Chicago, IL, September 19-22, 1993.

Does the U.S. trade deficit indicate our inability to compete internationally? The deficit is not due to unfair trade practices, nor is it due to high unit labor costs and low productivity. The trade deficit reflects an imbalance of national saving below investment. U.S. prosperity in a competitive world depends on our own productivity growth and our ability to maintain a stable economic environment.

THIS PAPER will discuss our trade deficit and what it implies about our ability to compete globally.

We've had this trade deficit for over a decade. Some people, and a number of policymakers, see this as a symptom that we've lost our edge in international competition. Here's their diagnosis of the problem: Foreign competitors are able to take markets away from U.S. producers because they have some important advantages. In particular, they have lower wages, superior technology, and "unfair" trade practices.

What's their prescription to fix the problem and return U.S. industries to competitive health? They'd like to see the government try to manage international competition by taking a more protectionist stance and targeting certain industries for special support.

My own view is that this analysis is off the mark. I do *not* think the trade deficit is due to lower wages,

superior technology, and "unfair" trade practices abroad. On the contrary, I think we can find the sources of the trade deficit in certain macroeconomic fundamentals—namely, our own government budget deficit and our investment and saving patterns. Moreover, I don't think the trade deficit is necessarily the best way to judge our competitiveness. There are more important factors to consider. In particular, I would point to price competitiveness and productivity.

DIMENSIONS OF THE TRADE DEFICIT

Let me begin by looking at just how bad the trade deficit is. First, I think it's a mistake to focus too much on the most recent numbers, which haven't been too good. The reason it's a mistake is that the source of the problem is more cyclical than it is structural. The U.S. has been in recovery for a while now. But many of our industrial trading partners are still in recession. So the recent bulge in our trade deficit is largely due to the fact that, as we continue to grow and import more, the weakness abroad is hurting our exports.

Now let me look at the longer view. Although the trade deficit has persisted for over a decade, the situation is much better now than it was in the mid-1980s. The merchandise trade deficit fell from a peak of $160 billion in 1987 to $96 billion in 1992. Relative to GDP, it declined from 3.5 percent to 1.6 percent. The current account deficit, which includes trade in services, improved even more dramatically. It dropped from a deficit of $167 billion in 1987 to $62 billion in 1992—or from 3.5 percent of GDP to 1 percent of GDP.[1]

Why the turnaround? Because over the past six years, U.S. exports have surged. From 1986 through 1992 the total value of U.S. merchandise exports

---

[1] See footnotes at end of text.

almost doubled, growing more than 12 percent per year.[2] In volume terms, exports grew almost as fast, averaging more than 10 percent per year.[3] A major source of strength in this export growth has been manufactures.[4] And it's notable that this sector has continued to show strength even during the worldwide economic slowdown of the past few years.[5] So the big picture on the trade deficit is that the situation is better than it was in the mid-1980s, because U.S. exports have surged since then.

UNFAIR TRADE PRACTICES

Now let me look at the problem of "unfair trade practices." By this I mean such things as government support of selected industries through export subsidies and trade protection. The evidence is clear that virtually all countries, including the U.S., impose at least some restrictions on imports and provide government support for exports. Still, there's *no* evidence that the U.S. trade deficits of the 1980s were caused by greater foreign trade barriers or other unfair trade practices. First of all, between 1981 and 1987, when the deficit was at its peak, the deterioration in our trade position was *pervasive*. It spread uniformly and roughly proportionately across capital goods, automotive products, and consumer goods. And the deterioration was roughly in proportion to each of our major trading partner's share of U.S. import and exports in 1981. If unfair foreign trade practices had caused the pervasive decline in the early 1980s, they would have had to change uniformly and suddenly around 1981, an unlikely conspiracy.

Of all the U.S. trading partners, Japan continues to be singled out for having the most unfair trading practices. But it's doubtful that such policies have been a major cause of U.S. trade deficits. First of all, the Japanese market has become somewhat more *open--* not more closed—over the past decade. Second, Japan's share of changes in the total U.S. non-oil merchandise trade deficit has been proportional to its U.S. trade share.[6] For example, in 1981, about 9 percent of our exports went to Japan, and about 20 percent of our imports came from Japan. That left us with a bilateral deficit of $16 billion. If the same shares prevailed in 1992, we would have had a bilateral deficit of $57 billion—which is in fact a little larger than the actual deficit of $51 billion. So I think there's not much evidence to say that restrictive trade practices have been the driving force behind changes in the U.S. trade deficit.

Of course, the doors to Japanese and other foreign markets aren't exactly wide open to U.S. exporters. But even if existing foreign restrictions on U.S. exports were completely removed, most estimates suggest we'd reduce our trade deficit by only modest amounts.[7]

PRODUCTION COSTS AND PRODUCTIVITY

Now let me look at our international competitiveness in terms of our production costs and productivity. Is there any evidence that U.S. price competitiveness declined during the 1980s? If we make the comparison in dollar terms, then the answer is: "Yes, price competitiveness *did* decline." Between 1980 and 1985 unit labor costs in dollars rose at an annual rate of 3.1 percent in the U.S., while unit labor costs fell in 10 of 11 other industrial countries.

But that information doesn't give us a complete picture. If we make the comparison in national currency terms, then unit labor costs actually *rose* in most of those other countries. Therefore, it was the appreciation of the dollar in the early 1980s, not underlying cost increases, that primarily caused U.S. manufacturers to lose price competitiveness to foreign producers during this period.

The fall of the dollar since the mid-1980s has made foreign unit labor costs measured in dollars now substantially higher than they were in 1980. Between the 1985 peak in the dollar and 1992, U.S. unit labor costs rose at only 1 percent per year, while costs in Japan, France, Germany, Korea, and Taiwan, for example, all rose at roughly 10 percent annually over the period 1985-92. Therefore, most of the apparent improvement in U.S. international competitiveness is due to changes in the value of the dollar. Furthermore, manufacturing in the U.S. now appears to have a significant cost advantage over manufacturing in other countries.

What about productivity? The U.S. had relatively *strong* productivity growth during the 1980s. Between 1980 and 1985, manufactures output per worker grew 3.3 percent annually in the U.S., compared to 4.0 percent in Japan, 2.3 percent in France, and 2.1 percent in Germany. Since the mid-1980s U.S. productivity has continued to keep pace and even exceed that in much of the rest of the world. From 1985 to 1992 U.S. manufacturing output per worker grew at 2.9 percent per year, compared to 2.3 percent in Japan, 0.8 percent in Germany, and 2.8 percent in France.[8]

SOURCE OF TRADE DEFICIT

Now that we can't blame the trade deficit on our competitor's lower labor costs, higher productivity, or unfair trade practices, where do we look for the source of it? The answer, I think, is in macroeconomic fundamentals. By definition, a country's trade balance is the mirror image of its pattern of saving and investment. So, for example, a country with more investment opportunities than its domestic saving can handle will borrow from abroad and run a trade deficit. This is true even if its costs are relatively low, its home

markets are protected, and its exports are subsidized. The converse also holds true: A country with high saving relative to investment will run trade *surpluses*—even if its markets are open and its products are regarded as "noncompetitive."

In the case of the U.S., the emergence and persistence of large trade deficits since the early 1980s can be attributed largely to changes in the nation's saving-investment balance. Over the 1960s and 1970s, the U.S. (gross) national saving rate roughly equaled the investment rate and remained constant at about 20 percent of GNP. As a result the current account remained approximately in balance. But in the early 1980s, the national saving rate fell, largely because of bigger government budget deficits.[9] The resulting net saving deficit led to higher real interest rates, the appreciation of the dollar, and the associated current account deficits that emerged in the early 1980s. In the second half of the 1980s the budget deficit turned around somewhat, interest rates and the dollar fell, and the current account deficit began to narrow. So it's primarily *macroeconomic developments* that explain the worsening of the U.S. trade balance in the early 1980s followed by its improvement later in the decade. To keep the trend of improvement going in the long run, we'll need further macroeconomic policy adjustments. Ideally, we'd accomplish this through either a fiscal contraction or an increase in private saving. Less ideally, we could accomplish it through a reduction in domestic investment. The current plans for reduced federal budget deficits are in the right direction.

CONCLUSION

In conclusion, I think the U.S. is in reasonably good competitive shape. U.S. exports have boomed and the trade deficit is lower than it was in the mid-1980s. More important, measures of labor costs and productivity, particularly in manufacturing, indicate resurgent U.S. price competitiveness. U.S. productivity growth in the 1980s has been comparable with and, in some cases better than, other industrial countries abroad. The continued existence of U.S. trade deficits reflects an imbalance of national saving below investment, not any fundamental decline in U.S. international competitiveness.

Of course, when you talk about competition, you're always talking about winners and losers. And there's no question that some industries are going to continue to face difficult times from foreign competitors. But the real winners will be consumers for whom foreign competition means better quality U.S. products. The experience of the U.S. automobile industry is a case in point. Moreover, in a dynamic competitive world economy, with new products, technologies, and production processes continually becoming available, there will always be some firms on the decline as others

are on the rise. The appropriate policy response to an industry that's losing ground to foreign competition is not to erect barriers to imports, but rather to facilitate the redirection of workers who lose jobs to more productive employment opportunities elsewhere. If the protectionist route is followed, newer, more efficient industries will have less scope to expand, and overall output and economic welfare will suffer.

And this brings me back to the main question of this conference: U.S. prosperity in a competitive world. The real issue of our long-term prosperity, of maintaining and improving American living standards, doesn't depend on how stiff the competition is abroad. It depends primarily on our *own* productivity growth and our ability to maintain a stable economic environment. The Federal Reserve has a role in this, of course. And that is to conduct a low-inflation monetary policy. But that's not enough. This country also must grapple with the hard issues of devising the means to boost productivity

- with policies that foster greater private capital formation,
- with policies that increase investment in infrastructure,
- with policies that expand research and development expenditures,
- with policies that improve the quality of education, and
- with policies that stimulate entrepreneurial activity.

To sum this all up: Our prosperity doesn't depend on distorting markets with industrial policies and protectionist barriers; instead it depends on improving our productivity and letting markets work to bring out the best in our natural and human resources.

REFERENCES

[1] In 1991 the trade balance deficit fell to almost $70 billion due to the cyclical decline of imports associated with the U.S. recession. The current account improved even more, to a $4 billion deficit, as the result of cash contributions of coalition partners in Operation Desert Storm.

[2] Annual export growth from 1986 to 1989 was a robust 17 percent; annual growth from 1989 to 1992 slowed largely due to slower economic growth in major U.S. export markets, but was still a relatively strong 7 percent.

[3] Annual export volume growth also slowed over this period, averaging 13 percent from 1986 to 1989 and 5.4 percent from 1989 to 1992.

[4] Manufacturers make up more than 60 percent of U.S. merchandise exports. Since 1986, the value of U.S. manufactured exports has more than doubled, rising at 14 percent per year, and the volume of manufactured exports has grown at an annual rate of 13 percent. The value of civilian aircraft exports, which account for about 13 percent of total manufactured exports, has grown at an annual rate of 16 percent since 1986.

[5] In 1991 and 1992, the export value of U.S. manufactures grew at an annual rate of almost 9 percent. Civilian aircraft exports grew at an 8 percent annual rate.

[6] Oil comprises about 10 percent of total U.S. imports, and including it in the calculation comparing the change in Japan's share of the U.S. deficit would have distorted the result, because there is virtually no trade in oil between the U.S. and Japan.

[7] It should be noted that Japanese imports of manufactured goods are indeed the lowest among industrialized countries, amounting to 6 percent of the total Japanese market compared to over 15 percent for both the U.S. and Germany. This is due less to explicit government tariffs and quantitative restrictions than it is to barriers associated with technical standards, and the practices of the wholesale and retail distribution system.

[8] In 1992 manufacturing output per worker grew 5.4 percent in the U.S., fell 9.1 percent in Japan; and grew 3.2 percent in France, and 0.4 percent in Germany.

[9] The government budget deficits rose by roughly two percentage points; the private saving and investment rates fell by about one percentage point each.

Exporting the truth on trade

SUSAN DENTZER

You don't need to pack it into a shipping container or load it onto a ship to have something to trade in the 20th century. Nowadays, a hefty portion of what countries sell to each other consists of services—everything from the professional skills of lawyers to licenses for nifty new technologies. As a result, last week the Commerce Department began publishing a new report on U.S. international trade in goods and services, a broader measure of trade flows than the traditional monthly statistics on merchandise trade. The new numbers constitute a better picture of reality that could blunt America's obsession with its trade deficit in goods. But given the difficulty of collecting services data, even this welcome attempt at verisimilitude is still a long way from perfect.

For years, the government has published monthly tallies of the goods America exports and imports—cars, farm products and assorted widgets. It also totes up the bottom line: If merchandise exports exceed imports, the nation is said to be running a trade surplus, and if the opposite is true, to be posting a trade deficit. But from now on, monthly numbers on services trade will be added into that mix—and since the United States typically runs a services surplus, the overall trade deficit looks smaller (chart). Experts have urged the government to make this change for years to yield a more accurate look at the economy. So have services firms like American Express, which have been eager to spotlight their share of global trade and the urgency of prying open foreign markets for their products.

Travelogue. Fair enough—but just what is a services export or import? The answers can be confusing. For example, the largest single category of U.S. services exports is travel—especially tourism—which totaled $56.5 billion in 1993, or about 30 percent of all services exported that year. But that doesn't mean that Americans spent this much money traveling abroad; rather, it means that foreign travelers spent that sum staying in hotels or sightseeing throughout the United States. Nothing was really "exported," but because foreigners paid Americans for a "product" made in the United States, their purchases were analogous to importing American goods and thus were recorded as U.S. exports. Conversely, when Americans went abroad last year, they "imported" $42.3 billion of travel services.

How does the government keep track of such expenditures? It's a lot harder than counting the shipment of goods, which the government does by sifting through roughly 2.5 million documents a year processed by the Customs Service. But since services aren't accompanied by bills of lading and the like, Uncle Sam has to rely instead on periodic surveys of people and companies that buy and sell them. For example, to garner data on patent royalties and license fees paid to U.S. firms, which last year amounted to $20.4 billion in services exports, the government requires all multinational corporations in the United States to fill out an extensive survey every five years. It then updates those results with more limited samplings annually.

Some surveys produce far better data than others. To help figure out how much travelers are spending, the government relies on voluntary passenger surveys carried out by international airlines. But according to a report by the National Academy of Sciences, in 1988 only half of the 200,000 survey cards that airlines handed out were turned in by passengers. What's more, only 37,000 cards—representing a tiny fraction of the 27 million people who traveled to and from the United States that year—contained useful information that could be plugged into the services statistics. The NAS has urged the government to try to improve the survey, including urging flight attendants to do a better job collecting the survey cards.

Plenty of other problems dog the services data as well. Worried that it may be missing some financial services exports—such as some of the lucrative fees that foreign companies pay U.S. investment houses for underwriting securities sales—the Commerce Department's Bureau of Economic Analysis is developing a new census to collect better information directly from firms. Moreover, the State Department is three years late in telling the bureau what it has been spending to run America's foreign embassies—a form of services "import" roughly estimated at $2.4 billion in 1993. And many countries' statistics for services exports and imports don't match up with the U.S. numbers, since few of America's trading partners try to collect services information in as much detail.

So just what do the government's new trade numbers really signify? For one thing, that services exports are rising—a fact that underscores U.S. competitiveness in areas like telecommunications. But the overall trade balance has less to do with competitiveness or access to foreign markets than with broader macroeconomic forces, notes Robert Lipsey, an economist at New York's Queens College and the National Bureau of Economic Research. Indeed, America's combined trade deficit is soaring chiefly because the U.S. economy is growing faster than the economies of its trading partners—and Americans are buying billions more dollars' worth of imported goods. For now, that's a story line that no new data on services will change.

Trading in the numbers

In the government's new statistical series, America's surplus in services trade partially offsets the yawning trade deficit in goods.

	Merchandise trade balance (in billions)	Services balance (in billions)	Combined trade balance (in billions)
1989	-$115.2	$24.9	-$90.3
1990	-$109	$30.7	-$78.3
1991	-$73.8	$45.9	-$27.9
1992	-$96.1	$56.4	-$39.7
1993	-$132.5	$55.7	-$76.8

Rod Little—USN&WR

Note: Negative numbers signify deficits.

USN&WR—Basic data: U.S. Dept. of Commerce

Cars and VCR's Aren't Necessarily the First Domino

Sylvia Nasar

Must commerce among nations always be a dog eat dog fight for absolute advantage? Economic Darwinians fear that America's loss of leadership in a few key industries is the beginning of an irreversible decline in competitiveness. A more sanguine school, which holds that industrialized economies will ultimately converge, maintains that Japan and Germany will catch up with the United States, but not surpass it.

As it turns out, reality isn't unfolding quite according to either script, some economists say. While the level of output per employee in Japan and Germany and the United States has converged since the 1950's, productivity in individual industries has begun to diverge.

Instead of catching up across the board, countries seem to be specializing in the things they do best. While Japan and Germany have surged ahead in some industries, the United States has widened its lead in others and stayed ahead, if by a narrower margin, in still others.

"If you lose one industry, there's no sign you'll lose them all," said Edward N. Wolff, an economist at New York University. "Just because Japan has taken over consumer electronics does not mean that Japan will triumph in mainframe computers or medical instruments."

A book by Professor Wolff and David Dollar, a colleague at the World Bank, called "Competitiveness, Convergence and International Specialization" will be published by M.I.T. Press this fall.

That pattern of specialization, which started to emerge after the early 1970's, said Dale W. Jorgenson, an economist at Harvard University, suggests that the United States still stands to gain from expanded world trade, but that it con-

tinues to face the possibility that trade conflicts will develop too.

"We can take some of their markets and they can take ours," said Professor Jorgenson. "So we will have to stamp out little moves toward protectionism and make sure our trading partners do too."

Productivity is a handy measure of an industry's competitive muscle. Industries with high levels of labor productivity tend to export a lot. "If you're the most efficient country in the world in making planes, you tend to dominate world aircraft trade," Professor Wolff said. "High productivity reflects how much investment you've poured into an industry as well as how sophisticated the technology you have."

'First Among Equals'

For 25 years after World War II, the overall level of productivity among industrialized countries did converge. Productivity grew faster in Germany and Japan than in the United States during the 1950's, 1960's and early 1970's. "The U.S. was once the dominant economy," said Professor Wolff. "Now it's the first among equals."

Using output per worker as a yardstick for productivity, the United States is about 45 percent more efficient than either Germany or Japan, which are roughly equal.

Of course, using that measure instead of output per hour understates Germany's efficiency and overstates Japan's because German workers put in fewer hours on the job than Americans while their Japanese counterparts put in more.

"Many parts of Japanese businesses operate below United States standards," said Mr. Jorgenson. "Japan has world class factories in many industries, but getting things to and out of the factory is incredibly inefficient." Wholesaling, retailing and company depart-

ments like transportation and billing use methods that in the United States are considered archaic, he said. "The best example is Narita Airport—logistically speaking, it's Idlewild 30 years ago."

But ever since the early 1970's, the gap in overall productivity has narrowed far more slowly. Why? After the first oil shock in 1973, Japan's overall productivity growth rate fell from 10 to 3 percent a year. United States productivity growth fell also, but only by 1 percentage point.

The fact that Japan was no longer catching up in overall productivity was masked, said Professor Jorgenson, by the vast appreciation of the dollar in the early 1980's. Even as Japan's domestic economy slowed, its exports exploded and the United States lost overseas markets and saw a flood of imports.

In any case, the United States and its main rivals have specialized in different industries. German bankers, it seems, are the world's most efficient. Small wonder. The United States has more than 12,000 banks, the Germans a dozen or two. Meanwhile, America's high-tech farms boast productivity 4 times as high as Japan's and 2.5 times as high as Germany's. Japan's electronics industry is twice as productive as Germany's and slightly ahead of United States electronics companies.

America's lead is actually growing in perhaps one-third of its industries including agriculture, wood products and food processing, which is really a clutch of industries that churn out everything from cigarettes to cereal to Coca-Cola.

Japan surged ahead in cars and trucks and, despite resurgent American competitiveness in steel and semiconductors, in metals and consumer electronics.

And in lots of industries, the United States is hanging on to its lead. That includes building materials, heavy machinery, computers.

Germany Slowing Down

Surprisingly, the United States widened its lead over Germany during the 1980's, not only in overall productivity but in most manufacturing industries. Mr. Wolff attributes that reversal from earlier decades to the fact that German industry didn't face the same cold blast of world competition spurred by a too-strong dollar that woke American manufacturers to the need to boost efficiency.

A second reason, perhaps more unexpected, is that the United States invested more in manufacturing than Germany did in the 1980's.

Mr. Wolff is convinced that countries specialize and achieve leadership in those industries where they invest heavily in new plants and equipment. Investment not only gives each worker more equipment to work with but it also puts the latest technology in his or her hands.

And research and development is just as important.

"The U.S. is still the leader in aircraft because of heavy R.&D. spending, some of which came via the Pentagon," said Professor Wolff. "Likewise, medical equipment research is heavily subsidized by the National Institutes of Health."

In the 1950's and 1960's Japan and Germany mainly caught up by imitating United States technology. But Americans should take note that, since the 1970's, new investment has played the primary role.

Who's the Most Efficient Producer?

Productivity of each country, measured in thousands of dollars worth of goods each worker produced. Based on gross domestic product and labor numbers from 1988, the most recent year available; calculations are shown in 1991 dollars.

	United States	Japan	Germany
Total productivity ▶	$56.3	$38.8	$39.9
Mining and oil and gas drilling	$242.5 ✓	$ 54.7	$ 26.5
Utilities	204.3 ✓	182.3	132.8
Transportation and communication	76.7 ✓	40.1	44.4
Manufacturing (see breakdown below)	66.9 ✓	52.2	36.2
Finance, Insurance and real estate	45.2	57.8	59.2 ✓
Agriculture, forestry and fisheries	42.7 ✓	9.1	17.5
Wholesale and retail sales, hotels and restaurants	41.2 ✓	24.0	26.4
Construction	38.7 ✓	34.1	27.8

Areas in manufacturing:

	United States	Japan	Germany
Petroleum and coal refining	$396.2 ✓	$321.0	$360.2
Machinery, except electrical	113.5 ✓	100.9	34.2
Chemicals, plastics and other synthetics	98.4	122.0 ✓	52.4
Cars, planes and other transportation equipment	76.7	90.5 ✓	36.2
Paper, printing and publishing	71.2 ✓	64.2	36.4
Steel, aluminum, copper and other metals	64.6	82.7 ✓	33.8
Scientific instruments	60.3 ✓	38.7	31.8
Electric machinery and electronic equipment	59.8	67.4 ✓	34.4
Food, beverages, tobacco	59.2 ✓	20.7	30.0
Stone, clay and glass products	57.9 ✓	44.6	39.0
Textiles	31.1 ✓	17.7	22.6

✓ Most efficient

Source: Edward N. Wolff, professor of economics, New York University

The Changing Relationship Between the State and the Economy in Mexico

Francisco Valdés-Ugalde

FRANCISCO VALDÉS-UGALDE is Re-searcher at the Institute for Social Research at the *Universidad Nacional Autónoma de México*. Formerly, he was Visiting Fellow at the Center for U.S.-Mexican Studies at the University of California, and Visiting Professor at the Center for Latin American Studies at The University of Connecticut and at Brown University.

A market economy cannot be created solely by reducing state economic intervention. State reform cannot be limited to economic matters. It has to address democratization of the political system.

The application of market reforms to the Mexican economy has included the reorganization of state structures and economic functions. The reforms have strained all aspects of state economic intervention. This process has involved both external and internal adjustment. For example, insofar as the outside world is concerned, economic policies from 1982 until the present have focused on Mexico's external debt-crisis management and on its economic integration with the rest of the world through trade liberalization and expansion of foreign direct investment (FDI). The North American Free Trade Agreement (NAFTA) has been one of the most important steps in this effort. With regard to domestic adjustment, vast state reforms have been set in motion. As a result of both processes, the Mexican State increasingly has faced a contradiction between market reform, on the one hand, and demands for economic development with social justice (as well as a democratic reform of the political system), on the other. I shall address key aspects of these reforms and their impact on the relationship between the state and the economy.

SOME HISTORY

Once the Mexican postrevolutionary state built its basic structures, its relationship to economic development was distinguished by two outstanding features: (1) a concentration of economic decisionmaking and power in the presidency; and (2) the adoption of social reforms, in order to achieve economic growth unaccompanied by increased inequity. This was the economic content of "revolutionary nationalism." It represented the economic statism of the contemporary Mexican State.

The Lázaro Cárdenas Presidency (1934–40) carried out extensive land reform. The peasantry and labor organized big unions which were affiliated with the Mexican Revolution Party—the progenitor of the PRI. And the government nationalized the oil companies. It also fostered economic growth with these reforms and gave birth to a significant number of modern enterprises and to a business class, which

also was aided by import substitution industrialization (ISI) strategy. But once the country had moved through this period of reform, and had sustained economic growth, "revolutionary nationalism" became an increasingly contradictory process. This contradiction was, and continues to be, expressed as the one between the antiliberalism (in the classical sense of anti-economic freedom) of the postrevolutionary Mexican State and the market-oriented reforms that the government began to set in motion in the 1980s.

Previously—between 1954 and 1970—economic growth reached the highest rates in Mexico's contemporary history. This growth was due to the success of recent policies and a favorable international business

> A new understanding between the public and private sectors gave birth to the idea that, in the long run, the economic importance of the government should be reduced and that of the private sector increased.

climate. Even though, in this period, state economic intervention grew, private enterprise also grew. Hence, market forces became more important. A new understanding between the public and private sectors gave birth to the idea that, in the long run, the economic importance of the government should be reduced and that of the private sector increased.

Some developing countries resisted the trend to market reform. They remained strongly in favor of policies that are protective of domestic industry and employment. Populism and socialism were extended widely throughout the Third World. Being anti-imperialist, they continued to be hostile to market-oriented reforms. Nevertheless, the 1970s saw a growing consensus about the importance of market-oriented policies. But the increasing importance of liberalism was not as widely accepted as it would prove to be later. Mexico, among other countries, experienced this conflict during the Echeverría and López Portillo Governments. From 1970 to 1982, under these administrations, state intervention was characterized by attempts to strengthen the weight of government in the economic process rather than to mitigate it. Echeverría's strategy of "shared development" and later, López Portillo's "alliance for production" deviated from the implicit goal of market privatization. They assumed that it was inconsistent with Mexican history and with problems with which the governing

alliance had to deal. One of these problems was the disagreement among the various economic actors and between them and the state about which economic and social policies were to be implemented. While business groups and organizations joined the chorus for neoconservatism and market reforms, trade unions demanded stronger state intervention in the attempt to improve income-distribution policies. They also insisted on a policymaking role. In turn, government demonstrated that it was torn by divisive attitudes between the nationalists in power and the technocrats who had been displaced from key policy positions.

Thus, from 1970 to 1982, the government sought a new equilibrium in economic policy among the state, the economy, and the society at large. But they failed to achieve that equilibrium. The essence of state economic intervention during this period lies in its refusal to give up ISI and, consequently, to redefine the division of labor between the state and the private sector. The overall result of these policies was, in the end, the opposite of their original purpose. The state came into increasing and intricate conflict with the private sector and failed to build a nationally centered economic model.

The end of this period was remarkable. President Luis Echeverría tried to modify these polarizing economic tendencies, because they put state legitimacy in peril. But he was not only incapable of creating economic peace, he actually stirred up a unified opposition. His administration ended being unable to govern. Six years later, in spite of President José López Portillo's efforts to moderate the consequences of the 1970–76 *sexenio*, by the end of his term, economic crisis and social conflict had reappeared. It ended in the 1982 bank nationalization. The economic alliance between the private and the public sector was broken. Economic problems became structural in nature. So too did the remedy.

A NEW MODEL

The central factors in this process of change we should consider are: (1) the changing size, organization, and operation of the productive and administrative structure of the government; (2) budgetary, fiscal, and taxation measures; (3) privatization policies; and (4) changes in economic legislation and social policy. I offer here an overview of these aspects—considering first, the de la Madrid Administration, and second, Salinas's.

From the first day of his term, President Miguel de la Madrid attempted to reorder state economic inter-

vention. As early as his second day in office, he sent a bill to Congress to open a new "economic chapter" in the Constitution—despite the opposition it raised among business representatives. But, only three months after the expropriation of private banks, this measure was seen as one following the same "state-centered economic path." Clearly, the purpose of this reform was to establish a difference between public and private responsibilities, in response to the demands of the business community. The state was to restrict economic intervention to "guidance" of the economic process and to intervene only in those "strategic areas" which were specified in the constitutional reform. In addition, new powers were granted to Congress. It could issue and approve economic legislation—powers previously granted solely to the Executive Office. This constitutional reform laid the foundation for policies of adjustment and privatization. Reform was meant to reshape the structure of the relationships among the state, the economy, and whole society.

Legal changes modified the structure of the federal government—from the ministries to state-owned enterprises. In the former, a huge redistribution of responsibilities took place. In the latter, the privatization process was set in motion. The reorganization of the state apparatus included the following changes: (1) from 1982 to 1994, 940 state-owned enterprises were sold off or eliminated; (2) the federal budget was significantly reduced by cutting government employment; (3) municipal reform relieved the central government of many of its budgetary obligations to local governments; and (4) decentralizing federal government transferred to state governments basic health services and education. The Salinas Government later deepened this last change.

Privatization policies, on the other hand, have led to the restructuring of private business groups. They actually have increased concentration within an already concentrated economic system. In 1990, the top ten economic corporations represented 56 percent of total sales and 53 percent of employment generated by the 119 main economic groups. Three stock-exchange firms concentrated 40 percent of stock-exchange operations before the privatization of the banks in 1991–93. Besides, the same individuals who control the "casas de bolsa" and banks control the main business umbrella organizations. These are a handful of individuals who comfortably preside over the relationship with the public sector. On the other hand, the 500 biggest enterprises (including the banks, but also PEMEX—another state-owned enterprise) generated only 2.8 percent of total employment in 1990.

The building up of a new model has to be understood within the context of a lack of private confidence. It was critical throughout the de la Madrid Administration, and was not really solved until 1987–88, when a stabilization pact was signed among the government, the private sector, and organized labor. Two elements contributed to this: (1) the conviction that legal and economic changes could lead to an expanded, though reordered state presence; and (2) the natural uncertainty that is produced by changing policies at all levels. In sum, all economic actors shared the same institutional instability.

The 1987 Economic Solidarity Pact responded to the new economic crisis of October–December 1987. It addressed the need to find a stable framework for policy consulting, implementation, and control. It was meant to control macroeconomic variables in the short run through the control of wages and prices. Once the critical period had passed, it also proved useful in the satisfaction of private demands for an expanded privatization policy. In fact, President Carlos Salinas de Gortari undertook just that policy.

The "pacto" established a format for policy negotiations that allowed the government to keep macroeconomic equilibria and to avoid unilateral actions on the part of single actors. It has worked to induce market reforms. But, for the same reasons, it has also worked to sustain the reform project within the old political structure.

THE POLITICS OF MODERNIZATION

In 1988 (and mainly from 1989 onward), the international climate for market-oriented reforms improved significantly. By the end of the 1980s, in contrast with 1982 (not to mention 1970 or 1976), the free-market mechanism was seen as the only way for domestic economies to become viable in the world economy. Consensus over "neoliberal" reforms, which support the engineering of the changes in the relationship between the state and society, was finally achieved.

State reform (along with economic reforms) was the key goal of Salinas's policies. It was meant to consolidate the modernization project that was initiated by his predecessor. It was presented by Salinas simultaneously as a break with the past of statism and as a continuity with the "original spirit" of the 1917 Mexican Constitution—the former being a distortion

of the latter. According to Salinas's views, state economic centralism turned government into a "proprietor" whose goal of social justice was distorted by the activities that stemmed from the management of state enterprises. This situation, said the President, would come to an end with privatization measures. State structure would then be remodeled with the attainment of social justice with specific social programs in mind—mainly, "the national solidarity program." Obviously, this is an ideological operation which, in Salinas's own words, allows for the deepening of privatization policies, justifying this before all of Mexico by claiming that the resources which would ensue from privatizations would be associated with social programs. In the same speech, Salinas asserted that this was the only way in which he could get congressional support to modify the constitution to privatize the banking sector.

> *A key role of government in postrevolutionary Mexico had been as arbiter between labor and capital.*

In contrast with Salinas's words, it can be said that a strong role for the state in the economy comes from the very "original" writing (not just the spirit) of the 1917 Constitution. Its goal was to moderate social inequity and stimulate economic growth. That principle gave birth to a system of state enterprises. Salinas's state reform established a different principle for economic organization. But it still claimed its origin in the ideology of the Mexican revolution. Nevertheless, Salinas's reform reshapes state structure in order to reduce its economic intervention and to foster private investment as a substitute for the past role of public investment. Salinas's reform of the state basically concentrated on the economy and on social policy. It dissociated these from political democratization. Its basic operation consisted of deactivating the constitutional commitment to social justice in the economic process, and of transforming it into a separate branch of state policy.

One of the major turning points of Salinas's policies was the reform of the Constitution's Article 27. Its objective was to set in motion certain structural changes in agricultural production: (1) officially finishing land distribution (excepting for that involved in previously filed demands); (2) giving definitive property rights to "ejidos" and small proprietors; (3) allowing companies to buy land; (4) separating urban states

from arable land and allowing communities to decide whether they would distribute the latter in individual parcels (or lots) among their members; and (5) allowing landowners of any kind to form productive associations or rent their land.

The *ejido* community assembly is meant to be the forum in which decisions on all matters concerning this law are made. The effects of this reform are still very uncertain. Potentially, this change is a turning point in agrarian social structure. But the question of whether it will succeed in increasing agricultural output has yet to be answered.

Fiscal policy has been another area of major reform. Fiscal adjustment (excluding extraordinary revenues due to privatizations) accounts for the 1991–94 surpluses. Besides, the new taxation policy (mainly precluding tax evasion) has shown remarkable results. It has increased tax revenues by 217 percent in the period from 1988 to 1993.

New economic rules and procedures have constituted another area of extensive changes. According to "neoliberal" economic theory, this area is fundamental to freer investment flows and simplified economic transactions. Among the most important is the new "automatic mechanism" for foreign investment. This mechanism has increased the number of operations (new investment as well as the constitution of new firms) that do not require previous government authorization. In 1994, Direct Foreign Investment (DFI) reached a stock of more than $50 billion. This figure surpasses by more than 100 percent total foreign investment in 1988. However, a large amount of new DFI has been located in the stock market and in trade, rather than in industrial or agricultural production. A heated debate has developed over the proper role for foreign investment in a country like Mexico. The December 1994 devaluation, preceded by capital flight and its impact on internal debt and confidence crisis, has intensified this debate.

Other economic regulations have been changed. By mid-1993, around fifty major changes had been made in different areas to encourage microeconomic activity. These areas include transportation, trade and port operations, health, tourism, mining, electricity, and petrochemicals. Besides, "systemic actions" have been taken in key areas to reduce transaction costs and encourage competitiveness. Such areas include investment, money and stock markets, weights and measures, competitiveness, and consumer rights.

A key role of government in postrevolutionary Mexico had been as arbiter between labor and capital.

In spite of the demands of the private sector to modify labor laws, the government has not attempted to change them. But everyday life in the working place has changed substantially. Economic adjustments have been made almost entirely on the backs of the laboring and middle classes. The proportion of wages in the GDP plummeted 12 percentage points between 1980 and 1990. Collectively bargained contracts have almost disappeared. Unemployment has remained at a very high level. Changes in the organization of labor have been possible without changing laws, and with the acquiescence of trade unions. Nonetheless, sooner or later, a new federal labor law will be sent to Congress. But the timing could vary because of the political calendar. In any case, future regulations will basically give structure to that which is already happening in the labor market.

> *If the economy cannot meet social needs, and the state cannot make this possible, the only thing we can expect is the polarity of a minimally modern Mexico.*

Privatization was one of the key policies of the Salinas Administration. Among businesses privatized were eighteen commercial banks, airlines, iron and steel works, sugar mills, and the substantial portion of *Conasupo*—the staples distributor. Total privatization revenues have yielded the equivalent of 6.5 percent of the GDP of 1991. Revenues for bank sales represent more than one-half of this percentage. At the outset of President Ernesto Zedillo's Government, and even before the December 1994 financial blow-up, the private sector has not managed to fuel the economy.

Social policy has been another area of major change. Traditionally, social welfare had been thought of as part of state action, combining strong government leadership, sectoral services (health, education, retirement, etc.) and subsidies (food, transport, etc.). The latter have been radically reduced, whereas specialized services have been rationalized. In addition, the National Solidarity Program (*Pronasol*) was introduced by the Salinas Government to deal with problems of poverty and social marginality. *Pronasol* has worked in the field as an organizer of social demand.

It emanates from grass-roots organizations, channeling funding to produce basic public goods—both in the countryside and in urban areas.

LIMITED SUCCESS

Economic adjustment has been achieved partly through the reform process. But the foundations for a new and balanced development have not yet been laid. This reveals a twofold problem: (1) A market economy cannot be created solely by reducing of state economic intervention; and (2) state reform cannot be limited to economic matters; it has to address democratization of the political system.

Privatization measures and the reduction of state economic intervention do not automatically constitute either the adequate entrepreneurial function or the appropriate governmental regulation. Efficient resource allocation does not spring only from these policies. It needs proper economic, social, and political equilibria which bring actors—both collective and individual—into a virtuous economic game. State and economic modernization in Mexico have not even come close to accomplishing their objectives. Mexico does not have a market economy in the modern sense of the word. Neither has it found an adequate way to focus on social justice. If the economy cannot meet social needs, and the state cannot make this possible, the only thing we can expect is the polarity of a minimally modern Mexico—one that is made up of a handful of giant enterprises and a few dozen technocrats on the one hand, and the vast impoverished majority of a backward Mexico on the other.

For Further Reading

The following book and speech may be of interest to readers who would like to explore the topics in this article more fully.

FRANCISCO VALDÉS-UGALDE, "From Bank Nationalization to State Reform; Business and the new Mexican Order," in MARIA LORENA COOK, KEVIN MIDDLEBROOK, and JUAN MOLINAR (eds.), *The Politics of Economic Restructuring: State-Society Relations and Regime Change in Mexico,* Center for U.S.–Mexican Studies, University of California, 1994.
CARLOS SALINAS DE GORTARI, "Speech to the members of the United States Business Round Table," June 10, 1990.

East Germany's Transitional Economy

Despite some initial successes for the East German worker and consumer, comprehensive improvement of the East German economy does not appear to be in the cards.

JOHN HALL AND UDO LUDWIG

John Hall is Professor of Economics and International Studies, Portland State University. Udo Ludwig is Senior Research Fellow at the Institute for Economic Research in Halle, Germany.

No one could expect East Germany's transition to a market economy to follow some predictable path. First of all, after four decades of development in a different and even conflicting economic system, its transition is inextricably linked to a reintegration into West Germany's economy. This is much more complex and problematic than, for example, Poland's or Hungary's return to a market system—a process that might be considered a more typical model.

One significant result of unification is that some East German families are benefiting from rising family incomes and enjoying substantial increases in their bundle of consumer goods with greater choice, despite the difficult problems. Moreover, the unified system now offers greater stability through the overarching umbrella of West German institutions, including a major currency—the Deutschmark. In addition, West Germany's well-developed social welfare system—an integral part of its social market economy—is a safety net to catch East Germans, if they happen to stumble as a result of their integration into the more productive West German economy.

Emerging problems

After four years of unification, some economic indicators look promising. Labor productivity in industry increased from an estimated 30 percent of the West German level at the start of unification to 50 percent in 1994. In 1993, the growth rate of output in East Germany was greater than 6 percent, and rivaled the rapid growth rates of some developing economies in East Asia. Nevertheless, problems which suggest that East Germany will fail to recover its historical losses relative to West Germany can be seen beneath the surface. This is a pattern that was evident at the end of World War II and that was only aggravated by the forty-year experiment with planned socialism.

According to conventional economic wisdom, East Germany's economic problems are rooted in the German Monetary Union that became effective on July 1, 1990. That is when East Germany changed to the market and adopted the German mark as its currency. The logical sequence of that story ran as follows: When unification began, East Germany's economy exhibited lower levels of labor productivity than did West Germany's. Its infrastructure was antiquated, its industrial structure was old-fashioned. Its rapid union with the more productive West German economy was expected to result in precipitously declining employment, as real output fell. These were thought to be the inevitable consequences of newly created markets, and the normal outcomes of a new market system.

Perhaps more important, the initial losses inflicted by the adoption of a market system aggravated the

 From *Challenge*, September/October 1994, pp. 26-32. © 1994 by M. E. Sharpe, Inc., Armonk, NY 10504. Reprinted by permission.

Table 1 **Public Sector Transfers to East Germany**
(In Billion Deutschmarks, Current and Rounded)

Year	1991	1992	1993	1994 (est.)
Total Transfers	129.2	150.3	162.9	165.5
of which:				
Unemployment Insurance	20.9	30.6	32.1	28.5
Pensions	—	1.5	4.9	7.0
Total Transfers as % of East German GDP	71.4	64.4	59.1	55.0

Source: *Die Lage der Weltwirtschaft und der Deutschen Wirtschaft*, Herbst 1993.

losses that the Eastern Laender (five new states) had suffered since the Second World War and had never overcome. Moreover, West Germany's unification policies did not even seem to address those problems. Rather than promoting economic equalization between East and West, unification policies seemed to subordinate the East to the West. Those problems have been compounded by the fact that the transformation extends well beyond the economic system and reaches deeply into the political and social systems as well.

West Germany's financial burden

Since its inception, unification has been an expensive proposition that tended to grow more expensive over time. It has required the transfer of subsidies and investments from West to East in amounts that the Bonn Government deems "massive." In 1993, transfers amounted to sizable portions of East German output. Roughly 20 percent of the total transfers went to support labor market policies, by and large in the form of unemployment insurance. In addition, pensions (often induced by forced early retirements) accounted for another 3 percent (see *Table 1*).

The transfer of funds can be viewed as a useful measure of West Germany's commitment to unification and a market economy in East Germany; however, it is typically presented in a distorted light. On the one hand, transfers are regarded as West Germany's responsibility and burden; on the other hand, they are considered the essential means of transforming the East German economy.

Closer examination of the intra-German financial flows reveals a peculiar pattern. Transfers of funds from West to East Germany are not new phenomena; they occurred as inter-German flows, when Germany was separated into two nations. For example, close to 2 billion Deutschmarks were paid annually to the

East German (GDR) government for transit rights to the geographic island of West Berlin. The West Berliners also paid the East Germans to dispose of their garbage in East German dumps. West German families often transferred funds to family members in East Germany. There was also an active prisoner trade. Since 1977, the West German government has paid upwards of 96,000 Deutschmarks to buy a prisoner from an East German jail.

In addition to transfers, there was an active merchandise trade. In 1985, the total of inter-German trade amounted to 15.5 million Deutschmarks; East German exports to West Germany accounted for 49 percent of the total. Several important sectors in East Germany relied on exports to West Germany (and, in effect, the European Community). Some exports (listed in cardinal order of value) were: textiles and apparel; fuels; chemicals; steel; ferrous and nonferrous metals; electrical engineering products; and processed wood products (including furniture).

Prior to the start of German unification in 1990, the methods used to transfer funds from West to East, and the ways in which goods flowed from East to West, were many. West Germans imported established product lines from East Germany. With respect to types of products and their quality, these must have contributed something to the utility maximization of the discerning West German consumers, and to the profit maximization of competitive West German firms.

But East German merchandise exports to West Germany have stagnated since unification, while West German exports to the East have increased

Table 2 **Inter and Intra-German * Merchandise Trade**
(in Thousand Deutschmarks, Current)

Year	Total Trade	Imports from West Germany	Exports to West Germany
1985	15,537	7,901	7,636
1989	15,309	8,104	7,205
1990	29,600	21,324	8,275
1991	55,718	46,733	8,985
1992	74,684	63,530	11,154

* Viewed as West German imports into East Germany, and East German exports to West Germany.
Sources: "Kein Gewinn von Marktanteilen im innerdeutschen und Aussenhandel", in *Konjunkturbericht* 5-7/93, Institut fuer Wirtschaftsforschung Halle; and Ingrid Haschke, "Der Innerdeutsche Handel im Strukturwandel," *Kunjunkturbericht* 5-6/93, Institut fuer Wirtschaftsforschung Halle.

markedly (see *Table 2*). In effect, the East German market serves as a newly opened frontier—a market for expanding West German exports. While this might serve to improve the material standard in East Germany, the implication of the burgeoning trade

Table 3   **Total Capital Formation in** *
Two States and East Germany
(Public plus Private Investment)
(in Billions of Deutschmarks, Current, and Rounded)

	North Rhine Westphalia	Bavaria	Five New States
1988	97.6	93.5	
1989	107.1	102.5	
1990	119.6	115.6	
1991	133.5	130.5	87.2
1992	—	—	108.1
1993	—	—	124.3

* Total capital formation is assumed to come into federal states as flows. There is no measure to account for that portion of capital formation that might also be generated and invested internally, within states.
Sources: Volkswirtschaftliche Gesamtrechnungen der Laender, Investitionsdaten. Statistischen Landesamt Baden-Wuertemberg, Stuttgart, 1993; *Volkswirtschaftliche Gesamtrechnungen,* FS 18, Reihe 1.3 und Reihe 3, Statisches Bundesamt, Wiesbaden 1993 and 1994.

imbalance is that East Germany will be left with the difficult (if not nearly impossible) task of developing a market economy in the face of stagnating exports to West Germany. Those exports, which could most effectively bring about demand management policies to promote microeconomic restructuring in East Germany, appears to be closed to expansion.

Changing German transfers

Prior to unification, trade in goods and services (as well as financial flows) were regarded as inter-German trade and transfers. With unification, East Germany is now the eastern region of a unified Germany. Trade and transfers between the East German region and the former West Germany are now part of intra-German economic activity. With respect to intraregional transfers, does East Germany fare well or poorly, relative to other federal states?

Large financial flows, in the form of private and public investments, production and consumption subsidies, and other transfers are found throughout Germany. The division of Germany into regions, and the organization the five new states (Laender) as the East German region of the new Germany, has caused a curious pattern to emerge. The total of private and public investments in East Germany (primarily flowing from West to East) is not so massive as it is proportional, at least when compared to the levels of private and public investments in other regions of unified Germany.

The 1991 population of the five new Laender of East Germany (excluding West Berlin) is 16.4 million. This compares to the 17.5 million people living in the industrialized state of North Rhine Westphalia, located in the North Rhine and Ruhr Valleys. It is a

region noted for traditional industries such as coal mining, chemicals, metallurgy, and numerous forms of steel fabrication (including automobile manufacturing and machine building).

Bavaria serves as a useful, contrasting example. With its smaller population of 11.6 million, it is a federal state that advanced its relative position in cold-war West Germany and functioned as a magnet that attracts advanced industries. Numbered among them are aerospace, defense, and (some related) advanced electronics and semiconductor industries. An examination of capital formation that stemmed from flows of private- and public-sector investments into East Germany shows that these flows were proportional rather than massive. In considering that East Germany is now composed of five new federal states which are not represented as single states (such as North Rhine Westphalia and Bavaria), the investments are proportionately smaller; they have to be split among five recipients (see *Table 3*).

Private-sector commitments

West German investment in East Germany increased significantly from 1991 to 1993. Moreover, increased investment also seemed to be fostered by sending less capital out of Germany as foreign direct investment. West German private investment in East Germany nearly doubled in current Deutschmarks—

Table 4   **German Foreign Investment and**
West German Investment in East Germany
(In Billions of Deutschmarks, rounded)

Year	1991	1992	1993
Total German Foreign Direct Investment (est.) [1]	31	24	17
West German Investment in East Germany [2]	19	29	33
Total	50	53	50

1. Does not include purchase of foreign stocks.
2. Includes long-term credits and reinvestment of profits.
Sources: Deutsche Bundesbank Zahlungsbilanzstatistik, February 1994; *Wirtschaft in Zahlen,* Bonn, 1993.

from 19 billion in 1991 to 33 billion in 1993. During the same period, total German foreign direct investment declined from 31 billion Deutschmarks in 1991 to 17 billion in 1993. There appears to be a real shift from direct foreign investment to domestic investment in East Germany (see *Table 4*).

Per capita and spatial equalization

How large should German private investments in East Germany be in order to promote an equalization

Table 5 **Births and Deaths in East Germany and West Germany** (Actual Figures)

	In Five New States plus East Berlin			Former FRG
Year	Live Births	Deaths	Difference	Live Births
1988	215,734	213,111	+2,623	677,259
1989	198,922	205,711	-6,789	681,537
1990	178,476	208,110	-29,634	727,199
1991	107,769	202,427	-94,658	722,250
1992	87,030	187,083	-100,053	718,730

Source: *Zur Wirtschaftlichen und Sozialen Lage in den Neuen Bundeslaendern Sonderausgabe*, April 1993.

of investment activity and, ultimately, of economic activity? To promote investment equalization, the amount should, in principle, be at least as proportionately large as German private investments are in West Germany; it should be even greater, if the East is to catch up. The East German states represent less than 20 percent of the total population of unified Germany—a declining share. In 1939, East Germany's population was 29 percent of the total German population that lived within the present borders of unified Germany. A 20-percent share of population fails to account for the fact that the East German region suffered a decline in population—a secular trend that started after the end of World War II and extended through the forty years of planned socialism. Moreover, it now continues, either in the face of, or perhaps more realistically as a result of, unification policies.

A 1993 study conducted by the German Institute for Economic Research (DIW) in West Berlin shows that Eastern Germany's population share (relative to the German total and in actual numbers) is expected to continue to decline until the year 2040, even under the more optimistic of the two scenarios. This decline can be attributed to emigration, a fall in East German birth rates, and marked increases in the ratio of deaths over live births. A detailed study would be required to determine the exact causes of the sharp declines in live births. Even though East Germans of child-bearing age may well have emigrated to West Germany, we do not see corresponding increases in live births in West Germany (see *Table 5*).

More realistically, a decrease in live births reflects the citizenry's perception of economic uncertainty. But changing family policy appears to be more important. East German women are forced to accept conservative West German policies. In the first instance, these policies throw a disproportionate

number of women out of work altogether. In 1989, the participation rate for women in the total labor force was 49 percent. In 1992, this share had already fallen to 44.8 percent. In addition to squeezing women out of the labor force, there has been a simultaneous failure to provide accessible, affordable child care—a service previously available in East Germany.

Table 6 **Private, Public, and Foreign Investments in Germany** (in Billion Deutschmarks, Current and Rounded)

	1991	1992	1993
Total Investment in Corporate Sector in Unified Germany *	411	429	402
of which:			
West Germany	353	356	318
East Germany	58	73	84
East Germany as percentage of total	14%	20%	21%
General Government [2] (in Unified Germany)	75	85	86
of which:			
West Germany	61	66	65
East Germany	14	19	21
East Germany as percentage of total	19%	22%	24%

1. Includes companies, financial institutions, plus public corporations, excluding housing.
2. Includes public investment in roads, public buldings, public hospitals, public schools, and the like.
Sources: *Volkswirtschaftliche Gesamtrechnungen Fachserie 18*, 1992; for Year 1993, *Vierteljahresergebnisse der Inlandsproduktberechnung*, 4. Vierteljahr, 1993 (preliminary document); *Wirtschaft in Zahlen*. Bonn, Bundesministerium fuer Wirtschaft, 1993.

With respect to geographic area, East Germany's five new Laender account for 30 percent of the land area of unified Germany. For per capita investment to be equalized on an annual basis, it would require that Eastern Germany receive close to 30 percent of total German private investment.

Both private and public investment is needed, if regional equalization is to be furthered. In 1993, East Germany received 21 percent of private-sector investment and 24 percent of public-sector investment. This can be interpreted as a firm commitment to a per capita equalization of investment. But the share is closer to the level of population engendered by a secular trend of emigration for over fifty years (see *Table 6*).

Transfers of stocks

Funds are flowing from West to East, presumably in order to promote economic integration, regional equalization, and, thereby, German unification. But there is a reverse transfer of stocks. Compared to flows of funds, transfers of stocks are characteristically lumpy and often permanent.

Privatization through the *Treuhandanstalt* (the institution created in autumn 1989 to serve as the holding company of state-owned, productive and property assets of the GDR) can be considered successful because of its rapidity and completeness (certainly when compared to other Central and East European economies in transition). But a curious feature lingers. Through *Treuhandanstalt* privatization, the productive assets (stocks) of the previous East German nation (and which are now geographically located in the East German region) essentially were transferred from East German to West German ownership.

Of the thousands of firms privatized through *Treuhandanstalt*, a total of 819 were bought by foreigners. This amounted (as of January 1994) to a financial obligation on their part of just over 20 million Deutschmarks. Foreigners taking over East German firms also assumed responsibility for 146,786 salaried employees and wage workers. In all, this amounts to less than 7 percent of the privatized firms and less than 4 percent of the 4 million salaried employees and wage workers. By March 1994, only 242 firms, with 92,754 employees, remained under the control of *Treuhandanstalt*. Management buy-outs (MBOs) by East German workers have not occurred often. In real terms, this means that a share greater than 90 percent of East Germany's productive assets fell into the hands of West German corporations and entrepreneurs.

In addition to the transfer of stocks of productive assets, 40 percent of the land surface of the former GDR fell to *Treuandanstalt*'s portfolio. These included *Volkseigen Gueter* (public lands). Most of these were state forests. Another portion were *Staatsgueter* (state-owned farms). It appears that all of this stock was transferred to the ownership portfolios of West Germans.

Sandwiching the East German economy

Rules for property restitution were spelled out clearly in Article 41 of Germany's Unification Treaty.

Property that had been taken over during the GDR days were to be returned as property rather than as financial compensation (*Rueckgabe vor Entschaedigung*). With the start of unification, this initially slowed investment in East Germany, because the return of properties takes some years to sort out. But more important than the slowing of investment flows from West to East is the transfer (and portending transfer) of these types of stocks from East to West. By 1994, 2,170,000 claims had been filed for the return of real estate (typically lots, houses, and apartment buildings).

The effects of claims against, and actual transfers in, real estate on East Germany's economic future have already been measured and forecasted. The DIW reports that the *Mittelstand*—those people who own the medium-sized firms that played such an important role in West Germany's postwar reconstruction and, especially, in the increase of labor demand—has failed to take form and rescue the East German economy. Above all, there has been a failure to reverse the continuing trend of the loss of factories. While a discernible *Mittelstand* does exist in East Germany, it tends to be concentrated in secondary activities such as food processing (baking and meat packing), cabinetmaking, plastics, and repair services.

East Germany's *Mittelstand* is characterized by firms with less than twenty employees. Only 10 percent of the total has 200 to 500 employees. Thus the East German *Mittelstand* tends to be composed of small businesses (proprietorships) rather than middle-sized firms. As a result, these firms are not in the mainstream of the East German economy, with respect to earnings, assets, or number of employees. A major cause of the *Mittelstand's* aborted growth is a shortage of capital—a condition that is related to East Germans entering unification, by and large, without equity in the form of property assets.

Stock of human capital

A significant transfer of human capital (also defined as a stock) has occurred. In the first instance, these were workers who migrated from East German industries to West Germany in search of higher wages and better job prospects. They were part of an exodus that accelerated in 1989 and 1990, just before and at the beginning of unification. Between the Fall of 1989 and the Fall of 1990, East Germany lost 600,000 employed persons to West Germany. In July of 1991, 415,000 East German *Pendlers* (table leg makers)

were commuting to West Germany. Reports emphasize that, of young males between the ages of eighteen and thirty—those who composed the backbone of technical labor employed in East German industry, and who were the best qualified of this generation—moved from East to West shortly before and at the onset of unification. A detailed sectoral study reveals the significant and presumably permanent loss of skilled workers in East German shipyards. The major exodus of East Germany's best technical and skilled workers took place before the end of 1991.

While the East-to-West transfer of human capital stock is important to consider, another important loss has damaged and reduced East Germany's stock of regional wealth, as a result of unification. While the loss in industrial output is significant (down in 1993 to less than 40 percent of the 1989 level), perhaps the loss with the greatest implication for the future of the East German economic region is the destruction of the careers of the significant portion of their educated workers. The German Academy of Sciences, nearly all universities and professional schools (*Hochschulen*) in their previous incorporated forms, as well as academic and enterprise research-oriented centers have been liquidated. Vast numbers of those specialists affected by closures and dismissals have been unable to reclaim meaningful employment either in East Germany or even in the whole of unified Germany.

In 1990, a West German specialist on the subject of the role of human potential in research and development filed a report on the stock of human (intellectual) capital in East Germany—a stock composed of 140,200 people. This included the research and development potential in state-owned enterprises, agricultural research institutes, the Academy of Sciences, and universities and colleges. It estimated that 45 to 68 percent of the intellectual potential that had been devoted to research and development in the GDR could be assimilated by unified Germany.

More detailed statistical evidence reports on the fates of the 18,000 East German scientists who had been employed by the East Berlin-based German Academy of Sciences. The pattern for these scientists can be extrapolated and applied to other fields. It illuminates the prospects for research and development (as well as advanced teaching) in East Germany. Of the 18,000 scientists affiliated with the German Academy of Sciences, about 2,000 (or less than 12 percent) were included in the newly created Scientists' Integration Program (*Wissenschaftlerintegrationsprogram*). Scientific integration means

that their work could continue until 1996. Another portion is temporarily being funded in the Federal Jobs Program (*Arbeitsbeschaffungsmassnahmen*), but their possibilities for advanced research are limited, especially when research centers are being closed, reorganized, or simply made inaccessible. At the most, an estimated 20 percent of the original 18,000 research scientists who were inherited by unified Germany are continuing to work in their fields, or have been moved to related fields. No more than 10 percent of the original 18,000 have secure jobs.

The effects of significant losses in the stock of human capital, either through emigration or through termination inside East Germany, are significant. The DIW has assessed the destruction of research and development potential in East Germany. It concludes: "the likelihood is great that, for a long time, East Germany will remain a weakly developed economic region (*schwach entwickelte Region*) and there, above all, the majority of activities shall remain as an extended workshop bench (*verlaengerten Werkbank*)."

Facing a stacked deck

Ostensible commitments to unification on the part of the directors of unification policies appear to be no more than chest-beating. A clearer view shows that the price paid for East Germany's share of the investment pie also means the transfer out of title to productive assets, stretches of forests, farmland, real estate, the emigration of the best portion of the technical work force, as well as the liquidation of a sizable portion of the region's research and development potential. In principle, economic equalization does not have to take place in the new Germany. In many national economies, some regions often lag behind relative to others. In numerous cases, they are the beneficiaries of transfers (certainly an integral dimension of the workings of the European Union). But, for historical reasons, East Germany should be viewed differently.

By its geographic location and through Allied policy, East Germany was designated as that German region, that portion of the German population, and that part of the German economy, that would pay most heavily for the Nazis' catastrophic invasion of the Soviet Union. Under political duress, the region was strategically absorbed by the Soviet Union; it

then contributed (and rather heroically) toward propping up the Soviets for forty years of the postwar cold-war era. It was an economic system on the slow road to eventual liquidation.

Since 1945, East Germany has suffered losses, according to numerous economic indicators (even with respect to vital statistics). After more than four decades under Soviet domination, the unraveling of its planned socialism and its simultaneous integration with West Germany offers Eastern Germany the first good historical opportunity to reverse the relative and (in some cases) real declines. After four years of unification, there are no clear indicators that those policies designed by a unified Germany to reverse East Germany's historical losses are either sufficient in size and scope or capable of effectively addressing the problems. Because of its geographic location, losses appear to be continually inflicted on the East German region, population, and economy. It has been dealt an unfair hand.

Can a Socialist Republic Find Happiness Trading in a Capitalist World?

David L. James

David L. James is President of Business Strategies International, a consulting and venture development firm for the Asia Pacific region located in San Francisco, CA. Economic data in this article are 1993 estimates derived from the *World Bank Atlas 1995*, and CIA *World Factbook* reports.

Unrelenting economic forces in an interdependent world are causing China and Vietnam, two socialist republics, to turn to foreign investment and export-led international trade as a means of building economic strength and independence in a world of capitalist market economies. The irony of this notwithstanding, businesspeople elsewhere need to assess the risks and rewards of trade and investment with these two countries. This article provides a brief review of China's and Vietnam's relevant background and their recent responses to change – and a list of concerns for their trading and investment partners.

WITH APPROVAL of the General Agreement on Tariffs and Trade (GATT) by the United States, the world's principal trading nations enter a new chapter in their economic relationships. Implementation of GATT and establishment of the World Trade Organization (WTO) are underway. New issues and disagreements will arise, and the new chapter is unlikely to be less tumultuous and contentious than the last.

One of the interesting questions soon to arise is whether the WTO will play ball with two emerging economic stars – China and Vietnam – that have political ideologies and agendas radically different from those of the general membership of the WTO. The corollary is also interesting: whether these two countries will play ball with the WTO. China is already a powerful player and wants admission to the league. Although a trade war loomed, when this article went to press, between China and the U.S. over the pirating of music and computer software by China, it is in the interests of both parties eventually to reach some accommodation.

On a purchasing power parity basis, China has the third largest economy in the world ($2.49 trillion) after the U.S. ($6.39 trillion) and Japan ($2.63 trillion). China's trade accounts are also substantial, with exports of $92 billion and imports of $104 billion in 1993. Vietnam, on the other hand, is presently just a sand lot player (a GDP of perhaps $73.7 billion, exports of $2.6 billion, and imports of $3.1 billion), but it has the potential to become a standout in the blink of an economist's eye.

To deduce the future role of international trade for China and Vietnam, one needs to consider broadly their more recent history and the character of their people. To determine whether to invest time, energy, and money in trade and investment with these countries, businesspeople elsewhere need also to look behind political rhetoric and observe economic behavior.

CONCURRENCE AND CONTRAST

China and Vietnam are socialist republics with Marxist/Leninist ideologies, each governed by a strong central bureaucracy. Each has seized upon economic reform, with export-led international trade and regulated direct foreign investment, as the key to strength and independence in an increasingly interdependent world. Ironically, each has a long history of distrust of foreign relationships.

6. INTERNATIONAL ECONOMICS

China introduced economic reforms in 1978, two years following the deaths of Mao Ze-dong and Zhou En-lai, and in 1992 China's leadership endorsed "faster, bolder" economic growth. Vietnam, as a result of the crumbling power of its patron, the Soviet Union, and peace efforts of the United Nations in Cambodia, adopted a course of social and economic reform, known as "Doi Moi," in 1990. The difference in the present economic policies of the two countries is largely a matter of duration of the effort, not the direction.

Economic reform is clearly paying off for each country. China's economic growth has averaged more than 10 percent over the past decade. For Vietnam, unofficial estimates are that economic growth has averaged 8 percent since 1992, and inflation has dropped from 84 percent in 1991 to about 10 percent currently.

When it comes to interaction with the outside world, the two countries each have long histories of conflict and xenophobia. In modern times, China's historic resistance to foreign influence intensified as a result of Japanese aggression that commenced in the 1920s and erupted in the Sino-Japanese War in 1937. Japan was finally ousted at the conclusion of World War II, but conflict continued as civil war broke out in 1945 between the Nationalist Party under Chiang Kai-shek and the Communist Party under Mao Ze-dong. The Communists won that war, and the Nationalists moved their government to Taiwan. China under Mao withdrew further from the world community, and a period of isolation and anti-intellectualism – dubbed the Cultural Revolution – prevailed for the next two decades. China's gradual opening to the world in recent times can be traced to the rise of Deng Xiaoping as paramount leader commencing in 1978.

Vietnam's resistance to foreign influence goes back to long periods of domination by Chinese dynasties from the north and, during the past century, to French colonial occupation that commenced in 1858. Anticolonialist sentiment steadily grew among the Vietnamese, spurred by news of the Russian revolution and the Kuomingtang revolution early in the present century. Ho Chi Minh, perhaps Vietnam's best known political figure, became active in the anticolonialist movement in 1919 and gradually rose to power in Vietnam's communist movement. Following Japanese occupation of Vietnam during World War II, the French sought to reassert control over the country and wound up in a nine-year war with communist forces supported by the Soviet Union and, ironically, in part by China. The conflict ended in 1954 with the division of the country into the Democratic Republic of Vietnam (North Vietnam) and the Republic of South Vietnam. The United States, pursuing a global policy of containment against communist influence, began supporting South Vietnam militarily, and itself became embroiled in all-out war, finally withdrawing in 1975. For fifteen years following the American withdrawal, Vietnam allied itself with the Soviet Union and continued in military conflict, occupying Cambodia and confronting China. Finally, in 1990, no longer able to count on Soviet support, Vietnam entered upon its present course of social and economic reform.

The character of the people of the two countries is similar as well – resolute and determined, pragmatic, entrepreneurial, possessing a strong work ethic. After generations of deprivation, there is a thirst for a higher standard of living and a willingness to sacrifice for it.

In terms of size, however, the two countries are dramatically different. China has the largest population in the world (1.2 billion) and a land area that is the third largest after Russia and Canada, slightly larger than the United States. Vietnam has a sizable but much smaller population (70 million), and in land area it is smaller than California.

China's vast size makes it difficult to govern, especially from the center. This accounts in large measure for the government's resistance to foreign influences and its severe treatment of dissidents and political opposition. Vietnam's smaller size is more accommodating to centralized government, although the lingering effects of its north/south division during years of war following World War II occasionally strain the authority of its central government in Hanoi over its economic heart in Ho Chi Minh City (Saigon).

LEADING INDICATORS

One would think that these two socialist republics, with every political reason to limit interaction with the world community, would shun international trade and foreign investment. Instead, each is aggressively pursuing its international economic options. While mixed signals abound – from bureaucratic delays to canceled projects – astounding progress in being made.

Direct foreign investment tells an interesting story because the policies of China and Vietnam encourage export projects that earn foreign exchange, rather than merely generate domestic sales. These policies would seem to deter investors who seek to tap the large population and growing demand of each country. Yet in China direct foreign investment rose from $916 million in 1983 to $25.8 billion in 1993, the pace accelerating dramatically in 1992 and 1993. Total direct foreign investment stood at $110.9 billion at the end of 1993. In Vietnam, where foreign investment is in its infancy, total direct foreign investment stood at less than $3 billion seven years ago but is expected to reach $15 billion by the year 2000.

To accommodate foreign investment, China is reforming its capital markets and taking steps to make its currency fully convertible. The Bank of China is establishing credit systems to supplement the country's

cumbersome cash economy, expecting to have issued 200 million credit cards by the year 2000. China is also conforming accounting and legal practices to international standards. And it is giving priority to infrastructure projects that will facilitate expansion of trade, notably telecommunications and transportation. China's goal is to increase telephone service fourfold by the year 2000, from serving only 2 percent of the population presently to 8 percent by then. It also expects to invest $40 billion in new aircraft in the next two decades and to produce affordable automobiles for the masses, more than doubling present production by the year 2000.

For its part, Vietnam has enacted one of the most liberal foreign investment laws in the region and is reforming other laws and practices to accommodate investors. Among its priorities is improvement of physical infrastructure – roads, bridges, port facilities, telecommunications systems – that presently inhibits economic expansion. With the U.S. embargo on trade and investment with Vietnam now lifted, the World Bank and other lenders are providing expedited financing of numerous developmental projects in this war-ravaged country.

Aside from government policies and initiatives, the attitudes and appetites of the Chinese and Vietnamese are indicators of what lies ahead. Business managers, who are often essentially government bureaucrats, are eager to participate in joint ventures and market economy transactions. Workers in the cities and in villages crave the products that virtually everyone now sees on televisions or reads about in foreign publications. Satellite television, with international programming, is now widely available in China in spite of the government's efforts to outlaw satellite dishes. (Reruns of "Dallas" are especially popular currently.) Today there are about 600 television stations in China, an emerging cable system, 250 million television sets, and a growing number of videocassette players.

On a recent business trip to Ho Chi Minh City, I found that local businesspeople were eager to collaborate on virtually any form of business activity, and government representatives were willing to find ways to facilitate any promising project. In Vietnam "cooperation joint ventures," as opposed to equity joint ventures, are perhaps the most effective investment vehicles for foreigners presently. In a typical cooperation joint venture, the foreign partner supplies machinery, raw materials, and technology; the Vietnamese partner (often a state owned enterprise) supplies labor and plant facilities. By contrast, in China the most effective investment vehicles are equity joint ventures, largely because the laws governing equity joint ventures are clear and easily understood by foreign investors.

POTHOLES AHEAD

On the road to international trade expansion for China and Vietnam, four significant potholes lie ahead. Here is a list of them, with a forecast of how each will play out in the near term.

1. *Ideological Concern*. As socialist republics with Marxist/Leninist ideologies, China and Vietnam each have a genuine concern that exposure to the influence of Western democratic nations through international trade and investment will undermine their political powers and authority, destabilizing their society and interrupting economic growth. This is a particular concern of China, whose vast size makes governing especially difficult and whose political leadership is undergoing change with the anticipated passing of Deng Xiaoping. For each country, a concern about the impact of foreign influence will continue to unsettle relations with its foreign investors and trading partners for years to come.

2. *Social Unrest*. Rapid change and exposure to foreign influence are already testing the social fabric of these two countries. This is especially true of China, which is further along the road of development. There is a growing disparity in China in the incomes of rural and urban classes, and growing awareness among the population of the disparity between domestic standards of living and those of industrialized nations. Similar conditions are beginning to occur in Vietnam as well. However, the governments of the two countries are moving to relieve such disparities and spread the wealth. It is probable that standards of living will rise rapidly enough, and broadly enough, to avoid governmental action that would curtail international trade expansion.

3. *Bureaucratic Bottlenecks and Corruption*. As in other developing countries emerging from highly bureaucratic command economies to market economies, business managers in China and Vietnam have exceptionally close ties with counterparts in government ministries and agencies. Most business activities are operated as state-owned enterprises. As a result, bureaucratic delays continue to inhibit market responses, and competition is often suppressed. Moreover, corruption flourishes where the power to grant permits or provide access to materials or markets has monetary value. It is likely that these problems will inhibit rather than deter the development of China's and Vietnam's international trade.

4. *Bad Habits*. As a number of foreign investors and creditors have found to their distress, some entities in China and Vietnam have failed to meet their commitments to deliver products, repay loans, or honor lease agreements and other contractual obligations. (Some borrowers would seem to take seriously the facetious

quip, "A rolling loan gathers no loss.") Generally, foreign parties are at greater risk when it comes to honoring commercial commitments. Lapses in such matters stem from weak legal and financial systems and from central governments too often willing to support inefficient enterprises in order to accomplish noneconomic goals. Lapses like these are the lingering bad habits of emerging market economies. One can expect that they will diminish over time but not be easily broken.

POSITIONED FOR THE INEVITABLE

China and Vietnam lie at the geographic center of the world's most vibrant economic region. By the year 2000, Asia is expected to have half the world's population and one-quarter of the world's GDP. As intraregional trade expands, Asia's economies, now growing at twice the rate of those of the rest of the world, are destined to dominate world economic growth for decades to come.

The future of international trade for China and Vietnam is not so much a matter of their admission to the WTO or any other trading group, or their election to join. It is a matter of inevitability. There is no reversing the conditions that are forcing them to interact with the rest of the world. Their governments cannot isolate their populations in this age of universal communications; they cannot compel their subjects to turn off their television sets and scrap their satellite dishes. Nor will they be able to resist the siren song of economic strength and international recognition that are the products of international trade in an increasingly connected world.

Table 1
Engines of Economic Growth
Selected Development Projects

	Project	Size (US$)	Current Status
CHINA			
	Beijing-Kowloon railroad line	5 billion	Completion 1995
	Guangdong expressway roads	15 billion	First phase completion 1995
	Three Gorges Dam, Yangtze River	10 billion	Site preparation begun
VIETNAM			
	Highway No. 1 rehabilitation	150 million	Feasibility studies underway
	Banking system modernization	50 billion	Project design
	Procurement systems design	460,000	Technical assistance underway

TOTAL OUTPUT, INCOME, AND SPENDING

GROSS DOMESTIC PRODUCT

In the first quarter of 1995, according to revised estimates, current-dollar gross domestic product (GDP) rose 4.7 percent (annual rate), real GDP (GDP in 1987 dollars) rose 2.7 percent, and the implicit price deflator rose 2.2 percent.

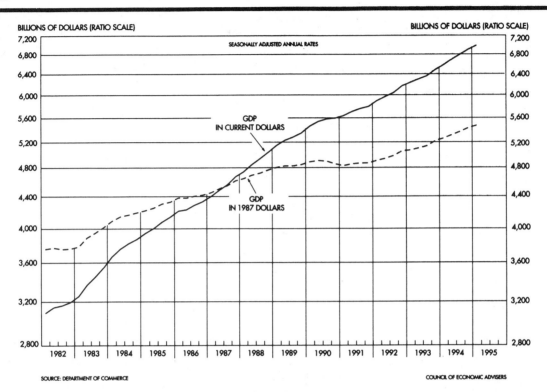

SOURCE: DEPARTMENT OF COMMERCE

COUNCIL OF ECONOMIC ADVISERS

[Billions of current dollars; quarterly data at seasonally adjusted annual rates]

Period	Gross domestic product	Personal consumption expenditures	Gross private domestic investment	Exports and imports of goods and services			Government purchases					Final sales of domestic product	Gross domestic purchases [1]	Addendum: Gross national product
				Net exports	Exports	Imports	Total	Federal			State and local			
								Total	National defense	Non-defense				
1986	4,268.6	2,850.6	717.6	−132.5	319.2	451.7	833.0	367.8	276.7	91.1	465.3	4,260.0	4,401.2	4,277.7
1987	4,539.9	3,052.2	749.3	−143.1	364.0	507.1	881.5	384.9	292.1	92.9	496.6	4,513.7	4,683.0	4,544.5
1988	4,900.4	3,296.1	793.6	−108.0	444.2	552.2	918.7	387.0	295.6	91.4	531.7	4,884.2	5,008.4	4,908.2
1989	5,250.8	3,523.1	832.3	−79.7	508.0	587.7	975.2	401.6	299.9	101.7	573.6	5,217.5	5,330.5	5,266.8
1990	5,546.1	3,761.2	808.9	−71.4	557.1	628.5	1,047.4	426.5	314.0	112.5	620.9	5,539.3	5,617.5	5,567.8
1991	5,724.8	3,902.4	744.8	−19.9	601.1	620.9	1,097.4	445.8	322.8	123.1	651.6	5,726.6	5,744.7	5,740.8
1992	6,020.2	4,136.9	788.3	−30.3	638.1	668.4	1,125.3	449.0	314.2	134.8	676.3	6,017.2	6,050.5	6,025.8
1993	6,343.3	4,378.2	882.0	−65.3	659.1	724.3	1,148.4	443.6	302.7	140.9	704.7	6,327.9	6,408.6	6,347.8
1994	6,738.4	4,628.4	1,032.9	−98.2	718.7	816.9	1,175.3	437.3	292.3	145.0	738.0	6,686.2	6,836.6	6,726.9
1982: IV	3,195.1	2,128.7	464.2	−29.5	265.6	295.1	631.6	281.4	205.5	75.9	350.3	3,241.4	3,224.6	3,222.6
1983: IV	3,547.3	2,346.8	614.8	−71.8	286.2	358.0	657.6	289.7	222.8	66.9	367.9	3,527.1	3,619.1	3,578.4
1984: IV	3,869.1	2,526.4	722.8	−107.1	308.7	415.7	727.0	324.7	242.9	81.9	402.2	3,818.1	3,976.2	3,890.2
1985: IV	4,140.5	2,739.8	737.0	−135.5	304.7	440.2	799.2	356.9	268.6	88.3	442.4	4,107.9	4,276.0	4,156.2
1986: IV	4,336.6	2,923.1	697.1	−133.2	333.9	467.1	849.7	373.1	278.6	94.5	476.6	4,355.4	4,469.8	4,340.5
1987: IV	4,683.0	3,124.6	800.2	−143.2	392.4	535.6	901.4	392.5	295.8	96.7	509.0	4,623.7	4,826.2	4,690.5
1988: IV	5,044.6	3,398.2	814.8	−106.0	467.0	573.1	937.6	392.0	296.8	95.2	545.7	5,027.3	5,150.7	5,054.3
1989: IV	5,344.8	3,599.1	825.2	−73.9	523.8	597.7	994.5	405.1	302.5	102.6	589.3	5,314.6	5,418.7	5,365.0
1990: IV	5,597.9	3,836.6	756.4	−71.6	577.6	649.2	1,076.5	436.5	322.5	114.0	640.0	5,621.8	5,669.5	5,630.0
1991: IV	5,796.6	3,955.7	756.8	−13.7	623.7	637.5	1,097.9	438.3	311.6	126.6	659.7	5,782.3	5,810.4	5,810.7
1992: IV	6,169.3	4,251.3	822.0	−42.2	649.2	691.4	1,138.1	454.8	316.0	138.7	683.3	6,160.0	6,211.4	6,167.0
1993: I	6,235.9	4,294.6	853.8	−49.6	646.8	696.4	1,137.1	446.9	307.0	139.9	690.2	6,215.8	6,285.5	6,243.9
II	6,299.9	4,347.3	869.7	−63.3	660.1	723.5	1,146.3	445.2	305.8	139.4	701.2	6,281.4	6,363.3	6,303.3
III	6,359.2	4,401.2	882.2	−77.0	649.0	726.0	1,152.9	442.7	299.0	143.6	710.2	6,345.4	6,436.3	6,367.8
IV	6,478.1	4,469.6	922.5	−71.2	680.3	751.4	1,157.2	439.8	299.1	140.7	717.4	6,469.2	6,549.3	6,476.2
1994: I	6,574.7	4,535.0	966.6	−86.7	674.2	760.9	1,159.8	437.8	291.7	146.1	722.0	6,550.6	6,661.4	6,574.0
II	6,689.9	4,586.4	1,034.4	−97.6	704.5	802.1	1,166.7	435.1	291.7	143.5	731.5	6,622.5	6,787.5	6,682.5
III	6,791.7	4,657.5	1,055.1	−109.6	730.5	840.1	1,188.8	444.3	300.5	143.8	744.5	6,729.1	6,901.3	6,779.6
IV	6,897.2	4,734.8	1,075.6	−98.9	765.5	864.4	1,185.8	431.9	285.3	146.6	753.8	6,842.4	6,996.1	6,871.3
1995: I [r]	6,977.4	4,782.1	1,107.8	−111.1	778.8	889.9	1,198.7	434.4	283.7	150.6	764.3	6,922.9	7,088.5	6,959.5

[1] GDP less exports of goods and services plus imports of goods and services.

Source: Department of Commerce, Bureau of Economic Analysis.

DISPOSITION OF PERSONAL INCOME

According to revised estimates, per capita disposable personal income in 1987 dollars rose in the first quarter of 1995.

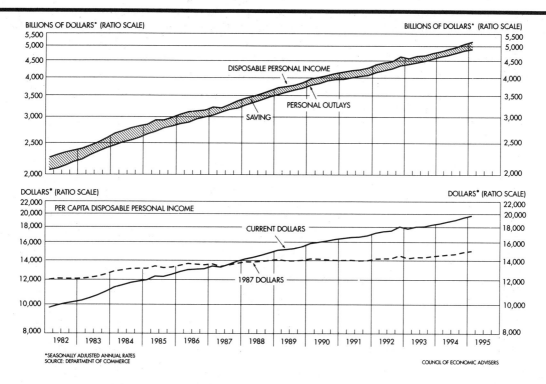

BILLIONS OF DOLLARS* (RATIO SCALE)

DISPOSABLE PERSONAL INCOME

PERSONAL OUTLAYS

SAVING

DOLLARS* (RATIO SCALE)

PER CAPITA DISPOSABLE PERSONAL INCOME

CURRENT DOLLARS

1987 DOLLARS

1982 1983 1984 1985 1986 1987 1988 1989 1990 1991 1992 1993 1994 1995

*SEASONALLY ADJUSTED ANNUAL RATES
SOURCE: DEPARTMENT OF COMMERCE

COUNCIL OF ECONOMIC ADVISERS

Period	Personal income	Less: Personal tax and nontax payments	Equals: Disposable personal income	Less: Personal outlays [1]	Equals: Personal saving	Disposable personal income in 1987 dollars (billions)	Per capita disposable personal income		Per capita personal consumption expenditures		Percent change in real per capita disposable personal income	Saving as percent of disposable personal income	Population, including Armed Forces overseas (thousands) [2]
							Current dollars	1987 dollars	Current dollars	1987 dollars			
	Billions of dollars						Dollars				Percent		
1987	3,802.0	512.5	3,289.5	3,147.5	142.0	3,289.5	13,545	13,545	12,568	12,568	− 0.1	4.3	242,860
1988	4,075.9	527.7	3,548.2	3,392.5	155.7	3,404.3	14,477	13,890	13,448	12,903	2.5	4.4	245,093
1989	4,380.3	593.3	3,787.0	3,634.9	152.1	3,464.9	15,307	14,005	14,241	13,029	.8	4.0	247,397
1990	4,673.8	623.3	4,050.5	3,880.6	170.0	3,524.5	16,205	14,101	15,048	13,093	.7	4.2	249,951
1991	4,860.3	623.7	4,236.6	4,025.0	211.6	3,538.5	16,766	14,003	15,444	12,899	− .7	5.0	252,688
1992	5,154.3	648.6	4,505.8	4,257.8	247.9	3,648.1	17,636	14,279	16,192	13,110	2.0	5.5	255,484
1993	5,375.1	686.4	4,688.7	4,496.2	192.6	3,704.1	18,153	14,341	16,951	13,391	.4	4.1	258,290
1994	5,701.7	742.1	4,959.6	4,756.5	203.1	3,835.7	19,003	14,696	17,734	13,716	2.5	4.1	260,991
	Seasonally adjusted annual rates												
1982: IV	2,746.8	372.1	2,374.7	2,190.9	183.8	2,832.6	10,189	12,154	9,134	10,895	− 0.5	7.7	233,060
1983: IV	2,965.8	371.6	2,594.3	2,417.9	176.3	2,960.6	11,033	12,591	9,980	11,390	7.2	6.8	235,146
1984: IV	3,242.5	413.4	2,829.1	2,606.5	222.6	3,118.5	11,925	13,145	10,649	11,739	1.0	7.9	237,231
1985: IV	3,456.7	448.8	3,007.9	2,828.7	179.2	3,178.7	12,565	13,278	11,445	12,095	1.8	6.0	239,387
1986: IV	3,647.8	478.5	3,169.3	3,018.2	151.1	3,266.2	13,121	13,522	12,101	12,472	− 1.7	4.8	241,550
1987: IV	3,918.5	528.6	3,389.9	3,220.1	169.8	3,335.8	13,907	13,685	12,819	12,615	5.2	5.0	243,745
1988: IV	4,195.2	542.0	3,653.2	3,496.7	156.4	3,443.1	14,850	13,996	13,814	13,020	3.2	4.3	246,004
1989: IV	4,469.4	605.1	3,864.3	3,715.5	148.8	3,480.9	15,558	14,015	14,491	13,053	1.8	3.9	248,372
1990: IV	4,759.1	625.2	4,133.9	3,957.7	176.2	3,519.0	16,467	14,018	15,283	13,010	− 1.7	4.3	251,035
1991: IV	4,934.2	631.2	4,303.0	4,078.4	224.6	3,552.1	16,957	13,998	15,588	12,868	.7	5.2	253,758
1992: IV	5,335.0	676.2	4,658.8	4,371.4	287.4	3,729.6	18,154	14,533	16,566	13,262	9.3	6.2	256,626
1993: I	5,255.5	657.3	4,598.2	4,413.7	184.6	3,658.9	17,874	14,222	16,693	13,283	− 8.3	4.0	257,262
II	5,364.5	685.9	4,678.6	4,464.6	214.0	3,701.3	18,141	14,351	16,856	13,335	3.7	4.6	257,908
III	5,395.9	695.4	4,700.5	4,518.2	182.3	3,708.4	18,174	14,338	17,017	13,425	− .4	3.9	258,635
IV.	5,484.6	707.0	4,777.6	4,588.2	189.4	3,747.8	18,421	14,451	17,233	13,519	3.2	4.0	259,356
1994: I	5,555.8	723.0	4,832.8	4,657.3	175.5	3,779.2	18,588	14,535	17,443	13,640	2.3	3.6	259,997
II	5,659.9	746.4	4,913.5	4,712.4	201.1	3,811.5	18,853	14,625	17,598	13,651	2.5	4.1	260,627
III	5,734.5	744.1	4,990.3	4,787.0	203.3	3,840.9	19,095	14,697	17,821	13,717	2.0	4.1	261,340
IV	5,856.6	754.7	5,101.9	4,869.3	232.6	3,911.0	19,473	14,927	18,072	13,853	6.4	4.6	261,999
1995: I ʳ	5,962.0	777.6	5,184.4	4,920.7	263.7	3,950.5	19,748	15,048	18,216	13,880	3.3	5.1	262,527

[1] Includes personal consumption expenditures, interest paid by persons, and personal transfer payments to rest of the world (net).

[2] Annual data are averages of quarterly data, which are averages for the period.

Source: Department of Commerce (Bureau of Economic Analysis and Bureau of the Census).

CONSUMER PRICES—ALL URBAN CONSUMERS

In May, the consumer price index for all urban consumers rose 0.3 percent seasonally adjusted (it rose 0.2 percent not seasonally adjusted). The index was 3.2 percent above its year-earlier level.

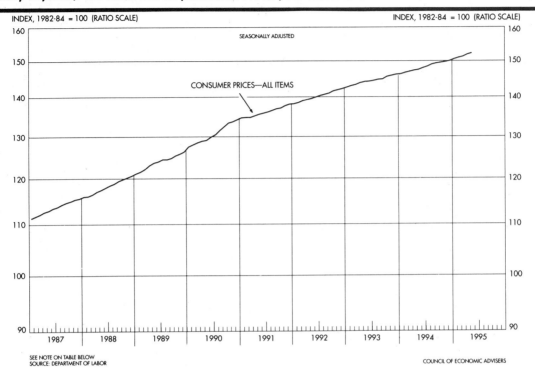

INDEX, 1982-84 = 100 (RATIO SCALE)   INDEX, 1982-84 = 100 (RATIO SCALE)

SEASONALLY ADJUSTED

CONSUMER PRICES—ALL ITEMS

SEE NOTE ON TABLE BELOW
SOURCE: DEPARTMENT OF LABOR

COUNCIL OF ECONOMIC ADVISERS

[1982–84=100, except as noted; monthly data seasonally adjusted, except as noted]

Period	All items [1]		Food	Housing							Transportation			Medical care	Energy [2]	All items less food and energy
	Not seasonally adjusted (NSA)	Seasonally adjusted		Total [1]	Shelter				Fuel and other utilities	Apparel and upkeep	Total [1]	New cars	Motor fuel			
					Total	Renters' costs (Dec. 1982=100)	Homeowners' costs (Dec. 1982=100)	Maintenance and repairs (NSA)								
Rel. imp.[3]	100.0	....	15.8	41.2	28.0	8.0	19.9	0.2	7.1	5.7	17.1	4.1	3.1	7.3	7.0	77.2
1985	107.6	....	105.6	107.7	109.8	115.4	113.1	106.5	106.5	105.0	106.4	106.1	98.7	113.5	101.6	109.1
1986	109.6	....	109.0	110.9	115.8	121.9	119.4	107.9	104.1	105.9	102.3	110.6	77.1	122.0	88.2	113.5
1987	113.6	....	113.5	114.2	121.3	128.1	124.8	111.8	103.0	110.6	105.4	114.6	80.2	130.1	88.6	118.2
1988	118.3	....	118.2	118.5	127.1	133.6	131.1	114.7	104.4	115.4	108.7	116.9	80.9	138.6	89.3	123.4
1989	124.0	....	125.1	123.0	132.8	138.9	137.3	118.0	107.8	118.6	114.1	119.2	88.5	149.3	94.3	129.0
1990	130.7	....	132.4	128.5	140.0	146.7	144.6	122.2	111.6	124.1	120.5	121.0	101.2	162.8	102.1	135.5
1991	136.2	....	136.3	133.6	146.3	155.6	150.2	126.3	115.3	128.7	123.8	125.3	99.4	177.0	102.5	142.1
1992	140.3	....	137.9	137.5	151.2	160.9	155.3	128.6	117.8	131.9	126.5	128.4	99.0	190.1	103.0	147.3
1993	144.5	....	140.9	141.2	155.7	165.0	160.2	130.6	121.3	133.7	130.4	131.5	98.0	201.4	104.2	152.2
1994	148.2	....	144.3	144.8	160.5	169.4	165.5	130.8	122.8	133.4	134.3	136.0	98.5	211.0	104.6	156.5
1994: May	147.5	147.6	143.5	144.3	159.7	168.1	164.8	131.0	122.6	133.9	132.8	135.4	95.4	209.9	102.7	156.2
June	148.0	148.1	143.9	144.4	159.8	168.5	164.9	131.5	122.6	134.7	133.7	135.9	96.1	210.7	103.0	156.7
July	148.4	148.5	144.7	144.7	160.2	168.5	165.3	131.3	122.8	134.2	134.7	136.5	98.8	211.5	104.4	157.0
Aug	149.0	149.1	145.4	145.1	160.9	169.2	166.1	131.2	123.0	133.0	136.0	136.9	101.8	212.4	105.9	157.4
Sept	149.4	149.4	145.7	145.4	161.3	169.1	166.8	131.6	122.6	133.1	136.2	137.5	101.1	213.3	105.3	157.7
Oct	149.5	149.6	145.8	145.7	161.8	169.7	167.3	130.8	122.6	132.8	136.3	137.6	100.4	214.3	105.0	158.0
Nov	149.7	149.8	146.0	145.9	162.2	170.2	167.7	131.2	122.9	132.4	136.3	137.4	101.1	215.2	105.5	158.3
Dec	149.7	150.1	147.1	145.9	162.3	170.1	167.8	132.7	122.7	132.1	136.6	137.6	101.3	216.2	105.4	158.5
1995: Jan	150.3	150.6	146.7	146.5	162.8	170.5	168.4	133.1	123.3	133.0	137.4	137.7	101.7	216.9	105.7	159.2
Feb	150.9	151.0	147.1	146.9	163.3	171.0	168.9	133.8	123.3	132.2	137.9	138.1	101.3	217.6	105.6	159.6
Mar	151.4	151.3	147.1	147.2	163.8	172.0	169.2	134.2	123.1	132.2	138.7	138.1	100.9	218.2	105.1	160.1
Apr	151.9	151.9	148.2	147.6	164.4	172.7	169.8	134.2	123.4	132.1	139.7	138.9	101.5	218.8	105.5	160.7
May	152.2	152.3	148.3	147.8	165.0	173.4	170.4	134.6	122.9	131.7	140.3	139.0	103.5	219.5	106.0	161.0

[1] Includes items not shown separately.
[2] Household fuels—gas (piped), electricity, fuel oil, etc.—and motor fuel. Motor oil, coolant, etc. excluded beginning 1983.
[3] Relative importance, December 1994.

NOTE.—Data incorporate a rental equivalence measure for homeownership costs (beginning 1983).

Source: Department of Labor, Bureau of Labor Statistics.

PERSONAL CONSUMPTION EXPENDITURES IN 1987 DOLLARS

[Billions of 1987 dollars, except as noted; quarterly data at seasonally adjusted annual rates]

Period	Total personal consumption expenditures	Durable goods				Nondurable goods						Services			Retail sales of new passenger cars (millions of units)	
		Total durable goods	Motor vehicles and parts	Furniture and household equipment	Other	Total nondurable goods	Food	Clothing and shoes	Gasoline and oil	Fuel oil and coal	Other	Total services[1]	Housing	Medical care	Domestics	Imports
1989	3,223.3	440.7	196.4	165.8	78.5	1,051.6	515.0	187.8	87.3	11.4	250.2	1,731.0	469.2	408.6	7.1	2.8
1990	3,272.6	443.1	192.7	171.6	78.7	1,060.7	523.9	186.2	86.4	10.5	253.8	1,768.8	474.6	424.6	6.9	2.6
1991	3,259.4	425.3	170.0	179.2	76.1	1,047.7	518.8	184.7	83.1	10.7	250.5	1,786.3	479.0	437.7	6.1	2.3
1992	3,349.5	452.6	181.8	193.3	77.5	1,057.7	514.7	193.2	85.6	11.2	253.0	1,839.1	485.2	454.3	6.3	2.1
1993	3,458.7	489.9	196.1	214.1	79.7	1,078.5	524.0	197.8	86.5	12.1	258.2	1,890.3	492.6	466.4	6.7	2.0
1994	3,579.6	532.1	208.2	238.7	85.2	1,109.5	535.6	208.8	87.2	11.9	265.9	1,938.1	501.3	479.0	7.3	2.0
1982: IV	2,539.3	272.3	123.7	96.4	52.3	880.7	458.3	135.7	73.4	10.5	202.8	1,386.2	411.0	327.8	6.0	2.5
1983: IV	2,678.2	319.1	151.6	109.3	58.1	915.2	467.1	147.7	76.9	11.4	212.2	1,443.9	419.7	334.8	7.4	2.6
1984: IV	2,784.8	347.7	164.3	118.7	64.8	942.9	475.1	154.7	79.0	11.1	222.9	1,494.2	431.3	344.9	7.7	2.6
1985: IV	2,895.3	369.6	173.9	128.6	67.1	968.7	488.2	161.7	79.5	11.4	228.0	1,557.1	438.1	359.1	7.0	3.1
1986: IV	3,012.5	415.7	193.6	141.4	80.7	1,000.9	496.9	171.9	84.6	12.4	235.2	1,595.8	444.8	372.0	7.7	3.4
1987: IV	3,074.7	404.7	183.6	145.9	75.2	1,014.6	502.4	174.5	85.4	11.9	240.4	1,655.5	457.0	390.7	6.6	3.3
1988: IV	3,202.9	439.2	197.7	160.3	81.2	1,046.8	518.0	182.8	87.5	12.0	246.4	1,716.9	465.6	403.0	7.5	3.0
1989: IV	3,242.0	436.8	188.3	167.9	80.5	1,058.9	515.6	190.9	88.6	12.0	251.8	1,746.3	471.3	411.8	6.2	2.6
1990: IV	3,265.9	433.2	182.1	172.3	78.8	1,057.5	525.8	184.5	84.6	9.5	253.1	1,775.2	475.9	429.4	6.6	2.4
1991: IV	3,265.3	427.7	171.6	181.2	74.9	1,040.4	514.9	182.8	82.4	10.7	249.7	1,797.3	481.4	444.7	6.1	2.2
1992: IV	3,403.4	468.8	188.2	202.0	78.6	1,074.2	522.0	198.7	86.0	11.3	256.3	1,860.4	487.8	459.0	6.4	2.0
1993: I	3,417.2	472.5	189.7	205.2	77.6	1,070.0	520.7	194.0	86.1	12.0	257.2	1,874.8	489.8	463.1	6.4	2.0
II	3,439.2	483.7	195.1	209.9	78.7	1,074.3	522.3	196.1	85.7	11.8	258.3	1,881.2	491.5	464.3	6.9	2.1
III	3,472.2	492.7	195.0	216.6	81.1	1,081.7	525.1	198.6	87.5	12.2	258.4	1,897.8	493.7	467.6	6.7	2.0
IV	3,506.2	510.8	204.7	224.6	81.5	1,088.0	528.1	202.4	86.6	12.2	258.8	1,907.4	495.4	470.4	7.1	1.9
1994: I	3,546.3	521.7	213.7	225.9	82.0	1,098.3	531.9	203.8	86.1	13.4	263.1	1,926.3	497.7	473.2	7.4	2.0
II	3,557.8	522.2	205.3	232.5	84.4	1,104.3	536.1	204.9	86.7	11.4	265.1	1,931.4	500.0	477.4	7.2	2.0
III	3,584.7	529.6	202.0	241.7	86.0	1,113.4	535.7	210.2	88.0	11.7	267.8	1,941.8	502.6	481.0	7.1	2.0
IV	3,629.6	554.8	211.9	254.5	88.4	1,121.9	538.5	216.4	88.2	11.1	267.6	1,952.9	505.0	484.4	7.4	1.8
1995: I r	3,643.9	550.0	203.2	256.6	90.3	1,128.2	541.1	216.6	90.3	11.5	268.7	1,965.7	507.4	486.9	7.0	1.8
II	....	....	....	....	....	....	....	....	....	....	....	....	....	....	6.9	1.8

[1] Includes other items, not shown separately.

Source: Department of Commerce, Bureau of Economic Analysis.

CONSUMER INSTALLMENT CREDIT

[Millions of dollars; seasonally adjusted]

Period	Installment credit outstanding (end of period)				Net change in installment credit outstanding[1]			
	Total	Automobile	Revolving	Other[2]	Total	Automobile	Revolving	Other[2]
1985: Dec	517,659	210,238	121,758	185,664	75,057	36,674	21,478	16,906
1986: Dec	572,006	247,772	135,825	188,408	54,347	37,534	14,067	2,744
1987: Dec	608,675	266,295	153,064	189,316	36,669	18,523	17,239	908
1988: Dec[3]	662,553	285,364	174,269	202,921	53,878	19,069	21,205	13,605
1989: Dec	717,200	291,531	199,162	226,508	(4)	(4)	(4)	(4)
1990: Dec	734,898	283,072	223,517	228,309	17,698	-8,459	24,355	1,801
1991: Dec	728,389	259,594	245,281	223,514	-6,509	-23,478	21,764	-4,795
1992: Dec	731,098	257,678	257,304	216,117	2,709	-1,916	12,023	-7,397
1993: Dec	794,300	282,036	287,875	224,389	63,202	24,358	30,571	8,272
1994: Dec	911,311	324,519	337,694	249,098	117,011	42,483	49,819	24,709
1994: May	836,936	298,278	305,528	233,130	13,594	5,260	4,268	4,066
June	847,715	303,526	309,472	234,717	10,779	5,248	3,944	1,587
July	854,469	305,193	313,591	235,685	6,753	1,666	4,119	968
Aug	869,628	309,721	321,365	238,542	15,159	4,528	7,773	2,857
Sept	879,961	315,162	322,823	241,976	10,333	5,441	1,459	3,434
Oct	891,603	318,036	327,707	245,860	11,642	2,875	4,883	3,884
Nov	904,757	323,447	334,843	246,467	13,154	5,411	7,136	607
Dec	911,311	324,519	337,694	249,098	6,554	1,072	2,851	2,631
1995: Jan	920,338	324,855	343,184	252,299	9,027	336	5,490	3,200
Feb	928,010	327,720	349,487	250,803	7,672	2,865	6,303	-1,496
Mar r	942,149	330,187	356,185	255,778	14,140	2,467	6,698	4,975
Apr p	953,188	332,693	362,644	257,850	11,039	2,506	6,460	2,073

[1] For year-end data, change from preceding year-end; for monthly data, change from preceding month.
[2] Outstanding loans for mobile homes, education, boats, trailers, vacations, etc.
[3] Data newly available in January 1989 result in breaks in many series between December 1988 and subsequent months.
[4] Because of breaks in series, net change not available.

Source: Board of Governors of the Federal Reserve System.

EMPLOYMENT, UNEMPLOYMENT, AND WAGES

STATUS OF THE LABOR FORCE

In June, employment rose by 166,000 and unemployment fell by 108,000.

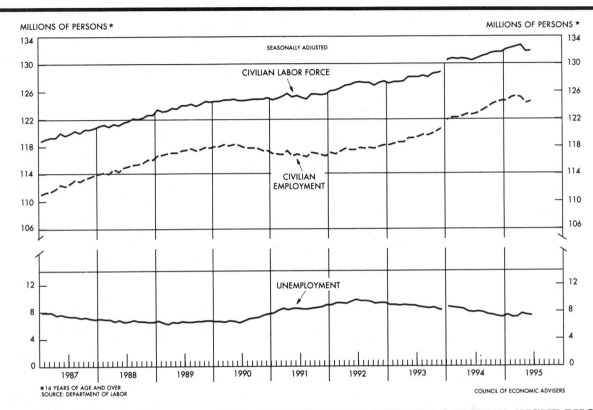

MILLIONS OF PERSONS *

SEASONALLY ADJUSTED

CIVILIAN LABOR FORCE

CIVILIAN EMPLOYMENT

UNEMPLOYMENT

★16 YEARS OF AGE AND OVER
SOURCE: DEPARTMENT OF LABOR

COUNCIL OF ECONOMIC ADVISERS

SELECTED MEASURES OF UNEMPLOYMENT AND UNEMPLOYMENT INSURANCE PROGRAMS

In June, the percentages of the unemployed who had been out of work for less than 5 weeks and for 5–14 weeks rose, while the percentages for 15–26 weeks and for 27 weeks and over fell. The mean duration of unemployment fell to 15.6 weeks and the median duration fell to 7.5 weeks.

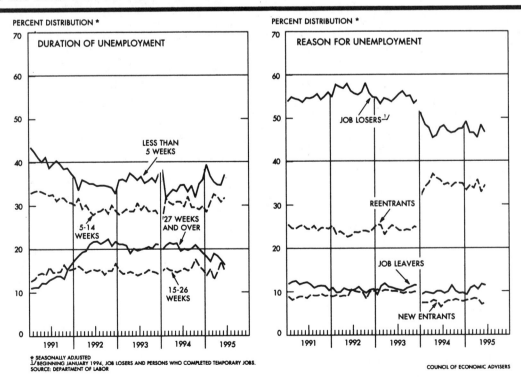

PERCENT DISTRIBUTION *

DURATION OF UNEMPLOYMENT

LESS THAN 5 WEEKS

5-14 WEEKS

'27 WEEKS AND OVER

15-26 WEEKS

PERCENT DISTRIBUTION *

REASON FOR UNEMPLOYMENT

JOB LOSERS ¹/

REENTRANTS

JOB LEAVERS

NEW ENTRANTS

* SEASONALLY ADJUSTED
1/ BEGINNING JANUARY 1994, JOB LOSERS AND PERSONS WHO COMPLETED TEMPORARY JOBS.
SOURCE: DEPARTMENT OF LABOR

COUNCIL OF ECONOMIC ADVISERS

Share of Aggregate Income and Mean Income in 1967 to 1992 Received by Each Fifth and Top 5 Percent of Households, by Race and Hispanic Origin of Householder

(Households as of March of the following year. Mean incomes are in 1992 CPI-U-X1 dollars)

Year	Number (thous.)	Percent distribution of aggregate income						Mean income (dollars)						Mean income (dollars)	Gini ratio
		Lowest fifth	Second fifth	Third fifth	Fourth fifth	Highest fifth	Top 5 percent	Lowest fifth	Second fifth	Third fifth	Fourth fifth	Highest fifth	Top 5 percent	Mean income (dollars)	Gini ratio
TOTAL															
1992	96,391	3.8	9.4	15.8	24.2	46.9	18.6	7,328	18,281	30,794	47,235	91,494	145,244	39,020	0.433
1991	95,669	3.8	9.6	15.9	24.2	46.5	18.1	7,482	18,695	31,055	47,340	90,783	141,672	39,064	0.428
1990	94,312	3.9	9.6	15.9	24.0	46.6	18.6	7,723	19,354	31,968	48,199	93,537	148,948	40,150	0.428
1989	93,347	3.8	9.5	15.8	24.0	46.8	18.9	7,944	19,688	32,727	49,504	96,772	156,350	41,321	0.431
1988	92,830	3.8	9.6	16.0	24.3	46.3	18.3	7,714	19,351	32,366	48,926	93,406	147,315	40,343	0.427
1987[1]	91,124	3.8	9.6	16.1	24.3	46.2	18.2	7,616	19,247	32,179	48,639	92,500	145,734	40,027	0.426
1986	89,479	3.8	9.7	16.2	24.3	46.1	18.0	7,391	19,013	31,817	47,931	90,723	142,123	39,375	0.425
1985	88,458	3.9	9.8	16.2	24.4	45.6	17.6	7,320	18,551	30,792	46,317	86,518	133,460	37,899	0.419
1984[2]	86,789	4.0	9.9	16.3	24.6	45.2	17.1	7,340	18,284	30,299	45,620	83,884	126,627	37,086	0.415
1983[2]	85,290	4.0	9.9	16.4	24.6	45.1	17.1	7,118	17,880	29,562	44,361	81,446	123,057	36,074	0.414
1982	83,918	4.0	10.0	16.5	24.5	45.0	17.0	7,030	17,788	29,445	43,792	80,319	121,364	35,675	0.412
1981	83,527	4.1	10.1	16.7	24.8	44.4	16.5	7,166	17,851	29,572	44,082	78,742	117,011	35,483	0.406
1980	82,368	4.2	10.2	16.8	24.8	44.1	16.5	7,347	18,287	30,176	44,456	79,265	118,452	35,907	0.403
1979[3]	80,776	4.1	10.2	16.8	24.7	44.2	16.9	7,595	18,891	31,147	45,707	82,028	125,102	37,073	0.404
1978	77,330	4.2	10.2	16.9	24.7	44.1	16.8	7,659	18,811	31,059	45,499	81,231	123,643	36,852	0.402
1977	76,030	4.2	10.2	16.9	24.7	44.0	16.8	7,403	18,223	30,145	44,168	78,763	120,492	35,741	0.402
1976[4]	74,142	4.3	10.3	17.0	24.7	43.7	16.6	7,445	18,227	29,976	43,531	77,045	117,389	35,245	0.398
1975[5]	72,867	4.3	10.4	17.0	24.7	43.6	16.6	7,262	17,840	29,268	42,529	75,088	113,948	34,398	0.397
1974[5][6]	71,163	4.3	10.6	17.0	24.6	43.5	16.5	7,523	18,699	30,133	43,520	77,106	117,201	35,397	0.395
1973	69,859	4.2	10.5	17.1	24.6	43.6	16.6	7,556	18,923	30,920	44,450	78,833	120,138	36,136	0.397
1972	68,251	4.1	10.5	17.1	24.5	43.9	17.0	7,214	18,637	30,414	43,660	78,385	121,489	35,663	0.401
1971	66,676	4.1	10.6	17.3	24.5	43.5	16.7	6,810	17,998	29,183	41,488	73,513	112,751	33,799	0.396
1970	64,374	4.1	10.8	17.4	24.5	43.3	16.6	6,767	18,327	29,514	41,604	73,663	113,065	33,974	0.394
1969	63,401	4.1	10.9	17.5	24.5	43.0	16.6	6,876	18,574	29,680	41,570	73,070	112,475	33,953	0.391
1968	61,805	4.2	11.1	17.5	24.4	42.8	16.6	6,721	18,019	28,577	39,868	69,823	108,102	32,600	0.388
1967[7]	60,446	4.0	10.8	17.3	24.2	43.8	17.5	6,184	17,134	27,357	38,275	69,362	110,559	31,662	0.399
WHITE															
1992	82,083	4.1	9.7	16.0	24.1	46.2	18.3	8,275	19,827	32,527	49,117	94,191	149,546	40,780	0.423
1991	81,675	4.1	9.9	16.0	24.1	45.8	17.9	8,434	20,142	32,660	49,099	93,268	145,404	40,713	0.418
1990	80,968	4.2	10.0	16.0	23.9	46.0	18.3	8,677	20,800	33,464	49,871	96,071	153,234	41,770	0.419
1989	80,163	4.1	9.8	16.0	23.8	46.3	18.7	8,892	21,186	34,371	51,219	99,573	161,174	43,042	0.422
1988	79,734	4.1	10.0	16.2	24.1	45.6	18.0	8,667	20,971	34,136	50,644	95,946	151,498	42,064	0.416
1987[1]	78,519	4.1	10.0	16.3	24.2	45.5	17.9	8,574	20,850	33,983	50,422	94,907	149,654	41,738	0.415
1986	77,284	4.1	10.0	16.3	24.2	45.4	17.8	8,257	20,498	33,497	49,653	93,168	146,053	41,015	0.415
1985	76,576	4.1	10.1	16.4	24.3	45.1	17.4	8,070	19,933	32,349	47,933	88,990	137,378	39,455	0.411
1984	75,328	4.3	10.2	16.5	24.4	44.6	16.8	8,128	19,718	31,895	47,220	86,118	130,016	38,616	0.405
1983[2]	74,170	4.3	10.3	16.5	24.4	44.5	16.8	7,940	19,295	31,087	45,916	83,666	126,462	37,581	0.404
1982	73,182	4.2	10.3	16.6	24.4	44.4	16.7	7,749	19,153	30,917	45,367	82,539	124,458	37,146	0.403
1981	72,845	4.4	10.4	16.8	24.7	43.8	16.3	7,924	19,217	31,162	45,620	80,930	120,277	36,970	0.397
1980	71,872	4.4	10.5	17.0	24.6	43.5	16.3	8,098	19,688	31,717	45,963	81,309	121,466	37,356	0.394
1979[3]	70,766	4.4	10.5	17.0	24.5	43.7	16.7	8,325	20,268	32,684	47,179	84,226	128,534	38,535	0.396
1978	68,028	4.4	10.5	17.0	24.5	43.6	16.6	8,322	20,081	32,514	46,885	83,290	127,153	38,218	0.394
1977	66,934	4.4	10.5	17.0	24.6	43.5	16.7	7,987	19,555	31,670	45,640	80,828	123,908	37,137	0.394
1976[4]	65,353	4.5	10.6	17.2	24.5	43.2	16.5	8,052	19,493	31,416	44,927	79,114	120,809	36,601	0.391
1975[5]	64,392	4.5	10.7	17.1	24.6	43.2	16.4	7,836	19,043	30,601	43,835	77,038	117,205	35,669	0.390
1974[5][6]	62,984	4.5	10.9	17.1	24.4	43.0	16.4	8,121	19,996	31,490	44,874	79,065	120,261	36,708	0.387
1973	61,965	4.4	10.8	17.3	24.5	43.1	16.4	8,150	20,302	32,400	45,913	80,892	123,479	37,533	0.389
1972	60,618	4.3	10.8	17.2	24.3	43.4	16.8	7,795	20,034	31,893	45,019	80,515	124,842	37,050	0.393
1971	59,463	4.3	11.0	17.4	24.4	43.0	16.5	7,341	19,242	30,482	42,708	75,345	115,752	35,023	0.389
1970	57,575	4.2	11.1	17.5	24.3	42.9	16.5	7,300	19,554	30,740	42,800	75,429	116,102	35,163	0.387
1969	56,602	4.3	11.3	17.6	24.3	42.5	16.4	7,442	19,934	31,037	42,852	75,004	115,890	35,253	0.383
1968	55,394	4.4	11.4	17.6	24.3	42.3	16.5	7,253	19,303	29,783	40,988	71,531	111,261	33,772	0.381
1967[7]	54,188	4.1	11.2	17.4	24.0	43.3	17.3	6,656	18,405	28,535	39,400	70,981	113,342	32,795	0.391

See footnotes at end of table.

Share of Aggregate Income and Mean Income in 1967 to 1992 Received by Each Fifth and Top 5 Percent of Households, by Race and Hispanic Origin of Householder

(Households as of March of the following year. Mean incomes are in 1992 CPI-U-X1 dollars)

Year	Number (thous.)	Percent distribution of aggregate income						Mean income (dollars)						Mean income (dollars)	Gini ratio
		Lowest fifth	Second fifth	Third fifth	Fourth fifth	Highest fifth	Top 5 percent	Lowest fifth	Second fifth	Third fifth	Fourth fifth	Highest fifth	Top 5 percent		
BLACK															
1992	11,190	3.1	7.8	14.7	24.8	49.7	19.2	3,930	9,853	18,625	31,474	63,178	97,430	25,409	0.471
1991	11,083	3.1	7.8	15.0	25.2	48.9	18.3	3,982	10,119	19,386	32,467	63,056	94,657	25,797	0.464
1990	10,671	3.1	7.9	15.0	25.1	49.0	18.5	4,124	10,475	20,020	33,376	65,207	98,651	26,637	0.464
1989	10,486	3.2	8.0	15.0	24.9	48.9	18.2	4,292	10,857	20,409	33,809	66,388	98,750	27,149	0.461
1988	10,561	3.3	7.7	14.6	24.7	49.7	18.7	4,398	10,321	19,433	32,914	66,294	99,845	26,657	0.468
1987[1]	10,192	3.3	7.9	14.8	24.4	49.7	19.3	4,241	10,267	19,327	31,860	64,980	100,601	26,135	0.468
1986	9,922	3.1	8.0	14.9	25.0	49.0	18.6	4,004	10,328	19,327	32,350	63,486	96,477	25,899	0.464
1985	9,797	3.5	8.3	15.2	25.0	48.0	17.6	4,406	10,511	19,118	31,453	60,568	88,783	25,211	0.450
1984	9,480	3.6	8.4	15.0	24.7	48.4	17.6	4,328	10,192	18,149	29,972	58,661	85,220	24,260	0.450
1983[2]	9,243	3.5	8.3	15.1	25.1	47.9	17.1	4,117	9,728	17,704	29,401	56,065	80,053	23,403	0.448
1982	8,916	3.6	8.6	15.3	25.5	47.1	17.1	4,124	9,894	17,692	29,437	54,404	79,192	23,110	0.442
1981	8,961	3.7	8.5	15.2	25.3	47.3	16.6	4,246	9,876	17,597	29,248	54,697	76,955	23,133	0.440
1980	8,847	3.7	8.7	15.3	25.2	47.1	16.9	4,388	10,309	18,263	30,043.	56,076	80,421	23,815	0.439
1979[3]	8,586	3.8	8.8	15.5	25.3	46.6	16.5	4,658	10,850	19,090	31,243	57,417	81,492	24,651	0.433
1978	8,066	3.9	8.7	15.6	25.3	46.5	16.5	4,889	10,902	19,519	31,606	58,082	82,617	24,998	0.431
1977	7,977	4.2	9.2	15.5	24.9	46.3	16.8	4,962	10,966	18,548	29,789	55,512	80,395	23,955	0.425
1976[4]	7,776	4.2	9.1	15.7	25.4	45.6	16.3	4,906	10,867	18,742	30,301	54,415	77,996	23,846	0.421
1975[5]	7,489	4.1	9.0	16.0	25.5	45.4	16.0	4,763	10,440	18,439	29,398	52,388	73,850	23,085	0.419
1974[5][6]	7,263	4.2	9.4	16.1	25.2	45.1	15.8	4,871	11,016	18,885	29,444	52,852	74,056	23,413	0.414
1973	7,040	4.1	9.4	16.0	25.1	45.5	16.6	4,893	11,245	19,110	30,007	54,435	79,463	23,937	0.419
1972	6,809	3.9	9.2	15.8	24.9	46.2	16.9	4,648	10,864	18,710	29,529	54,768	79,873	23,702	0.427
1971	6,578	4.0	9.4	16.1	25.1	45.4	16.4	4,450	10,518	18,161	28,242	51,133	73,737	22,500	0.419
1970	6,180	3.7	9.3	16.3	25.2	45.5	16.4	4,240	10,731	18,667	28,930	52,264	75,382	22,968	0.422
1969	6,223	3.9	9.7	16.5	25.1	44.7	15.9	4,366	10,868	18,456	28,053	49,824	71,051	22,313	0.411
1968	5,870	4.0	10.0	16.3	25.1	44.9	15.9	4,265	10,532	17,536	27,070	48,327	68,632	21,547	0.412
1967[7]	5,728	3.8	9.3	15.9	24.3	46.7	18.2	3,931	9,682	16,596	25,366	48,730	75,855	20,859	0.432
HISPANIC ORIGIN[8]															
1992	6,626	3.9	9.4	15.7	24.1	46.9	18.1	5,737	13,679	22,801	35,093	68,215	105,304	29,102	0.430
1991	6,379	4.0	9.4	15.8	24.3	46.5	17.7	5,926	14,032	23,460	36,111	69,202	105,519	29,741	0.427
1990	6,220	4.0	9.5	15.9	24.3	46.3	17.9	6,057	14,215	23,915	36,414	69,556	107,577	30,027	0.425
1989	5,933	3.8	9.5	15.7	24.4	46.6	18.1	5,971	15,116	24,942	38,653	73,764	114,967	31,672	0.430
1988	5,910	3.7	9.3	15.6	24.2	47.2	19.0	5,657	14,388	24,083	37,239	72,795	116,964	30,827	0.437
1987[1]	5,642	3.7	9.1	15.5	24.1	47.6	19.2	5,689	13,993	23,651	36,828	72,930	117,640	30,612	0.441
1986	5,418	3.9	9.5	15.8	24.8	46.1	16.9	5,744	14,030	23,464	36,737	68,344	100,089	29,664	0.424
1985	5,213	4.1	9.4	16.1	24.8	45.6	16.6	5,839	13,438	22,840	35,212	64,946	94,493	28,455	0.418
1984	4,883	3.9	9.5	16.2	24.9	45.5	16.9	5,527	13,565	23,076	35,535	64,953	96,446	28,531	0.420
1983[2]	4,666	4.1	9.6	16.3	24.8	45.2	16.4	5,612	13,143	22,197	33,754	61,549	89,127	27,251	0.413
1982	4,085	4.2	9.6	16.1	24.6	45.5	17.0	5,682	13,210	22,162	33,848	62,549	93,279	27,491	0.417
1981	3,980	4.4	10.3	16.6	24.7	44.0	15.9	6,243	14,667	23,818	35,369	62,951	91,257	28,610	0.398
1980	3,906	4.3	10.1	16.4	24.8	44.5	16.5	6,143	14,420	23,248	35,193	63,220	93,612	28,425	0.405
1979[3]	3,684	4.5	10.5	16.6	24.5	44.0	16.3	6,679	15,689	24,782	36,673	65,768	97,471	29,918	0.396
1978	3,291	4.7	10.7	16.9	24.9	42.8	15.5	6,757	15,514	24,441	36,110	62,075	89,811	28,979	0.385
1977	3,304	4.9	10.7	16.9	24.6	42.9	15.6	6,771	14,982	23,518	34,347	59,856	86,962	27,894	0.383
1976[4]	3,081	4.7	10.4	16.8	25.1	43.0	15.4	6,264	13,926	22,476	33,516	57,362	82,394	26,709	0.387
1975[5]	2,948	4.7	10.6	16.8	24.8	43.1	16.1	6,109	13,948	22,081	32,606	56,622	84,799	26,273	0.388
1974[5][6]	2,897	5.1	10.9	17.1	24.7	42.3	15.4	7,080	15,152	23,886	34,399	58,931	86,105	27,890	0.376
1973	2,820	5.1	11.1	17.1	24.7	42.0	15.0	7,184	15,828	24,279	35,111	59,604	85,277	28,402	0.371
1972	2,698	5.3	11.2	17.2	24.0	42.3	16.2	7,255	15,446	23,788	33,201	58,458	89,340	27,630	0.373

[1]Implementation of a new March CPS processing system.
[2]Implementation of Hispanic population weighting controls.
[3]Implementation of 1980 census population controls. Questionnaire expanded to show 27 possible values from 51 possible sources of income.
[4]First year medians are derived using both pareto and linear interpolation. Prior to this year all medians were derived using linear interpolation.
[5]These estimates were derived using pareto interpolation and may differ from published data which were derived using linear interpolation.
[6]Implementation of a new March CPS processing system. Questionnaire expanded to ask eleven income questions.
[7]Implementation of a new March CPS processing system.
[8]Persons of Hispanic origin may be of any race. Income data for Hispanic origin households are not available prior to 1972.

NOTE: The changes listed above are discussed in more detail in a paper, "Effects of the March Current Population Survey's New Processing System on Estimates of Income and Poverty," by Edward J. Welniak, Jr., published in the American Statistical Association Meeting Proceedings, 1990.

FEDERAL FINANCE

FEDERAL RECEIPTS, OUTLAYS, AND DEBT

In the first 8 months of fiscal 1995, there was a deficit of $133.2 billion, compared with a deficit of $164.7 billion a year earlier.

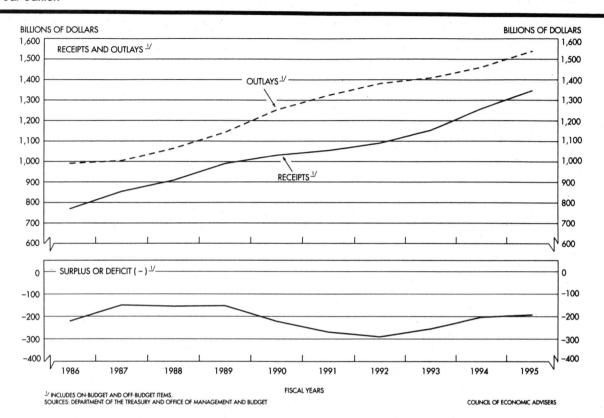

BILLIONS OF DOLLARS

RECEIPTS AND OUTLAYS [1]

OUTLAYS [1]

RECEIPTS [1]

SURPLUS OR DEFICIT (-) [1]

FISCAL YEARS

[1] INCLUDES ON-BUDGET AND OFF-BUDGET ITEMS.
SOURCES: DEPARTMENT OF THE TREASURY AND OFFICE OF MANAGEMENT AND BUDGET

COUNCIL OF ECONOMIC ADVISERS

[Billions of dollars]

Fiscal year or period	Total			On-budget			Off-budget			Gross Federal debt (end of period)	
	Receipts	Outlays	Surplus or deficit (-)	Receipts	Outlays	Surplus or deficit (-)	Receipts	Outlays	Surplus or deficit (-)	Total	Held by the public
1976	298.1	371.8	-73.7	231.7	302.2	-70.5	66.4	69.6	-3.2	629.0	477.4
1977	355.6	409.2	-53.7	278.7	328.5	-49.8	76.8	80.7	-3.9	706.4	549.1
1978	399.6	458.7	-59.2	314.2	369.1	-54.9	85.4	89.7	-4.3	776.6	607.1
1979	463.3	504.0	-40.7	365.3	404.1	-38.7	98.0	100.0	-2.0	829.5	640.3
1980	517.1	590.9	-73.8	403.9	476.6	-72.7	113.2	114.3	-1.1	909.1	709.8
1981	599.3	678.2	-79.0	469.1	543.1	-74.0	130.2	135.2	-5.0	994.8	785.3
1982	617.8	745.8	-128.0	474.3	594.4	-120.1	143.5	151.4	-7.9	1,137.3	919.8
1983	600.6	808.4	-207.8	453.2	661.3	-208.0	147.3	147.1	.2	1,371.7	1,131.6
1984	666.5	851.8	-185.4	500.4	686.0	-185.7	166.1	165.8	.3	1,564.7	1,300.5
1985	734.1	946.4	-212.3	547.9	769.6	-221.7	186.2	176.8	9.4	1,817.5	1,499.9
1986	769.1	990.3	-221.2	568.9	806.8	-238.0	200.2	183.5	16.7	2,120.6	1,736.7
1987	854.1	1,003.9	-149.8	640.7	810.1	-169.3	213.4	193.8	19.6	2,346.1	1,888.7
1988	909.0	1,064.1	-155.2	667.5	861.4	-194.0	241.5	202.7	38.8	2,601.3	2,050.8
1989	990.7	1,143.2	-152.5	727.0	932.3	-205.2	263.7	210.9	52.8	2,868.0	2,189.9
1990	1,031.3	1,252.7	-221.4	749.7	1,027.6	-278.0	281.7	225.1	56.6	3,206.6	2,410.7
1991	1,054.3	1,323.4	-269.2	760.4	1,081.8	-321.4	293.9	241.7	52.2	3,598.5	2,688.1
1992	1,090.5	1,380.9	-290.4	788.0	1,128.5	-340.5	302.4	252.3	50.1	4,002.1	2,998.8
1993	1,153.5	1,408.7	-255.1	841.6	1,142.1	-300.5	311.9	266.6	45.3	4,351.4	3,247.5
1994	1,257.7	1,460.9	-203.2	922.7	1,181.5	-258.8	335.0	279.4	55.7	4,643.7	3,432.2
1995 (estimates)	1,346.4	1,538.9	-192.5	995.2	1,246.9	-251.8	351.3	292.0	59.3	4,961.5	3,640.1
Cumulative total, first 8 months: [1]											
Fiscal year 1994	801.3	966.0	-164.7	580.1	781.7	-201.5	221.2	184.4	36.8	4,562.4	3,393.5
Fiscal year 1995	870.2	1,003.4	-133.2	635.9	812.1	-176.1	234.2	191.3	42.9	4,851.3	3,574.9

[1] Data from *Monthly Treasury Statement.*

Sources: Department of the Treasury and Office of Management and Budget.

NOTE.—Data (except as noted) are from *Budget of the United States Government, Fiscal Year 1996*, issued February 6, 1995.

U.S. INTERNATIONAL TRANSACTIONS

In the first quarter of 1995, the merchandise trade deficit rose to $45.1 billion, from $43.5 billion in the fourth quarter of 1994. The current account deficit fell to $40.5 billion, from $43.3 billion in the fourth quarter. (Series revised.)

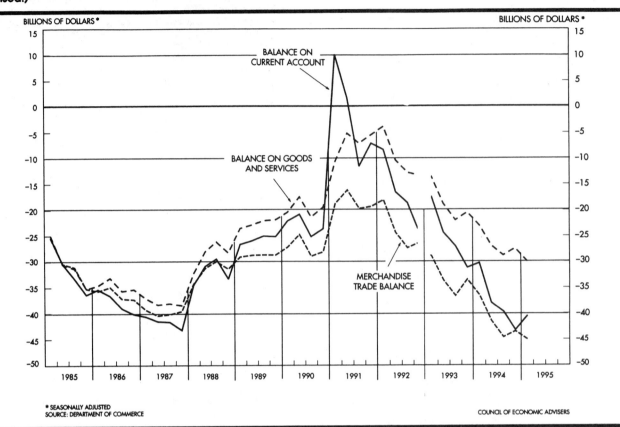

BILLIONS OF DOLLARS *

* SEASONALLY ADJUSTED
SOURCE: DEPARTMENT OF COMMERCE

COUNCIL OF ECONOMIC ADVISERS

[Millions of dollars; quarterly data seasonally adjusted, except as noted. Credits (+), debits (−)]

Period	Merchandise [1]			Services			Balance on goods and services	Investment income			Balance on goods, services, and income	Unilateral transfers, net [4]	Balance on current account
	Exports	Imports	Net balance	Net military transactions [2][3]	Net travel and transportation receipts	Other services, net		Receipts on U.S. assets abroad	Payments on foreign assets in U.S.	Net			
1981	237,044	−265,067	−28,023	−844	144	12,552	−16,172	86,529	−53,626	32,903	16,732	−11,702	5,030
1982	211,157	−247,642	−36,485	112	−992	13,209	−24,156	86,200	−56,412	29,788	5,632	−17,075	−11,443
1983	201,799	−268,901	−67,102	−563	−4,227	14,095	−57,796	84,778	−53,700	31,078	−26,719	−17,741	−44,460
1984	219,926	−332,418	−112,492	−2,547	−8,438	14,277	−109,200	104,075	−74,036	30,038	−79,161	−20,612	−99,773
1985	215,915	−338,088	−122,173	−4,390	−9,798	14,266	−122,095	92,760	−73,087	19,673	−102,422	−22,950	−125,372
1986	223,344	−368,425	−145,081	−5,181	−7,382	18,855	−138,789	90,858	−79,095	11,763	−127,026	−24,176	−151,201
1987	250,208	−409,765	−159,557	−3,844	−6,481	17,900	−151,981	99,239	−91,302	7,937	−144,045	−23,052	−167,097
1988	320,230	−447,189	−126,959	−6,315	−1,511	19,961	−114,824	127,414	−115,806	11,607	−103,217	−24,977	−128,194
1989	362,116	−477,365	−115,249	−6,726	5,071	26,558	−90,345	152,517	−138,858	13,659	−76,686	−26,134	−102,820
1990	389,303	−498,336	−109,033	−7,567	8,978	28,811	−78,810	160,300	−139,574	20,725	−58,085	−33,663	−91,748
1991	416,913	−490,981	−74,068	−5,485	17,957	33,124	−28,472	136,914	−122,081	14,833	−13,639	6,687	−6,952
1992	440,361	−536,458	−96,097	−3,034	20,885	37,862	−40,384	114,449	−109,909	4,540	−35,844	−32,042	−67,886
1993 ͬ	456,823	−589,441	−132,618	448	19,885	37,444	−74,841	119,248	−110,248	9,000	−65,841	−34,084	−99,925
1994 ͬ	502,485	−668,584	−166,099	2,148	19,330	38,410	−106,212	137,619	−146,891	−9,272	−115,484	−35,761	−151,245
1993: I ͬ	111,862	−140,821	−28,959	401	5,302	9,683	−13,573	28,950	−25,239	3,711	−9,862	−7,521	−17,383
II ͬ	114,131	−147,718	−33,587	90	5,389	9,315	−18,793	29,958	−27,893	2,065	−16,728	−7,609	−24,337
III ͬ	111,576	−148,181	−36,605	283	5,062	9,272	−21,988	29,931	−26,741	3,190	−18,798	−8,234	−27,032
IV ͬ	119,254	−152,721	−33,467	−326	4,131	9,172	−20,490	30,412	−30,376	36	−20,454	−10,722	−31,176
1994: I ͬ	118,445	−154,935	−36,490	−31	4,642	8,863	−23,016	30,942	−30,826	116	−22,900	−7,371	−30,271
II ͬ	122,730	−164,224	−41,494	376	4,647	9,548	−26,923	32,338	−34,623	−2,285	−29,208	−8,778	−37,986
III ͬ	127,384	−172,011	−44,627	1,124	4,792	9,904	−28,807	36,031	−38,564	−2,533	−31,340	−8,374	−39,714
IV ͬ	133,926	−177,414	−43,488	679	5,247	10,095	−27,467	38,307	−42,878	−4,571	−32,038	−11,239	−43,277
1995: I ͬ	138,059	−183,111	−45,052	621	4,523	9,885	−30,023	42,511	−45,209	−2,698	−32,721	−7,782	−40,503

[1] Adjusted from Census data for differences in timing and coverage; excludes military.
[2] Transfers under U.S. military agency sales contracts (exports) minus direct defense expenditures (imports).
[3] Quarterly data are not seasonally adjusted.
[4] Includes transfers of goods and services under U.S. military grant programs.

See p. 37 for continuation of table.

Glossary

This glossary of economic terms is included to provide you with a convenient and ready reference as you encounter general terms in your study of economics that are unfamiliar or require a review. It is not intended to be comprehensive, but taken together with the many definitions included in the articles themselves it should prove to be quite useful.

Absolute advantage: A condition that exists when one producer can produce a product more efficiently than the first producer. The two producers benefit when each produces the product in which it has an absolute advantage and trades part of its output for the other product.

Affirmative action program: A program devised by employers to increase their hiring of women and minorities; frequently mandated by government regulations.

Aggregate concentration: A measure of the proportion of the total sales of all industries accounted for by the largest firms in the country. There is no common standard for measuring the aggregate concentration ratio.

Aggregate demand: The total effective demand for the nation's total output of goods and services.

Aggregate supply: The total amount of goods and services available from all industries in the economy.

Allocation: A decision as to what is to be produced with the resources of an economy or who is to get what is produced.

Alternative indicators: A more realistic measures of economic progress than the traditional Gross National Product (GNP). GNP tells only how much a nation is producing, but not whether it is using up nonrenewable resources.

Annually balanced budget: A budgetary principle calling for the revenue and expenditures of a government to be equal during the course of a year.

Antitrust legislation: Laws that prohibit or limit monopolies or monopolistic practices.

Appropriate technology: A term used by economist E. F. Schumacher to describe methods and techniques that will render the highest productive capacity with the smallest possible level of resource usage.

Arbitrage: The simultaneous buying and selling of two or more currencies in different markets for purposes of gain. The most prevalent forms are exchange and interest rate.

Area chart: A chart in which filled areas compare the magnitude of data series, frequently over time.

Authoritarian (state) socialism: A command economy in which all of the means of production are in the hands of the state and decision making is centralized.

Automatic stabilizers: Changes in government payments and tax receipts that automatically result from fluctuations in national income and act to aid in offsetting those fluctuations.

Automatic transfer services (ATS): A type of account that provides for the depository institution to automatically transfer funds from the depositor's savings account to her or his checking account when it has been drawn down.

Automation: Production techniques that adjust automatically to the needs of the processing operation by the use of control devices.

Average costs: Total costs divided by the number of units produced.

Average propensity to consume (APC): The percentage of after-tax income that, on the average, consumers spend on goods and services.

Average propensity to save (APS): The percentage of after-tax income which, on the average, consumers save.

Average revenue: Can be computed by dividing total revenue by the number of units produced and sold.

Average total cost of production (ATC): The cost of all the inputs used per unit of output.

Average variable cost of production (AVC): The cost of all the variable inputs used per unit of output.

Balance of payments: An annual summary of all economic transactions between a country and the rest of the world during the year.

Balance of trade: The net deficit or surplus in a country's merchandise trade; the difference between merchandise imports and exports.

Bar chart: A chart, similar to a column chart turned on its side, used to compare sizes and amounts or emphasize differences in amounts, usually at the same point in time.

Barrier to entry: An obstacle to the entry of new firms into an industry.

Barter: Direct exchange of goods and services without the use of money.

Base period (base year): The reference period for comparison of subsequent changes in an index series; set equal to 100.

Basic deficit: The excess of import-type transactions over export-type transactions in a country's current, long-term capital and noninduced, short-term capital movements in the balance of payments.

Benefits principle: Levy of a tax on an individual to pay the costs of government service in proportion to the individual's benefit from the service.

Bilateral trade negotiations: Trade negotiations between two countries only.

Black market: Transactions that evade government controls and taxation, and are thus illegal.

Bond: A long-term, interest-bearing certificate issued by a business firm or by a government that promises to pay the bondholder a specified sum of money on a specified date.

Boycott: Refusal by consumers to buy the products or services of a firm.

Break-even point: The output level of a firm where total revenue equals total costs (TR = TC).

Buddhist economics: Popularized by British economist E. F. Schumacher, it is the systematic study of how to attain given ends with the least possible means. The aim is to maximize human well-being with a minimum of consumption.

Business cycles, phases: The phases of change an economy usually experiences from slump to recovery. The four typical phases used to describe economic activity in industrial nations are: depression, recovery, recession, and prosperity.

Business transfer payments: Outlay by business for which no good or service is exchanged, such as excise taxes, payouts under deferred compensation arrangements, gifts, and donations.

Capital: The means of production including factories, office buildings, machinery, tools, and equipment; alternatively, it can mean financial capital, the money to acquire the foregoing and employ land and labor resources.

Capital consumption allowances: The costs of capital assets consumed in producing GNP.

Capital equipment: The machinery and tools used to produce goods and services.

Capital gains: Net income from the sale of an asset, such as stocks.

Capitalism: An economic system based on the right of private ownership of most of the means of production, such as businesses, farms, mines, and natural resources, as well as private property, such as homes and automobiles.

Capital output ratio: The ratio of the cost of new investment goods to the value of the annual output produced by those investment goods.

Capital saving: The effect of an innovation or invention that lowers the share of capital (inventory, property, or money) relative to the share of labor used in a business or industry. (An example of a capital-saving device would be the use of leased equipment in business.)

Capital stock: The actual amount of physical capital and inventories in existence at a given time, or, in terms of business organizations, a source of funds used for capital.

Cartel: An industry in which the firms have an agreement to set prices and/or divide the market among members of the cartel.

Celler-Kefauver Act: The 1950 law that amends sections of the Clayton Act, which forbade mergers through stock acquisition only.

Central bank: A government institution that controls the issuance of currency, provides banking services to the government and to the other banks, and implements the nation's monetary policy; in the United States the Federal Reserve System acts as the central bank.

Central planning: A method of resource allocation in which top leadership makes the major decisions on production, distribution, and coordination.

Centrally directed (command) economy: An economic system in which the basic questions of what, how, and for whom to produce are resolved primarily by governmental authority.

Certificate of deposit (CD): A deposit of a specified sum of money for a specified period of time that cannot be redeemed prior to the date specified.

Chart: A graphic representation of statistical data or other information.

Check: A written order to a depository institution to pay a person or institution named on it a specified sum of money.

Circular flow diagram: A schematic drawing showing the economic relationships between the major sectors of an economic system.

Civil Aeronautics Board (CAB): A semi-independent regulatory body that is responsible for the economic regulation of commercial air transportation.

Civil Rights Act of 1964: Federal legislation declaring it unlawful to discriminate against a person on the basis of race, sex, or age.

Clayton Antitrust Act: Adopted in 1914 as a companion law to the Sherman Antitrust Act, it prohibits price discrimination by a seller where the effect may injure competitors; tying contracts and exclusive dealerships where the effect lessens competition; acquisition of stock of a rival business where the effect is to reduce competition; and interlocking directorates among competing firms of a certain size.

Collective bargaining: A process by which decisions regarding the wages, hours, and conditions of employment are determined by the interaction of workers acting through their unions and employers.

Collectivization: The process of consolidating small or individual holdings into larger, cooperatively run enterprises.

Collusion: An agreement or conspiracy, usually secret, among nominal competitors to engage in anticompetitive practices in violation of antitrust laws.

Commodity: An economic good.

Commodity markets: Large-scale, organized exchanges, similar to stock markets, where vast quantities of goods are exchanged.

Communism: According to Karl Marx, the last stage of economic development after the state has withered away and work and consumption are engaged in communally; today frequently used to designate state socialist economies.

Comparative advantage: Gains from international trade are maximized when each nation specializes in the production of those goods in which its comparative advantage is greatest (or comparative disadvantage least).

Complement: A product that is employed jointly in conjunction with another product.

Computer-integrated manufacturing (CIM): A system of integrating all the operations of different departments in a plant by means of a central computer and a network of workstatiom computers.

Concentration ratio: A measure of the extent to which a market or industry is dominated by a few firms. The most widely-used concentration ratios are those published by the Commerce Department as part of the various censuses of business.

Conglomerate merger: The joining of two firms that do not produce the same good or service (or close substitutes) nor outputs at different stages of the same production process.

Conspicuous consumption: The practice of consuming goods or services far beyond one's needs to demonstrate wealth, power and success. Thorstein Veblen coined the phrase in *Theory of the Leisure Class* (1899).

Constant dollar GNP (Real GNP): The value of GNP adjusted for changes in the price level since a base period.

Constant value: Refers to a national income account adjusted for price changes. What remains is a dollar measure that changes only because of changes in the quantities of goods and services.

Consumer equilibrium: The condition in which consumers allocate their income in such a way that the last dollar spent on each good or service and the last dollar saved provide equal amounts of utility.

Consumer price index (CPI): A statistical measure of changes in the prices of a representative sample of urban family purchases relative to a previous period.

Consumer Product Safety Commission (SPSC): A semi-independent federal agency created in 1972 to establish mandatory safety standards for products and to monitor the design, construction, contents, performance, and labeling of consumer products. A five-member commission, appointed by the president and confirmed by the Senate, which develops regulations to enforce standards and imposes product bans.

Consumer sovereignty: The theory that states that, in a free-market economy, the consumer determines which goods and services will be produced.

Consumer tastes and preferences: Individual liking or partiality for specific goods or services.

Consumer surplus: The difference between the total utility received from a product and the total market value of that product. The surplus is received by the consumer, but not at the expense of the producer.

Consumption: The amount spent by households on currently produced goods and services.

Consumption-investment mix: The percentage of shares of the national product going respectively to consumption and investment.

Convergence hypothesis: Contends that market economies and command economies are both changing in the direction of becoming identical.

Cooperative: Producer and worker cooperatives are associations in which the members join in production and marketing and share the profits. Consumer cooperatives are associations of consumers engaged in retail trade, sharing the profits as a dividend among the members.

Corporation: A business enterprise that is chartered by a state government or, occasionally, by the federal government to do business as a legal entity.

Correspondent bank: A bank in another city or country that a bank has an arrangement with to provide deposit transfer or other services.

Cost of living adjustment (COLA): A frequently used provision of labor contracts that grants wage increases based on changes in the consumer price index; often referred to in negotiations as the "escalator clause."

Cost of living index: *See* Consumer price index.

Cost-benefit analysis: A comparison of all the costs of a project to the value of the benefits of that project.

Cost-push inflation: A continuing rise in the general price level that results from increases in production costs.

Creative financing: Any new method to raise capital for an enterprise without use of bank loans, stock offerings, or other conventional steps. Also, the myriad new methods developed because of high interest rates for financing house purchases.

Credit card: An economic instrument extended by businesses and banks that allows the acquisition of something of value in exchange for the promise to return its equivalent (payment) at some time in the future.

Crowding out: The term given to the effect government has in reducing the amount of financial capital available for private investment.

Currency: That part of the money supply consisting of coins and paper bills.

Currency appreciation: An increase in the value of a country's currency relative to other currencies as a result of a decrease in its supply relative to the demand for it.

Currency depreciation: A decline in the value of a country's currency as a result of an increase in its supply relative to the demand for it.

Current value: GNP is normally defined in terms of current market value, or the quantities of various outputs—final goods and services—multiplied by their respective prices and summed together.

Cyclical balanced budget: A budgetary principle calling for the balancing of the budget over the course of a complete business cycle rather than in a particular fiscal or calendar year; over the course of the cycle, tax receipts and expenditures would balance.

Cyclical unemployment: The lack of work that occurs because the total effective demand for goods and services is insufficient to employ all workers in the labor force.

Debit card: An economic instrument issued by the creditor that shows the amount of debt to be incurred.

Deficit: A negative balance after expenditures are subtracted from revenues.

Deflation: A decrease in the general level of prices or an increase in the value of money in terms of goods and services.

Demand: The relationship between the quantities of a good or service that consumers desire to purchase at any particular time and the various prices that can exist for the good or service.

Demand curve: A graphic representation of the relationship between price and quantity demanded.

Demand deposits (checking accounts): Liabilities of depository institutions to their customers that are payable on demand.

Demand schedule: A table recording the number of units of a commodity demanded per unit of time at various money prices.

Demand theory: A plausible explanation of the manner in which purchasers of commodities respond to price changes. It is an empirical fact that consumers purchase more of a good or service at a low price than at a high price.

Demand-pull inflation: A continuing rise in the general price level that occurs when aggregate demand exceeds the full-employment output capacity of the economy.

Democratic (liberal) socialism: An economic system that combines state ownership of at least some of the means of production and a set of democratic political institutions.

Depository institutions: Financial institutions that maintain deposit account obligations to customers; includes commercial banks, savings banks, savings and loan associations, and credit unions.

Depreciation: Reduction in value, quality, and usefulness of a fixed asset (plant or equipment) because of physical deterioration, destruction, or obsolescence resulting from technological development.

Depression: *See* Business cycles, phases.

Deregulation: The process of eliminating government regulations and reducing the scope and power of regulatory bodies.

Derived demand: *See* Factor demand.

Design for manufacturability and assembly (DFMA): A system of designing products in which the design engineers consult with manufacturing personnel during the designing process to avoid designs that will be difficult or costly to manufacture.

Devaluation: A decrease in the value of a country's currency relative to other currencies due to an official government reduction in the exchange rate under a fixed rate system.

Diagram: A graph that shows the relationship between two or more variables that may or may not have values that can actually be measured; a graphic model.

Differentiated competition: An industry in which there are a large number of firms producing similar but not identical products; sometimes called monopolistic competition.

Differentiated products: Similar but not identical products produced by different firms.

Diminishing marginal utility: *See* Demand theory.

Diminishing returns: *See* Law of diminishing returns.

Direct controls: Government control of individual prices and wages, prohibiting increases without the authorization of the controlling agency.

Direct relationship: A relationship between two variables in which their values increase and decrease together.

Discount rate: The interest rate charged by the Federal Reserve on loans to depository institutions.

Discounting: Assigning a present value to future returns; making a loan with the interest subtracted in advance from the principal.

Discretionary fiscal policy: Fiscal policy measures activated by overt decisions.

Disposable income: The amount of after-tax income that households have available for consumption or saving.

Diversification: The process in which a business firm increases the variety of products it produces and sells, either by introducing new products into the same product line or market, or by going into new product lines or markets.

Dumping: Occurs when a nation sells export products in foreign countries more cheaply than the same products are sold domestically.

Dynamic efficiency: Efficiency over a period of time with changing resources and levels of technology.

Earned income: Wages, salaries, and other employee compensation plus earnings from self-employment.

Earned income tax credit (EITC): A federal tax credit for poor families with earnings that offset their tax liabilities and, for the poorest, provides a tax subsidy.

Econometrics: A subdiscipline of economics that describes the ways in which statistics and modeling can be combined to explain economic relationships. Such a model relates economic theory to actual economic events.

Economic concept: A word or phrase that conveys an economic idea.

Economic good: Any good or service that sells for a price; that is, not a free good.

Economic growth: An increase in the production capacity of the economy.

Economic imperialism: The practice of expansionism where control of a country is maintained through economic power rather than through political action or military force.

Economic model: A simplified representation of the cause and effect relationships in a particular situation. Models may be in verbal, graphic, or equation form.

Economic profits: Earnings on invested capital that are in excess of the normal rate of return.

Economic rent: Any payment to an owner of a productive resource that is an amount in excess of the payment needed to keep the resource in its current use.

Economic surplus: A margin of output over and above consumption needs that can be allocated to investment for intensive growth.

Economies of scale: Decreasing costs per unit as plant size increases.

Effective demand: The desire and the ability to purchase a certain number of units of a good or service at a given price.

Efficiency: Maximizing the amount of output obtained from a given amount of resources used for a given amount of output.

Elastic (demand): A demand condition in which the relative size of the change in quantity demanded is greater than the size of the price change.

Elasticity ratio: A measurement of the degree of the response of a change in quantity to a change in price.

Employee involvement (EI): Various programs for incorporating hourly-wage workers in decision making; may involve decisions on production methods, work scheduling, purchase of capital equipment, etc.

Entrepreneur: A business innovator who sees the opportunity to make a profit from a new product, new process, or unexploited raw material and then brings together the land, labor, and capital to exploit the opportunity, risking failure.

Environmental Protection Agency (EPA): A department within the executive branch charged with enforcing the nation's laws relating to the improvement and maintenance of a good environment.

Equal Employment Opportunity Commission (EEOC): An independent federal agency established in 1965 to prohibit employment discrimination on the basis of race, color, national origin, religion, sex or physical limitation. The enforcement body for the equal employment provisions of the Civil Rights Act of 1964.

Equation of Exchange: *See* Quantity equation.

Equilibrium: Applies to virtually all economic units in the economy, to the relationships among them, and to the economy as a whole; when aggregate demand is just equal to aggregate supply. Equilibrium positions occur in three levels of economic analysis—analysis of individual decision makers, market analysis, and analysis of an entire economic system.

Equilibrium price: The price at which the quantity of a good or service offered by suppliers is exactly equal to the quantity that is demanded by purchasers in a particular period of time.

Equilibrium quantity: The quantity of a good that the producers are willing to supply and the consumers are willing to purchase at a given price.

Equity (housing): The owner's share of the value of property or other assets, net of mortgages or other liabilities.

Excess demand: Occurs when a commodity price is below the equilibrium.

Excess reserves: Reserves of depository institutions over and above the legally required minimum on deposit with the Federal Reserve.

Excess supply: Occurs when a commodity price is above the equilibrium.

Exchange rate: The value of a nation's currency measured in the number of units of a foreign currency for which it can be exchanged.

Excise taxes: A tax on a particular type of good or service; a sales tax.

Export (X): Domestically produced good or service sold abroad.

Extensive growth: Economic growth that results from an increase in population and in proportionate quantities of other factor inputs; does not generally raise a country's standard of living.

External costs: Costs of the production process that are not carried by the producer unit or by the purchaser of the product and are therefore not taken into consideration in production and consumption decisions. Air pollution represents an external cost of production.

External economies: Benefits that accrue to parties other than the producer and purchaser of the good or service; benefits for which payment is not collected.

Externalities: Exists when the decisions of the producers or consumers of a good or service impose direct costs or benefits on persons or firms other than the decision maker. Also called spillover effects, neighborhood effects, or external costs or benefits.

Factor demand: The demand for a factor of production, not because it directly provides utility, but because it is needed to produce finished products that do provide utility.

Factor incomes: The return to factors of production as a reward for productive activity.

Factor market: A market in which resources and semifinished products are exchanged.

Factor share: The part of national income received by a particular factor of production.

Factors of production (factor inputs): Land, labor, and capital, synonymous with production inputs.

Fair Labor Standards Act: The federal Wage and House law adopted by Congress in 1938 that set a minimum wage for most American workers. It also mandates overtime pay beyond an eight hour work day or over 40 hours a week.

FED: Federal Reserve System.

FED Board of Governors: The governing body of the Federal Reserve System consisting of seven members appointed by the president for 14-year terms.

Federal Communications Commission (FCC): An independent federal agency that regulates radio and television broadcasting and interstate and foreign telephone and telegraph services. A seven member commission, appointed by the president to seven year terms, grants broadcast licenses, and regulates common carriers in the communications industry.

Federal Deposit Insurance Corporation (FDIC): A U.S. government agency that insures deposits up to $100,000 in savings and commercial banks if a participating bank fails.

Federal funds market: The market among depository institutions for temporary transfer of excess reserves from one institution to another.

Federal Open Market Committee: A committee consisting of the Federal Reserve Board and the presidents of five regional Federal Reserve banks that decides on the purchase or sale of government securities by the Federal Reserve to implement monetary policy.

Federal Reserve Board of Governors: The governing body of the Federal Reserve System consisting of seven members appointed by the U.S. president for 14-year terms.

Federal Reserve System (FED): The central bank of the United States; a system established by the Federal Reserve Act of 1913 to issue paper currency, supervise the nation's banking system, and implement monetary policy.

Federal Trade Commission (FTC): The federal agency responsible for enforcement of antitrust laws in conjunction with the Antitrust Division, Department of Justice. The FTC, with a five member governing board and national network of offices, attempts to counter deceptive actions and practices and anticompetitive behavior among business through its regulations.

Financial capital: The money to acquire the factors of production.

First-tier wage industry: An industry in which both the firms and the unions have extensive market power, and as a result wages in the industry are above the average for all industries.

Fiscal federalism: Tax collection and disbursement of funds by a higher level of government to lower jurisdictions.

Fiscal policy: The use of federal government spending, taxing, and debt management to influence general economic activity.

Fixed costs: Production costs that do not change with changes in the quantity of output.

Food and Drug Administration (FDA): An agency within the U.S Health and Human Services (HHS) Department that is responsible for the protection of the public from health hazards posed by harmful or mislabeled foods, cosmetics, medical devices, and drugs.

Foreign sector: Economic transactions with nations abroad.

Foreign-exchange market: A set of institutions, including large banks in the world's financial centers, private brokers, and government central banks and other agencies, that deal in the exchange of one country's money for another's.

Fourth world: The poorest countries of the underdeveloped regions that do not have intensive growth or any valuable export resources.

Free enterprise: A microeconomic concept referring to a business firm privately owned and operated for profit. Under the free enterprise system most of the goods and services are provided by the private sector.

Free good: A production or consumption good that does not have a direct cost.

Free trade: International trade that is unrestricted by government protectionist measures.

Freely-fluctuating exchange rates: An exchange-rate system by which the relative values of different currencies are determined by demand and supply rather than by government fiat.

Frictional unemployment: The lack of work that occurs from time lost changing jobs.

Fringe benefits: Non-wage returns to workers for labor services; includes time off with pay for holidays, vacations, and sick leave, retirement benefits, health care, and similar benefits.

Full employment: Employment of nearly everyone who desires to work. In practice, an unemployment level of not more than 4–5 percent is considered full employment.

Full employment aggregate demand: The level of total effective demand that is just sufficient to employ all workers in the labor force.

Full Employment and Balanced Growth Act (1978): A federal law enacted by Congress that set forth national goals for employment, economic growth, and development.

Functional finance: The use of fiscal policy to stabilize the economy without regard to the policy's effect on a balanced government budget.

Functional income distribution: The shares of total income distributed according to the type of factor service for which they are paid, e.g., rent as a payment for land, wages for labor, and interest for capital.

Gandhian economics: Gandhi developed economics that combined ethics with economics in order to maximize the welfare of all. His system was committed to the pursuit of truth (dharma) rather than self-interest (artha).

General Agreement on Tariffs and Trade (GATT): An organization established in 1947 composed of most non-Communist nations. GATT negotiations have periodically reduced tariffs for all member nations under the most favored nation principle, which extends any tariff concession one nation extends to another to all participating countries.

Giveback: Withdrawal of a labor benefit prior to the end of a collective bargaining agreement by mutual agreement of the employer and the union, normally to avoid closure of plants due to business losses.

Gold standard: A monetary system under which a country defines its currency as a given weight of gold. The system provides a mechanism by which anyone can exchange any form of domestic currency and gold at that official value and does not interfere with domestic or international movement of gold. By 1936, all countries had abandoned the gold standard.

Government Spending (G): Spending by the various levels of government on goods and services, including public investment.

Great Depression: A period of worldwide economic crisis during the 1930s that closed banks, created 25 percent unemployment, and led to government intervention in the U.S. economy.

Great Leap Forward: A 1958 attempt by the Chinese leadership to accelerate the rate of economic development by maximizing investment in industrial growth, which resulted in an economic and food crisis.

Gross National Product (GNP): The sum of the values of all goods and services produced during the year.

Gross investment or gross private domestic investment (I): Private sector spending on capital equipment, increased stocks of inventories, and new residential housing.

Headcount index: The percentage of the population below the poverty line.

High-technology: Production processes that utilize modern techniques and are capital-intensive with a large investment in equipment per worker.

Horizontal merger: The joining of two firms that produce the same good or service, or close substitutes.

Household: An economic unit consisting of an individual or a family.

Human capital: Labor that is literate, skilled, trained, healthy, and economically motivated.

Hyperinflation: A condition in which prices rise faster and faster and people spend more money before it buys less; also known as runaway inflation.

Hypothesis: A tentative explanation of an event; used as a basis for further research.

Implicit interest: Income that derives from the use of capital but is not paid as interest but rather as a part of accounting profits.

Implicit wages: Income that is the result of labor input but is not received in the form of wages or salaries, but in some other form such as net proprietor's income (profits).

Import (M): Good or service purchased from foreign suppliers.

Import-competing industry: A domestic industry that produces the same or a close substitute good that competes in the domestic market with imports.

Incentive: A motivation to undertake an action or to refrain from undertaking an action; in a market economy profits are the incentive to produce.

Income: The return to a factor of production as a reward for productive activity.

Income effect: The change in demand of a good or service as a result of a change in the consumer's income.

Incomes policy: Any policy that has an effect on real income, the purchasing power of individuals' money incomes.

Increasing costs: A rise in average production costs as the quantity of output of the good increases.

Index number: A percentage or ratio of two observations, the denominator being the base item in a cross section or the base period in a time series. The observations could be prices, quantities, or values.

Index of leading economic indicators: An index that includes 12 economic variables that have been found to have a historical tendency to precede the turning points of the level of Gross National Product. The index is a composite of those 12 indicators.

Indexing: A system of adjusting incomes in line with inflation.

Indicative planning: A method used by governments to improve the performance of the economy by providing economic information in the form of forecasts or targets for industries and, possibly, providing incentives for selected industries.

Indicators: Statistical time series, or groups of series, used by economists to predict future economic activity. Most indicators may be categorized as coincident, lagging, or leading.

Indirect taxes: Taxes that are ultimately paid in full or in part by someone other than the business from which the tax is collected; not income taxes.

Individual Retirement Accounts (IRA): A personal savings investment account on which income taxes are not paid until the money is withdrawn at or after age 59 1/2 or death.

Industrial production index: A monthly measurement of physical output, compiled and published by the Board of Governors of the Federal Reserve System.

Industrial Revolution: Dramatic technological and social changes that occurred in the nineteenth century that altered economies, began the process of mass production and led to the modern industrial age.

Industry consortium: A combination of firms in an industry to carry out a common purpose.

Inelastic Demand: A demand condition in which the relative size of the change in the quantity demanded is less than the size of the price change.

Infant industry argument: The contention that it is economically justified to provide trade protection to a new industry's early stages of growth until it can compete with established foreign rivals.

Inflation: A continuously rising general price level, resulting in a loss of the purchasing power of money.

Infrastructure: An economy's stock of capital—much of it publicly owned—that provides basic services to producers and consumers. Includes highways, electric power, water supplies, educational facilities, health services, etc.

In-kind income: Income in a form other than money.

Institutions: Decision-making units, established practices, or laws.

Intensive growth: Economic growth that results from increased productivity and raises a country's standard of living.

Interdependence: The relationship between individuals and institutions in a country or between countries that arises because of specialization of production.

Interest: A factor payment for the use of capital.

Internalize external costs: The process of transforming external costs into internal costs so that the producer and consumer of a good pay the full cost of its production.

International Monetary Fund (IMF): An organization established in 1946 to assist in the operation of the world monetary system by regulating the exchange practices of countries and providing liquidity to member countries that have payment problems.

Interstate Commerce Act of 1887: 19th century law enacted by Congress to curb monopolistic and discriminatory shipping practices to railroads and to prohibit arrangements among competing railroads for sharing traffic and earnings. The law also created an Interstate Commerce Commission.

Interstate Commerce Commission (ICC): A regulatory body established in 1887 to regulate railroads, interstate trucking, inland water transport, and other transportation firms.

Inventories: The value of finished and semifinished goods and raw materials in the hands of producers and distributors.

Inverse relationship: A relationship between two variables in which the value of one decreases as the value of the other increases.

Investment: Spending by businesses on currently produced goods (I) in national income accounting and development economics; in finance, the purchase of stocks, bonds, and other titles to property.

Invisible hand: A concept used by Adam Smith that states that individuals who freely pursue their own self interests will automatically promote the interests of society.

Job action: A concerted action by employees to disrupt production or distribution in order to put pressure on employers to grant concessions.

Junk bonds: Bonds that are issued paying higher than normal interest rates because they have a greater risk of default.

Jurisdictional dispute: Conflicts between unions as to which one shall represent a certain group of workers.

Just-in-time: A system that provides for raw materials and subassemblies to be delivered by suppliers to the location where they will be processed at the time they are needed rather than being stored in inventories.

Keogh Plan: A tax sheltered retirement account for those who are self-employed.

Keynesian economics: The body of macroeconomic theories and policies that stem from the model developed by John Maynard Keynes.

Kinked demand curve: An analytical approach using certain assumptions to explain price rigidity in oligopolistic markets.

L: A measure of the money supply that includes M3 plus commercial paper, savings bonds, and government securities with maturities of 18 months or less.

Labor: All human resources including manual, clerical, technical, professional, and managerial labor.

Labor force: All members of the working-age population who are either employed or seeking or awaiting employment.

Laffer curve: An economic model developed by economist Arthur Laffer that purports to show a relationship between marginal tax rates and the level of total tax revenue.

Laffer Effect: The impact of cutting marginal tax rates postulated by economist Arthur Laffer who says the release of revenue into the economy will stimulate new production and therefore result in more tax revenues at lower rates.

Laissez-faire: A concept of nonintervention by government developed by the eighteenth-century French physiocrats in reaction against mercantilism and incorporated into classical economic writings by Adam Smith and others.

Land: All natural resources including fields, forests, mineral deposits, the sea, and other gifts of nature.

Law of demand: The quantity demanded of a good or service varies inversely with its price; the lower the price the larger the quantity demanded, and the higher the price the smaller the quantity demanded.

Law of diminishing returns: The common condition in which additional inputs produce successively smaller increments of output.

Law of Supply: The quantity supplied of a good or service varies directly with its price; the lower the price the smaller the quantity supplied, and the higher the price the larger the quantity supplied.

Leading indicator: An economic measurement or time series of one aggregate of economic activity that precedes a change in total economic activity. Leading indicators include new durable goods orders, average weekly state unemployment insurance claims, and new building permits.

Learning curve: A diagram showing how labor productivity or labor costs change as the total number of units produced by a new plant or with new technology increases over time.

Less developed countries (LDCs): Nonindustrialized countries, primarily located in Africa, Asia, or Latin America, generally characterized by poverty income levels, a labor force primarily employed in

agriculture, extensive underemployment, illiteracy, and high rates of population growth.

Leverage: A concept used to describe the effect of an increase in sales or the price on a firm's profits. There are two kinds of leverage: operating leverage, which looks at the ratio of fixed costs for a firm, and financial leverage, which is defined as the proportion of the firm's assets that have been raised by borrowing.

Limited liability: A legal provision that protects individual stockholders of a corporation from being sued by creditors of the corporation to collect unpaid debts of the firm.

Line graph: A graph in which points on a line show the relationship of two variables.

Liquidity: The degree of ease with which an asset can be converted into cash without appreciable loss in value.

Long run: A period of time long enough for all factors of production to be variable (but not so long, however, that the basic technology in use can be changed).

Long-term capital: Direct investment in plant and equipment or portfolio investments in stocks and bonds.

Lorenz curve: A diagram showing the distribution of income among groups of people; an indicator of the degree of inequality of income distribution.

Macroeconomics: The area of economic studies that deals with the overall functioning of an economy, total production output, employment, and the price level.

Marginal analysis: An analytical technique frequently used in economics in which small increments in quantities are examined.

Marginal cost: The addition to total cost from the production of an additional unit of output.

Marginal revenue: The rate at which total revenue varies as sales quantity varies and can be thought of as the difference in revenue between selling an additional unit and not selling that unit.

Marginal tax rate: The incremental tax burden due to an incremental change in the tax base.

Marginal utility: The amount of satisfaction a consumer derives from consuming one additional unit (or the last unit consumed) of a particular good or service.

Marginalist school: A significant development in Neoclassical economic theory that led to the market theory of supply and demand, the acceptance of the equilibria concept and possible expansion of economic theory through the use of differential calculus.

Market: *See* Marketplace.

Market concentration: A measure of the number of firms in an industry.

Market economy: An economic system in which the basic questions of what, how, and for whom to produce are resolved primarily by buyers and sellers interacting in markets.

Market system: An economic system that relies predominantly on a market mechanism to determine allocation of scarce resources, production techniques, pricing, distribution of goods and services to members of society, and so on.

Marketplace (market): A network of dealings between buyers and sellers of a resource or product (good or service); the dealings may take place at a particular location or they may take place by communicating at a distance with no face-to-face contact between buyers and sellers.

Marxism: An economic theory and philosophy named for Karl Marx (1818-1883), the founder of "scientific" socialism and leader of the revolutionary movement to overturn capitalism. Marxian economics use the labor theory of value wherein the value of the commodity consists of capital (raw materials and depreciation), variable capital (labor), and surplus value (profit).

Maximum profit level: The output level of a firm where the revenue from one additional unit of production (marginal revenue) is equal to the cost of producing that unit (marginal cost).

Medicaid: A federally subsidized, state-administered program to pay for medical and hospital costs of low-income families.

Medium of exchange: *See* Money.

Mercantilism: A doctrine that dominated policies in many countries from the sixteenth to the eighteenth centuries which held that exports should be maximized and imports minimized to generate an inflow of gold, and exports of machinery and technology should be prohibited to prevent competition from foreign producers.

Merger: A contractual joining of the assets of one formerly independent business firm with another, frequently by the purchase by one company of a controlling share of the stock of another company.

Merit goods: Result when intellectually or morally elite groups override individual preferences.

Microeconomics: The area of economic studies that deals with individual units in an economy, households, business firms, labor unions, and workers.

Minimum wage laws: Federal or state laws that prohibit employers from paying less than a specified hourly wage to their employees.

Mixed economy: An economic system in which the basic questions of what, how, and for whom to produce are resolved by a mixture of market forces with governmental direction and/or custom and tradition.

Model: A simplified representation of the cause and effect relationships in a particular situation. Models may be in verbal, graphic, or equation form.

Monetarism: Economic theory that emphasizes the importance of changes in the money supply and their impact on the aggregate economy. Closely linked to economist Milton Friedman, monetarism employs the equation of exchange ($PQ = MV$) as an analytical device.

Monetarists: Those who believe that changes in the money supply have a determinative effect on economic conditions.

Monetary Control Act: Officially known as the Deposit Institutions and Monetary Control Act of 1980, the law extended the Federal Reserve Board's control over the economy and lifted some restrictions on savings deposits.

Monetary policy: Actions of the Federal Reserve Board to produce changes in the money supply, the availability of loanable funds, or the level of interest rates in an attempt to influence general economic activity.

Money: A commodity that is accepted by common consent in payment for goods and services and as settlement of debts and contracts.

Money market mutual fund: An investment fund that pools the assets of investors and puts the cash into debt securities that mature in less than one year; short-term bank CDs, commercial paper of corporations, 6-month Treasury bills.

Money multiplier: The ratio of the maximum increase in the money supply to an increase in bank reserves. Determined by the required reserve ratio.

Money supply: There are four measures of the money supply used by the Federal Reserve System. M1 is the narrowest definition with L the broadest in scope:

M1: A measure of the money supply that includes currency in circulation, demand deposit accounts, negotiable order of withdrawal (NOW) accounts, automatic transfer savings (ATS) accounts, traveler's checks, and checkable money market accounts.

M1-A: A measure of the money supply that includes currency in circulation and demand deposit accounts in commercial banks only.

M1-B: A measure of the money supply that includes currency in circulation and checkable deposit accounts in commercial banks, savings banks, savings and loan associations, and credit unions.

M2: A measure of the money supply which includes M1 plus savings deposits, small time deposits (CDs), and certain money market mutual funds.

M3: A measure of the money supply which includes M2 plus large time deposits (CDs).

L: M3, plus other liquid assets such as term Euro-dollars held by non bank U.S. residents, bankers' acceptances, commercial paper, Treasury bills and other liquid government instruments, and U.S. savings bonds.

Monopolistic pricing: Setting a price above the level necessary to bring a product to market by restricting the supply of the product.

Most-favored nation clause: Any tariff reduction (called tariff concession) that one member grants to another that must also be extended to other members.

Multilateral trade negotiations: Simultaneous trade negotiations between a number of countries.

Multinational company: A firm based in one country with operations in one or more additional countries.

Multiplier: The ratio of the ultimate increase in income, caused by an initial increase in spending, to that initial increase.

National debt: The amount of money owed by the government of a country through the practice of borrowing.

National economic plan: A plan drawn up by a national planning board or agency covering a specific period of time setting forth economic goals to be achieved and providing for actions in the public and private sectors to achieve these goals.

National income (NI): The total of all incomes earned in producing the Gross National Product.

National income accounts: The collective name for various macro-economics measurements such as GNP and national income.

National Labor Relations Board: Independent regulatory agency empowered to prevent and remedy unfair labor practices by employers or by union organizations and to ensure fair union representation.

Nationalized industries: Industries that have been transformed from private to public ownership.

Natural monopoly: An industry in which the economies of scale are so extensive that a single firm can supply the whole market more efficiently than two or more firms could; natural monopolies are generally public utilities.

Natural rate hypothesis: The hypothesis that there is a long-run level of real gross national product (GNP) that exists independent of the inflation rate.

Near MONEY: Assets with a specified monetary value that can be readily redeemable as money; savings accounts, certificates of deposit, and shares in money market mutual funds.

Negative Income Tax: An income maintenance plan that would provide a guaranteed minimum income for eligible families with no other income, and a supplement for families with incomes below a predetermined level.

Negotiable Order of Withdrawal (NOW) Accounts: Savings and loan bank customer accounts on which checks can be drawn.

Neomercantilists: Contemporary advocates of mercantilist trade policies to restrict imports, maximize exports of consumer products, and restrict exports of capital equipment and technology to prevent competition from foreign producers.

Net exports (X × M): The value of goods and services exported minus the amount spent on imported goods and services.

Net value: The market value of a worker's output after subtracting the other production costs, such as raw materials.

Nonearned income: Dividends, interest, capital gains, and other non-labor income.

Nontariff barriers: Restrictions on imports resulting from requirements for special marking, test, or standards enforced on imported goods or the time delays in clearing them for importation.

Normal rate of return: The rate of earnings on invested capital that is normal for a given degree of risk.

Occupational Safety and Health Administration (OSHA): An agency of the U.S. Department of Labor created to encourage employers and employees to reduce workplace hazards and enforce on-the-job safety and health standards.

Oligopoly: A shared monopoly in which there is no explicit agreement among the firms.

Open-market operations: The purchase or sale of government securities by the Federal Reserve to implement monetary policy.

Opportunity cost: Real economic cost of a good or service produced measured by the value of the sacrificed alternative.

Partnership: A nonincorporated business enterprise with two or more owners.

Patent: A form of property rights giving an inventor of a new product design or process (or the owner of the patent, if sold) the sole legal right to use, not use, or dispose of the invention.

Per capita real income: Individual personal income, mostly wages, stated in noninflationary monetary units. It is calculated by dividing the total national income (or GNP) by the population size.

Perfect competition: *See* Pure competition.

Perfectly elastic (demand): A demand condition in which the quantity demanded varies from zero to infinity when there is a change in the price.

Perfectly inelastic (demand): A demand condition in which there is no change in the quantity demanded when price changes.

Personal consumption expenditures (C): Spending by households on goods and services.

Personal income distribution: The pattern of income distribution according to the relative size of people's income.

Phillips curve: A statistical relationship between increases in the general price level and unemployment.

Planned obsolescence: The practice of producing goods or services that are deliberately designed to limit use, thereby requiring replacement or repair.

Population density: The average number of people per unit of land area.

Poverty gap: The aggregate income shortfall of the poor as a percentage of aggregate consumption.

Poverty line: The family income level below which people are officially classified as poor.

Predatory business practice: Any action on the part of a firm carried out solely to interfere with a competitor.

Price discrimination: Selling a product to two different buyers at different prices where all other conditions are the same.

Price elasticity of demand: The relative size of the change in the quantity demanded of a good or service as a result of a small change in its price.

Price indexes: Indicators of the general level of prices and attempts to average price changes of individual goods and services into a composite that will reflect the net effect of all the price changes upon the general level of prices. *See also* Consumer Price Index and Producer Price Index.

Price leadership: A common practice in shared monopoly industries by which one of the firms in the industry, normally one of the largest, changes its prices, and the other firms follow its lead.

Price level: The average level of money prices, a general indicator of the state of the economy.

Price stability: A constant average level of prices for all goods and services.

Priority sectors: Those parts of the economy that decision makers want to expand most rapidly and therefore favor with scarce inputs.

Privatization: The process of selling government assets to private buyers and/or relinquishing government services to the private sector.

Producer Price Index (PPI): Replaced the Wholesale Price Index as the most important monthly measure of prices at the wholesale level. PPI is really three indexes: one for producer finished goods, one for intermediate, and one for crude commodities. The PPI usually refers to the finished goods index.

Product differentiation: A device used by business firms to distinguish their product from the products of other firms in the same industry.

Product market: A market in which finished goods and services are exchanged.

Production inputs: The factors of production used in producing a good or service.

Production Possibility Frontier (PPF): Frequently used by economists to explain the costs to the economy of producing more of one good in terms of the resultant lost quantities of other goods.

Productivity: A ratio of the amount of output per unit of input.

Profits: The net returns after subtracting total costs from total revenue. If costs are greater than revenue, profits are negative.

Progressive income tax: A tax rate that increases as the income on which the tax is based grows larger.

Progressive tax system: A system of taxation based on increasing marginal tax rates at higher levels of income.

Promissory note: (IOU) a written obligation to pay a specified amount at a specified time.

Property tax: A tax levied on real estate, including the land and structures on it.

Proportional tax: A levy that takes the same proportion in taxes from low and high incomes.

Proprietorship: A business enterprise with a single private owner.

Prosperity: *See* Business cycles, phases.

Protectionism: Measures taken by the government in order to limit or exclude imports that compete with domestic production.

Protectionist measures: Actions taken by the government in order to limit or exclude imports that compete with domestic production.

Public utility: An industry that produces an essential public service such as electricity, gas, water, and telephone service; normally, a single firm is granted a local monopoly to provide the service.

Public Utility Commission: A regulatory body whose members are appointed by government to set rates and services provided by public utility firms.

Pure competition: A condition prevailing in an industry in which there are such a large number of firms producing a standardized product that no single firm can noticeably affect the market price by changing its output; also an industry in which firms can easily enter or leave.

Pure monopoly: An industry in which there is only one firm.

Pure public good: A good or service that is collectively consumed.

Quality-of-work-life program: An activity that attempts to improve the workplace environment of a business, encourage employee participation and counter worker alienation, and absenteeism.

Quantity demanded: The amount of a good or service that consumers would purchase at a particular price.

Quantity Equation (Equation of Exchange): The quantity of money (M) times the velocity of its circulation (V) equals the quantity of goods and services transacted (T) times their average price (P), normally written PQ = MV.

Quantity theory of money: *See* Quantity equation.

Quota: A limit on the quantity or value of a good that can be imported in a given time period.

Rate discrimination (price discrimination): Charging different customers different rates for services of equal production cost.

Rate level: The general level of rates (prices) of a regulated company.

Real capital: The buildings, machinery, tools, and equipment used in production.

Real flow: Involves the physical movement of goods and services and/or the use of factors of production.

Real income: *See* Price level.

Real interest rate: The quoted interest rate calculated on an annual basis and adjusted for changes in the purchasing power of money during the duration of the loan.

Real investment: The purchase of business structures and capital equipment; investment measured in dollars of constant value to adjust for inflation.

Real output: The value of output adjusted for changes in prices; the volume of output.

Recession: *See* Business cycles, phases.

Reciprocal Trade Agreement Act (1934): Federal law in effect from 1934 to 1962 that empowered the president to reduce tariff barriers by as much as 50 percent on a reciprocal basis with other countries through negotiated treaties. Extended 11 times, the law enabled the United States to reduce tariffs by more than 75 percent.

Recovery: *See* Business cycles, phases.

Regressive tax: A levy that takes a higher proportion from low incomes in taxes than it takes from high incomes.

Residual accounts: Short-term capital transfers and monetary gold transactions that compensate for the imbalance in a country's basic balance in its international payments.

Resources: The inputs that are used in production. Includes natural resources (minerals, timber, rivers), labor (blue collar, white collar), and capital (machinery, buildings).

Revaluation: An increase in the value of a country's currency relative to other currencies due to an official government increase in the exchange rate under a fixed rate system.

Revenue: The receipts from sales of goods and services.

Sales tax: A tax levied on the value of a good or service when exchanged.

Say's Law: A theory of the French economist J. B. Say, which holds that when goods or services are produced, enough income is generated to purchase what is produced, thereby eliminating the problem of overproduction.

Scarcity: The limited resources for production relative to satisfy the wants and needs of all the people in the world.

Scientific method: A procedure used by scientists to develop explanations for events and test the validity of those explanations.

Securities and Exchange Commission (SEC): Independent federal agency established under the Securities Exchange Act of 1934 that regulates brokers, investment companies, stock exchanges and the actions of corporate officers in the securities industry.

Shared monopoly: An industry in which there are only a few firms; more specifically, an industry in which four or fewer firms account for more than 50 percent of industry sales.

Sherman Antitrust Act: The 1890 antitrust law that makes restraint of trade and other monopolistic practices such as price fixing a misdemeanor.

Shift in demand: A change in the quantity of a good or service that would be purchased at each possible price.

Shift in supply: A change in the quantity of a good or service that would be offered for sale at each possible price.

Short run: A period of time so short that the amount of some factor inputs cannot be varied.

Short-term business cycles: Fluctuations in economic activity, particularly prices, production, and employment.

Social indicators: Noneconomic statistics that reflect a country's standard of living.

Social Security: A federal program of social insurance, introduced in 1935, that now provides retirement, disability, and medical care to eligible participants.

Socialism: An economic system that involves state ownership of the means of production, equitable distribution of incomes, and economic planning.

Specialization: Concentrating the activity of a unit of a production resource—especially labor—on a single task or production operation. Also applies to the specialization of nations in producing those goods and services that their resources are best suited to produce.

Speculators: People who purchase goods or financial assets in anticipation that prices will rise and they can sell at a profit; speculators can also speculate on a fall in prices.

Stagflation: A term created to describe a situation of simultaneous economic stagnation, high unemployment, and inflation.

State (authoritarian) socialism: A command economy in which virtually all of the means of production are in the hands of the state and decision making is centralized.

Stationary state: A condition of no change; a static economy with no growth.

Statistics: The data on economic variables; also the techniques of analyzing, interpreting, and presenting data.

Stock option: The right to purchase a specific amount of a corporation's stock at a fixed price. Often part of the compensation package for a company's top executives.

Strike: A collective refusal by employees to work.

Structural unemployment: The lack of work that occurs because of changes in the basic characteristics of a market, such as a new substitute product, a change in consumer tastes, or new technology in production.

Substitution effect: *See* Law of demand.

Supply: The relationship between the quantities of a good or service that sellers wish to market at any particular time and the various prices that can exist for the good or service.

Supply curve: A graphic representation of the relationship between price and quantity supplied.

Supply schedule: A table recording the number of units of a good or service supplied at various possible prices.

Supply-side economics: An approach to macroeconomic problems that focuses on the importance of increasing the supply of goods and services.

Surplus: A positive balance after expenditures are subtracted from revenues.

Taft-Hartley Act: A federal law, also known as the Labor-Management Relations Act of 1947, that seeks a balance of power between labor and management; protects the public from economic harm in labor disputes; and allows the president injunction powers in strikes that threaten the public safety and well-being. The law restrains the power of unions by amending the Wagner Act of 1935.

Tariffs: Taxes placed on imports either by value (ad valorem duty) or per unit of quantity (specific duty); also, the whole schedule of a country's import duties.

Tariff quota: A combination of a limited quantity or value of a good that can be imported free of duty or at a low tariff and high tariffs imposed on amounts exceeding the limit.

Technology: The body of skills and knowledge that comprises the processes used in production.

Terms of trade: The ratio of average export prices to average import prices.

Theory of the firm: In microeconomics, the analysis of the decision-making process of firms—all firms are assumed to maximize profits.

In economic theory, a firm is defined as any organizationally separate production unit.

Third World: The underdeveloped, nonaligned nations in Asia, Africa, and Latin America.

Time series: The changes in the values of a variable over time; a chart in which time—generally years—is one of the variables.

Total cost: The sum of fixed cost and variable cost.

Total revenue: The sum of receipts from all of the units sold; price × quantity.

Total utility: The amount of satisfaction a consumer derives from all of the units of a particular good or service consumed in a given time period.

Trade adjustment assistance: Supplementary unemployment payments to workers who have lost their jobs because of import competition and assistance to firms in shifting to other types of production.

Trade balance: Exports minus imports (net exports).

Trade-off: The choice between alternative uses for a given quantity of a resource.

Traditional economy: An economic system in which the basic questions of what, how, and for whom to produce are resolved primarily by custom and tradition.

Transfer payments: Expenditures for which no goods or services are exchanged. Welfare, Social Security, and unemployment compensation are government transfer payments.

Treasury bill: A short-term, marketable, federal government security with a maturity of one year or less.

Trust: A combination of producers in the same industry under one direction for the purpose of exerting monopoly power.

Unbalanced growth: Directing a country's capital resources into one or a limited number of industries to promote growth in those industries at a more rapid rate than growth of industry in general.

Underemployed: Workers who cannot obtain full-time employment or who are working at jobs for which they are overqualified.

Unfavorable balance of trade: The deficit in a country's merchandise trade when imports during the year are greater than exports.

Union shop: A firm in which all workers must belong to the union that represents their bargaining unit.

Unit of measurement (standard of value or unit of account): A common denominator of value in which prices are stated and accounts recorded.

Unitary elasticity (demand): A demand condition in which the relative change in the quantity demanded is the same as the size of the price change.

Urbanization: Migration of the population from rural areas to cities.

Utility: The amount of satisfaction a consumer derives from consumption of a good or service.

Value added: The difference between the value of a firm's sales and its purchases of materials and semifinished inputs.

Variable: A quantity—such as number of workers, amount of carbon dioxide, interest rate, amount of cropland, etc.—whose value changes in relationship to changes in the values of other associated items.

Variable costs: *See* Average variable cost of production.

Velocity of money circulation (V): The average rate at which money changes hands.

Venture capitalist: An individual or firm that provides financing for new business ventures for a share in the returns if the business succeeds.

Vertical equity: Fair differentiations of treatment of individuals at different levels.

Vertical merger: The joining of two firms in which the output of one firm is an input of the other firm.

Vertically integrated: Separate divisions of one company producing the different stages of a product and marketing their output to one another.

Vicious circle of poverty: The pattern of economic stagnation that results from a lack of surplus of production to invest in capital goods to increase productivity.

Wage (salary): A factor payment for labor service.

Welfare economics: A branch of economic study concerned with how an economic system attempts to maximize the welfare of its people; studies the principles by which alternative economic objectives can be ranked in terms of social welfare.

Welfare state (democratic socialism): An economic system that is committed to the security of its population in the areas of income, health care, job security, and providing for old age.

Wholesale Price Index (WPI): Replaced by the Producer Price Index in 1978; it was one of the best known of the price indexes. A statistical composite measure of price movements in wholesale, or primary, markets.

Workfare: A program that requires nonexempt welfare recipients to work at public service jobs for a given number of hours a month.

World Bank (International Bank for Reconstruction and Development—IBRD): A specialized agency of the UN that began operations in 1945 first to help countries rebuild facilities destroyed in World War II and subsequently to help finance development of the LDCs.

SOURCES

The Encyclopedic Dictionary of Economics, Fourth Edition, 1991. Dushkin Publishing Group/Brown & Benchmark Publishers, Guilford, CT 06437.

The Study of Economics: Principles, Concepts, and Applications, Turley Mings, 1991. Dushkin Publishing Group/Brown & Benchmark Publishers, Guilford, CT 06437.

(1996–1997)

Credits/ Acknowledgments

Cover design by Charles Vitelli

1. Introduction to Macroeconomics

Facing overview—*New York Times* photo by Ruby Washington.

2. Measuring Economic Performance

Facing overview—TRW Inc. photo.

3. Fiscal Policy and the Federal Budget

Facing overview—Federal Reserve Bank photo.

4. Money, Banking, and Monetary Policy

Facing overview—New York Stock Exchange photo by Edward Topple.

5. Unemployment, Inflation, and the Business Cycle

Facing overview—Photographer unknown.

6. International Economics

Facing overview—United Nations photo by Y. Nagata.

ANNUAL EDITIONS ARTICLE REVIEW FORM

■ NAME: _____ DATE: _____

■ TITLE AND NUMBER OF ARTICLE: _____

■ BRIEFLY STATE THE MAIN IDEA OF THIS ARTICLE: _____

_____

_____

_____

_____

■ LIST THREE IMPORTANT FACTS THAT THE AUTHOR USES TO SUPPORT THE MAIN IDEA:

_____

_____

_____

_____

_____

_____

■ WHAT INFORMATION OR IDEAS DISCUSSED IN THIS ARTICLE ARE ALSO DISCUSSED IN YOUR TEXTBOOK OR OTHER READING YOU HAVE DONE? LIST THE TEXTBOOK CHAPTERS AND PAGE NUMBERS:

_____

_____

_____

_____

_____

_____

_____

■ LIST ANY EXAMPLES OF BIAS OR FAULTY REASONING THAT YOU FOUND IN THE ARTICLE:

_____

_____

_____

_____

_____

■ LIST ANY NEW TERMS/CONCEPTS THAT WERE DISCUSSED IN THE ARTICLE AND WRITE A SHORT DEFINITION:

_____

_____

_____

_____

_____

*Your instructor may require you to use this Annual Editions Article Review Form in any number of ways: for articles that are assigned, for extra credit, as a tool to assist in developing assigned papers, or simply for your own reference. Even if it is not required, we encourage you to photocopy and use this page; you'll find that reflecting on the articles will greatly enhance the information from your text.

We Want Your Advice

ANNUAL EDITIONS:
MACROECONOMICS 96/97
Article Rating Form

Here is an opportunity for you to have direct input into the next revision of this volume. We would like you to rate each of the 45 articles listed below, using the following scale:

1. **Excellent: should definitely be retained**
2. **Above average: should probably be retained**
3. **Below average: should probably be deleted**
4. **Poor: should definitely be deleted**

Your ratings will play a vital part in the next revision. So please mail this prepaid form to us just as soon as you complete it.
Thanks for your help!

Annual Editions revisions depend on two major opinion sources: one is our Advisory Board, listed in the front of this volume, which works with us in scanning the thousands of articles published in the public press each year; the other is you—the person actually using the book. Please help us and the users of the next edition by completing the prepaid article rating form on this page and returning it to us. Thank you.

Rating	Article	Rating	Article
	1. Economics of My Times and Yours		24. The Future of Money
	2. Economic Report of the President: A Review		25. Bank Failure: The Financial Marginalization of the Poor
	3. Revisionism in the History of Supply-Side Economics		26. Our NAIRU Limit: The Governing Myth of Economic Policy
	4. Economic Possibilities for Our Grandchildren		27. Technology and Unemployment: A World without Jobs?
	5. The Economy You Can't See		28. Flexibility Trap: The Proliferation of Marginal Jobs
	6. Taking the Measure of Economics		29. The Real Un(der)employment Rate
	7. Services: A Future of Low Productivity Growth?		30. Only a Paper Boon
	8. The Economy's Barometer		31. Has Our Living Standard Stalled?
	9. The Real Truth about the Economy		32. As Parties Skirmish over Budget, Greenspan Offers a Painless Cure
	10. Sustainable Development: Conventional versus Emergent Alternative Wisdom		33. The Long Wave in Inflation and Real Interest Rates
	11. What's in Store? The GOP Contract for Tax Cuts and a Balanced Budget		34. Consolidating Capitalism
	12. The Pitfalls of a Balanced Budget		35. Power and Policy: The New Economic World Order
	13. Budget Blaster		36. Global Growth Is on a Tear
	14. Saving, Economic Growth, and the Arrow of Causality		37. From GATT to WTO: The Institutionalization of World Trade
	15. Taxpayers Are Angry. They're Expensive, Too		38. United States Trade Policy after the Cold War
	16. True Tax Reform: Encouraging Saving and Investment		39. Down in the Dumps: Administering America's "Unfair" Trade Laws
	17. Europeans Shrug as Taxes Go Up		40. U.S. Trade Deficits and International Competitiveness
	18. The Inequality Express		41. Exporting the Truth on Trade
	19. Activist Monetary Policy for Good or Evil? The New Keynesians vs. the New Classicals		42. Cars and VCR's Aren't Necessarily the First Domino
	20. The Fed: Wrong Turn in Risky Traffic		43. The Changing Relationship between the State and the Economy in Mexico
	21. It's Not Broke: So Don't Fix It: Why the Federal Reserve Should Not Be Reformed		44. East Germany's Transitional Economy
	22. Banking: Real Risks Require Real Reforms		45. Can a Socialist Republic Find Happiness Trading in a Capitalist World?
	23. Should the Feds Have Greater Control over State Banks?		

(Continued on next page)

ABOUT YOU

Name_____ Date_____
Are you a teacher? ☐ Or student? ☐
Your School Name _____
Department _____
Address _____
City _____ State _____ Zip _____
School Telephone #_____

YOUR COMMENTS ARE IMPORTANT TO US!

Please fill in the following information:

For which course did you use this book? _____
Did you use a text with this Annual Edition? ☐ yes ☐ no
The title of the text? _____
What are your general reactions to the Annual Editions concept?

Have you read any particular articles recently that you think should be included in the next edition?

Are there any articles you feel should be replaced in the next edition? Why?

Are there other areas that you feel would utilize an Annual Edition?

May we contact you for editorial input?

May we quote you from above?

ANNUAL EDITIONS: MACROECONOMICS 96/97

BUSINESS REPLY MAIL

First Class   Permit No. 84   Guilford, CT

Postage will be paid by addressee

**Dushkin Publishing Group/
Brown & Benchmark Publishers**
Sluice Dock
Guilford, Connecticut 06437